Almighty God
A Study of the Doctrine of Divine Omnipotence

STUDIES IN PHILOSOPHICAL THEOLOGY

Edited by: H.J. Adriaanse & Vincent Brümmer
Advisory Board: John Clayton (Lancaster), Ingolf Dalferth (Tübingen), Jean Greisch (Paris), Anders Jeffner (Uppsala), Christoph Schwöbel (London)

Editorial Formula:
'Philosophical theology is the study of conceptual issues which arise in views of life, in religious thinking and in theology. Such conceptual issues relate to the logical coherence between and the presuppositions and implications of fundamental concepts in human thought, as well as the effects which historical and cultural changes have on these aspects of human thinking.'

1. Hent de Vries, *Theologie im Pianissimo & zwischen Rationalität und Dekonstruktion,* Kampen, 1989
2. Stanislas Breton, *La pensée du rien,* Kampen, 1992
3. Christoph Schwöbel, *God: Action and Revelation,* Kampen, 1992
4. Vincent Brümmer (ed.), *Interpreting the Universe as Creation,* Kampen, 1991
5. Luco J. van den Brom, *Divine Presence in the World* (in preparation)
6. Marcel Sarot, *God, Passibility and Corporeality,* Kampen, 1992
7. Gijsbert van den Brink, *Almighty God,* Kampen, 1993

Almighty God
A Study of the Doctrine of Divine Omnipotence

Gijsbert van den Brink

Kok Pharos Publishing House
Kampen – The Netherlands

This study was defended as a dissertation for the doctorate at the University of Utrecht. Supervisor was Prof. Dr. Vincent Brümmer.

CIP-GEGEVENS KONINKLIJKE BIBLIOTHEEK, DEN HAAG

© 1993, Kok Pharos Publishing House,
P.O. Box 130, 8260 GA Kampen, The Netherlands
1996, second print
Cover Design By Rob Lucas
ISBN 90 390 0024 7
NUGI 632

To my parents

CONTENTS

Preface

At the completion of my doctoral dissertation after a good four years working on it, most of the time as a research assistent (*assistent in opleiding*) at the Faculty of Theology of the University of Utrecht, I would like to thank all those who have co-operated in one way or another to its present result. Since this moment coincides with the end of my study in theology, I implicitly include all others who contributed to my theological education over the years.

First of all, I want to express my gratitude towards my supervisor, Prof. Dr. Vincent Brümmer; he has been a *promotor* to me in many senses of the word ever since we met in the time that I was an undergraduate student. He not only encouraged me to qualify in philosophical theology, but also prompted me to publish papers, and stimulated me to communicate with specialists about the theme of my project. In his criticism of my drafts he was always so much milder than I had expected, that I gradually came to believe in the project myself. I consider it an exceptional privilege to have had such a supervisor.

I thank Dr. Luco J. van den Brom and Dr. Andy F. Sanders for their readiness to function as co-promotors. The former shares a wide range of common interests with me, and was always prepared to guide me skilfully through specific issues relevant to my inquiry. The latter generously offered me the opportunity to finish this book by taking over my teaching obligations in Groningen, and in an admirably short time mastered the book's contents. As to both of them, I have profited much from their constructive criticisms. My co-supervisor Dr. Christoph Schwöbel made many valuable comments on the manuscript as a whole, which resulted among other things in a much more balanced structural composition of the present study. I also wish to thank Dr. Marcel Sarot, who has been my *sparring partner* for all the time that I have worked on this book. His continuous fellowship, which was not at all tempered by the fact that we are slightly different kinds of personalities and belong to different confessional traditions, has been of great significance to me. Apart from our many discussions his erudite and accurate reading of my text saved me from many errors.

I am grateful to Prof. Dr. David Brown (Durham), Prof. Dr. C. Graafland (Utrecht) and Prof. Paul Helm (London) for their willingness to participate in the examining-committee, as well as for the various ways in which they encouraged and helped me to complete my study. Prof. F. van der Blij (Utrecht), Prof. R. van den Broek (Utrecht), Prof. F.W. Golka (Oldenburg), Prof. Eberhard Hermann (Uppsala), Dr. F.G. Immink (Doorn), Prof. Anders Jeffner (Uppsala) and Dr. Ann Loades (Durham) all commented on smaller or larger parts of the text at various stages of its incubation period. My colleague Drs. Eef Dekker (Utrecht) found time for a critical reading of the entire manuscript, notably in the busy final stage of his own dissertation. I am highly indebted to all these people for their helpful advice and friendly suggestions.

My colleagues Drs. Gerbrandt van Santen and Drs. Anja Kosterman contributed considerably to the good atmosphere within our Philosophy of Religion-section of the Department of Philosophy of Religion and Ethics. Throughout the years, my research was considerably facilitated by the professional and benevolent help of the staff of the liberary centre at De Uithof (BCU). The *Gereformeerde Bond in de Nederlandse Hervormde Kerk*, the *Fonds legaat "Ad Pias Causas"* and the *Stichting Aanpakken* sponsored the publication of this dissertation. Part of chapter 3 has previously appeared as "Descartes, Modalities, and God," *International Journal for Philosophy of Religion* 33 (1993), 1-15, and is re-used here by permission of this journal's publisher.

I come to my parents, who have continuously and warm-heartedly supported my theological studies from the very beginning. It is to them that I dedicate this book, in deep gratitude for their wisdom and care. Furthermore, it is difficult to imagine what would have become of this study without the continual love, patience, and even assistance of my wife Gerie-Anne.

Finally, this book is basically a book about God. Speaking about God is the most perilous and at the same time the most urgent task of the theologian, especially in a secularizing world like ours. I therefore conclude by expressing the hope that my words nowhere stop short of doing justice to the truth of God. It is He, to whom belongs all the power and the glory, who graciously gave me all I needed to finish this study.

Utrecht, February 1993   Gijsbert van den Brink

1

Methodological Preliminaries

It is difficult to find the beginning. Or, better: it is difficult to begin at the beginning. And not try to go further back.

Ludwig Wittgenstein[1]

1.1 INTRODUCTION

1.1.1 *Divine power and the scope of the present study*

The phrase "Almighty God," which I have chosen as a title for the present study, has functioned for many centuries and in many cases still functions as one of the most common forms of addressing God in Christian prayer. Indeed, almightiness or omnipotence has certainly been the most prominent of all attributes traditionally ascribed to God. Both in the Nicene and in the Apostles' Creed it is the only divine property which is explicitly mentioned, in both cases even at the very outset. It is hard to over-estimate the impact of this conspicuous presence in the most ecumenical of all confessions on the Christian mind and spirituality, the more so since the claim that God is omnipotent went virtually unchallenged in Christian theology for many centuries.

In our century, however, especially since the first World War, this situation has changed dramatically. Instead of ranking as the *primus inter pares* among the divine perfections, omnipotence now serves as one of the most contested of all. Different kinds of modifying and qualifying proposals with regard to the doctrine of divine omnipotence have been put forward.[2]

---

[1] L.Wittgenstein, *On Certainty*, Oxford 1969 (ed. G.E.M. Anscombe & G.H. von Wright), 62e §471.

[2] I think of the following examples from Protestant continental theology: H. Cremer, *Die christliche Lehre von den Eigenschaften Gottes*, ed. H. Burkhardt, Giessen 1983², 77-84; E. Brunner, *The Christian Doctrine of God*, London 1949, 248-255, cf. 294-297; K. Barth, *Church Dogmatics* II.1, ed. G.W. Bromiley & T.F. Torrance, Edinburgh 1957, 490-607; more radical proposals for revision came from D. Bonhoeffer, *Letters and Papers from Prison*, London 1970¹², esp. 122; Paul Tillich, *Systematic Theology* I, Chicago 1951, 273-276, and Jürgen Moltmann, *The Trinity and the Kingdom of God*, London 1981, esp. 191-222; in the Netherlands, H.J. Heering borrowed some insights from Tillich in his "God de almachtige," in: H.J. Heering, W.P. ten Kate & J. Sperna Weiland (eds.), *Dogmatische verkenningen*, Den Haag 1968, 74-84; see also his "Schepping en almacht," *Wending* 17 (1962), 328-339; H. Berkhof's concept of God's power as "defenceless superior power" has in turn been influenced by Heering, see Hendrikus Berkhof,

The more radical revisions often go hand in hand with straightforward and sometimes vehement rejections of the traditional notion.[3] Let me by way of example quote process theologian Charles Hartshorne, who expresses this rejection most eloquently.

> All I have said is that omnipotence as usually conceived is a false or indeed absurd ideal, which in truth *limits* God, denies to him any world worth talking about: a world of living, that is to say, significantly decision-making, agents. It is the *tradition* which did indeed terribly limit divine power, the power to foster creativity even in the least of the creatures. No worse falsehood was ever perpetrated than the traditional concept of omnipotence. It is a piece of unconscious blasphemy, condemning God to a dead world, probably not distinguishable from no world at all.[4]

What happened in the theological tradition (Hartshorne explicitly mentions Thomas Aquinas in this connection) is the following:

Christian Faith, Grand Rapids 1986[2], 140-147 (see further on this concept E. Schillebeeckx, "Overwegingen rond Gods 'weerloze overmacht'," *TvTh* 27 (1987), 370-381; I.J. Hesselink, "The Providence and Power of God," *RJ* 41 (1988), 108-111; D.J. Louw, "Omnipotence (Force) or Vulnerability (Defencelessness)?" *Scriptura* 28 (1989), 41-58); see also F.O. van Gennep, *De terugkeer van de verloren Vader*, Baarn 1989, 416-439. For English revisions of the doctrine of omnipotence, see e.g. Paul G. Kuntz, "The Sense and Nonsense of Omnipotence," *RS* 3 (1967), 525-538; id., "Omnipotence: Tradition and Revolt in Philosophical Theology," *NS* 42 (1968), 270-279; John Macquarrie, "Divine Omnipotence," *Proceedings of the Seventh Inter-American Congress of Philosophy* I, Quebec 1967, 132-137; Paul Fiddes, *The Creative Suffering of God*, Oxford 1988, 144-173; D.W.D. Shaw, "Omnipotence," *SJRS* 13 (1992), 103-113.

[3] There is a somewhat longer tradition of rejecting omnipotence in the Anglo-Saxon "finitist" tradition, especially among philosophers. It starts from John Stuart Mill, *Three Essays on Religion*, London 1874, esp. 176-186, and includes among others F.C.S. Schiller, *Riddles of the Sphinx*, London 1894[2], 309-324; William James, *A Pluralistic Universe*, London 1909; C.E. Rolt, *The World's Redemption*, London 1913, 1-61 (from a theological perspective); H.G. Wells, *God the Invisible King*, New York 1917; W.M. Thorburn, "Omnipotence and Personality," *Mind* 29 (1920), 159-185; for early criticism of this tradition, see C.F. d'Arcy, "The Theory of a Limited Deity," *PAS* 18 (1917-18), 158-184 (cf. Schiller's reply: "Omnipotence," *ibid.*, 247-270), and G.H. Joyce, *Principles of Natural Theology*, London 1923, 412-438, esp.421-426. Later finitist accounts include E.S. Brightman, *A Philosophy of Religion*, New York 1946[3], 276-341 (with a historical survey of finitism, 286-301) and Peter Bertocci, *Introduction to the Philosophy of Religion*, New York 1951, 408-441. Cf. on this "modern Marcionism" also A. van Egmond, *De lijdende God in de Britse Theologie van de Negentiende Eeuw*, Amsterdam 1986, 210 (esp. the literature mentioned in note 51), 238.
  The following well-known books, written from widely divergent traditions and perspectives, are also among those rejecting omnipotence: A.N. Whitehead, *Process and Reality*, Cambridge 1929, esp. 519f.; D. Sölle, *Suffering*, London 1975; and Harold Kushner's best seller *When Bad Things Happen to Good People*, New York 1981.

[4] Charles Hartshorne, *Omnipotence and other Theological Mistakes*, Albany 1984, 18. A similar allegation is to be found already in Rolt, *World's Redemption*, 13, where he claims that the conception of omnipotence which is accepted by most Christians (viz. omnipotence as infinite force) "... is immoral, irrational and anti-Christian, and from this fruitful source have sprung some of the worst travesties of the Christain Faith which have ever hindered the Gospel of God."

2

Without telling themselves so, the founders of the theological tradition were accepting and applying to deity the *tyrant* ideal of power. "I decide and determine everything, you (and your friends and enemies) merely do what I determine you (and them) to do. Your decision is simply mine for you. You only think you decide: in reality the decision is mine.[5]

This analogy between God and the tyrannical monarch is "perhaps the most shockingly bad of all theological analogies, or at least the one open to the most dangerous abuses."[6] According to Hartshorne, "'brute power' is ... practically efficacious, for good or ill, and has to be reckoned with. The one thing we need not and ought not to do is - to worship it!"[7] Since this is precisely what happened in the ascription of omnipotence to God, this word "has been so fearfully misdefined, and has so catastrophically misled so many thinkers, that I incline to say that the word itself had better be dropped."[8]

For others, however, the omnipotence of God as traditionally conceived is still almost a matter of self-evidence. In this way, Wolfhart Pannenberg says: "The word 'God' is used meaningfully only if one means by it the power that determines everything that exists."[9] And Keith Ward is hardly less emphatical in stating that

> ... God is such that he cannot fail to exist; he is an "absolutely necessary being", and he necessarily possesses the property of omnipotence, ... in the sense of having the power to create or destroy all possible creatable and destructible (all contingent) things. The presupposition of Biblical theism is that there exists a necessary being which necessarily possesses the power to create or destroy all contingent

---

[5] Ibid., 11. Cf. Hartshorne, *The Divine Relativity*, New Haven 1948, 50. The idea that the ideal of a tyrant was projected upon God by classical theism stems from Whitehead. Cf. the famous accusation in his *Process and Reality*: "When the Western world accepted Christianity, Caesar conquered; ... the deeper idolatry, of the fashioning of God in the image of the Egyptian, Persian, and Roman imperial rulers was retained. The Church gave unto God the attributes which belonged exclusively to Caesar." (corrected edition, New York 1978, 342). This accusation has been endorsed by Jürgen Moltmann in his *Trinity*, 249f.; cf. also David E. Jenkins, *God, Miracle and the Church of England*, London 1987, 28.

[6] Hartshorne, *Man's Vision of God and the Logic of Theism*, Hamden (Conn.) 1964[2], 203. Since no conceivable tyrant can ever make all the decisions of its subjects, it is (especially in the previous quotation) rather the analogy of the hypnoticist or puppeteer which Hartshorne seems to have in mind. Cf. *Omnipotence*, 12: "Is it the highest ideal of power to rule over puppets who are permitted to think they make decisions but who are really made by another to do exactly what they do? For twenty centuries we have had theologians who seem to say yes to this question."

[7] Hartshorne, *Divine Relativity*, 155; cf. ibid., 52: "Upon the ... rotten foundation of the worship of mere power or absoluteness we ought to build no edifice, sacred or profane."

[8] Hartshorne, *Omnipotence*, 26.

[9] W. Pannenberg, *Basic Questions in Theology* I, London 1970, 1; cf. 156f. Pannenberg is indebted for this definition to Rudolf Bultmann, "Welchen Sinn hat es von Gott zu reden?," in: id., *Glauben und Verstehen* I, Tübingen 1954[2], 26; cf. Bultmann's *Essays Philosophical and Theological*, London 1955, 92: "To the idea of God as such belongs the *idea of omnipotence*."

3

things.[10]

Still others, on the other hand, hold that precisely because of this inextricable connection between the concept of omnipotence and the concept of God, we cannot believe that God exists at all. For them, the only way to give up the unpalatable classical omnipotence-doctrine is by jettisoning belief in God as such, and embracing atheism instead.[11]

In the light of this widespread contemporary reflection on the nature of God's power, and its influence on people's over-all evaluation of Christian faith and the Christian tradition, it comes as a surprise to discover that relatively few monographs have been devoted to the theme. In contrast to the myriad of (mostly philosophical) recent articles and papers on the scope and conceivability of omnipotence, as well as to the still more manifold cases of scattered loose remarks made in the context of some related theme,[12] I know of only a few full-length scholarly works studying and evaluating the classical conception of God's power and its alternatives.[13] One might contrast here the much larger number of recent volumes devoted to the doctrine and concept of divine omni*science*.[14] Again, there are numerous books which discuss God's power from the perspective of the problem of evil, but only few of them extensively examine the role of the omni-

---

[10] Keith Ward, *Divine Action*, London 1990, 9.

[11] J.M.E. McTaggart, *Some Dogmas of Religion*, London 1906, 186-260; Roland Pucetti, "The Concept of God," *PQ* 14 (1964), 237-245; Antony Flew, *God and Philosophy*, London 1966, esp. 41-47. As to the Dutch situation we can refer to R.F. Beerling, *Niet te geloven*, Deventer 1979, 102-113; cf. also Karel van het Reve's essay "De ongelofelijke slechtheid van het opperwezen," in: D. van Weerlee et al., *Het verschijnsel godsdienst*, Amsterdam 1986, 26-32.

[12] As to the former, I refrain from giving a survey here since many of them are discussed below. As to the latter, I have not made any effort to list or discuss the large number of passages which briefly mention the theme as a side-issue, and which usually either easily dismiss or simply endorse the classical concept of God as omnipotent.

[13] H.A. Redmond, *The Omnipotence of God*, Philadelphia 1964 gives a rough survey of what theologians, philosophers, poets and biblical writers have said about omnipotence, ending with a chapter on "what may we believe today?"; the scope of this book is too universal to satisfy the requirements of an in-depth study. Daniel L. Migliore, *The Power of God*, Philadelphia 1983, has only one chapter on "the power of God in the church's theology" (60-74); David Basinger, *Divine Power in Process Theism*, Albany 1988, although containing some interesting insights pertaining to the classical doctrine of omnipotence, concentrates (as the title indicates) on the process concept of divine power. Anna Case-Winters, *God's Power*, Louisville 1990 is the only monography I know of which seriously and systematically investigates classical thinking on the divine omnipotence (though even this study restricts itself to only one representative of classical thought, viz. John Calvin). Sometimes larger sections on the omnipotence-theme are included in studies of the classical doctrine of God as a whole (as in Barth's *Church Dogmatics*, cf. note 2). Finally, there are some monographies dealing with God's power from the perspective of biblical theology, which will be mentioned in chapter 2.

[14] Let me mention only the - to my knowledge - most recent volume of William Lane Craig, *Divine Foreknowledge and Human Freedom. The Coherence of Theism: Omniscience*, Leiden 1991, which contains an extensive bibliography.

potence-doctrine.[15]

How is this remarkable omission to be explained? One underlying reason is presumably that for many people what they think about omnipotence is decided at a very basic, pre-reflective level. As a result, for some it is a matter of self-evidence that God is omnipotent, whereas for others it is a matter of equal self-evidence that He is not, or that He does not exist since if He did He would be omnipotent, which is unbelievable. In this way, either the doctrine of omnipotence or its denial often functions as a firmly held presupposition in the heart of someone's world view rather than in its periphery, where it would be more open to rational scrutiny. However this may be, the present study is intended to help changing this situation. As to my own view, I disagree with all of the three positions outlined above. I will argue that the classical doctrine of divine omnipotence is sustainable, but that, on its most plausible interpretation, it does not depict God's omnipotence as a matter of self-evidence or necessity. Rather, it is suggested that the best reason to believe that God is omnipotent is because He has revealed Himself as such, and that the way in which His omnipotence should be interpreted is determined by this revelation. In other words, the doctrine of God's omnipotence - or, as I prefer to say, almightiness - is not a matter of course but a matter of faith. It belongs to the very core of Christian faith to believe that *God*, the sole source of all truth, goodness and beauty, is almighty, rather than the forces of falsehood, evil and ugliness.

So what I envisage to do in this book is to take up challenges like those of Hartshorne as well as rather robust definitions like those of Pannenberg and Ward, and see whether they are sustainable in the light of this criterion. My procedure will not be a very direct one, however, since I am primarily interested in the classical conception of divine omnipotence for its own sake. Therefore, I shall take ample time to study this conception as such. In the course of this it will turn out how it differs from preconceived philosophical notions of omnipotence. Then, I return to the contemporary challenges and trace the intellectual problems by which they are inspired, in order to examine whether they indeed force us to revise or reject the traditional view, or whether (parts of) this view can be retained. These reflections lead me to the following strategy for the book as a whole. In the rest of this first chapter, I try to sort out methodological issues, explaining and defending some basic assumptions from which I start and the criteria I use in this study. I begin by making some general remarks on method in

---

[15] John Hick, *Evil and the God of Love*, London 1977[2]; David R. Griffin, *God, Power, and Evil*, Washington 1990[2]; J.B. Hygen, *Guds allmakt og det ondes problem*, Oslo 1973; perhaps I may also refer to the work of the Dutch theologian A. van de Beek, *Why? On Suffering, Guilt, and God*, Grand Rapids 1990. It should be noted that my observations are restricted to the realms of scholarly work which came to my attention during the past five years. These include publications from the Anglophone and Dutch-speaking world, parts of the German and French literature, and a still smaller portion of Scandinavian and Italian publications.

science and (philosophical) theology (§1.1.2), which are intended as a provisional elucidation of the academic locus of the present study. Then, since I will largely ignore epistemological questions with regard to the divine omnipotence in the course of this study, I account in advance for the epistemological assumption that it is possible to know that God exists, and that this knowledge may be taken as a given in scholarly work (§1.2). A further assumption which I take into consideration in advance is that it is of primary importance for our inquiry to keep in mind that the affirmation of the divine omnipotence has received the status of a *church doctrine*. I try to find out what is implied by this doctrinal status, and what kind of methodological criteria for its study follow from it (§1.3).

In the second chapter, I investigate the theological-philosophical tradition from a historical point of view. I do not intend to write a complete history of the doctrine of divine omnipotence, but rather select three highly debated historical issues, in order to find out what is precisely implied by the traditional doctrine and what is not. After having explained my reasons for these selections (§2.1), I examine the origins of the doctrine (§2.2), its development in medieval thought (§2.3), and what I see as its intended consummation in early modern times (§2.4).

In chapter three, I switch from the historical to the analytical approach, joining the discussion as to whether "omnipotence" is a coherent concept at all, and if so how it should be spelled out. After the introduction (§3.1), I first analyse the concept of power and some of its cognates (§3.2), and then try to find out what happens when we qualify this concept by means of the logical operator "omni" and apply it to God (§3.3). It will turn out that this operation leads to a number of very complicated conceptual problems, which do not lend themselves for simple and unambiguously convincing solutions. So I conclude that "omnipotence" is probably not a coherent concept, and should better be substituted by "almightiness" as this notion arises from the biblical revelation; in what I consider to be one of the most crucial sections of the present study, I analyse the similarities and differences between these two concepts of omnipotence and almightiness (§3.4). Finally, I show how formulating the power of God in terms of almightiness rather than omnipotence helps us to solve one of the most basic conceptual problems which beset the classical doctrine of God's power, viz. the relation between God's power and the laws of logic (§3.5).

In chapter four, I return to the contemporary challenges sketched out above, and I attempt to show that they do not force us to reject or revise the traditional notion of almightiness. In the introductory section I trace the two most important intellectual pressures behind these challenges (§4.1), which I then study in turn. First, I examine whether and how human creaturely freedom and responsibility in earthly affairs can be seen as compatible with God's almightiness (§4.2). Then, I ask for the way in which this same relation should be conceived in soteriological affairs, thus joining and trying to illuminate the classical debate concerning "freedom and grace" (§4.3). Finally, I defend and elaborate the doctrine of divine almightiness in a way which makes it tenable and even plausible in view of what is no doubt its most influential contemporary disclaimer, viz. the problem of evil (§4.4).

1.1.2 *Method in science and theology*

The present study wants to be read as a study in philosophical theology, a discipline which can roughly be located somewhere on the borderline between systematic theology and philosophy of religion. Now both in contemporary systematic theology and in present-day philosophy of religion there is a large variety of methodological principles of inquiry. It is not clear in advance what kind of guiding axioms should be held and what kind of criteria should be applied to theorizing activities in either of those fields, since systematic theologians as well as philosophers of religion simply disagree with each other on this issue.[16]

As a result of this predicament, anyone who starts reading a study in one of those disciplines is uncertain as to what kind of prior assumptions and normative criteria the author endorses - unless they are spelled out in advance. Since we may duly expect this uncertainty to be even greater in the discipline of philosophical theology, which covers the borderline between systematic theology and philosophy of religion, I intend to spell out in advance my methodological assumptions and criteria in the remainder of this chapter. It should be stated at the outset, however, that my argument is not exhaustive in this respect. I do not offer many conclusive arguments for or against particular options which are available in the literature. I only intend to give some reasons as to why I reject some of them and embrace others, and why I take them to be intellectually respectable. After having done that, I shall further take their acceptability for granted.

In a sense, the "problem of presuppositions" is germane to scientific[17] inquiry in general. In contemporary philosophy of science, it is

---

[16] See e.g. the recent debate concerning the different definitions of philosophy of religion and its relations to theology in *TJTh* 5 (1989), 3-56 (papers from the Canadian symposium on the relationship of the philosophy of religion to theological studies, edited by A.H. Khan). As to systematic theology, cf. the complaint of Gordon Kaufman that "the contemporary theological scene has become chaotic... There appears to be no consensus on what the task of theology is or how theology is to be pursued." G.D. Kaufman, *An Essay on Theological Method*, Missoula 1979[2], ix. In order to see that the European situation on the borderline between philosophy and theology is not much better, it suffices to compare the vastly divergent approaches followed in the books which appear (along with the present study) in the series *Studies in Philosophical Theology*. The specifically Dutch methodological differences are nicely illustrated by the unpublished papers of H.J. Adriaanse ("Theses on Philosophy of Religion and Theology") and V. Brümmer ("Theology and Philosophical Inquiry"), held at the "Symposium on the Nature and Rationality of (Philosophical) Theology" which was organized by the *Netherlands Network for Advanced Studies in Theology* (Philosophy of Religion Section), Utrecht 9 September 1992.

[17] Here and in what follows I take the words "science" and "scientific" as covering the whole range of academic disciplines rather than merely the natural sciences; thus, they should be read as on a par with the Dutch "wetenschap" and "wetenschappelijk."

widely - though still not generally - acknowledged that no inquiry which pretends to be scientific can be free from various kinds of axiomatic presuppositions. It belongs to the very nature of scientific research to operate with the help of such presuppositions. These presuppositions include both assumptions derived from the results of previous scientific research, and what might be called pre-scientific assumptions. Of course opinions differ widely about the epistemological status of such presuppositions, their influence on the scientific quality of the performed inquiry and on its conclusions, etc. But without taking certain things for granted scientific activity (let alone scientific progress) would be impossible.[18]

To give only one brief example, a physicist engaged in certain very specific investigations in the field of quantum mechanics cannot critically re-examine in advance all existing theories which are fundamental to quantum mechanics as a whole, even though these theories are constitutive for the very meaningfulness of her own inquiry. Instead, she simply has to take the fundamentals of quantum mechanics for granted, lest she get lost in all kinds of preliminary issues. Without simply accepting this preceding scientific tradition as a piece of "normal science" she cannot even get her own research off the ground! Even if we imagine our physicist to be a genius in her discipline, and capable of accounting critically for all the fundamentals of quantum mechanics before devoting herself to the proper subject of her investigations, there would still remain other, even more fundamental axioms to be accounted for. Take, for example, the axiom that the physicist's senses are not deceiving her when she is conducting her inquiries, and that, therefore, the physical world which she observes is real, i.e. has existence independently of her observations. It will require completely different capacities and modes of argument to account for the reasonableness of this particular axiom. In fact, it is notoriously difficult to give objective grounds for the belief that our senses are on the whole reliable, and that something like the "physical world-in-itself" really exists.[19] Or take the axiom that all processes in the universe are rationally ordered, so that there must be a rational solution to any scientific problem we encounter.[20] Our physicist

---

[18] Cf. e.g. Nicholas Wolterstorff, *Reason within the Bounds of Religion* Grand Rapids 1984[2], 63-70 for a helpful discussion of the different types of beliefs which must be presumed in the process of theory-weighing. Cf. also M. Polanyi's theory of tacit knowing: "All explicit knowledge is rooted in, i.e. necessarily depends for its application and understanding on, tacit knowing," Andy F. Sanders, *Michael Polanyi's Post-Critical Epistemology*, Amsterdam 1988, 21.

[19] Notably, especially as a result of the rise of quantum mechanics, questions about the ontological status of the physical world have received a new urgency; cf. e.g. Russell Stannard, *Grounds for Reasonable Belief*, Edinburgh 1989, 45-68.

[20] See for the axiomatic and heuristic character of this basic assumption e.g. Alistair MacKinnon, *Falsification and Belief*, The Hague 1970, 28-46; T.F. Torrance, *The Ground and Grammar of Theology*, Belfast 1980, 131f.; id., *Divine and Contingent Order*, Oxford 1981; the point is also forcefully pressed in the recent work of Lesslie Newbigin. See his *Foolishness to the Greeks*, Grand Rapids 1986, 70f., where he concludes his argument with the statement: "Thus science is

would certainly be unable to deal extensively with the intricacies of these and similar guiding axioms without being compelled to give up her task as a researching physicist and becoming a full-time philosopher.

The impossibility of arguing extensively for all the a priori assumptions which play a role beneath the surface of a scientific inquiry, however, cannot be an excuse for disregarding them altogether. On the contrary, it is extremely important to be as conscious as possible of the nature and the implications of one's presuppositions. Therefore, even though we cannot argue exhaustively in support of our a priori's, it is appropriate to be as explicit as possible about them at the very outset. Irrespective of the way in which we interpret the relationship between science and theology, at least in this respect the same is vital for scientific inquiry as well as for theology. All too often academic studies of both sorts suffer from a lack of clarity about the nature and implications of the framework which the author takes for granted. The danger of such absence of any account of the author's basic assumptions is, of course, that, precisely because they are kept hidden and implicit, those assumptions may be allowed to play an all too crucial role in the subsequent inquiry.[21]

In order to avoid this danger (as well as the opposite risk of getting totally absorbed by methodological issues[22]), I will devote the next sections to an examination of some of my basic guiding assumptions. Obviously, the goal of this procedure cannot be to get rid of those assumptions. As is argued in contemporary hermeneutical theory, that would not only be impossible, but also undesirable.[23] Instead, the purpose is to approach them in a critical way, developing, moulding and when necessary even revising them by means of new outside material. I can give an example of such revision from my own work. One of the assumptions with which I started my inquiry - an assumption too specific to be discussed in the present chapter - was, that the philosophical concept of divine omnipotence squares neatly with the biblical notion of divine almightiness, and properly functions

---

sustained in its search for an understanding of what it sees by faith in what is unseen. The formula *credo ut intelligam* is fundamental to science" (71); his *The Gospel in a Pluralist Society*, London 1989, 20; and my "Lesslie Newbigin als postmodern apologeet," *NTT* 46 (1992), 312. Finally, for a witness who can hardly be suspected of theological bias, see Nicholas Rescher's conclusion in his *Rationality: A Philosophical Enquiry*, Oxford 1989, 230: "It is a fact of profound irony that assured confidence in the efficacy of reason requires an act of faith."

[21] Cf. A.E. McGrath, *The Genesis of Doctrine*, Oxford 1990, 87: "It is precisely when the ideological component to frameworks of rationality is ignored or denied that its influence is at its greatest." McGrath particularly shows this to be the case in historicist and relativist strands of contemporary sociology of knowledge (90-102).

[22] Cf. in this connection Paul Avis, *The Methods of Modern Theology*, Basingstoke 1986, 203-209 for a well-balanced treatment of the topic of methodology in theology, rejecting both the dismissal (e.g. by Karl Barth and Paul Holmer) and the overvaluation of methodical questions.

[23] See e.g. H.G. Gadamer, *Philosophical Hermeneutics*, Berkeley 1977 (tr. and ed. David E. Linge).

as its logical elaboration and theoretical support. This was the thrust of an article which I wrote in the initial phase of my inquiry, and which has only recently been published.[24] Further study, however, led me to the conclusion that this assumption was misguided, and that there exist some crucial dissimilarities between both concepts which should not be overlooked (see on this §3.4).

As to the more general assumptions to be discussed here, I have not found such reasons for revision in the course of the inquiry. They have especially to do with the nature of philosophical theology and its methods for analysing religious statements. As indicated above, the theorizing in philosophical theology takes place somewhere on the borderline between theology and philosophy. But the essential question is of course where exactly. The precise point of departure which we adopt will have important implications for the method to follow and the criteria to use. Both of these must be appropriate to the object of inquiry, but even so more options than a single one are open. Therefore, clear and reasoned choices are necessary indeed.

In brief, we have to make prior decisions with regard to a number of much-discussed questions in both philosophy and theology. I will arrange these questions according to the generality of their scope, and divide them into two sections. Since the doctrine of divine omnipotence is primarily a piece of religious language, I start with an investigation of the epistemological status of religious language. After having sketched the most popular view on this issue in both post-Enlightenment philosophy and contemporary theology (§ 1.2.1), and after having argued against its tenability (§ 1.2.2), I reject some of its proposed modifications (§ 1.2.3), and then try to expound in brief a theory of religion which I consider to be epistemologically more recommendable (§ 1.2.4). Next, in section 1.3 I discuss those particular elements of religious systems which we are primarily concerned with in the present study, viz. doctrines. I will argue that some current accounts of the nature of doctrine must be qualified as reductionist and therefore inadequate (§ 1.3.1), and trace briefly the main lines along which to my mind an alternative should be construed (§ 1.3.2). This will lead us quite naturally to an examination of the character and criteria of systematic theological investigation in doctrine (§ 1.3.3). Finally, since the structure of this book is largely determined by these criteria, I will be able to present an outline of the different stages of the subsequent inquiry as this emerges from the preceding discussion (§ 1.4).

---

[24] See G. van den Brink, "Allmacht und Omnipotenz," *K&D* 38 (1992), 260-279; the article was written in the midst of 1989.

1.2 THE EPISTEMOLOGY OF RELIGIOUS BELIEF

1.2.1 *The nature and problems of modern foundationalism*

An inquiry concerning the omnipotence of God seems first of all to presuppose in some way or another the existence of God. Since this book is not about the existence of God, and since to presuppose it is, of course, a rather basic and pivotal decision, I will try to account for this presupposition in advance, and to indicate precisely *in which way* it underlies this study. In doing this, however, we should keep in mind from the very beginning that the question of God cannot be discussed in isolation from the whole religious way of life. If someone asks me "Do you believe in God?," what is asked for is not simply whether I endorse a particular proposition, but whether I live and interpret my life within an overall religious perspective. Nevertheless, it is possible to examine the epistemological status of certain affirmations which are made within and inspired by this religious perspective. In this way, we may ask whether it is possible to *know* that God exists, and, therefore, to take the existence of God as a starting point in scientific inquiry. Is it possible at all to know whether religious statements are true?

From the Enlightenment onwards, the standard answer to these questions has generally been in the negative. According to the prevailing epistemological theory throughout the Western tradition since Aristotle, there are only two categories of propositions that may count as justified true beliefs, i.e. that may claim the status of "knowledge":

1. propositions that are self-evident
2. propositions that are appropriately inferred from self-evident propositions.

As is clear from this structure, the first category consists of propositions which are foundational to propositions of the second category. From this relationship the theory derives its name: *foundationalism*. Actually, foundationalism is the general term for a whole family of epistemological theories, all of which share the above structure in some form or another. Concrete foundational theories differ with regard to what kind of beliefs are regarded to be self-evident, what kinds of inference are considered to be correct etc., but they all agree that knowledge-claims are only justified with regard to a proposition p if p can be subsumed within either category 1 or 2. As Alvin Plantinga observes, "foundationalism is a *picture* or total way of looking at faith, knowledge, justified belief, rationality, and allied topics."[1] It has been an enormously popular picture, and remains the dominant way of thinking about these topics, despite a growing awareness of its substantial deficiencies. Common to all foundationalists is the idea that the

---

[1] Alvin Plantinga, "Reason and Belief in God," in: Alvin Plantinga & Nicholas Wolterstorff (eds.), *Faith and Rationality*, Notre Dame 1983, 48.

house of genuine science is firmly based upon a foundation of indubitable certitudes which are known non-inferentially.[2]

In the history of Western thought up to the Enlightenment, the proposition "God exists" was usually regarded, along with many other belief statements, to belong to the first category, i.e. to the class of foundational, non-inferential beliefs which are not in need of external justification. One famous statement of John Calvin may suffice to illustrate this point:

> There is within the human mind, and indeed by natural instinct, an awareness of divinity. This we take to be beyond controversy. To prevent anyone from taking refuge in the pretense of ignorance, God himself has implanted in all men a certain understanding of his divine majesty.[3]

The interesting point about this quotation in the context of our discussion is not so much the expressed view in itself, as the fact that Calvin takes this view to be not only true, but even "beyond controversy." The belief in the general human awareness of divinity, along with the more fundamental belief which is included in it, viz. the belief in the existence of God, functions as a kind of "background belief," i.e. as an axiomatic, often unspoken conviction which is not tested upon its credentials anymore, but implicitly functions itself as a test for the acceptability of all possible kinds of other convictions.[4]

Now what happened in the Enlightenment (and was, in fact, already initiated in its anticipating movements like Cartesian philosophy) can be described as a shift from assumption to argument.[5] The belief in the existence of God lost its axiomatic status, and could only be upheld if *reasons* were produced for it; in the light of the new anthropocentric basic convictions, such reasons should be independent of the Christian faith.[6] In other words: if the proposition "God exists" could be granted the status of knowledge, this could no longer be the case because of its belonging to the body of self-evident propositions. The only way to save this fundamental theo-

---

[2] Wolterstorff, *Reason within the Bounds*, 29.

[3] John Calvin, *Institutes of the Christian Religion*, I 3 1 (ed. J.T. McNeill, Philadelphia 1960, 43).

[4] See for the nature and function of a background belief various so-called "holist" treatments of the justification of beliefs, e.g. W.V.O. Quine and J.S. Ullian, *The Web of Belief*, New York 1978²; Clark N. Glymour, *Theory and Evidence*, Princeton 1980 (though Glymour appears to be a critical holist, 145-152); see further Wolterstorff, *Reason within the Bounds*, 61-66; for a theological application of the concept, see Ronald F. Thiemann, *Revelation and Theology*, Notre Dame 1985, 11-14, 99-102.

[5] This shift is meticulously demonstrated in Michael J. Buckley, *At the Origins of Modern Atheism*, Yale 1987.

[6] Thiemann, *Revelation and Theology*, 11-14 offers some interesting evidence for this thesis from the writings of Descartes. In general, I am indebted to Thiemann's insightful treatment of the impact of foundationalism upon the structure of modern philosophical and theological discourse.

logical proposition from being degraded to mere "opinion" was to infer it from other beliefs. Since, there was only one way out for the science that wanted to include the existence of God in its axioms (let us call this science "theology"), and that was to find arguments for it by deducing it from other propositions that were regarded to contain indubitable knowledge.[7]

The most noteworthy result of this shift from assumption to argument was the rise of what is often called "philosophical theism," or simply "theism."[8] Here, the question whether it is rational to believe in the existence of God was to be decided by means of evidential arguments based on general human experience. Of course, formal arguments for the existence of God had been presented already in the Middle Ages. Their function in the Middle Ages, however, was unmistakably different from what the arguments were intended to do in the Enlightenment. According to the modern conception, arguments for the existence of God are a posteriori proofs drawing on universal aspects of human experience, which, if succesful, form the sole validation of God's existence. In classical theology, by contrast, the arguments (for example Aquinas' famous "five ways") functioned as explanatory devices for conceptually elucidating the Christian faith, in accordance with the medieval principle of *fides quaerens intellectum*.[9] They simply illustrated and confirmed on an intellectual level what was already known with intuitive certainty. Attempts to establish the existence of God in the tradition of philosophical theism continue to be undertaken up to the present.[10]

A second argumentative strategy adopted in order to establish the existence of God as appropriately inferred knowledge centred around the

---

[7] A primary example of this procedure can be found in Locke; see Nicholas Wolterstorff, "The Migration of Theistic Arguments," in: R. Audi & W.J. Wainwright (eds.), *Rationality, Religious Belief, & Moral Commitment*, London 1986, 38-81, esp. 81 n.63. But one may also think of Kant's inferring the existence of God (though not as a piece of knowledge) from the demands of practical reason and morality.

[8] Cf. Ingolf U. Dalferth, "Historical Roots of Theism," in: Dalferth et al., "Traditional Theism and its Modern Alternatives," papers held at the 9th European Conference on Philosophy of Religion, Aarhus 1992 (unpublished).

[9] See for this interpretation, among others, David B. Burrell, "Religious Belief and Rationality," in: Delaney (ed.), *Rationality and Religious Belief*, 84-115; cf. also Thiemann, *Revelation and Theology*, 166. This interpretation yields a solution to Plantinga's embarrassment (Plantinga, "Reason and Belief in God," 47) about two apparently conflicting lines in Aquinas' thought on the justification of belief in God's existence. Given the above interpretation, Aquinas' "five ways" are not at odds with his assurance that there is a sort of intuitive or immediate grasp of God's existence, which offers us sufficient warrant for belief in God on its own. Here Aquinas' approach corresponds to Calvin's "beyond controversy." It should be added, however, that the more traditional interpretation of the "five ways," which sees them as structurally in line with the enterprise of philosophical theism, continues to have its advocates; cf. e.g. Anthony Kenny, *What is Faith?*, Oxford 1992, 43, 63-74.

[10] To mention only one of the most well-known of them: Richard Swinburne *The Existence of God*, Oxford 1979.

notion of revelation. According to the proponents of this approach, the propositional contents of revelation have a status comparable to that of the foundational, self-evident beliefs in science. From the foundation of revelation all kinds of religious truths can appropriately be inferred. In this strategy, the doctrine of revelation is moulded in such a way as to function as a variation of epistemological foundationalism.[11]

Now either of these attempts tends to overlook the fact that epistemological foundationalism - the theory which functions as one of the most influential background beliefs in academic research - is a very peculiar doctrine. It is always difficult to offer a well-balanced evaluation of an all-pervasive paradigmatic framework like foundationalism, since there is simply no position-neutral viewpoint from which to approach the issue. Reasons for and against the theory can only be derived from a textured web of belief, in which we are already entangled. As is generally known, paradigms usually don't shift as a result of knock-down arguments, but in far more subtle ways.[12] Nevertheless, we should indicate in a few words the most salient shortcomings of foundationalism, especially of its modern version which has been dominant since the Cartesian revolution in philosophy.[13] Let us define this "modern foundationalism" as that member of the family which (1) includes in its body of self-evident foundational propositions only propositions of two sorts, viz. analytical truths and incorrigible beliefs (such as, respectively, "2+2=4" and "I seem to see a tree"), and (2) explicitly denies that the proposition "God exists" belongs to either of those sets.[14]

---

[11] The "father" of this latter approach is again John Locke, see esp. his *An Essay Concerning Human Understanding*; for a reconstruction of his theory of revelation, see Thiemann, *Revelation and Theology*, 17-24. In subsequent discussions (24-43), Thiemann deals with theologians as diverse as Friedrich Schleiermacher and Thomas F. Torrance as other representatives of this line of reasoning.

[12] Cf. Thomas Kuhn, *The Structure of Scientific Revolutions*, Chicago 1970[2].

[13] In the present-day philosophical scene there are indications of the gradual collapse of the foundationalist paradigm as the reigning (meta-)epistemological theory. That something like a paradigm shift - to use the Kuhnian term - is taking place, is clear from the writings of many leading philosophers. Cf. for a useful survey Richard J. Bernstein's "Introduction" to his *Philosophical Profiles*, Cambridge 1986, 1-20. See also his *Beyond Objectivism and Relativism*, Philadelphia 1983. Highly influential is also Richard Rorty, *Philosophy and the Mirror of Nature*, Princeton 1979. As Nancey Murphy and James Wm. McClendon, Jr., "Distinguishing Modern and Postmodern Theologies," *MT* 5 (1989), 191-214, esp. 199-201 neatly show, the breakdown of epistemological foundationalism is a characteristic feature of contemporary postmodern thought. On the other hand, however, Timm Triplett, "Recent Work on Foundationalism," *APQ* 27 (1990), 93-116 shows that foundationalism is by no means dead. Nevertheless, it is clear that *anti*-foundationalism cannot simply be discarded as an invention of only one or two American Christian philosophers, as some of its critics have suggested.

[14] This definition concurs roughly with Plantinga's ("Reason and Belief in God," 58f.), and differs from Wolterstorff's proposal (Wolterstorff, "Introduction," in: Plantinga & Wolterstorff (eds.), *Faith and Rationality*, 3) to label this version "classical foundationalism." I find this latter name misleading, since "classical" usually refers to the pre-Enlightenment period. "Classical foundationalism" therefore should better be equated with Plantinga's "ancient and medieval founda-

Now first, modern foundationalism (like all its other versions) consists in a particular theory of what it is to know something which is *itself* neither self-evident nor warranted by adequate inferential procedures. In other words, it does not satisfy its own criteria for knowledge, a fact which underlines its paradigmatic and elusive character. As a normative model for theorizing foundationalism does not pass its own test for real knowledge. Of course this argument is not a straightforward refutation of foundationalism, but it shows its peculiar epistemological status: According to its own standards for justification foundationalism cannot claim to be a form of justified true belief, i.e. of knowledge, and therefore it should be considered as merely a form of "opinion"!

Second, foundationalism cannot in the end avoid a troublesome appeal to intuition. Actually, this appeal forms the Achilles heel of the theory since it occurs at its most crucial juncture, viz. at the very "foundation" of its foundational beliefs. In order to decide which propositions can be considered "self-evident" and which not, we must in some way appeal to what is grasped by us immediately and intuitively. But then the question becomes urgent who are meant by "us" in the previous sentence. For it is not at all clear in advance that intuition is a culture-neutral or even character-neutral category. We have already seen that in pre-Enlightenment theological thought the proposition "God exists" was included into the body of self-evident beliefs, whereas in modern theology it is almost generally excluded.

Furthermore, the mere existence of different varieties of foundationalism, disagreeing on the question of what *kinds* of beliefs can be classified as self-evident, indicates that the deliverances of human intuition are not fixed. To mention two extreme positions in this context: sense datum theorists would insist that apart from analytical truths only sense data can count as self-evident, whereas "revelatory positivists"[15] would at least also include revealed truths. Both positions differ in this respect from modern foundationalism: the first by narrowing, the latter by widening the range of self-evident beliefs. In brief, it is clear that any kind of universally shared intuition of what counts as self-evident is simply missing.[16]

Thirdly, as Alvin Plantinga has pointed out, even if we concede to

---

tionalism."

[15] See Simon Fisher, *Revelatory Positivism?*, Oxford 1988, esp. 306-338. Fisher concludes that both the theology of W. Herrmann and the earliest writings of Karl Barth (i.e., those predating his break with liberalism) are rightly characterised as "revelatory positivist" (335); although he rejects this kind of positivism, Fisher does not succeed in presenting a clear alternative (336-338).

[16] For a critique of intuitionism (though in a somewhat different context), see Vincent Brümmer, *Theology and Philosophical Inquiry*, London 1981, 90-94. See also Richard Rorty, "Intuition," in: *The Encyclopedia of Philosophy*, vol.3, New York 1967, 204-212, and Rorty's fundamental and influential critique of foundationalism as a whole, *Philosophy and the Mirror of Nature*, passim. Cf. in this connection Wittgenstein's remark: "At the foundation of well-founded belief lies belief that is not founded" (Wittgenstein, *On Certainty*, 33e §253).

modern foundationalism that theological statements are never self-evident, it is not clear why only self-evident propositions should be allowed to function as the foundations for our knowledge.[17] For obviously this restriction (like the foundationalist theory as a whole) is neither self-evident nor inferentially derivable from propositions that are self-evident. Therefore, as long as foundationalism does not provide some reason for this restriction, it seems to be "no more than a bit of intellectual imperialism on the part of the foundationalist."[18] Actually, this arbitrary restriction can only be interpreted as indicating the foundationalist's *commitment* to reason (since "self-evident" always means: self-evident to reason).[19] And since "it is obviously impossible to *argue* for the reliability of reasoning without relying on reason to do so,"[20] it is equally impossible for the foundationalist to offer any non-circular justification for his conviction.[21] Therefore, according to his own standards the foundationalist cannot claim that his theory of knowledge is the only rational one.

Fourthly and lastly, as D.Z. Phillips argues, modern foundationalism does not do justice to the primary language of religious belief, because it can at best assign a hypothetical status to this language.[22] Since belief in God is excluded from the set of self-evident beliefs, it can only claim to be a form of knowledge when there is enough external evidence to establish it. The amount, the force and the balance of the evidence, however, always remain open to discussion. For even if the theist would grant that during the last centuries all alleged evidence for the existence of God has been entirely undermined (for example by the development of science), it could always be insisted that new evidence might emerge in the future which will show that the existence of God is as likely as it was thought to be in the Middle Ages. In short: the existence of God is doomed to remain a question of probability and tentativeness.

Now this way of dealing with the existence of God seems overtly at variance with the way in which religious believers speak about God's existence. For clearly to religious believers the existence and reality of God is

---

[17] Plantinga, "Is Belief in God Rational?," in: Delaney, *Rationality and Religious Belief*, 7-27, esp.25f. It might be useful to note that my account of foundationalism differs from Plantinga's in that I don't distinguish between self-evident and incorrigible beliefs as two different sorts of belief which make up the foundations of true knowledge. As Plantinga himself (ibid., 20) observes, under close scrutiny the principle of incorrigibility boils down to that of self-evidence. Therefore, self-evidence can be considered as the only criterion for foundational knowledge.

[18] Plantinga, "Is belief in God rational?," 26.

[19] Plantinga, ibid, 24-27; cf. for the crucial role of commitment in the justification of science Herman Koningsveld, *Het verschijnsel wetenschap*, Meppel 1980[5], 83-90.

[20] William P. Alston, "Christian Experience and Christian Belief," in: Plantinga & Wolterstorff (eds.), *Faith and Rationality*, 119.

[21] Cf. Brümmer, *Theology*, 137: "...anyone can justify his answer to the ultimate questions only by a circular argument - by a petitio principii."

[22] See D.Z. Phillips, *Faith after Foundationalism*, London 1988, esp. 3-12.

inescapable.[23] Many religious believers would even insist that it belongs to the very character of faith to put trust and hope in God precisely in the absence of empirical evidence. When overwhelming empirical evidence for God's existence would be available, they argue, faith would become super-fluous (and, indeed, many believers think this will be the case in the es-chaton). So it is precisely in the absence of decisive empirical evidence that the believer attests to the prevenient and undeniable reality of God. Being the sovereign measure of all things for the believer, God cannot be made subject to measurement, to the assessment of probabilities. For surely, that would imply making Him subject to criteria of assessment which would be endowed with greater authority than God Himself. It seems that foun-dationalists who put God's existence to the test will at best be left in the end with the God of the philosophers, the real God having eluded them. As Basil Mitchell says, the defender of the rationality of religious belief is placed in a dilemma here.

> For, to the extent that he attempts to indicate how faith can be rationally defended, he is led to characterise faith in a way which fails to satisfy the religious mind; but if he portrays faith as it characteristically operates in the life and thought of believ-ers, he describes something inevitably incommensurate with the only sort of jus-tification that is available.[24]

1.2.2 *Modifying strategies: cognitivism and experientialism*
It is for reasons such as those given above that I reject the foundationalist's paradigm in the present study. Now this decision commits us to look for an alternative frame of reference. Philosophers who have challenged foun-dationalism in recent times do not agree among themselves about what kind of alternative (if any) should be put forward in its place. Since the only purpose of the present section is setting the stage for my discussion of one particular Christian doctrine, I need not review all current proposals, but may limit myself to two of the more influential ones. Both of these alter-natives advocate a widening of the foundations of knowledge. The first wants to acknowledge certain religious propositions as foundational, the second certain religious core-experiences. Let us discuss these options in turn.

---

[23] Cf. Phillips' reference to Psalm 139 ("Whither shall I go from thy Spirit? or whither shall I flee from thy presence?" etc.), *Faith after Foundationalism*, 9f. Of course this does not contra-dict the fact that sometimes believers don't experience God's reality, but rather suffer from His hiddenness and absence. Of course such experiences are not in themselves part of religious faith as trusting reliance on God, but are to be explained as assaults on, testings of or doubts about the faith (cf. e.g. Mark 9:24). In this way, however, they are inextricably bound up with faith, as smoke is bound up with fire (John Calvin).

[24] Basil Mitchell, *The Justification of Religious Belief*, London 1973, 116; see also 142 for a summary of Mitchell's solution to this dilemma.

The first option seems to be advocated by Plantinga.[25] After having concluded that there is no sound argument against the inclusion of religious beliefs into the body of foundational propositions, Plantinga simply declares some of them to be foundational, and goes on to point out why other candidates are not acceptable for serving as foundations, how religious beliefs that are foundational relate to others that are not, etc. Thus, apart from other beliefs which we cannot and need not justify by appealing to more basic beliefs, there are also some religious beliefs which enjoy this status.[26]

Being construed along these lines, Plantinga's epistemology amounts to a revised and updated version of the same foundationalism he purports to be "both false and self-referentially incoherent."[27] In fact, this alternative turns out to be merely the youngest member of the same foundationalist family. The only new element in it is the admission of a number of religious beliefs to the foundations of human knowledge (or the human "noetic structure," as Plantinga prefers to put it), as a result of extending the number and sorts of beliefs which may count as foundational (or "basic"). From such basic religious beliefs, it is suggested, all kinds of other religious beliefs can properly be inferred. So there is a shift in the contents of the foundations, but the overall *structure* of the foundationalist paradigm is kept intact. This can be illustrated from the interesting fact that Plantinga continues to employ foundationalist metaphors, which evoke the picture of a building of rational convictions firmly resting on a foundation of basic beliefs. According to Plantinga, any foundational proposition "must be capable of bearing its share of the weight of the entire noetic structure."[28]

I do not contest that this alternative forms an enormous amelioration in comparison to modern foundationalism. In fact, Plantinga reshapes foundationalism in such a way that the first three of the four objections against modern foundationalism stated in the previous subsection do no longer apply. By emphasizing that foundationalism is a basic picture of rationality rather than a theory of knowledge which is itself a piece of knowledge, he eliminates the first objection. By dropping the condition of self-evidence as

---

[25] Unfortunately, I have not been able to make use of Plantinga's most recent work on epistemology (to be collected in a forthcoming book announced as *Warrant*), which is reported to be much more subtle than the earlier work from which I quote. For this reason my formulation is cautious here.

[26] As examples of such beliefs Plantinga lists propositions like "God is speaking to me," "God has created all this," "God disapproves of what I have done," "God forgives me." The statement "God exists" can be inferred adequately from such propositions: "It is not the relatively high-level and general proposition *God exists* that is properly basic, but instead propositions detailing some of his attributes or actions"; Plantinga, "Reason and Belief in God," 81. Cf. the text on a sticker produced by evangelicals, circulating in the Netherlands a couple of years ago: "Jesus lives, I talk with him every day."

[27] Ibid., 90. Admittedly, Plantinga gives this verdict on *modern* foundationalism, but it is clear that his arguments against it apply to the structure of foundationalism as a whole.

[28] Plantinga, "Is Belief in God Rational?," 13.

a neutral standard which universally yields the same results, he meets both the second and the third of the objections made above (and in part raised by Plantinga himself) against modern foundationalism.

What I find somewhat worrying, however, is Plantinga's continued adherence to the foundationalist paradigm, which makes it unclear how he can face the fourth objection against modern foundationalism which we pointed out above. Does Plantinga's epistemology, treating religious foundational propositions as epistemologically on a par with all kinds of other ones, sufficiently take into account the structural differences between scientific knowledge and religious belief? Of course religious belief claims have cognitive dimensions, and therefore religious belief systems are not like self-enclosed autonomous monads, totally immune from external criticism. This does not imply, however, that religious belief is like a set of scientific hypotheses aimed at explaining the phenomena of the world. Rather, it is, to use Wittgenstein's idiom, a different "form of life,"[29] which cannot be assessed by means of scientific standards of rationality, since it has its own standard of rationality. Hence, attempts to make its intelligibility conditional upon external grounds or generally accessible evidence or common criteria for rationality are doomed to misconstrue its real nature. Religion is not built upon a number of basic propositions which give support to the whole enterprise.

Although there certainly are basic propositions in religion - things taken for granted, which are constitutive to the very possibility of the religious language game - these do not receive their credibility from external evidence, but are held fast by all that surrounds them. "They are not the bases *on* which our ways of thinking depend (foundationalism), but are basic *in* our ways of thinking."[30] In order to avoid the confusions which are bound up with vertical building metaphors ("basic," "foundational" etc.) in epistemology, we had better use other terms, like for example Norman Malcolm's "framework proposition":

> We do not *decide* to accept framework propositions... We do come to adhere to a framework proposition, in the sense that it shapes the way we think. The framework propositions that we accept, grow into, are not idiosyncrasies but common ways of speaking and thinking that are pressed on us by our human community.[31]

---

[29] Whether Wittgenstein himself considered religion as a form of life is a matter of debate. It has recently been contested by Fergus Kerr, *Theology after Wittgenstein*, Oxford 1986, 29-31, and re-affirmed by Vincent Brümmer, "A Dialogue of Language Games," in: id., (ed.), *Interpreting the Universe as Creation*, Kampen 1991, 9, who denies that this identification has fideistic consequences.

[30] Phillips, *Faith after Foundationalism*, 123; cf. also, for a comparison of the ways in which such basic propositions function in religion and in perception, id., *Religion Without Explanation*, Oxford 1976, 163-181.

[31] Norman Malcolm, *Thought and Knowledge*, Ithaca 1977, 203.

Here, Malcolm is in line with Wittgenstein, who focused on the wonderful way in which children ordinarily receive a world picture.[32]

In the biblical tradition one such framework proposition is no doubt the proposition that God exists. As is clear from the way belief in God's existence functions in the Bible (never in a hypothetical, argumentative context, but always as a "background belief"), it is not supported by any external epistemological warrants, but only by the practice of religious life and worship in all its diverse aspects. Thus, any (meta-)epistemological theory that claims to do justice to the real nature of religious belief should start from the practice of religious life and worship itself,[33] instead of from some exterior judging faculty. Within religious worship, basic propositions and conceptions don't have the isolated position bestowed upon them by any foundationalist epistemology. Rather, they are embedded in all kinds of practices, rituals, doctrines, experiences, etc. Since it is the whole set of these elements which forms the "plausibility structure"[34] of belief in God, it is arbitrary to single out one of those elements, and grant it epistemological priority. There are neither cognitive statements nor inner experiences which can adequately be described as the grounds or epistemological warrants of religious belief.

As to doctrinal statements (like the proposition "God exists"), we have already argued against their epistemological isolation, but we must now turn to the second influential alternative of modern foundationalism, which may be called "experientialism," since it hinges on the epistemological isolation of religious *experiences*.[35] In considering this set of theories, it will again turn out how difficult it still is to break away from the enchantment of the foundationalist paradigm. In many recent theories of religion since Schleiermacher, experience is considered as the source and core aspect of religious belief. All other aspects (cognitive, moral, psychological, social, institutional etc.) of religion are to be explained in terms of (or as derivable from) experiences.[36] According to George Lindbeck, im-

---

[32] Cf. e.g. the following fragment (§144) from *On Certainty*: "The child learns to believe a host of things. I.e., it learns to act according to these beliefs. Bit by bit there forms a system of what is believed, and in that system some things stand unshakeably fast and some are more or less liable to shift. What stands fast does so, not because it is intrinsically obvious or convincing: it is rather held fast by what lies around it" (21e).

[33] Cf. L.J. van den Brom, *God Alomtegenwoordig*, Kampen 1982, 17. Daniel W. Hardy & David F. Ford, *Jubilate*, London 1984; F.G. Immink, "Theism and Christian Worship," in: G. van den Brink, L.J. van den Brom & M. Sarot (eds.), *Christian Faith and Philosophical Theology*, Kampen 1992, 116-136.

[34] Peter Berger, *The Heretical Imperative*, New York 1979. Cf. Newbigin, *Foolishness*, 10-18.

[35] Interestingly, as noted in n.26 above, according to Plantinga in the last resort it is not the proposition "God exists" which is basic to the noetic structure of religious believers, but rather such propositions as: "God is speaking to me," "God forgives me" and other experience-indicating utterances.

[36] Cf. e.g. Berger, *Heretical Imperative*, 127-156 for a survey of the "experiential tradition" since Schleiermacher.

portant twentieth century adherents of this line of theorizing are, amongst others, Rudolf Otto, Mircea Eliade, and, in a more moderate fashion, Karl Rahner and Bernard Lonergan.[37] No doubt, the list could be extended. As to the Dutch theological climate the work of H.M. Kuitert comes in mind. Whatever the many and important variations between their theories and theologies, all of these thinkers locate what is basic to religion on the level of experience. Thus, the claim that in one way or another experiences are basic to religion, so that in the final analysis doctrinal truth claims can be reduced to inner experiences, is widely accepted, sometimes even without argument.[38] Indeed, the further claim that the various religions are diverse symbolizations of one and the same core experience is hardly less popular.[39] In this connection, Ronald Thiemann is certainly right in stating that "the most pervasive form of foundationalism in modern theology is that which seeks to ground theological language in a universal religious experience."[40]

The problem with this variety of modern foundationalism is not so much that it cannot be proved - since offering conclusive proofs is a highly difficult and therefore doubtful enterprise on this level - but that it is unable to deal adequately with the large variety of interrelations between the different phenomena that have their place in religious life. By narrowing down this variety to a kind of one-way traffic from the bottom of experience to all other phenomena, the fact that the nature of religious experience is also often shaped by those other phenomena (for example religious language and behaviour, doctrines, liturgy etc.) is blurred. In the next subsection I shall elaborate this criticism in some detail when presenting my own alternative to foundationalism.

---

[37] George A. Lindbeck, *The Nature of Doctrine*, Philadelphia 1984, 21, 24. Lindbeck's conclusion seems hardly exaggerated: "The habits of thought it [the experiential tradition] has fostered are ingrained in the soul of the modern West, perhaps particularly in the souls of theologians" (21). According to McGrath, *Genesis of Doctrine*, 20, Lindbeck's criticism of the experiential-expressivist theory "may well be judged to be the most significant long-term contribution he has made to the contemporary discussion of the nature of doctrine."

[38] See e.g. H.M. Vroom, *Religions and the Truth*, Grand Rapids 1989, 327, 340f., 369; at the same time, Vroom acknowledges that "religious experience pure and simple does not exist; experience is always interpreted" (384).

[39] See e.g. David Tracy, *Blessed Rage for Order*, New York 1975, esp. 91-109, where he speaks of religion as disclosing the "limit-dimension" (93) of "our common human experience" (106). This religious dimension is articulated symbolically and metaphorically (108) by means of religious language on the level of self-conscious belief. John Hick is a representative of this view as well, the core experience being in his case the experience of the Transcendent. Although Hick is all too aware of the irreducible plurality of religious experiences, he considers them to be experiences of one and the same object, which is only formally describable (e.g. as "the Transcendent"). Cf. his *An Interpretation of Religion*, London 1989.

[40] Thiemann, *Revelation and Theology*, 73.

1.2.3 *The network of religious belief*

Our rejection of the two modifications of modern foundationalism in the previous subsection makes clear that our own solution must entail a more radical departure from foundationalism. To explicate its main line, we will draw upon George Lindbeck's highly influential study on doctrinal development. Lindbeck emphasizes "the degree to which human experience is shaped, molded, and in a sense constituted by cultural and linguistic forms."[41] According to Lindbeck, becoming religious resembles acquiring a language. In the same way as without a language of some kind we cannot actualize our normal human capacities for thought, we cannot have religious experiences without being skilled in the practices and the language of a given religion. It is worth quoting Lindbeck at greater length here:

> There are numberless thoughts we cannot think, sentiments we cannot have, and realities we cannot perceive unless we learn to use the appropriate symbol systems... To become a Christian involves learning the story of Israel and of Jesus well enough to interpret and experience oneself and one's world in its terms. A religion is above all an external word, a *verbum externum*, that molds and shapes the self and its world, rather than an expression or thematisation of a pre-existing self or pre-conceptual experience. The *verbum internum* (traditionally equated by Christians with the action of the Holy Spirit) is also crucially important, but it would be understood in a theological use of the model as a capacity for hearing and accepting the true religion, the true external word, rather than (as experiential-expressivism would have it) as a common experience diversely articulated in different religions.[42]

In this view, there is no such thing as an unmediated, uninterpreted religious core experience or object which gives rise to different interpretations and religions. The experiences evoked by religions, so the argument goes, are as varied as the religious systems themselves. To classify Buddhist compassion, Christian love and French Revolutionary *fraternité* as different exemplifications of one and the same experience is like classifying apples, Indians and the Moscow square as exemplifications of the same natural genus of "red things."[43] So the problem with the experiential outlook (as well as with the cognitivist approach) is, that it singles out certain specific elements of religion as more fundamental than others, instead of acknowledging the fact that all those elements are intelligible only from within the whole of the religious framework, since they relate to each other in often highly subtle and complicated ways.

---

[41] Lindbeck, *Nature of Doctrine*, 34.

[42] Ibid.

[43] Lindbeck, *Nature of Doctrine*, 40. See for a parallel argument against the idea of a preconceptual unity of all *mystical* experience S.T. Katz, "Language, Epistemology and Mysticism," in: id., (ed.), *Mysticism and Philosophical Analysis*, London 1978, 22-71. Similarly, Grace M. Jantzen, "Could There be a Mystical Core of Religion?," *RS* 26 (1990), 59-72 argues that the very question which forms her title has emerged from mistaken post-Enlightenment parameters.

Moreover, in the experiential perspective as well as in its cognitivist counterpart, it is ultimately the human individual who decides from an allegedly neutral viewpoint on the truth of religion. In this sense, both models constitute typical examples of the Cartesian legacy which is usually referred to as the "turn to the subject." In the Cartesian perspective, the human self is seen as being in a position to decide on its own upon how to take the world - as if it were not itself irreducibly part of that world. The human person is depicted as "the self-conscious and self-reliant, self-transcendent and all-responsible individual," who is "able to view the world from somewhere else - as if one were God, as it were."[44] This conception of the human self as the isolated and autonomous starting point of all true knowledge is underlying epistemological foundationalism in all its varieties. As such, it has permeated not only post-Enlightenment philosophy, but has also functioned as the hidden paradigm behind many forms of modern theology up to the present. "Time and again ... the paradigm of the self turns out to have remarkably divine attributes. The philosophy of the self that possesses so many modern theologians is an inverted theology which philosophers today are working hard to destroy."[45]

Lindbeck tries to overcome these serious shortcomings by developing his "cultural linguistic" theory of religion, which combines the competing emphases of the other two approaches without resorting to the "complicated intellectual gymnastics"[46] he finds in the allegedly hybrid constructions of Karl Rahner and Bernard Lonergan. This approach concentrates upon the respects in which religions resemble languages together with their correlative forms of life and are thus similar to complete cultures. So Lindbeck offers what could be called a holist[47] or comprehensive account of religious belief. In such an account, the affirmation of God's existence is neither a basic or appropriately inferred proposition, nor a datum derived from human religious experience. Nevertheless, it is a theologically indispensable element, which derives its plausibility from the ways in which it functions within the whole network of religious practices, beliefs and experiences.

---

[44] Kerr, *Theology after Wittgenstein*, 5, 16.

[45] Kerr, *Theology after Wittgenstein*, 23; Kerr offers a radical critique of this "modern philosophy of the self," which according to him has decisively influenced such diverse contemporary theologians as Karl Rahner, Hans Küng, Don Cupitt, Schubert Ogden, Gordon Kaufman and others (3-27). Among the few theologians who oppose the emphasis on the self-conscious and autonomous individual from resolutely anti-Cartesian assumptions Kerr reckons Karl Barth and Eberhard Jüngel (8f.). Whether Kerr's attempt to jettison the Cartesian legacy necessarily initiates the "end of metaphysics," as he suggests (136-141), is a question we will take up in the next section.

[46] Lindbeck, *Nature of Doctrine*, 17.

[47] See for a holist account of epistemology W.V.O. Quine, "Two Dogmas of Empiricism," *PR* 60 (1951), 20-43, reprinted in id., *From a Logical Point of View*, London 1980³, 20-46. It is perhaps helpful to add that the use of the term "holism" in this connection should not be confused with one of the other connotations it has got in recent discourse (e.g. in New Age).

Now how do we deal with the obvious objection of relativism in this connection? Doesn't "anything go" according to this anti-foundationalist account of the nature of religious belief? If theistic belief cannot be grounded upon basic truths lying at its bottom, but is contextually determined, how can we argue for its truth? Lindbeck is not entirely clear here, but I think in answering this question it is important to point out two things. First, as we will see in more detail in the next section, although religious belief is not *grounded* in certain ontological truth-claims it certainly makes such truth-claims, because such truth-claims are constitutive to its very rationality. It would, for example, be irrational to pray to God without being committed to the truth-claim that He exists. And second, defending a particular belief claim is not necessarily the same as grounding it. To quote an example of Anthony Kenny, my belief in the existence of Australia is not grounded upon other, more basic beliefs. Although I certainly acquired it on the basis of reasons, I have by now forgotten most of them. Nevertheless, when my belief in the existence of Australia is challenged, I am perfectly able to defend it by offering reasons for it. In the words of Kenny himself:

> None the less I can defend the belief to others by offering considerations which, while not providing reasons for me because they are not better known to me than the conclusion is, might reasonably provide reasons for other people whose noetic structure did not afford the existence of Australia.[48]

In the same way, belief in the existence of God can be *defended by*, although it is not *grounded in* rational considerations concerning the ontological implications which are constitutive to this belief. The way in which such a defence is structured is open to public discussion according to common standards of rationality. The cogency of my arguments for the existence of God, the reliability of my personal experience of God etc. can all be discussed to a certain extent irrespective of the ultimate position I have adopted. But now consider the situation in which believers have to admit that all their adduced reasons for the existence of God are ill-formed. In that case, since they know better that God exists than that they were certain about their adduced reasons, they are not obliged to give up this belief in God. Their faith in God does not depend upon those reasons, because it is far more deeply embedded in the whole network of their thinking, acting, and interpreting the world than those reasons are. Only when this context changes, for example, because believers are no longer able to interpret important segments of their world in terms of their faith, or

---

[48] Kenny, *What is Faith?*, 25f. The distinction between founding and defending belief claims is also put forward by G. Gutting, *Religious Belief and Religious Skepticism*, Notre Dame 1982, 41f., who draws the following corollary: "The claim of groundlessness implies only that the belief is immune to the criticism that one is not entitled to a religious belief because one has no sufficient evidence for it" (42). What it does *not* imply is that no external criticism and no justificatory rational defence is possible.

because their belief system is no longer consistent, their belief in God is going to be endangered.[49]

Thus, certainly talk of rational justification is not out of order in the case of religious belief. But it is the mistake of foundationalism to confuse rational justification with causal explanation, as if a belief were justified only when its origin, source and cause has been identified in a way which is universally acceptable.[50] Rather, it is the whole context of practices, beliefs and experiences which forms the context of justification and clarification of the proposition: "God exists."

In this sense, dealing with the omnipotence of God presupposes the affirmation of God's existence. It is in spelling out the way in which the doctrine of divine omnipotence - or any other doctrine - functions within the Christian view of life that the inner rationality of this view of life, including its affirmation of God's existence can be elucidated. Spelling out these functions is what I intend do in the present study. First, however, we must consider in somewhat more detail what is implied in this activity of spelling out the functions of a doctrine. What kind of thing is a doctrine, what does it mean to say that a doctrine has functions, and what does it mean to spell out those functions? It is to these questions that we turn next.

1.3 DOCTRINES AND THE TASK OF SYSTEMATIC THEOLOGY

1.3.1 *Reductionist accounts of doctrine*
In the previous section we joined such postmodern[1] thinkers as Phillips and Lindbeck in briefly sketching a theory of religion which is not affected by the foundationalist paradigm. Since in what follows we are going to deal not with a particular religion as a whole but with a theological doctrine, we must now explore to some extent the nature of those specific components of religious world views which are called doctrines. Only if we grasp the concept of doctrine we are able to proceed along appropriate lines in our study of the doctrine of God's almightiness. Indeed, it will turn out that our exploration of the nature of doctrine quite naturally leads us to a discussion of the criteria which should function in the study of doctrine as undertaken in systematic theology. If we want our method to be properly geared to the object of our inquiry, we must make use of these criteria, although we must at the same time take into consideration that the present study is in

---

[49] Cf. in this connection the five criteria that any view of life has to meet if it is to fulfil the function of a view of life, mentioned by Brümmer, *Theology*, 139-143: freedom from contradiction, unity, relevance, universality, and impressiveness.

[50] Here I paraphrase the apt formulations of Thiemann, *Revelation and Theology*, 43f.

[1] For my use of the term "postmodern" (indicating the break with philosophical thought forms stemming from the Cartesian and Enlightenment traditions) as distinct from its use in other (e.g. continental deconstructivist) circles, see my "Lesslie Newbigin," 303-306.

philosophical theology rather than in systematic theology in general. Now what does an account of doctrine in line with a non-foundational epistemology of religion amount to?

One of the most important insights of postmodern philosophy of religion is, that doctrinal statements in religion resemble grammatical rules in languages.[2] From this point of view, the primary function of doctrinal statements as communally authoritative teachings is not to make ontological truth claims, neither to express religious experiences or religious dimensions of common human experience, but to clarify the usage rules for religious discourse within a particular religious tradition. And theology, as the activity of clarifying these rules, does not consist in a free theoretical pursuit of speculative truth irrespective of its relevance to the community of believers, but is entirely concentrated upon the beliefs and practices of that very community. As such, the theologian is not primarily engaged in the first-order activity of making material statements about God, man, the world etc., but in the more practical second-order activity of structuring *talk* about these matters in an organized fashion.

In distinction from many of those who have made the "linguistic turn,"[3] however, I want to stress the inclusive rather than exclusive character of picturing doctrines as grammatical rules and theology as a way of clarifying their interrelations. It is important to be aware of the variety of tasks doctrines fulfill within a religious community. In regulating religious speech and practice they function as rules assessing what can and what cannot be properly said, as directives indicating what kind of attitudes are correct under what kind of conditions, but also as referential claims as to what is ontologically true, and as indicators of the sorts of experience that may count as authentic in different situations. As Kathryn Tanner tells us:

> Theology may be called to do many different things within the context of a Christian form of life - to make first-order claims about God and world, recommend courses of action, criticize or support the practice of the community, regulate the church's belief and action, police itself etc.[4]

All attempts to reduce this rich plurality and multiplicity of doctrinal schemes and to isolate one particular function as fundamental result in theories which must be characterized as, indeed, reductive.

Usually, such theories which emphasize only one particular function

---

[2] It should be noted, however, that the metaphor of theology as grammar is not an invention of postmodern philosophers (among whom Wittgenstein must be mentioned first of all), but can be traced back via J.G. Hamann to at least Martin Luther. See Kerr, *Theology after Wittgenstein*, 146, n.1. The broader metaphor of doctrines as rules is even older (cf. the phrase *regula fidei*, which goes back to the patristic period).

[3] See for the theological use of this term e.g. the survey of David B. Burrell, "Theology and the Linguistic Turn," *Communio* 6 (1979), 95-112.

[4] Kathryn Tanner, *God and Creation in Christian Theology*, Oxford 1988, 13.

Usually, such theories which emphasize only one particular function of doctrines take them to be informative propositions or truth claims about objective realities. Here, the focus is on the ontological content of doctrines rather than on the (other) functions doctrines fulfill in the community of believers. As Charles Wood observes with regard to the Christian tradition, "theology has typically been concerned with the *content*, to the neglect of the *function*, of doctrine," i.e., to the neglect of "the way doctrine actually serves ... as an instrument for the regulation of the church's existence."[5]

In our days, however, the opposite reduction is more frequently propagated. Especially among those who are expanding on the theological applications of Wittgenstein's philosophical legacy it is often claimed that theological doctrines entirely lack ontological content.[6] The theologian who is analyzing a particular doctrinal statement should be content with spelling out the various ways in which it functions in religious practice and discourse. If he wants to specify in addition what is actually claimed to be the case in reality by that particular doctrine, he is simply confused about the nature of doctrine. According to D.Z. Phillips, for example, it is a confusion to construct the reality of God as if He were a physical object.[7] Now surely the reality of God is not of the same order as the reality of physical objects. But this is not to say that God has no reality at all independent from the religious belief-system in which He is worshipped.

Instead, it is inherent in for example the Christian faith to assert that the divine reality is in a certain sense more real than any created realities. It is exactly when we turn to the practice of Christian discourse itself and consider its grammar, that we come across the ascription of maximal (or necessary or perfect) reality to God. It is not at all clear why the grammar of Christian belief should prohibit us from labelling this reality as the highest possible *ontological* reality - as in fact many classical theologians have done. On the contrary, it is precisely because in the eyes of the believer God is more real than anything else in the universe, that he believes in God and worships Him. Of course it may be true that God has often been conceived naturalistically, and that believers, overlooking God's transcendence, often try to relate themselves to God as though He were part of our natural world. Nevertheless, *abusus non tollit usus*: the failures of believers to grasp the uniqueness of God does not imply that the proper use of religious language cannot or does not *refer* to the ontological reality of God. The problem which recurs time and again in Phillips' writings is, that he disregards the undeniable relations between the religious language game and the "real-world" language.[8]

---

[5] Charles M. Wood, *Vision and Discernment*, Atlanta 1985, 91.

[6] It is still a matter of dispute whether Wittgenstein himself denied that religious language has ontological implications; cf. the literature cited in §1.2 n.29 above.

[7] Phillips, *Religion Without Explanation*, 171; id., *Faith after Foundationalism*, 203.

[8] Cf. the excellent critique of Phillips' view in W. Proudfoot, *Religious Experience*, Berkeley

Phillips is right, as we saw in section 1.2, in warning against a confused portrayal of those relations, as if ontological statements (i.e., statements in "real-world" language) constitute the foundation of our religious language and practices. He rightly opposes "that strong tradition in which propositions about the existence of God are treated as the *presuppositions* of religion."[9] In the same vein, he had pointed out in an earlier study that "the relation between religious beliefs and non-religious facts cannot be that between what is justified and its justification, or that between a conclusion and its grounds."[10]

However, all this does not imply that propositions pertaining to extra-religious facts do not belong to religious belief at all. On the contrary, although truth claims about objective realities independent of the grammar of doctrine do not function as the presuppositions or foundations of religious belief, they certainly function in some way or another within religion. As such diverse thinkers as Kai Nielsen and Edward Henderson have persuasively argued, religious discourse and practice is inextricably bound up with belief in the ultimate nature of things.[11] To quote Henderson:

> It is not the same thing to say that religious beliefs cannot be *justified* by reference to realities outside of religious life or by philosophical arguments and proofs (non-foundationalism) as to say that theistic language does not refer to a God who exists in himself independently of the life of faith...[12]

It is certainly a form of reductionism to hold that doctrines only function as the regulative or grammatical principles of the internal language of faith,

---

1985, 200-212.

[9] Phillips, *Faith after Foundationalism*, 202 (italics by the author; Phillips does not, as I will propose below, distinguish presuppositions from grounds of belief).

[10] D.Z. Phillips, *Faith and Philosophical Enquiry*, New York 1971, 101.

[11] Kai Nielsen, "Religion and Groundless Believing," in: Frederick Crosson (ed.), *The Autonomy of Religious Belief. A Critical Inquiry*, Notre Dame 1981, 93-107; Edward Henderson, "A Critique of Religious Reductionism," *PRA* 8 (1983), 429-456. I owe these references to a paper of Brian Hebblethwaite, "God and Truth," Presidential Address SST, Oxford 1989, which is to my knowledge as yet unpublished (see p.18). Both authors do not succumb to the temptation of isolating the truth claims of religious (especially theistic) belief in a foundationalist fashion from the actual forms and practices of religious life. Cf. for example Nielsen's avowal: "I agree, of course, that religion can have no ... philosophical or metaphysical foundations. I do not even have a tolerably clear sense of what it means to say that there is some *distinctive philosophical* knowledge that would give us 'the true grounds' of religious belief."; ibid., 104f.

[12] Henderson, "A Critique of Religious Reductionism," 440. See also his careful but convincing classification of Phillips as a 'reductionist', 442-446; although "Phillips' discussions are so subtle," Henderson can see "no other interpretation of his views than to say that he understands the reality of God to consist wholly in the practical value theistic language has in structuring the lives that use it, giving them their peculiar values, outlooks, attitudes, and characters," 443. Phillips' subtlety is in the fact that he does not deny the appropriateness of talk about God's objective reality as such, provided only that the implications of such talk are not permitted to transcend the scope of the religious language game.

while denying that they also deal with the ontological nature of entities external to that language of faith.

1.3.2 *A multi-functional view of doctrine*

That the last-mentioned form of reductionism is not inherent in the adoption of "grammar" as a basic metaphor for the nature of doctrine and theology, becomes clear when we turn once again to Lindbeck's cultural-linguistic approach, in order to find out what it yields with regard to the nature of doctrine. Just like Phillips and other Wittgensteinians, Lindbeck views doctrines as grammatical rules for structuring (or, rather, discovering the structure of) religious language. Correspondingly, he labels his approach as the "regulative or rule theory of doctrine." However, in distinction from Phillips and others, Lindbeck seems to present his theory as inclusive rather than exclusive. Lindbeck is aware of the referential function religious utterances have according to many religious believers, and he considers it "crucial for our argument to ask whether the picture we have sketched does justice to what religious people themselves maintain."[13] As a result, he concludes that

> ... a religion can be interpreted as possibly containing ontologically true affirmations, not only in cognitivist theories but also in cultural-linguistic ones. There is nothing in the cultural-linguistic approach that requires the rejection ... of the epistemological realism and correspondence theory of truth, which, according to most of the theological tradition, is implicit in the conviction of believers that when they rightly use a sentence such as "Christ is Lord" they are uttering a true first-order proposition.[14]

The difference between a cognitivist and a cultural-linguistic account is in the fact that the latter stresses the indissoluble interwovenness of first-order propositions with the concrete religious activities of adoration, proclamation, obedience, promise-making etc. In this connection, Lindbeck incorporates J.L. Austin's notion of a "performatory" use of language into his theory: "a religious utterance, one might say, acquires the propositional truth of ontological correspondence only insofar as it is a performance, an act or deed..."[15]

Lindbeck gives an illuminating example of this performatory character of religious language: When St. Paul tells us that no one can say that Jesus is Lord, except by the Holy Spirit (1 Cor. 12:3), he means that "the only way to assert this truth is to do something about it, i.e., to commit oneself to a way of life."[16] To put this in the words of Brümmer,

---

[13] Lindbeck, *Nature of Doctrine*, 66.

[14] Ibid., 69.

[15] Ibid., 65; cf. John L. Austin, "Performative Utterances," in his *Philosophical Papers*, Oxford 1970², 232-252.

[16] Lindbeck, *Nature of Doctrine*, 66.

propositional talk about God can never be existentially neutral: "The question of God's factual nature is therefore never an *existentially neutral* question which we can disconnect from the question about the way of life which we are to lead in the presence of God."[17] In this way, doctrinal statements are closely bound up with the *praxis pietatis*.

Thus, Lindbeck's approach has important advantages in comparison with the traditional Wittgensteinian account of doctrine. Nevertheless, there are some passages in Lindbeck which raise serious doubts about whether he really succeeds in doing justice to what is maintained by religious believers themselves. For after having granted that there is room for first-order propositions within a cultural-linguistic perspective on religion, Lindbeck goes on to assert that

> ... technical theology and official doctrine, in contrast, are second-order discourse about the first-intentional uses of religious language. Here, in contrast to the common supposition, one rarely if ever succeeds in making affirmations with ontological import... Just as grammar by itself affirms nothing either true or false regarding the world in which language is used, but only about language, so theology and doctrine, to the extent that they are second-order activities, assert nothing either true or false about God and his relations to creatures...[18]

The most puzzling phrases in this quotation are doubtlessly "rarely if ever" and "to the extent that." Clearly, such ambiguous expressions leave some room for doctrinal first-order statements. But since Lindbeck does not decide between "rarely" and "if ever" and neither specifies to *what* extent theology and doctrines are second-order activities, the reader remains uncertain about his criteria here. In any case, it is clear that Lindbeck wants to minimize the referential function of doctrinal utterances.[19]

His hesitations in this respect are probably attributable to his knowing all too well that minimizing the referential function of doctrines means deviating from what most religious believers themselves consider to be the nature of doctrine. To take up Lindbeck's previous example, it is quite clear that Paul believed that Christ's Lordship is objectively real irrespective of the faith or lack of faith in those who hear or say the words "Christ is Lord."[20] So this statement at least seems to function as a doctrine with an unambiguously specifiable referential content. It is certainly not merely a private commitment to or an alignment of the believer with Christ, since the believer will claim that the statement has consequences for other people (including non-believers) as well. Lindbeck's theory of doctrine hardly accounts for these aspects. In this connection, Brian Hebblethwaite

---

[17] Vincent Brümmer, *Speaking of a Personal God*, Cambridge 1992, 59.

[18] Lindbeck, *Nature of Doctrine*, 69.

[19] Cf. also Lindbeck's "agnostic" interpretation of Aquinas' account of analogy, 66f.

[20] As Lindbeck himself considers in his refutation of the experiential view of doctrine; ibid., 66.

seems correct in his observation that Lindbeck makes an all too "minimal concession to realism."[21]

After all, it turns out that Lindbeck fails in maximally exploiting the integrative capacities of his cultural-linguistic theory. For that reason, L.J. van den Brom proposes to *extend* the cultural-linguistic approach of religion to encompass not only vocabulary (i.e. the stories, concepts, rites, symbols etc. of a religion) and grammar (i.e., the rules for interrelating the vocabulary), but also implicit and explicit truth claims. According to Van den Brom, Lindbeck's distinctions "are more like the various aspects of religious language in the way that speech acts always fulfil several functions at the same time. Although a speech act may be primarily constative, or primarily expressive or prescriptive, it is never one of these at a time."[22]

Van den Brom's proposal should be interpreted so as to apply to the theory of doctrine too. Here also, the reductionist usage of isolating one particular function blinds us to the rich variety of functions that doctrines have. The precise number of functions varies from doctrine to doctrine, and, perhaps, from time to time. Thus, "practical doctrines" (as Lindbeck calls them) structure religious life and thought, but have no referential function. Theoretical doctrines, on the other hand, usually have a referential function, and a language-guiding function as well. Often, they also have an experiential function because of their expressing religious experiences. The most important function of all doctrines is no doubt the doxological function. Actually, all doctrinal construct formation rises from doxology i.e. from the practice of religious worship and spirituality.[23] It is because God is worthy of worship that believers talk about Him at all. In this way, doxology is constitutive for doctrine and theology.[24]

Within such a multi-functional view of doctrine, the role of ontological truth claims is neither overestimated nor underestimated. On the one hand, it is denied that they form the *foundations* of religious belief and practices; on the other hand, it is denied that they do not function at all within religious life and thought. One of the ways in which they function, is certainly as the *implications* of religious practice and belief. We cannot

---

[21] Hebblethwaite, "God and Truth," 21. See for similar criticism of Lindbeck's argument Luco J. van den Brom, "Hermeneutics as a Feedback System for Systematic Theology," in: *Proceedings of the Seventh European Conference on Philosophy of Religion*, Utrecht 1988, 178-182.

[22] Van den Brom, "Hermeneutics," 182.

[23] This crucial relation between doctrine, dogmatics and doxology has often been recognized in Christian theology; cf. e.g. Wolfhart Pannenberg, *Basic Questions in Theology* Vol. I, London 1971, esp. the articles "What is a Dogmatic Statement?" (182-210) and "Analogy and Doxology" (211-238). See also the literature quoted in §1.2 n.33, and Geoffrey Wainwright, *Doxology*, London 1980.

[24] As a result, doctrine and theology are typical 'insider' phenomena. Outside the context in which the community of faith tries to make sense of its encounter with and experience of God, they seem "barren and lifeless, in that they link with the worship and spirituality of the community" (McGrath, *Genesis of Doctrine*, 12).

praise God for His goodness or trust Him as our Almighty Father without implying that God exists. The relation between religious practice and ontology is, however, even closer than that of an implication. For since it is impossible to trust God for His almightiness while at the same time denying that He really is almighty, the ontological truth claim implied in the sentence "God is almighty" functions as a *constitutive presupposition* for the meaningfulness of the religious practice.

It is important not to misunderstand the term "presupposition" in this connection as akin to "foundation." Constitutive presuppositions are not identical with external foundations.[25] The latter are assumed to support bodies of religious practice and belief, whereas the former are primarily *derived* from those bodies. Talk of constitutive presuppositions instead of foundations guarantees the independence of religious practice from external grounds, without precluding the possibilities of clarification and self-correction in the communication with other forms of life. In this way, ontological truth claims function as the constitutive presuppositions of religious life.[26] One of the functions of doctrine certainly is to spell out these ontological presuppositions.[27]

Thus, a multi-functional view of doctrine guarantees that ontological claims are neither detached from their context in the practice of religious life and worship, nor totally absorbed by that context. It is precisely at this point, that the possibility for dialogue between science and theology emerges. Surely, God is not an explanatory hypothesis, as Phillips insists. Nevertheless, for the believer belief in God *does* provide explanations of reality. To quote Hebblethwaite's clear example: "... surely the perspective of faith in God, the Father Almighty, maker of heaven and earth, provides, among other things, an explanation of the existence of the world."[28] At this level, the domains of science and religion touch each other and interact with

---

[25] This is not to say that there are no *internal* foundational relationships within the Christian form of life, e.g. between different doctrines; in this way, it is of course quite justified to hold that God as creator is the *ground* of the universe, or that God's will is the foundation of morality.

[26] One may wonder how these constitutive presuppositions relate to Norman Malcolm's "framework propositions" (see above, §1.2 n.31). I tend to view the latter as peculiar instances of the former. As Malcolm uses the term, framework propositions are a sort of transcendental concepts which tie together the whole scheme of religious life and thought, and which cannot be denied without causing the collapse of the entire practice of religious worship. This is the way a statement like "God exists" functions in theistic religions. Statements like "The material world exists," "There has been a past," "There are other minds" etc. have a similar function in other contexts. See for this similarity e.g. Alvin Plantinga, *God and Other Minds*, Ithaca 1967. Note, however, that only *some* of the ontological truth claims which play a role in religion possess such a pivotal function in religious life and practice.

[27] Here I disagree with the view, popularized in the Netherlands by C.A. van Peursen (cf. his *Cultuur in stroomversnelling*, Kampen 1992⁸), that the ontological worldview has been rendered out of date by the functional worldview. Twentieth-century people still want to know how things ultimately are!

[28] Hebblethwaite, "God and Truth," 17.

each other in specific ways, since religion does not strictly confine itself to the meaning as opposed to the explanation of things (i.e., to how things *ought* to be as opposed to how things factually *are*).

1.3.3 *Criteria for systematic theology*

As will be clear from the foregoing discussion, it is in my view the task of (especially: systematic) theology to unfold the diverse functions of and relations between doctrines in a systematic way. From the perspective of a non-foundational account of religion and doctrine, this task is primarily a descriptive one. As Ronald Thiemann argues, "a descriptive theology makes normative proposals but does not seek to justify those proposals by developing a foundational explanatory theory. 'Description' is an interpretive activity which seeks to illuminate the structures embedded in beliefs and practices."[29] In this way, Christian theology tries to elucidate the grammar (or, if you want: the logic) of Christian faith. It is engaged in the Anselmian enterprise of *faith seeking understanding* rather than in the enterprise of faith seeking foundation. As far as the search for understanding is concerned with the *justification* of faith, the material justifying conditions are internal to the Christian theistic framework. Thus, theology of this kind "seeks to uncover the patterns of coherent interrelationships which characterize the beliefs and practices of that complex phenomenon we call the Christian faith."[30] It re-describes the internal structures, the presuppositions and the implications of this faith.

Now as long as theology is in this way squarely located within the Christian tradition and community, there is nothing wrong with its occasionally concentrating upon the ontological implications and presuppositions of Christian belief and worship. This concentration is even necessary, since one of the essential aspects of Christian faith is its belief in the *ontological priority* of God to the Christian religious framework. Therefore, as Ingolf Dalferth explains, the question of the relation between faith and ontology certainly belongs to the body of theological themes. This question is conditional upon the truth claims which are ingredients of the faith, and for that reason it should not be ignored.[31] So providing its reliance upon the whole set of beliefs, attitudes and practices which constitute the Christian framework, the involvement of theology in ontology is entirely legitimate. If we define its parameters correspondingly, we can even use the (in both post-Kantian and Wittgensteinian circles notorious) term "metaphysics" as a substitute for ontology here.[32]

---

[29] Thiemann, *Revelation and Theology*, 72.

[30] Ibid., 75.

[31] Ingolf U. Dalferth, *Existenz Gottes und Christlicher Glaube*, München 1984, 31. "Zu die ... theologisch ausdrücklich zu thematisierenden Problemen gehört insbesondere die *ontologische Problematik*. Sie ist mit dem Wahrheitsanspruch des Glaubens gesetzt und kann von der Theologie infolgedessen nicht ignoriert werden."

[32] Especially in continental theology, there are signs of a revaluation of metaphysics as a

In brief, we can define Christian systematic theology as the activity of spelling out the diverse functions fulfilled by doctrines as the linguistic rules for proper Christian speech-acts, including the constative (or referential or ontological or metaphysical) functions which are - together with other, for example prescriptive and expressive ones - part of the "illocutionary force" of these acts.[33] Now the next question is, of course, how to establish what may count as *proper* Christian discourse. What criteria must be employed in deciding whether a particular doctrine or a particular interpretation or use of it is acceptable or not? An answer to this question is suggested by our previous account of the nature of doctrine and theology. I would like to propose three criteria, which follow more or less from our previous discussion.[34]

First of all, since doctrines are embedded in a specific religious tradition and should not be abstracted from this tradition in a speculative way, they should be in harmony with that tradition. This harmony may be creative in character rather than repetitive, but in the end theology is a communal rather than an individual enterprise, and the acceptability of theological proposals is always judged by a community of believers.[35] In this way, Christian theology has to be in creative harmony with the beliefs of the church, i.e. with the community of faith which confesses Jesus Christ as Lord.

In Christian theology, a minimum condition for such harmony is concordance with the Bible, since the recognition of the Bible as the primary standard of authority (the *norma normans*, as the traditional term formulates) is an essential ingredient of Christian identity. The lack of unanimity as to *how* the Bible functions as authoritative canon should not distract us from the fact *that* it actually does so one way or another.[36] Further, in the tradition of the Christian faith, the Bible has been actualized and interpreted continuously, and the most widely accepted results of these activities have been laid down in credal documents. A theologian who

---

distinctive theological enterprise. See, besides the book of Dalferth quoted in the previous note, e.g. W. Pannenberg, *Metaphysics and the Idea of God*, Edinburgh 1990, and W. Kasper, "Zustimmung zum Denken. Von der Unerlässlichkeit der Metaphysik für die Sache der Theologie," *ThQ* 169 (1989), 257-271.

[33] See for this terminology e.g. Brümmer, *Theology*, 9-33.

[34] Although I differ in details from both of them, I am indebted to Vincent Brümmer, "Metaphorical Thinking and Systematic Theology," *NTT* 43 (1989), 213-228 and to Ronald Thiemann, *Revelation and Theology*, 92-94 for my list of criteria.

[35] "The views of theologians are doctrinally significant, in so far as they have won acceptance within the community"; McGrath, *Genesis*, 11.

[36] See for this plurality in uses of the Bible as authoritative standard for theology David Kelsey, *The Uses of Scripture in Recent Theology*, Philadelphia 1975; for the authoritative status of Scripture as ingredient in Christian identity cf. Kelsey's conclusive remark: "The answer to which our entire analysis of 'authority' for theology points is this: Taking these writings [viz. of the Bible] as 'scripture', and even as 'canon', is an integral part of certain ways of becoming a Christian." (164).

refuses to take such documents seriously, runs the risk of becoming irrelevant to the community of believers that *does* take them seriously. In this way, post-biblical traditions of interpretation and actualization function as additional standards of authority. Although these traditions always function within a kind of feedback system with the Bible itself and are therefore corrigible, they are at the same time indispensable as more or less authorized ways of interpreting and actualizing the biblical text. According to Christians, the authoritative sources of their tradition contain the truth about God, man and the universe, i.e., the truth about what is ontologically real. Thus, when systematic theology focusses on this first criterion, it emphasizes the truth-claiming functions of doctrines.

It is for this reason that in studying (even in *philosophically* studying) the doctrine of divine omnipotence we cannot avoid investigating the authoritative sources of the Christian tradition. If we want to know which notion of divine omnipotence may count as authentically Christian, we must take our starting point in the biblical view of almightiness as interpreted and handed down in the Christian tradition. For clearly, it is this view which has been accepted as authoritative within the community of believers, and any proposal for reinterpreting the doctrine concerning God's power today should be in harmony with it. Otherwise our proposals cannot claim to be authentically Christian. In this way, the concepts of authority, community and authenticity hang closely together. For this reason I shall start my study of the omnipotence-doctrine with a rather detailed account of how the biblical confession of God as almighty has been interpreted and elaborated in the Christian tradition (chapter 2). And for the same reason, at several places in the present study I shall reject notions of divine power which turn out to deviate substantially from this authoritative notion (see for example section 3.4).

A second criterion for systematic theology can be labelled as "comprehensive conceptual coherence." A well-known and hermeneutically inescapable problem with respect to the authority of the Bible has always been, that it is easy to select a particular strand of ideas from it, and construct a complete theology around it, thereby neglecting other and equally authoritative strands of biblical thought. Therefore, a requirement for acceptable doctrine formation is a comprehensive rather than selective dealing with the authoritative texts. Every factor which might have a bearing on the content of the doctrine should be accounted for, none should be neglected.

However, to account for all relevant factors does not simply mean listing them without forgetting any. Such an approach would probably result in a highly incoherent specimen of theology. Incoherent doctrinal proposals are unacceptable because of their unintelligibility. If, for example, a doctrine concerning God's power states on the one hand that nothing is impossible for God to do (appealing to for example Luke 1:37) and on the other hand attributes weakness and inability to Him (for example with reference to 1 Cor.1:25 or 2 Tim.2:13), without any efforts being made to relate both statements to each other, it is unintelligible what the doctrine is all about and what it wants us to believe or to do. For that reason, it is inadequate. The different concepts which play a role in a particular *locus* of theology should be carefully attuned to each other. In this way, the second criterion particularly emphasizes the role of doctrines as regulative principles for proper Christian speech. It is concerned with the (coherent) *meaning* of Christian talk, rather than with its *truth*.

As to the present inquiry, it is incumbent upon us to interpret the doctrine of omnipotence in a way which is not only internally consistent and coherent with all what we claim to know in other contexts, but which also fulfills the requirement of comprehensiveness by doing maximal justice to all considerations which are relevant in relation to God's power. If we meet paradoxical strands of thought concerning God's omnipotence, we must do our utmost to find out whether, and if so how, these hang together with each other in a coherent way. This is a concern which we will have to keep in mind during the whole course of this study. At every stage, contradictory and incohesive claims with regard to God's power should be avoided. I will give special attention to this criterion, however, in the third chapter, in which I try to analyse the concept of omnipotence in a consistent and comprehensively coherent way.

A third criterion for the formulation of acceptable doctrinal proposals is their "adequacy to the demands of life."[37] A nagging problem with the criterion of comprehensive coherence is, that in a conceptually coherent and comprehensive doctrinal theory it is still often unavoidable that certain aspects are highlighted, whereas others are allotted only a secondary role. This is due to the fact that in the process of relating different aspects to each other in order to attain coherence, often one underlying model has to be constructed in terms of which all aspects are to be explained. But the choice of one "key model"[38] rather than another necessarily implies a certain amount of one-sidedness. In other words: the requirements of comprehensiveness and of conceptual coherence are competing requirements. As a result, the ideal of a doctrine which is completely comprehensive as well as completely conceptually coherent is seldom if ever realized.

At this point, our third criterion comes in. Sometimes, the acceptability of a theological theory is co-determined by the degree to which it enables us to cope adequately with the demands of life. An illuminating example in the sphere of the subject of the present study is offered by Sallie McFague. In the past, McFague argues, the doctrine of divine almightiness had a clear sense; people were almost unceasingly threatened by lethal epidemic diseases, oppressed by feudal lords, in danger of being killed in

---

[37] Brümmer, "Metaphorical Thinking," 226.
[38] See for this term Brümmer, "Metaphorical Thinking," 222f.

war etc. In this situation, discourse which stressed the providential care and the ultimate total control of God was of great help in facing the demands of life. On the other hand, in our present "nuclear age" situation, in which we have the power to destroy ourselves and the whole ecosystem in which we live, such discourse would be quite counterproductive, since it obscures our human *responsibility*. Therefore, *we* need to jettison the classical doctrine of divine omnipotence and sovereignty, and replace it by concepts, metaphors and models which emphasize a sense of mutuality, shared responsibility, reciprocity and interdependent love between God and human beings, human beings and their environment, etc.[39]

Now the point of quoting this example is not to argue that McFague is correct in her appraisal of the doctrine of divine omnipotence. Actually, her judgement seems to be solely based upon the third criterion, without taking into account the other criteria. Such a selective procedure is too easy to be convincing. Nevertheless, the view McFague offers anticipates some of the issues we have to discuss later on. For clearly, one of the practical demands of life is that in numerous situations with which life confronts us we have to *act*. What the McFague-example shows us is not only how the actual cultural situation can be relevant to the task of theology in doctrine formation, but also that we are in permanent need of life-guiding principles which enable us to act in proper ways. One of the functions of doctrine is to offer such principles, as orientational devices which have to work in different practical situations. In this way, a doctrine of omnipotence which is adequate to the demands of life should allow for responsible human agency and should enable us to deal with experiences which seem to contradict it, such as the experience of suffering and evil. It is to these practical challenges to the doctrine of God's power that we will turn in chapter 4.

Clearly, it is not so much the propositional *truth* or the conceptual *meaning* of the doctrine which is primarily at stake here, but rather its practical *relevance* as a life-guiding principle. It should be noted that this criterion may ask for the doctrinal accentuation of particular aspects of a doctrine rather than others, without thereby implying that those other aspects are false. For example, in some situations it is appropriate to high-light the compassion and love of God, whereas in other situations His wrath and righteousness should be emphasized. As Luther once pointedly remarked,

> ... if I profess with the loudest voice and clearest exposition every portion of the truth of God except precisely that little point which the world and the devil are at that moment attacking, I am not confessing Christ, however boldly I may be professing Christ. Where the battle rages, there the loyalty of the soldier is proved. To be steady on all battle fronts besides is mere flight and disgrace if he flinches

---

[39] Sallie McFague, *Models of God*, London 1987, 14-21; cf. 29f.

at that point.[40]

To relate this to McFague's example: according to her, in the present situation "that little point" is our human responsibility for the continued existence of the earth. Sometimes, some aspects or interpretations or uses of doctrines need to be emphasized more than others. In applying this criterion, however, we should keep in mind that for two reasons this criterion can never be used in isolation from the other ones.

First, the recognition of an entirely *independent* criterion to secure the relevance of Christian faith and doctrines in the present situation would suggest that Christian faith does not in itself entail its validity and relevance for today. And, as Christoph Schwöbel observes in this connection,

> ... this would be an implicit challenge to the claim to universal validity of Christian faith which is grounded in the ontological character of the Christian assertions... This would deprive the whole enterprise of systematic theology of its basis. Therefore it is necessary to interpret the present validity and relevance of Christian faith as an *implication* of the universality of the fundamental truth claims of Christian faith.[41]

However, this point can also be turned on its head: in order for its claim to universality to be meaningful, it must be possible to show wherein the relevance of Christian faith in the present situation consists. In this sense, the criterion of adequacy to the demands of life is justified as long as it functions in constant interaction with the other ones.

Second, what the demands of life amount to differs not only from culture to culture and from time to time, but also from person to person. Moreover, people differ not only about the question of what they think to be the "demands of life" which they have to face, but also about how to cope with these demands adequately. Thus, the notion is necessarily "person-relative."[42] In this way, for Christians both the demands of life and the most adequate responses to them will at least partly be shaped by the content of their Christian faith. So clearly, the criterion of adequacy to the

---

[40] Quoted by Lindbeck, *Nature of Doctrine*, 75; the original is in WA-B 3, 81f.

[41] Christoph Schwöbel, *God: Action and Revelation*, Kampen 1992, 19. For similar criticism of the "adequacy to the demands of life" criterion, see Wilfried Härle, "Lehre und Lehrbeanstandung," *ZEK* 30 (1985), 304-305. Cf. also Lindbeck's plea for intratextuality as opposed to reconceptualisation of the Christian faith: "Intratextual theology redescribes reality within the scriptural framework rather than translating Scripture into extrascriptural categories. It is the text, so to speak, which absorbs the world, rather than the world the text." (ibid., 118). Instead of "redescribing the faith in new concepts," Lindbeck's postliberal method "seeks to teach the language and practices of the religion to potential adherents," 132.

[42] See for the notion of "person-relativity" George I. Mavrodes, *Belief in God*, New York 1970, 32-40. Person-relativity has to be distinguished from sheer relativism. As to the demands of life, we have seen already that some of them are common to all of us, such as the need for action-directing devices.

demands of life can never function in isolation from the other criteria.

As it seems to me, this last conclusion can be extended. The criteria we have listed can only function fruitfully in continuous interaction with each other and by carefully attuning them to each other. In this process all criteria are necessary, and none of them is sufficient on its own. Of course the degree of usefulness and the significance of each criterion in relation to the other ones depends upon the concrete doctrines that are under scrutiny. For instance, practical doctrines are in general to a higher degree conditional upon the actual cultural situation than theoretical ones.[43] But the final results which are reached in this weighing process depend upon what can be described as authentic communal and, in the end, personal decisions.[44] Despite this interrelatedness of the criteria for acceptable doctrine formation in systematic theology, to a certain extent it is possible to study theological doctrines from the perspective of one of those particularly. In fact, different sub-disciplines of systematic theology are related to the criterion with which they are especially concerned in their investigations. In his essay on the character of theological study, Charles M. Wood distinguishes between three dimensions of theology, viz. what he calls historical theology, philosophical theology, and practical theology.

According to Wood, all of these dimensions are engaged in the one project of examining the validity of the Christian witness, but they differ with regard to the criteria they endorse. First, historical theology "appeals to elements of its own past to vindicate the Christian authenticity of its life and message: to 'tradition' generally, perhaps, or more specifically to scripture ..."[45] Obviously, this indication of the criterion of historical theology is in line with our first criterion. Further, philosophical theology aims to "clarify the conditions of meaningful and appropriate thought and speech," and to "display the sorts of meaning the discourse and activity of Christian witness involve, including the sorts of claims to truth which that witness can make."[46] Although Wood admittedly does not use our terminology, it is clear that his description of the task of philosophical theology is largely related to our second criterion. Finally, "the distinctive assignment of practical theology might be ... described as that of enabling those who bear Christian witness to perceive the place at which they stand, and to relate their witness to that context."[47] No doubt, "that context" is closely connected with the "demands of life" which formed the core of our third

---

[43] Cf. Lindbeck's "taxonomy of doctrines," *Nature of Doctrine*, 84-88.

[44] It should be noted that, as a matter of fact, the structural ambiguity of the criteria and their mutual relations, as well as their ultimate reliance upon communal and personal authentic commitment is not a *hindrance* to theology. On the contrary, it is precisely this ambiguity which does not only make theology possible, but even prompts theological clarification and decision-making.

[45] Wood, *Vision and Discernment*, 42.

[46] Ibid., 46.

[47] Ibid.,48.

criterion. In this way, the various criteria for doctrine are closely related to different strands or dimensions of systematic theology.

1.4. AN OUTLINE OF THE INQUIRY

The survey of the different criteria and dimensions of systematic theology given above enables me to explain the methodological structure of the subsequent inquiry and to show the latter's integrity more precisely than I could do at the end of §1.1.1. As indicated above, I consider my inquiry as a study in "philosophical theology." As Wood points out, this term must not be confused with others that have often served as synonyms, such as "natural theology" and "philosophy of religion." Philosophical theology differs from the latter in that its primary interest is in theology rather than in philosophy, and from the former in that it neither restricts its scope to *part of* the field of systematic theology nor necessarily starts from the data of natural reason as opposed to those of revelation. In clarifying its distinctive quality Wood comments:

> Just as historical theology is so named because its principal methods are those of historical study, so the adjective "philosophical" here discloses the methodological orientation of this branch of theological inquiry. And just as historical theology is not just another name for the historical study of Christian witness, but is rather the use of historical study for theological purposes, so philosophical theology is not just the philosophical study of that witness. If it were, it might find its proper context within the philosophical study of religion generally. However, in philosophical theology, that philosophical study is put to a theological use.[1]

In this sense, I will structure my inquiry. Its primary focus is on the employment of philosophical categories, such as conceptual clarification, the search for consistency and coherence, comprehensiveness, meaning and truth. Such an inquiry cannot be executed, however, in total disregard of other criteria and dimensions of theology. As Vincent Brümmer argues: "All three dimensions are essential. Systematic theology can be approached from any of these perspectives, but it becomes defective when it is reduced to one of these and ignores the others."[2] The question of truth, for example, is not only a matter of comprehensive conceptual coherence, but also of correspondence with the tradition, and of adequacy to the practical demands of life. Thus, making truth claims in systematic theology should not, as Wood suggests, be taken as a distinctive enterprise of *philosophical* theology. Actually, as suggested above, if the making of truth claims is to

---

[1] Ibid., 45; it should be added, that this definition is of course stipulative. To describe philosophical theology along these lines is not to say that any other definition of it is always wrong.

[2] Brümmer, *Personal God*, 157.

be restricted to one particular dimension of theology at all, Wood's "historical theology" would be the most plausible candidate. However this may be, because of the unfissionable connections of our second criterion with the others, it would be wrong to employ it in complete isolation.

Therefore, in the subsequent inquiry we will make use of all criteria, although the second criterion will be predominant. Our leading question will be, whether within the Christian community we should continue to speak of God as omnipotent and if so, in what sense or senses. In order to find an answer to this question, we will take the following steps.

Firstly, we will briefly survey the *history* of the doctrine of divine omnipotence. This will be done in chapter 2. We will especially examine the roots of the doctrine in patristic theology, its elaboration in scholastic thought, and its intended consummation in early modern philosophy. The upshot of this procedure will be, that we are able to list the most important theological notions which were generally implicit in the classical Christian claim that God is omnipotent. In this chapter, we will principally rely upon our first criterion and follow the methods of Wood's historical dimension of theology.

Secondly, we will rather extensively discuss the question of the doctrine's self-consistency and internal coherence. I first examine the conceptual meaning and content of some power-related concepts, including the concept of "omnipotence." Then, I try to sort out the conceptual implications of the application of "omnipotence" to the doctrine of God, and conclude that some of these are highly problematic. My contention will be that the problems here stem from a deviation from the original functions and intentions of the omnipotence-doctrine. In elaborating this contention, I distinguish between almightiness and omnipotence, and try to show that the biblically rooted notion almightiness can avoid the conceptual problems elicited by the application of "omnipotence" to the doctrine of God. The criteria of this second part are distinctively those of philosophical theology, viz. conceptual coherence and comprehensiveness.

Thirdly, we will test whether the doctrine of divine omnipotence is capable of dealing satisfactorily with some almost universally acknowledged problems which it seems to elicit. More particularly, we will investigate whether it can cope with the necessity of emphasizing human responsibility and freedom, and with one of the most widely acknowledged anomalies of Christian faith, viz. the problem of evil.[3] In the light of these demands of life, both of which seem to conflict with what is held in the classical doctrine of divine omnipotence, important qualifications of this doctrine

---

[3] According to Sallie McFague, *Metaphorical Theology*, London 1983, 140f. anomalies are "the most serious criteria for assessing a system," since "theologies ... will continue to function and gain support as long as the anomalies can be endured"; McFague's further remark, that the question of evil counts as "the most constant and serious anomaly to Christian belief" (143), is of course widely accepted in contemporary theology and philosophy.

have been proposed in recent times. The question is, whether these alternatives really are more adequate with regard to the demands of life (as well as, of course, with regard to the other criteria), and therefore merit our support. I hope to show that this is not the case, and that the classical idea of omnipotence should be modified in other ways than those usually advocated. In this way, I hope to arrive at a conception of divine power which is authentically Christian, conceptually coherent and comprehensive, and practically adequate to the demands of life - in short, at a conception which enables us to adequately confess God as the almighty "God of power and might"[4] today.

---

[4] Cf. Janet Martin Soskice, "God of Power and Might," *The Month* 21 (1988), 934-938; "This title, redolent of the language of liturgy, scripture and Creed, shows that it is the God of the theologians, of Abraham, Isaac and Jacob, whose power is under discussion" (934).

2

Historical Location

If we want the systematician to do thorough "Quellenforschung" then he cannot do his work as a systematician... If the relevance of history is to be shown, then both the historian and the systematician will have to do their separate jobs and rely on each other. But such a teamwork is only possible if both the historian and the systematician show their solidarity with each other and to a limited degree (and undoubtedly as amateurs) work in each other's field.

E.P. Meijering[1]

2.1 INTRODUCTION

Before offering a systematic account of the doctrine of divine omnipotence, I will first inquire into the theological considerations which have historically been involved in the ascription of omnipotence to God. For in spite of its apparent simplicity - what else could "omnipotent" mean than "being able to do all things"? -, the historical development of the doctrine has had many ramifications. In this chapter, I will not enter into all of them, but select three different issues which have been of crucial significance for the development of the doctrine of divine omnipotence. Before doing that, however, the decision to include a rather detailed separate historical chapter in an otherwise systematic study stands in need of some additional explanation. Let me point out in this section first why I have made this decision, second why I have selected the three issues to be discussed below, and third how these issues relate to the systematic discussion which follows.

Apart from the more general motives given in the previous chapter, my decision to include a historical chapter has been inspired by what I have come to see as a serious deficiency in many present-day discussions of the concept and doctrine of divine omnipotence. In most of these discussions a study of the doctrine's historical ramifications is either lacking, or rather confined in scope.

In the first case, the result is sometimes a striking uncertainty as to the basic characteristics of the traditional view of God's power. In this way, Alvin Plantinga tentatively suggests on the basis of some rather superficial observations that "there is not any one conception of God's omnipotence

---

[1] E.P. Meijering, "What Could Be the Relevance?," in: id., *God Being History*, Amsterdam 1975, 148.

common to classical theists."[2] In the light of the many traditional quarrels on details of the doctrine of divine omnipotence, this conclusion is no doubt right. But at the same time it blurs the underlying distinctive objectives and intentions of the Christian conceptualization of divine power as accepted by all or most classical theists. In this chapter, I will try to trace the nature and development of these objectives and intentions.

In the second case, these objectives and intentions are to some extent distorted since their description rests on too narrow a basis. Anna Case-Winters' recent study is a case in point here. In describing what she calls "the classical model," Case-Winters focuses exclusively on John Calvin's view of divine power.[3] But clearly paradigmatic examples should not be equated with the cumulative tradition as a whole, and it is only the latter which determines what may count as "classical thought." Now although Case-Winters makes some attempts to connect Calvin's arguments with those of preceding thinkers, the result of her self-imposed limitation is a rather imprecise and incomplete picture of what might be labelled "the classical model." For example, the use of the doctrine of omnipotence as a conceptual instrument against the strongly influential Graeco-Arabic necessitarianism is overlooked, because Case-Winters does not specify with sufficient precision how Calvin's conception of omnipotence relates to the medieval traditions before him. Consequently, it remains unclear what exactly is involved in Calvin's rejection of the medieval distinction between God's *potentia absoluta* and *potentia ordinata*, etc. Placing Calvin squarely in the tradition here would have resulted in a more informed account of "the classical model," and would probably have made clear that this view cannot adequately be characterized by merely stating that it conceives of God's power as "power in the mode of domination and control."[4] Especially if we concentrate, as Case-Winters proposes, on the mode rather than the scope of the divine power, we are unfair to both Calvin and classical theism as a whole when we isolate this power from the other divine attributes.

In order to avoid these kinds of deficiencies, in what follows I will not content myself with a superficial or too selective inspection of historical issues. Rather than burdening my systematic account with lengthy historical digressions by postponing these until the point where they are going to bear upon my systematic argument, I consider it more appropriate to discuss the historical issues in advance.

---

[2] Alvin Plantinga, "Reply to the Basingers on Divine Omnipotence," *PrS* 11 (1981), 28f. The tentativeness of his argument is illustrated by his use of phrases like "to seem to" (3 times), "I do not know" and "I know of no" (3 times), "my guess is," etc.

[3] Case-Winters, *God's Power*, 39-93.

[4] On Calvin's dismissal of the *potentia absoluta - ordinata* distinction, see ibid., 42-45, and below, §2.3.5. Case-Winters summarizes the scholastic debates on divine omnipotence in a brief section (41-46) included in the chapter on Calvin. On the characterization of the classical view as "power in the mode of domination and control," see ibid., 64-66, and passim.

Behind these more or less practical considerations, however, lies the deeper motive which I already pointed to at the end of the previous chapter. Careful study of its historical ramifications helps us to see what functions the omnipotence-doctrine has fulfilled, and so prepares the ground for answering the question which functions it should fulfill today. As Vincent Brümmer argues, whether the proposals of philosophical theologians are acceptable or not "does not depend on their logical coherence alone, but also on whether they are ... recognizably consonant with the religious 'cumulative tradition' which constitutes the horizon of understanding of the believing community."[5] One important condition for such consonance with the cumulative tradition is no doubt that the proposed conceptualizations of faith do justice to the deepest intentions of the tradition *as such*, rather than to popular (and possibly superficial or even misconceived) interpretations of this tradition. The community of believers wants its horizon of understanding to be in harmony with what was *really* ingrained in her tradition. This can only be discovered, however, by way of careful and detailed historical analysis.

As to the present study, this historical analysis will be confined to three issues, which I believe together give an adequate idea of the nature and functions of the classical doctrine of omnipotence. In exploring respectively the origin, development and culmination of the doctrine, the case studies in this chapter review three of the most pivotal discussions which moulded its concrete form. First, we examine the rise of the concept of omnipotence in Christian discourse. Its first well-known affirmation is in the Apostles' Creed, but what is the meaning of the concept there, and where does it stem from? Is the affirmation of God's omnipotence inspired by biblical motives, or does it rather have a Greek background, as is often suggested with regard to the classical divine attributes in general? The answers to these questions will turn out to bear heavily on our systematic account, especially at the point where we will find systematic reasons for a careful distinction between a biblical and a philosophical conception of omnipotence (§3.4).

Secondly, we will study the development of the doctrine in the Middle Ages from the perspective of the history of the distinction between God's absolute and ordained power. The hermeneutical significance of this distinction as a mirror in which crucial shifts in patterns of medieval thinking are reflected, has been increasingly acknowledged in recent research. We trace the different meanings and values the distinction was meant to convey from the early Middle Ages down to the Reformation period, and in doing so try to distinguish between proper applications and distortions of this distinction. This historical exploration will turn out to be systematically useful as well, since it shows us the doctrinal and spiritual problems which

---

[5] Brümmer, *Personal God*, 153.

arise as soon as God's power is conceived of in isolation of His other properties. In §3.3 it will become clear that these problems are in fact *conceptual* problems concerning the literal notion of omnipotence, and that they
therefore cannot be solved as long as this notion is left unqualified.

Thirdly, we will investigate the problem of the relation between the
divine omnipotence and the ontological status of so-called "eternal truths."
The problem here is not so much that the truths in question are allegedly
eternal, but that they usually are also claimed to be necessary, which seems
to imply that they are not included in the scope of God's omnipotence. Does
the classical view of God's omnipotence reckon with the existence of entities of any sort besides God, which have a comparable independent ontological status? Here we especially concentrate upon the arguments of
Descartes, who answered this question in a very untraditional way, and in
doing this intended to bring the doctrine of omnipotence to its proper culmination. In §3.5 this same issue will recur from a systematic perspective,
and I will attempt to show there how the conceptual problems in which
Descartes came to be entangled can be solved when we start from a biblical
conception of God's power as almightiness rather than from its philosophical interpretation as omnipotence.

In short, the upshot of our historical survey will hopefully be, that
we have a clearer picture of the most fundamental functions and characteristics of the traditional or classical view of divine omnipotence, in the light
of which we can then test this view on its comprehensive coherence and
religious adequacy, pondering in this process the main contemporary criticisms of it. Thus, in what follows in this chapter we are not interested in
giving accurate historical reconstructions for their own sake, but in the
systematic impact and relevance of the described historical positions. It is
precisely this systematic interest which adds to the need for accuracy and
detail in historiography rather than reducing it.

2.2 DIVINE POWER IN THE EARLY CHURCH

2.2.1 *Almightiness, omnipotence, and providence*
In a well-known article, Peter Geach argued that there is an important difference in Christian theology between the concepts of "almightiness" and
"omnipotence."[1] Whereas the ascription of the first term to God, which
comes in the creeds of the Church, suggests God's having power *over* all
things, the second expression is at home rather in formal theological trea-
tises, and indicates God's ability to *do* everything. According to Geach, the
doctrine of God's almightiness is not only authentically Christian, but also
in our time "indispensable for Christianity, not a bit of metaphysical lug-

---

[1] P.T. Geach, "Omnipotence," *Philosophy* 43 (1973), 7-20; now included in id., *Providence
and Evil*, Cambridge 1977, 3-28. I quote from the latter publication.

gage that can be abandoned with relief."[2] The doctrine of God's omnipotence, on the other hand, should be evaluated exactly the other way round. Geach has no objections against paying God a metaphysical compliment in calling Him "omnipotent." But as soon as

> ... people have tried to read into "God can do everything" a signification not of Pious Intention but of Philosophical Truth, they have only landed themselves in intractable problems and hopeless confusions; no graspable sense has ever been given to this sentence that did not lead to self-contradiction or at least to conclusions manifestly untenable from the Christian point of view.[3]

In this way, Geach stipulates a strict distinction between the concepts of almightiness and omnipotence.

Whether the assertion that God is omnipotent is as wrong-headed as Geach claims, is a question we will take up in later chapters. Apart from that charge, however, Geach also seems to make — albeit in part implicitly — an historical observation. He suggests that the original meaning of the Latin word *omnipotens* is to be found in the sphere of "having power over." As a result of the later scholastic distortion of the term, however, its meaning shifted towards "being able to do all things." Thus, Geach considers the concept of almightiness as an unquestionable part of traditional Christian belief in God, whereas according to him the doctrine of divine omnipotence should be regarded as a *corpus alienum*, an unauthentic later intrusion, of which Christian belief should in consequence be radically purified. In the present section, I want to review the historical accuracy of this description of the course of events.

As Geach himself indicates, the Latin *omnipotens* derives from the Greek word *pantokrator*. The history of this Greek term in turn dates back to the Septuagint, where it served some 170 times as the translation of the Hebrew divine names *Sebaoth* and (less frequently) *Sjaddai*. The Old Testament connotations of these words are still manifest in the New Testament use of *pantokrator*.[4] All these terms are used predominantly in solemn liturgical settings, have covenantal overtones,[5] and point to the power which God is confessed to have over all things.[6] As D.L. Holland argues, in the biblical context *pantokrator* indicates "the capacity for, not the exercise of power."[7] At least the concept does not imply any ceaseless sustaining, pre-

---

[2] Ibid., 5.

[3] Ibid., 4.

[4] Once by Paul (2 Cor.6:18, at the end of a series of O.T. quotations), and nine times in the book of Revelation (1:8; 4:8; 11:17; 15:3; 16:7, 14; 19:6, 15; 21:22).

[5] See P. Smulders, "'God Father All-Sovereign'. New Testament Use, the Creeds and the Liturgy: An Acclamation?," *Bijdragen* 41 (1980), 6.

[6] W. Michaelis, "Pantokrator," in: G. Kittel (ed.), *TDNT* III, ed. G.W. Bromiley, Grand Rapids 1965, 915 (footnote 11 contains a mistranslation from the German).

[7] D.L. Holland, "Pantokrator in New Testament and Creed," in: E.A. Livingstone (ed.), *Studia*

serving and governing providential activity of God, but rather God's ability to do all the things He wants to do in history.

Therefore, at first sight it seems that Geach's intuition is wrong, since in the sources of the Christian tradition God's power is articulated more in terms of omnipotence than in terms of almightiness. We should be careful, however, not to identify the distinction between God's capacity for and actual exercise of power with Geach's distinction between God's "being able to do all things" and His "having power over." A closer examination of the historical development of words denoting God's power in the different classical languages shows, that we should distinguish between the following three aspects of meaning.[8]

1. God's power as universal dominion and authority[9] over all and everything. God is the all-ruling, all-sovereign Master of the universe, the Most High, who has the whole world in His governing hands and is in control of all that happens in nature and history. This is the biblical meaning of *pantokrator*, coined by the translators of the LXX as a universalization of the Old Testament title "Lord of hosts (of Israel)" (*YHWH Sebaoth*). In Greek, this idea is expressed by the verb *kratein* followed by a genitive case.[10] In English, it approaches nearest to the proper meaning of the word "power."

2. God's power as shown in the creation and preservation of the world. This is power of a fully actualized sort. It is not executed, so to speak, from a distance, but it is intimately bound up with all parts of creation, in God's continuous activity of sustaining and backing up the universe. Although the dimension of divine government and ruling is by no means excluded from this connotation, the Almighty is not conceived of primarily as the sovereign dominator of the universe, but as the "Provident," embracing it in His loving and sustaining care.[11] In post-biblical Greek, this second notion could be incorporated in the meaning of *pantokrator*,

---

Evangelica Vol.VI, Berlin 1973, 255-259. Cf. Michaelis, ibid.

[8] Here, as well as in much of the following, I am indebted to the excellent study of A. de Halleux, "'Dieu le Père tout-puissant'" *RThL* 8 (1977), 401-422 (the article is reprinted in his *Patrologie et oecuménisme*, Leuven 1990, 68-89, but I quote from the original publication). De Halleux does not make as neat a distinction between the three types of divine power as seems appropriate, however.

[9] In this definition "dominion" points to God's power as such, "authority" to His power as far as acknowledged by others. See on the concept of divine authority Donald D. Evans, *The Logic of Self-Involvement*, London 1963, 170-173. Evans is aware of the fact that the biblical writers did not distinguish sharply between authority and power (172f.); the same, I would add, holds for most early Christian writers.

[10] C. Capizzi, *Pantokrator*, Roma 1964, 24, 155. Capizzi's study, although often deficient in its references (cf. Holland, "Pantokrator," 259 n.2), is an invaluable compilation of occurrences of the word, including its antecedents, cognates and derivatives, in antiquity.

[11] "Dès lors, le 'Tout-puissant' n'est plus conçu comme le Souverain, dominateur de l'univers qu'il a créé ..., mais plutôt comme le Provident qui l'entoure de sa sollicitude, comme le 'Sauveur' qui le maintient dans l'existence... ". De Halleux, "Dieu le Père," 410.

because of the fact that *kratein* followed by an accusative case means "to hold" (rather than "to reign"). In Latin, the term "omnitenens" was invented to express the same nuance.

3. God's power as the capacity to realize all possible states of affairs. This type of power is clearly not actual, but virtual. It pertains to the realm of God's theoretical potentialities rather than to His sovereign lordship or providential activity. The claim usually made in this connection is, that since Gods power is infinite, nothing is impossible for Him to perform. This conception of divine power is covered perfectly well by the Latin term *omnipotens*. Its equivalent in Greek is the word *pantodynamos*.[12]

Let us for the sake of clarity refer to these three types of divine power respectively as A-power (power as authority), B-power (power as back-up), and C-power (power as capacity). From this tripartite distinction it is evident why clear-cut divisions between God's "capacity for" and "actual exercise of" power are ambiguous. For such divisions can be meant to articulate either the difference between A-power and B-power (in which case B-power is the most actual one; in this way, the distinction is used by Holland), or the difference between A-power and C-power (in which case A-power is actual).[13] As to Geach's distinction between almightiness and omnipotence, it is clear that the former can be equated with A-power and the latter with C-power. Thus, it appears that both Geach and Holland point to A-power - although by means of different and seemingly mutually excluding descriptions[14] - as the primary connotation of divine power in the main sources of the Jewish-Christian tradition.

In this, both are certainly correct, as even a cursory view of names for God in this tradition brings to light. Several of the most frequently used divine names and titles in Old Testament, LXX and New Testament, as well as in intertestamental apocrypha and pseudephigrapha, etymologically have to do with power in the meaning of dominion and authority.[15] In Jewish

---

[12] A. Forcellini, *Lexicon totius latinitatis*, Vol.3, eds. F. Corradini & J. Perin, Padoue 1940, 488, s.v. *omnipotens*. Cf. Capizzi, *Pantokrator*, 157-174; De Halleux, "Dieu le Père," 420.

[13] In this latter way, *pantokrator* is often said to indicate the exercise of power rather than its possession; cf. e.g. C.H. Dodd, *The Bible and the Greeks*, London 1954[2], 19.

[14] Cf. for a definition of the biblical *pantokrator* in line with Geach's notion of almightiness, and at face value almost literally contradicting Holland's quoted definition (above, n.7), J.N.D. Kelly, *Early Christian Creeds*, London 1972[3], 137: "*Pantokrator* is in the first place an active word, conveying the idea not just of capacity but of actualization of capacity." But the contexts of both quotations are different: whereas Holland (or rather Michaelis, whom he is paraphrasing) is comparing A-power with B-power, Kelly contrasts A-power with C-power. Capizzi apparently did not grasp this difference, as is clear from his criticism of Michaelis (*Pantokrator*, 33).

[15] Cf. any lexicographical, exegetical or theological dictionary on e.g. *adonai, sebaoth, kurios* and *despotas*. The original meanings of *sjaddai* and *el(ohim)* are less certain, but these terms also acquired connotations of power in a rather early stage, as is clear from their oldest translations. For a general survey, see e.g. Cyril H. Powell, *The Biblical Concept of Power*, London 1963, 41-45, 72f.

literature from the intertestamental period the concept of God even becomes almost synomymous with that of power. The Targumim, for example, use "power" as a euphemistic paraphrase for YHWH, the most proper name of God which should not be pronounced. Next, in hellenistic Judaism the divine power becomes a kind of hypostasized intermediary between God (who is "pure being") and human beings.[16] In brief, the predominance of the attribute of power in the Judaeo-Christian concept of God is too conspicuous to escape notice. Or, to put it more succinctly with Powell's opening sentence: "The God of the Bible is the God of *power*."[17]

Since we are primarily interested in the ascription of omnipotence to God rather than of power in a broadly general sense,[18] in the section that follows we will examine more thoroughly the divine title *pantokrator*. More specifically, we will try to analyse the interplay during the first centuries between the three different connotations of *pantokrator* we discovered above, in order to clarify the development of the concept of divine omnipotence in early Christian theology.

2.2.2 *Pantokrator in Greek and patristic literature*

It has often been assumed that the biblical notion of divine power as universal dominion was implied in the inclusion of the epithet *pantokrator* in the early Christian creeds.[19] A straightforward line was supposed to run from the biblical meaning of the word to its patristic and credal applications.[20] As recent research has brought to light, however, the historical development of the ideas associated with *pantokrator* was much more complicated. To be sure, the sources of patristic use of the term are to be found in the Judaeo-Christian tradition, and not in one or other of the ancient pagan cults. As Montevecchi concludes:

> From the Old Testament the name *Pantokrator* passed in the Christian liturgy as indicating the only God, and more precisely the Father: in the first Christian wit-

---

[16] Walter Grundmann, *Der Begriff der Kraft im neutestamentlichen Gedankenwelt*, Stuttgart 1932, 11f., who points to the use of *dynamis* as a divine name by Jesus in Mt.26:64, Mk.14:62. Cf. his article "*dynamai ktl.*," in: Kittel (ed.), *ThDNT* Vol.2, Grand Rapids 1964, 284-317; Case-Winters, *God's Power*, 26f.

[17] Powell, *Biblical Concept*, 5.

[18] For a biblical-theological exposition of the latter theme, see e.g. Pierre Biard, *Puissance de Dieu*, Paris 1960.

[19] The term *pantokrator* (or its Latin counterpart) is standard in all known early Christian credal texts, both Eastern and Western; the latter group includes pre-R creeds dating from the second century (R being the authoritative old Roman baptismal creed and the principal ancestor of the Apostles' Creed). Its place is usually at the end of the triple sequence "God Father Almighty," a phrase which is hardly attested in other patristic texts. For a survey, see Smulders, "'God Father All-Sovereign'."

[20] See e.g. Michaelis, "Pantokrator," 914 n.12; O. Montevecchi, "Pantokrator," in: *Studii in onore di A. Chalderini et R. Paribeni*, Milan 1957, 418; and (though less explicitly) Kelly, *Early Christian Creeds*, 136-139.

nesses there is no word which expresses more effectively than this one the continuity between the Old and New Testament, the grafting of Christianity on to the old trunk of Judaism, the identity between the God of the prophets "who has the name Pantokrator" and "the Father of our Lord Jesus Christ."[21]

Notwithstanding this attested biblical and definitely non-Greek origin of the title, however, already in the time of the formation of the early Christian baptismal creeds which preceded the Apostles' Creed, other intuitions came to play an important role behind the ascription of the title *pantokrator* to God, namely intuitions which lie in the sphere of B-power.[22] This shift towards a widening of the connotation of *pantokrator* was particularly invoked by the prevailing hellenistic philosophical climate, which was permeated by popular Platonico-Stoic ideas on the preservation of the world. Although the debate about the degree to which patristic theology was substantially influenced by Greek philosophy of some sort, is of course still going on,[23] such influence seems undeniable with regard to the interpretation of what it means for God to be *pantokrator*.

In his important study, Hommel has shown that verbs like *sozein*, *sunechein, periechein, diakratein, kubernan* in combination with accusatives like *ta panta, ta hola* etc. were used abundantly in Greek philosophy to indicate the sustaining function of the divine Providence.[24] Hommel succeeds in tracing this terminology even back to the great Milesian philosophers Anaximander and Anaximenes.[25] Later on, Plato's *Timaeus* promoted the idea of God's (i.e. the Demiurge's) preservation of what was created by Him.[26] The Middle Stoic thinker Posidonius introduced it from both Anaximander and the *Timaeus* into Stoic circles, and seems to have

---

[21] "Dall' Antico Testamento il nome *Pantokrator* è passato nella liturgia cristiana per indicare il Dio unico e precisamente il Padre: nei primi testi cristiani non c'è parolo che più efficacemente di questa esprima la continuità tra l'Antico e il Nuovo Testamento, l'innestarsi del Cristianesimo sul vecchio ceppo del giudaismo, l'identità tra il Dio dei profeti 'che ha nome Pantokrator' e il 'Padre del Signor nostro Gesù Cristo'." Montevecchi, "Pantokrator," 418, after having shown that practically all non-Christian uses of the term are later than (and thus possibly influenced by) the LXX. Capizzi, *Pantokrator*, 70, concurs with Montevecchi's judgment.

[22] Hildebrecht Hommel makes a case for the presence of B-power intuitions even in three of the *pantokrator*-texts in Revelation (1:8, 4:8, 11:17); see H. Hommel, "Pantokrator," in: Harald Kruska (ed.), *Theologia Viatorum* Vol.V, Berlin 1954, 337-340. But his conclusion that these texts as a consequence "stoischen Geist atmen" (339) certainly goes too far (cf. Holland, "Pantokrator," 261).

[23] Cf. e.g. E.P. Meijering, "Wie platonisierten Christen?," in: id., *God Being History*, 133-146.

[24] H. Hommel, "Pantokrator"; revised version in id., *Schöpfer und Erhalter*, Berlin 1956, 81-137. The meaning of the last-mentioned verb in the list is slightly deviating, emphasizing the *governing* activity of the deity; but this notion is always closely connected with that of preservation.

[25] Hommel, "Pantokrator," 329-331.

[26] See e.g. *Timaeus* 41 A: "... those works whereof I am framer and father are indissoluble save by my will." R.G. Bury (ed. + tr.), *Plato* 9 (LCL), London 1981, 89. Cf. Hommel, "Pantokrator," 322.

used the simple *kratein* as a further synonym. Being especially popular in the Stoa, the concepts found a widespread use in all strands of religio-philosophical hellenistic thinking, including for example Philo.[27] In this process the meaning of the old divine epithet *pankratès* (imputed primarily to Zeus) changed from "all-mighty" or "all-sovereign" towards "all-sustainer."

It is this new use of *kratein* with the accusative in the sense of "to sustain, to preserve, to hold" which entered also in Christian discourse.[28] As a result, the title *pantokrator* was given an additional meaning besides the traditional one that stemmed from the LXX. The earliest Christian writers illustrated God's being *pantokrator* by referring to biblical examples of His sovereign power and authority, such as the Exodus, the remission of sins, and above all the creation of the world.[29] But a first indication of the shift of meaning in the direction of B-power had already been present in the Jewish letter of (Pseudo-)Aristeas (first century B.C.), in which God is invoked as "the *pantokrator* of all the goods He has created." Here, the term *pantokrator* obviously aims at God's preserving activity.[30] Even more precise is the *Epistle to Diognetus* (ca. 175 AD), where God's being *pantokrator* is explicitly distinguished from His being *pantoktistès* (creator of all).[31] Instead of describing God's sovereign power as exemplified in creation, the term *pantokrator* is now more and more going to point to a continuous relationship between God and the world. This newer connotation is clearly stated or at least alluded to in many of the most prominent fathers, including Irenaeus, Clement of Alexandria, Origen, Athanasius, Cyril of Jerusalem, Gregory of Nyssa, and Augustine.[32]

Let us illustrate this patristic application of the term by expanding a little upon two of its most unambiguously clear examples. The first one is still rather early. Theophilus, bishop of Antioch in the late second century, writes in his principal work that God is called

> ... Demiurge and maker (*poiètès*) because He Himself is the creator (*ktistès*) and maker of the universe (*toon holoon*)... But He is called *Pantokrator* because He Himself holds (*kratei*) and embraces (*emperiechei*) all things (*ta panta*). The heights of heavens, the depths of the abysses, and the extremities of the earth are in His hand; there is no place withdrawn from His action.[33]

---

[27] On the influence of Posidonius on Philo's conception of the divine power(s), see for example Grundmann, *Begriff der Kraft*, 38.

[28] A good example is in Revelation 2:1.

[29] See for examples De Halleux, "Dieu le Père," 408f.

[30] *Ad Philocratem Epistula* 185; cf. Hommel, "Pantokrator," 338, 370 and De Halleux, "Dieu le Père," 409f.

[31] *Epistula ad Diognetum* 7, 2; ET: K. Lake, *The Apostolic Fathers with an English Translation* 2 (LCL), London 1913, 362.

[32] See the lists of quotations (with exact references) in Hommel, "Pantokrator," 349-352; Capizzi, *Pantokrator*, 55-64; Holland, "Pantokrator," 260; De Halleux, "Dieu le Père," 409f. Even more frequent was the use of *kratein* with the accusative in connection with the sustaining power of God, cf. Hommel, ibid.

[33] Theophilus, *Ad Autolycum* 1, 4; see G. Bardy (ed.), *Trois livres à Autolycus*, (SC 20), Paris

Here, the definition of *pantokrator* has shifted entirely towards B-power, apparently in consequence of the now established special meaning of *kratein* + acc. Moreover, the vocabulary undeniably reflects Stoic influence. As Capizzi rightly concludes:

> This definition of *Pantokrator*, deduced from the construction *kratein* with acc. in connection with a composite of *periecho*, makes one think of the conserving function of the God-Kosmos of the Stoics rather than of the universal dominion of the Sebaoth-Pantokrator as underlined in the Septuagint.[34]

Our second example is from the books Gregory of Nyssa wrote against Eunomius. One of the things Eunomius is reproached for by Gregory, is his refusal to ascribe the title of *pantokrator* to the Son. In connection with this, however, Gregory seems to disagree with the very meaning Eunomius assigns to the title, since Eunomius takes it not as indicating providential activity, but tyrannical authority.[35] Perhaps it is against this purportedly false interpretation that Gregory writes a short treatise on the term, which results in the following definition:

> So when we hear the name *pantokrator*, our conception is this, that God sustains in being all things, both the intelligible and those which have a material nature. For for this cause, He controls the circle of the earth, for this cause He holds the ends of the earth in His hand, for this cause He encloses the heavens with the span [of His hand], He envelops the waters in His hand, He encompasses all intelligible creature in Himself, in order that all things should stay in being, encapsulated by his embracing power.[36]

Notwithstanding these clear instances of *pantokrator* in the sense of B-power, we should be careful not to overemphasize either their universality or the degree to which they betray Stoic influence upon early Christian representations of God's power. Firstly, the older meaning has never been completely abandoned in favour of the newer one. In many cases, *pantokrator* remains to be used in contexts which suggest or even explicitly state

---

1948, 64.

[34] Capizzi, *Pantokrator*, 76: "Questa definizione di P. dedotta dalla costruzione di *krateo* c.acc. unito a un composto di *periecho*, fa pensare alla funzione conservatrice del Dio-Kosmos degli stoici piuttosto che al dominio universale sottolineato dal *Sebaoth-Pantokrator* dei Settanta."

[35] Cf. De Halleux, "Dieu le Père," 417 n.108.

[36] Gregory of Nyssa, *Contra Eunomium* 2, 126; cf. W. Jaeger (ed.), *Gregorii Nysseni Opera* II, Leiden 1960, 366. In the translation, which is my own, all verbal phrases beginning with *peri* are rendered with English 'en'- or 'em'-verbs (as a result, the allusion to Isa.40:12 becomes less clear). Capizzi, *Pantokrator*, 79, correctly differentiates in his commentary on this passage between an *external* relationship of God and the universe (God "holds the world in His hands" etc.) and an *internal* relationship (God "encompasses all things in Himself"). The latter aspect was sometimes (e.g. by Gregory the Great) transformed into a doctrine of divine omnipresence, see ibid., 80f. In other contexts (e.g. in Stoic philosophy), the internal relationship between God and the universe had pantheistic consequences.

its original connotation in the sphere of A-power. The overtones of "all dominating," "all controlling" etc. always reverberate through the later applications of the term. Sometimes the word is even explicitly unfolded in two directions, *viz.* both that of A-power and that of B-power. Cyril of Jerusalem for instance, giving a special catechetical lecture on the term in the middle of the fourth century, defines it in the following dual paraphrase: "*Pantokrator* is He who supports all things, who has authority over all things."[37] The same ambiguity is obvious from Latin translations of *pantokrator*, which hesitate between the Jupiter-epithet *omnipotens* and the specially forged neologism *omnitenens*.[38] When the latter is used, it is clear that the translator was aware of the B-power connotation of the word *pantokrator*.[39]

Secondly, although many patristic authors have passages on divine preservation in which similar terms are used as in hellenistic and especially Stoic circles,[40] it is not true that all of them changed their concept of *pantokrator* as a result of the mutual contacts. Contrary to what is generally suggested for example, Origen as far as I can see never directly *equates* God's being *pantokrator* with His sustaining activities.[41] This is the more remarkable, since Origen reflected more upon the nature of divine power than any of his contemporaries, his preoccupations with the theme even culminating in, as Capizzi has it, "a whole theology of divine 'pantocracy'."[42] The same seems to be true in the case of Athanasius. Although

---

[37] Cyril of Jerusalem, *Catecheses* 8, 3. (PG 33, 628A). See on the accusative *panta* in the first clause as superior to the variant reading *pantoon* Capizzi, *Pantokrator*, 118 n.2. In Kelly (*Early Christian Creeds*, 137) this clause is rendered with "who rules all things." Although this translation blurs the specific content of *kratein* + acc., it is in accordance with the overall tendency of Cyril's lecture; cf. also De Halleux, "Dieu le Père," 416.

[38] The latter word we come across for the first time in Pseudo-Tertullianus, *Carmen adversus Marcionem* V 9, 5 (PL 2, 1089A). Pseudo-Tertullianus' poem dates from the middle of the fourth century. The term was picked up by Rufinus (PG 14, 1239C), Augustine (see below), and a pupil of the latter, Prosper Aquitanus (PL 51, 467BC; 510B). That the term was intentionally constructed to give a precise rendering of *pantokrator* in Latin has been observed by Forcellini, *Lexicon totius latinitatis* Vol.3, s.v.

[39] See on this point Capizzi's useful appendix "Excursus: *Pantokrator e omnipotens*," in: id., *Pantokrator*, 155-174; Hommel, "Pantokrator," 353-363; De Halleux, "Dieu le Père," 419-421.

[40] M. Spanneut, *Le stoïcisme de pères de l'Eglise de Clément de Rome à Clément d'Alexandrie*, Paris 1957, especially 269, 325f.; fortunately, Spanneut avoids the pitfall of confusing influence with sheer parallelism (11).

[41] The passage mentioned in Hommel ("Pantokrator," 325, 351; *De Principiis* II 9 1), though very interesting in that it limits the divine power, doesn't have the word *pantokrator*. Those listed by Capizzi (*Pantokrator*, 56; cf. also 72, 160) do, but in none of the cases there is a good reason for interpreting them as intending B-power, since they do not deal with divine preservation. The instance adduced by De Halleux ("Dieu le Père," 410; *Excerpta in Psalmos* 23, 10), finally, does not at all warrant his conclusion that Origen expressly affirms the newer meaning of *pantokrator* ("Origène affirme expressément que le Sauveur peut être justement qualifié de *pantokratôr* parce qu'il régit (*krateî*) providentiellement tous les êtres...," ibid.).

[42] Capizzi, *Pantokrator*, 62: "... presenta tutta una teologia della 'pantokratoria' divina...".

Athanasius has the verb *kratein* + acc. in texts on divine preservation, in his use of the term *pantokrator* A-power notions are clearly dominant.[43]

Thirdly and most importantly, however, the idea of God as holding and supporting the universe is of course not altogether alien to the Christian tradition in itself, but on the contrary deeply embedded in it. Although neither the term *pantokrator* nor one its Hebrew originals is used in biblical (or LXX) statements on God's preserving activities, the presence of such statements as such is indubitable.[44] Communicating in Greek, what else could the patristic authors be expected to do than use the current Greek terminology in describing the modes of divine preservation? That in doing this they took over certain fixed expressions which had a Stoic background is not denied here. What *is* denied is, that this Christian adoption and employment of such Stoic phrases should be branded as unauthentic, or even as a regrettable betrayal of own roots. Rather, the Stoic concepts offered a good opportunity for expressing a basically Jewish-Christian idea in the hellenistic culture. Being Greek is not by definition on a par with being non-Christian. Moreover, "we fail to do justice to the pressures confronting early Christian thinkers if we represent them as simply incorporating pre-existing philosophical or civil views of the divine attributes (such as omnipotence) in their thinking."[45]

In brief, then, early Christian literature displays a shift in the use of the word *pantokrator* from connoting only A-power towards including in its meaning B-power notions as well. This shift is partly due to the influence of Greek and especially current Stoic religio-philosophical ideas, but at the same time accords with certain strands of biblical thought. Let us now consider the impact of this development upon the meaning of the term *pantokrator* in the context which was pre-eminently responsible for its becoming generally known, viz. in the Apostles' Creed.

2.2.3 *Pantokrator in the Apostles' Creed*

Illuminating and to a high degree convincing observations concerning the meaning of *pantokrator* in the Apostles' Creed have recently been made by De Halleux.[46] His argument, in part parallel to that of Holland (though he does not mention the latter), runs as follows. As has been recognized before,[47] the combination of the words *pater* and *pantokrator* is very rare in

---

[43] Capizzi, *Pantokrator*, 57f.; Hommel, "Pantokrator," 349, 351.

[44] See Hommel, "Pantokrator," 323f. for a short and inexhaustive enumeration of OT-texts on God's keeping the created universe in existence. B.W. Farley, *The Providence of God*, Grand Rapids 1988, 32-34, has a list of both OT and NT references. Some of these texts (e.g. Hebr.1:3) play a decisive role in many patristic arguments.

[45] McGrath, *Genesis of Doctrine*, 5.

[46] De Halleux, "Dieu le Père," 408-417.

[47] Cf. Holland, "Pantokrator," 264f.; Kelly, *Early Christian Creeds*, 132f.; P. Smulders comes to the same conclusion with regard to the standard credal formula *theon patera pantokratora* as a whole, see his "The *Sitz im Leben* of the Old Roman Creed," in: E.A. Livingstone (ed.), *Studia*

pre-nicene patristic literature. This suggests that their juxtaposition in many credal texts must have been intentional, and that therefore one coherent exegesis should be given of both terms together.[48] One common interpretation does not fulfill this condition. According to it, the creeds want to say that God, the loving Father of Jesus Christ, is at the same time the all-sovereign Master of the universe.[49] But this interpretation "joins two contrasting images in a hardly satisfying paradox."[50]

The contrast between these images is mitigated, however, when we understand the title *pantokrator* in line with the popular use of *kratein* with the accusative case, that means as signifying B-power rather than A-power. In that case, the connotation of loving care connects both images. That *pantokrator* can be explained in this way, is clear from the instances given in § 2.2.2 above. Actually, its function in the Creed has often been explained in this way, especially in theological commentaries.[51]

Now both interpretations of *pantokrator* of course don't necessarily exclude one another. But a very powerful argument for the hypothesis that the B-power interpretation at least played an important role in the Creed's ascription of the title to God, can be derived from the meaning of the preceding word *pater*. It is generally acknowledged, that the original primary intention of this term was to designate neither the relationship between God and Jesus Christ as His Son, nor the relationship between God and the individual believer as one of His adopted children,[52] but the relationship between God and the world as His creation. Kelly's commentary is to the point here. After having considered the other possible interpretations, he continues:

Patristica Vol.XIII, Berlin 1975, 411 ("... this form is so rare as to be virtually nonexistent apart from the Creeds"); cf. id., "God Father All-Sovereign," 3, 7.

[48] Contrary to Kelly, *Early Christian Creeds*, 132, who argues against taking the two words together. His argument is refuted by Holland, "Pantokrator," 264.

[49] This interpretation is sometimes corroborated by the assumption of an anti-marcionite tendency in the first article. De Halleux, "Dieu le Père," 411 offers some cogent arguments against this assumption. See for a defence of it Holland, *Pantokrator*, 262-266. The 'paradox-interpretation' has also entered into theological commentaries on the Creed, e.g. in W. Pannenberg, *The Apostles' Creed in the Light of Today's Questions*, Philadelphia 1972, 31-33.

[50] De Halleux, "Dieu le Père," 411: "... réunit deux images contrastées en un paradoxe peu satisfaisant."

[51] See for instance Martin Luther's explanation of the first article in his *Smaller Catechism* (WA 30-1, 292-294); Hommel, "Pantokrator," 358-366 traces this explanation back via Peter Lombard to the Latin fathers, and points to the influence Luther in turn exerted in this respect on later generations (364). See also Ulrich Zwingli's account in his *De providentia Dei anamnema*: "Through God's power all things exist, live, and act, nay all things are in Him, who is everywhere present..." (quoted in Farley, *Providence*, 145). A contemporary Dutch example is in A.A. van Ruler, *Ik geloof*, Nijkerk 1969, 29 ("In one word: this is God's omnipotence, that He embraces all as a whole").

[52] See F. Kattenbusch, *Das Apostolische Symbol* I, Leipzig 1894, 530 on the decline of this aspect in early Christian theology.

When we turn to the period of the Creed's formation, it is clear that neither of these interpretations represents the whole, or even the most important part, of what was in the minds of its authors. It would be gravely misleading, of course, to exclude them... Most often, however, where the term "Father" was used at this time, the reference was to God in His capacity as Father and creator of the universe... To Christians of the second century this was beyond any question the primary, if by no means the only, significance of the Fatherhood of God.[53]

Interestingly, Kelly makes the further comment that this "was a belief which they shared ... with Hellenistic Judaism as well as with enlightened religious people generally."[54] Indeed, the old Greek vocabulary of God as "maker (*poiètès*) and father of this universe,"[55] transformed into Stoic theology by Posidonius, had conquered the entire hellenistic world, including the intellectual Jewish circles (Philo). Thus the Christian use of the name "Father" along these lines reflected the general theological phraseology of the period in which the Creed was shaped.

If the name *pater* in the Creed pointed to the divine work of creation indeed, the motive for its being followed by the term *pantokrator* is clear. Both in Greek and biblical settings references to God's creative activities were often, and as it were naturally, succeeded by statements on divine preservation.[56] Taking *pantokrator* at least as *including* B-power, the framers of the credal phrase *pater pantokrator*, rather than identifying in a somewhat tortuous construction the NT "Father of Jesus Christ" with the OT (or, more precisely, LXX) "Lord of the universe," simply conformed to this common practice. Since this procedure enabled them to find a common starting-point in communicating their Christian faith to those who didn't share it, it is possible that they even had missionary aims with their wording, comparable to those of Paul on the Areopagus.[57] In this sense, Hommel concludes that the first article in its very formulation tries to link up with the still manifest Greek religio-philosophical heritage.[58]

---

[53] Kelly, *Early Christian Creeds*, 134f. Evidence for this claim is given by means of quotations from Clement of Rome, Justin, Irenaeus, Theophilus of Antioch, and Novatian. See for more patristic material Holland, "Pantokrator," 264, and De Halleux, "Dieu le Père," 412.

[54] Ibid.; cf. 139: "... the best Jewish and pagan thought of the age would have heartily endorsed it."

[55] Plato, *Timaeus* 28C (ed. R.G. Dury, 50f.).

[56] Hommel, "Pantokrator," 322f. In fact, the whole of Hommel's article is an inquiry into occurrences of the dual determination of God as creator and sustainer ("Schöpfer und Erhalter") in fixed formulas.

[57] Acts 17:16-34; especially the quotations in verse 28 form a highly interesting parallel in this respect. In the first (perhaps a paraphrase rather than a quotation), Paul concurs with the Greek idea of divine omnipresence, which was, as we saw above (n.36), closely connected with that of divine preservation. In the second, he affirms the global extension of God's fatherhood.

[58] Hommel, "Pantokrator," 378: "... denn dass im Hellenismus der Glaube an 'Gott den Vater, Schöpfer und Erhalter aller Dinge' als vorsokratisch-platonisch-stoisches Erbe lebendig war und dass sich der erste Artikel hieran sogar in seiner Formulierung angeschlossen hat, möchte als Ergebnis der vorliegenden Untersuchung zu buchen sein."

However this may be, it is clear that already in a rather early stage after its formation, the original function of the phrase *pater pantokrator* changed as a result of the all pervasive christological and trinitarian controversies. Generally, these struggles led in the early fourth century to a transition in the function of the creeds from local liturgical (and specifically baptismal) acclamations towards conciliar and doctrinal declarations of orthodox belief with far more than local authority.[59] More particularly, the repudiation of Arianism and other christological heresies entailed some crucial shifts in the interpretation of the first article of what came to be the Apostles' Creed.

First, the term *pater* could no longer be used to refer indiscriminately to God's relationship with His creation and creatures on the one hand and with Christ on the other hand. For the conviction had settled, that the generation of the Son was irreducible to any other form of divine production.[60] As a result, the Fatherhood of God became more exclusively related to the generation of the Son rather than to the creation of the world. In accordance with the crystallization of the trinitarian dogma, the meaning of the title "Father" came to be restricted to God's intra-trinitarian relationship with the Son. "As soon as one thinks of the Father, one also thinks of the Son," Cyril of Jerusalem seems to repeat an early orthodox slogan.[61] Only "in an improper sense"[62] can God be called the Father of many; by nature and in truth He is the Father of only One.

Second, when this change in the content of the word *pater* had established itself, every reminiscence of the divine act of creation had disappeared from the Creed. This fact is the most likely explanation for the relatively late addition to the first article of the phrase *creatorem coeli et terrae* ("creator of heaven and earth"). As Kelly[63] suggests, those whose task it was to expound on the creed may have become conscious of an awkward gap in its teaching. As a result, the clause on God as creator probably crept in the creed quite casually and spontaneously.

---

[59] Kelly, *Early Christian Creeds*, 205; De Halleux, "Dieu le Père," 415.

[60] In the *Symbolum Nicaenum*, the affirmation that Jesus was God's "only-begotten Son" had been specified by the explicit assurance that He was "begotten, not made." Cf. A. & G.L. Hahn, *Bibliothek der Symbole und Glaubensregeln der alten Kirche*, 1897³, repr. Hildesheim 1962, 161 (§142).

[61] Cyril of Jerusalem, *Catecheses* 7, 4 (PG 33, 609A; NPNF II 8, 45); cf. before Cyril Athanasius, *Orationes contra Arianos* 1, 33 (PG 26, 80B); and after him Rufinus, *Expositio symboli* 4 (CCL 20, 138; NPNF II 3, 544): "Patrem cum audis, Filii intellige Patrem" ("When you hear the word 'Father', you must understand by this the Father of a Son"). The main argument for this claim is, that no one can be described as father unless he has a son (*ibid.*). Kelly comments: "This type of interpretation, and this identical argument to support it, became almost routine in subsequent centuries" (*Early Christian Creeds*, 134).

[62] Cyril, *Catecheses* 7, 5 (ibid.; the Greek word is a technical term coined by Aristotle: *katachrèstikoos*).

[63] *Early Christian Creeds*, 374.

58

Third, in an earlier stage already the semantic modification of the word *pater* had had repercussions on the exegesis of the contiguous *pantokrator*. For it was not clear why reference should be made to God's preservation of the world without any foregoing accentuation of the world's being created by God. Consequently, we see patristic commentators hesitate in explaining the word. We mentioned already the double-edged comment of Cyril, according to whom God is called *pantokrator* both because of His supporting all things and because of His having power over all things.[64] Others, like Theodore of Mopsuestia, simply skip the explanation of the title.[65] But the prevailing attitude becomes to fall back upon the biblical meaning of the term, and explain it in terms of A-power.

This tendency seems to have been reinforced again by the outcome of the christological debate. As we saw already in Gregory's writing against Eunomius, the Arians denied that the title *pantokrator* belonged to the Son as well as to the Father. Instead, they considered the Son to be only one of the powers (*dynameis*) of the Father *pantokrator*. Over against this Arian reduction, Athanasius emphasized the universal authority and dominion of the Lord Jesus,[66] obviously supported by biblical data like Mt.28:18, John 16:15 (which text he explicitly mentions), 17:10, and Rev.1:8, 4:8 etc.[67] Thus, it became a hallmark of orthodox belief to regard the Son as well as the Father as *pantokrator* in this sense of "having universal dominion."[68] In the end, this development even culminated in the representation of the Son as the pre-eminent bearer of the title *pantokrator* in byzantine iconography. This explains the widespread portraying of Christ as the all-dominating *Pantokrator* in eastern medieval mosaics.[69] Although the use of *pantokrator* in this connotation reflects what had by then become its common meaning, awareness of the former B-power meaning of the word survived up to the end of the byzantine empire.[70]

In this section, we have made a case for the thesis that, contrary to

---

[64] See above, n.37.

[65] Theodore of Mopsuestia, *Homilia catechetica* 2, 10; see R. Tonneau and R. Devreesse (eds.), *Les Homélies Catéchétiques de Théodore de Mopsueste*, Roma 1949, 41 (cf. 21, 23).

[66] Athanasius, *Orationes contra Arianos* 1, 33 (PG 26, 80AB); 2, 23-24 (PG 26, 197AB); cf. *ibid.*, 1, 5 (PG 26, 21B); *Epistula ad Serapionem* 2 ("Pantocrator is the Father and Pantocrator is the Son as John said, 'that which was and is and is to come, the Pantocrator'"; PG 26, 611).

[67] Texts like these seem to have formed the bridge between the attribution of *pantokrator* to the Father and to the Son. Cf. Capizzi, *Pantokrator*, 47-50. Especially the pertinent passages from the Apocalypse were used to support the orthodox doctrine of consubstantiality; cf. already Origen, *De Principiis* I, 2 10 (SC 252, 134).

[68] The point is also highlighted e.g. by Athanasius' contemporary Silvanus; see R. van den Broek, "The Theology of the Teachings of Silvanus," *VC* 40 (1986), 12-16.

[69] See on the use of the term in byzantine art Capizzi, *Pantokrator*, 189-203, 309-325; J.T. Matthews, *The Pantocrator*, New York 1976.

[70] See for examples De Halleux, "Dieu le Père," 417f.; Matthews, *Pantocrator*, 26f. (Symeon of Thessalonika, 14th century).

what is often assumed, the original meaning of the word *pantokrator* as used in the ancestors of the Apostles' Creed lay in the sphere of B-power. As a result of certain doctrinal developments in connection with the christological controversies, however, it came to be interpreted more and more in terms of A-power, although testimony of its B-power overtones continued to be extant for a long time. We will now try to sketch the further development of early Christian thought on God's power in the Western church, as reflected in the rise and function of the divine title *omnipotens*. It is especially the analysis of this development which will enable us to test the claim of Peter Geach expounded in § 2.2.1, that the ascription of omnipotence (in the sense of C-power) to God cannot properly be considered as authentically Christian.

2.2.4 *The power and potentialities of the* **omnipotens**

The fact that the Latin word *omnipotens* became its standard translation, offers additional evidence for the ultimate comeback of the A-power meaning of *pantokrator*. But at the same time knowledge of the alternative rendering *omnitenens* (i.e., knowledge of the original B-power meaning of *pantokrator*) did not fade away completely, although this translation itself, apart from some sporadic instances, fell into disuse. A fine example of both the preference for *omnipotens* and the abiding sensitivity to the more precise *omnitenens* is to be found in Augustine. We will examine this example in some detail, because it shows us another important shift in the prime sort of power attributed to God, namely the shift from A-power to C-power.

In his *Confessions* Augustine refers to God as "the omnipotent, all-creating and all-sustaining maker of heaven and earth."[71] From the sequence of the three adjectives it is clear that Augustine is aware of the different meanings of *omnipotens* and *omnitenens*. The former he clearly takes as indicating God's capacity to do all things, the latter as the second actualization of this capacity (the creation of all things being its first actualization). In his commentary on St. John's gospel Augustine further clarifies the way in which he sees the relation between both terms. Here, he concedes that *omnitenens* is the word which answers best to the Greek *pantokrator*. Nevertheless, according to Augustine, when the translators preferred *omnipotens*, this was because they considered it to have the same value (*tantumdem valere*) as *omnitenens*.[72] This theory is very plausible indeed. For the Latin participle *potens* was used traditionally as a means to denote the domain of several Roman divinities. Jupiter for example had been called *rerum omnium potens*, in the sense of: master of all things.[73]

---

[71] Augustine, *Confessiones* XI 13, 15 (CSEL 33, 290): "... te deum omnipotentem et omnicreantem et omnitenentem coeli et terrae artificem". A similar phrase is in *De Genesi ad litteram* 4, 12 (CSEL 28 1, 108). Cf. De Halleux, "Dieu le Père," 420.

[72] Augustine, *Tractatus in Johannis Evangelium* 106, 5 (CCL 36, 611).

[73] See Forcellini, *Lexicon totius latinitatis* 3, 782 (s.v. potens).

The term *omnipotens*, attributed to, for example, Jupiter, Neptune and Fortuna,[74] was synonymous with this phrase. In other words: *omnipotens* in this original context did not signify the capacity to do things, but the actual dominion over things, not C-power but A-power. Since this aspect of ruling and governing over things was clearly present in the Greek *pantokrator* as well, as we saw above even in its B-power interpretation, the translators were not completely unjustified in choosing *omnipotens* as its equivalent.

What happened, however, was of course that the word *omnipotens* became to be interpreted more literally as "being able to do all things" (*qui omnia potest*). Instead of effectively exercised power, this second interpretation signified the virtual (i.e., not actually realized) capacity or ability to do things. Although probably not original,[75] this connotation was indeed inherent in the Latin word, but it was alien to the Greek *pantokrator* and, as a matter of fact, to the intentions of the framers of the creeds. In Greek, it was expressed by the adjective *pantodynamos*. Thus, it is interesting that Augustine, although knowing perfectly well of these different nuances of *pantokrator* and *omnipotens*, in commenting on the Creed didn't hesitate to unfold the meaning of the word *omnipotens* in terms of C-power. "But who is omnipotent, then He who can do all things!," he exclaims at one point.[76]

Once this is said, the famous philosophical puzzles arise which are bound up with the classical concept of divine omnipotence. For now of course we can imagine all sorts of hypothetical actions, and ask with respect to each of them whether God really is able to perform this particular action. Augustine did not evade such questions or reject them as improper. In one of his sermons, for example, he argues that God is omnipotent in the sense that He is able to perform everything that He wills.[77] Yet he continues,

> I can tell you the sort of things He could not do. He cannot die, He cannot sin, He cannot lie, He cannot be deceived. Such things He cannot. If He could, He would not be omnipotent.[78]

In Augustine's view, statements like these were not of a completely different order than the traditional expositions on God's power, that linked it with for example the theme of creation. In another sermon,[79] Augustine

---

[74] Ibid., 488.

[75] According to M. Leumann et al., *Lateinische Grammatik* 1, München 1963, 310, *possum* is etymologically a contraction of *potis sum* (*potis = Lord).

[76] Augustine, *De Trinitate* IV 20, 27 (CCL 50, 197): "Quis est autem omnipotens, nisi qui omnia potest."

[77] Augustine, *Sermo* 213 (PL 38, 1060f.); see also *Enchiridion* 24, 96 (CCL 46, 100): "Neque enim ob aliud veraciter vocatur omnipotens nisi quoniam quidquid vult potest."

[78] "Nam ego dico quanta non possit. Non potest mori, non potest peccare, non potest mentiri, non potest falli. Tanta non potest: quae si posset, non esset omnipotens"; cf. Kelly, *Early Christian Creeds*, 138. See also Augustine's *Sermo de Symbolo ad catechumenos* I 2 (CCL 46, 185f.).

[79] Augustine, *Sermo* 214 (PL 38, 1066ff.).

first of all teaches that belief in God's almightiness amounts to believing that God is the creator of the universe, a connection he also emphasizes in other contexts.[80] But a few paragraphs later he goes on to discuss problems of divine omnipotence in a more speculative vein, taking 2 Tim.2:13 ("He cannot deny Himself") as his starting point. "If God can be what He does not will to be, He is not omnipotent."[81] Of course such a statement quite naturally leads to questions, especially pertaining to the interpretation of the word "can." Not surprisingly then, remarks like this one, relating God's power to God's will in one way or another, set the scene for vehement quarrelling in the *philosophia christiana* of the Middle Ages (cf. the next section). In the course of time, along these lines "He who can do all things" became the sole generally accepted (but variously interpreted) definition of the word *omnipotens*, at the cost of the original purport of the underlying *pantokrator*.

In connection with this, many modern commentators suggest that the transition from taking God's omnipotence primarily as A-power (or even B-power) to its definition as C-power, has been responsible for the nestling of a lot of hopelessly intricate conceptual problems in the Christian tradition, all of which are alien to the authentic motives Christians had in confessing the omnipotence of God. In the beginning of this section we already quoted the objections of Peter Geach. The appraisal of André de Halleux is equally negative. De Halleux concludes that the Latin conception of God as the omnipotent not only deviates from the Helleno-Christian B-power interpretation of the Greek *pantokrator*, but "is also unfaithful to the biblical acceptation" of this word.[82]

In my opinion, however, this negative appraisal of the shift which we were able to trace so clearly in Augustine, is unjustified. Talk of God's power in the sources of the Christian tradition was from its beginning much more diversified and variegated than it suggests. Although metaphors of God as the all-sovereign King and Ruler of the universe were surely dominant, images stressing God's ongoing loving and preserving care for His creation also belonged to it, as well as statements defining the precise scope of God's potential capacities. In other words: neither A-power nor B-power nor C-power can be discarded as a later intrusion in the early Christian belief in God and doctrine of God. Rather, all three of them formed an integral part of both. Let us, in addition to what was said earlier at the evaluation of B-power, give some arguments for this claim with regard to

---

[80] Often with polemical motives against those who denied God's *creatio ex nihilo* (Manicheans, Marcionites etc.); see e.g. his *De fide et symbolo* 2, 2 (CSEL 41, 4-6), and cf. E.P. Meijering, *Augustine: De Fide et Symbolo*, Amsterdam 1987, 25-37; C. Eichenseer, *Das Symbolum Apostolicum beim heiligen Augustinus*, St. Ottilien 1960, 181-187.

[81] "Si ergo potest esse quod non vult, omnipotens non est" (PL 38, 1068).

[82] De Halleux, "Dieu le Père," 422: "De toute façon, la conception latine de l'*omnipotens* ... est aussi infidèle á l'acception biblique ...".

C-power.

We noticed already, that it was possible for Augustine to pass over smoothly from a discussion of God's power as actualized in the work of creation to an argument which pertained to the notion of C-power. Although Augustine knew perfectly well that the original intention of the Creed did not square with this C-power notion, he did not hesitate to ascribe to God omnipotence in exactly this C-power sense of infinite capacity to realize all theoretically possible states of affairs. Moreover, he dealt with some specific "philosophical" questions which are inevitable once the divine power is interpreted in terms of C-power.[83] Now there are two facts which form together a better explanation for Augustine's behaviour in this respect than the simple assumption of carelessness or of the false understanding that is alleged to be found in later Latin writers in general.[84]

First, it is by no means true that Augustine or other later Latin writers were the first to formulate a "philosophical" doctrine of omnipotence.[85] Although the framers of the Creed had in mind something other than C-power in calling God *pantokrator*, theologians before them had already explicated their ideas on God's theoretical capacities. A clear example is Origen, in his rebuttal of Celsus' attack on what he thought to be the Christian idea of divine omnipotence. According to Origen, Celsus ascribes to the Christians the view that "God can do all things," but he understands neither the meaning of "can," nor that of "all things."[86] For when Christians say that God can do all things, they mean "all that He can do without ceasing to be God." And this important restriction excludes for example acts of injustice. Possibly, it might be objected (for example by someone like Geach) that Origen in these sections, although defending a Christian point of view, was influenced by Greek philosophy in the very fact that he entered the field of philosophical debate. Were discussions on the scope of the divine omnipotence not current in hellenistic religious philosophy?[87] As a Christian believer, Origen should simply have refused

---

[83] For example, Augustine deals with the question of whether it belongs to God's omnipotence that He can change the past; see his *Contra Faustum* 26, 5 (CSEL 25, 732f.) and cf. the comments of Meijering, *Augustine*, 29f.

[84] See for the latter explanation J. Kunze, *Glaubensregel, Heilige Schrift und Taufbekenntnis*, Leipzig 1899, 93: "Die späteren Lateiner verstehen es meist falsch; selbst Augustin, sermo 213,1 erklärt: omnipotens est ad facienda omnia quae voluerit." Cf. the criticism of Eichenseer, *Symbolum Apostolicum*, 180.

[85] Eichenseer, *Das Symbolum Apostolicum*, 180.

[86] Origen, *Contra Celsum* 3, 70 (SC 136, 158-161). Cf. 5, 14; 5, 23f. See the translation and notes in H. Chadwick, *Origen: Contra Celsum*, Cambridge 1953, 175, 274f., 281f. In general, Origen endorsed the B-power interpretation of the divine omnipotence (cf. n.41 above).

[87] See for a survey R.M. Grant, *Miracle and Natural Law in Graeco-Roman and Early Christian Thought*, Amsterdam 1952, 127-134. Grant cites among others the elder Pliny (first century A.D.), who has a list of things which according to him God cannot do (129). One century later, Galen presented a similar list against the Jewish idea of omnipotence. The lists contain events which are contrary to nature (God Himself dying, recalling the dead, making a horse out

to speculate about God's abstract capacities, and should rather have stuck to the confession of God's almightiness in the sense of A- and B-power.

Against this objection, however, it should be pointed out that even Origen was not the first to deal with questions concerning the precise scope of C-power. Both Clement of Alexandria and Clement of Rome had done so before him.[88] Moreover, it is undeniable that the first incentives to reflection on God's hypothetical capacities occur in the biblical literature. As Simo Knuuttila argues:

> In the Christian tradition it was realized very early that ... the possibilities of God must be assumed to be greater in number than what happens in the actual world. The source of this idea was the Bible, where the actual world is in many places not taken as an exhaustive manifestation of God's omnipotence.[89]

In addition, Knuuttila lists the following texts: Gen. 18:14; Matt. 19:26, 26:53; Mark 10:27, Luke 1:37, 18:27.[90] Phrases like "nothing is impossible for God," recurring in most of these texts, clearly say something not about God's actualized power, but about the scope of God's capacity to perform all kinds of theoretically possible actions. The Greek word for "(im)possible" used in these texts by resp. the LXX and the NT is *(a)dynatos* or one of its cognates, the root of which corresponds to that of *pantodynamos*, the Greek equivalent of the Latin *omnipotens*. Comparison of these texts with biblical sayings mentioning things that are *not* possible for God to do (for example Hebr. 6:13, 6:18; 2 Tim. 2:13, Tit.1:2), must inevitably provoke reflection on the compatibility of both strands of the biblical tradition. Thus, as we saw already in Augustine, often a text belonging to either strand became the starting point for conceptualizing divine C-power.

Secondly, the fact that ideas on God's actual and potential power are intertwined so closely in both Greek[91] and Christian traditions, evokes the question whether this is sheer coincidence. Contrary to that suggestion, I

---

of ashes etc.), as well as logical impossibilities (making twice ten unequal to twenty etc.) On the other hand, especially Stoic philosophers like Posidonius held that God was omnipotent in a more literal sense, although to the Stoics God was of course totally immanent in the cosmos. Apparently, their stress on divine power as B-power did not prevent them from conceiving of it as C-power as well.

[88] Clement of Alexandria, *Stromateis* V, 12, 82 (GCS 15, 381, 1-3); almost a century earlier yet (ca. 96 A.D.) is 1 Clemens 27:2: "He who has commanded not to lie shall much more not be a liar Himself. For nothing is impossible with God save to lie" (tr. K. Lake, *The Apostolic Fathers* 1, London 1975, 55).

[89] S. Knuuttila, "Time and Modality in Scholasticism," in: id. (ed.), *Reforging the Great Chain of Being*, Dordrecht 1981, 199.

[90] Ibid.; he could have added other texts, as e.g. Jer. 32:17, Job 42:2 and Mark 14:36. See also the discussion in Rebecca D. Pentz, *A Defense of the Formal Adequacy of Saint Thomas Aquinas' Analysis of Omnipotence*, unpublished diss. Univ. of California, Irvine 1979, 5-15, esp.10f.

[91] Cf. the case of Stoic philosophy, above n.87.

would argue that there is a kind of implicative relation between A-power and C-power.[92] If we take a closer look at the biblical texts just quoted, it becomes clear that nowhere propositions on C-power like "nothing is impossible for God" stand on their own. When they are used by people in prayer, they function as a sort of additional argument to obtain what is prayed for. When they are used by God or one of His representatives in prophecy, they function as a guarantee that a particular promise will be fulfilled.[93] In both cases, they stand in relation to a concrete event which is hoped for or promised. Thus, the context is not one of abstract philosophical reasoning, but of the living communication between God and man.

In this context, affirmations of divine C-power like "nothing is impossible for God" seem to function as expressives of trust (when uttered by people praying) or as commissives (when uttered by God), rather than as constatives.[94] Nevertheless, that being the case, such affirmations logically seem to presuppose the factual state of affairs that nothing is impossible for God indeed. If that is true, there is an "undeniable implication" between the expressive or commissive elements of the speech act on the one hand, and the constative illocution on the other hand.[95]

Against this it might be argued, however, that the relation of A-power and C-power is of another sort, since surely the implication here is logically deniable. For it is possible to imagine a God who has created the universe, and keeps on to rule over it as its sovereign Lord, but who nevertheless lacks C-power. This would be the case if God had done and did all those things, but if He was not able to do only one innocent logically possible thing, for example creating a red stone. Perhaps God once had this particular power, but then voluntarily gave it up for some reason. At any rate, such a state of affairs does not seem to be *logically* impossible. From a religious point of view, however, it completely misses the point. For in the context of prayer and promise the power of the God who has done such wondrous things as creating the universe, and who goes on to keep it in being and to rule over it, must be infinite. Therefore, even if it would be true that there is no *undeniable implication* between A-power on the one hand and C-power on the other hand, there certainly is a *contextual implication* between them. In the context of prayer and promise, it is inconceivable (or at least inappropriate to suggest) that there would be anything which an all-creating and all-sovereign God could not bring about.

---

[92] Here I disagree with Hygen, *Guds allmakt*, II.10 (cf. 187), who argues that the notion of C-power is not authentically Christian.

[93] Jeremiah 32 offers an illuminative example of these different functions. In vs.17 Jeremiah starts his prayer for the deliverance of Israel with an appeal to God's unlimited abilities: "No thing is impossible for Thee." In vs.27 God answers him, promises him that what he has prayed for will come about (vs.37ff.), and underlines this promise with the assurance: "No thing is impossible for Me."

[94] See on these distinctions Brümmer, *Theology*, 10-25.

[95] See Brümmer, *Theology*, 28f. on undeniable implications between different illocutions.

Moreover, even if someone would deny this implication there remains a very close connection between the concepts of A-power and C-power. For if God is *pantokrator* in the sense of having A-power, He certainly does many things. But in order to do things, it is necessary to be able to do these things. Thus, if God is *pantokrator*, He must have the capacity to do all what is implied in governing the universe. The reverse of course is not necessarily true: It is perfectly possible that God has the capacity to do all things, but deistically refrains from actualizing this capacity, or refrains from actualizing this capacity in many cases. In this way, Eichenseer is correct in arguing that the concept of *pantokrator* includes that of *pantodynamos*, whereas this inclusion does not hold the other way round.[96] As a result, reflection on the range of God's potentialities is not out of order from the point of view of A-power, but follows naturally from it. This explains why A-power claims and C-power claims often go hand in hand.

We conclude that apart from an historical argument, there is also a logical argument against the thesis that ascribing C-power to God distorts the authentic character of Christian belief. These arguments are together sufficiently cogent to falsify this view of Geach and others. In the same way as it is in general much too easy to play off the God of the philosophers against the God of the Bible, it is too simple to isolate the doctrine of God's almightiness from reflection on the realm of God's capacities and possibilities for action.[97] At the same time, Geach is right in carefully distinguishing the concepts of almightiness (A-power) and omnipotence (C-power) from each other, and in what follows it will turn out how important it is not to overlook the differences between these concepts (see especially §3.4)

2.2.5 Conclusion

Let us finally summarize the main conclusions of § 2.2. We do more justice to the biblical and patristic sources if we distinguish between three rather than only between two different concepts of divine power. The mutual relations between these three concepts, as well as their translatability in terms of each other, can be illustrated by means of the following sketch of their semantic fields.

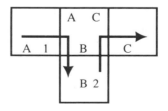

---

[96] Eichenseer, *Symbolum Apostolicum*, 178: "Das *pantokrator* schliesst das *pantodynamos* ein, aber nicht umgekehrt." For a similar assessment of the relation between both Greek concepts, see F. Kattenbusch, *Apostolische Symbol*, 533.

[97] For more argumentation on this point, see my paper "Allmacht und Omnipotenz."

In this diagram, the letters A, B and C stand for what we have called A-, B-, and C-power respectively. That means, A corresponds with the Hebrew *Sebaoth*, B with the Greek *pantokrator* and C with the Latin *omnipotens*. The square in which the fields overlap each other represents that aspect of meaning which the three concepts have in common. This aspect can be defined as follows: power as all-sovereign dominion over and actual government of the world. This connotation is present to some degree in all three concepts. But apart from this overlap, each concept has its specific significance, which it does not share with either or both of the others. In the case of A, this specific significance is: the liberating military power of the Lord of Israel's hosts.[98] In the case of B it is: the preserving power of the God who keeps the world in being in His solicitude. And in the case of C: the virtual power of the God for whom nothing is impossible to do.

We have observed two shifts of emphasis in the Jewish-Christian conception of divine power: from A to B (1), and from B to C (2). But we have also seen that these are indeed only shifts of emphasis. In the course of the development towards one particular conception of God's power, the other conceptions were never completely forgotten. Despite some people's preference for one of the three aspects, we have shown that it is at least historically (and in part also logically) unsound to play them off against one another. In the next section, we shall investigate how in the form of a new conceptuality precisely the balancing of God's actual and potential powers continued to be an important concern, which in the Middle Ages even moved to the centre of an increasingly passionate theological and philosophical debate.

At the same time, however, and more importantly, it is clear that the present section also gives rise to a systematic question. For the different understandings of God's omnipotence in early Christian theology reflect a deeply rooted interest in the very *nature* of power. What exactly is power, what sorts of powers might be distinguished, and why is it so important to have power? Moreover, what does it mean to ascribe all the power there is to one particular being? And does it make a difference if this being is *God*? It is to questions like these that we have to return in the conceptual-analytic part of our inquiry (chapter 3). As to the present section, we may conclude that this at least is true in the Geach-thesis, that authentic Christian reflection on the nature of God's power can never take place in speculative abstraction from the concrete experience of its governing and preserving actuality.

---

[98] See for the connotations of the Old Testament title *Sebaoth* most recently H.-J. Zobel, "Seba'ot," in: G.J. Botterweck, H. Ringgren & H.-J. Fabry (eds.), *TWAT* VI, Lieferung 8-10, Stuttgart 1989, c.876-892.

2.3 THE ABSOLUTE AND ORDAINED POWER OF GOD

2.3.1 *The rise and original function of the distinction*

In the previous section we quoted the view of Augustine, that God is called omnipotent for no other reason than that He can do what He wills.[1] Since the early Middle Ages, the question is raised whether indeed the ascription of omnipotence to God does not mean more than this. If God's omnipotence simply means that He can do what He wills, does this imply that God is *only* able to do the things He wants to do, and therefore unable to do things which He does not want to do? Since it seems to be the case that God does only and all those things which He wants to do, it would follow from this that God is not able to do other things than He actually does! This conclusion, however, was quite unsatisfactory to orthodox ears. Even in the case of human beings it is clear that they are able to do other things than they want to do - so how much more in the case of God! To bind God's power exclusively to His will seems to limit Him in a way which denies His freedom and therefore detracts from His perfection.

This uneasiness with the Augustinian position[2] was the main reason for the genesis of the famous distinction between God's absolute and ordained power. The history of the meaning and functions of this distinction since its origination is as intriguing as it is complicated. During the first half of our century some important research was done in this field.[3] More recent studies, based on a broader supply of primary texts, come to a more detailed and to some extent more varied representation.[4] Surely investigations have not yet been completed. In what follows we will try to offer a survey of the semantic and hermeneutic vicissitudes of the distinction as far as these have been elucidated by now. Perhaps it is good to note at the outset that it is not my intention simply to offer an account of the distinction's career which is as neutral as possible.[5] Instead, I want to de-

---

[1] See §2.2, n.77.

[2] Augustine's position is not entirely unambiguous, however. In other places Augustine knows of "eine Dimension des göttlichen Könnens, die ausserhalb des faktischen Verhaltens Gottes liegt," so that "die *potentia Dei* von Augustin nicht nur als Ausführungsorgan des göttlichen Willens ... verstanden [wird]." B. Hamm, *Promissio, Pactum, Ordinatio*, Tübingen 1977, 492.

[3] For references, see my paper "De absolute en geordineerde macht van God," *NTT* 45 (1991), 204 n.1.

[4] H.A. Oberman, *The Harvest of Medieval Theology*, Cambridge (Mass.) 1963, 30-56; R.P. Desharnais, *The History of the Distinction between God's Absolute and Ordained Power and its Influence on Martin Luther*, Washington 1966 (unpublished dissertation, Catholic University of America). But see above all: F. Oakley, *Omnipotence, Covenant and Order*, Ithaca 1984, and W.J. Courtenay, "The Dialectic of Divine Omnipotence in the High and Late Middle Ages," in: T. Rudavsky (ed.), *Divine Omniscience and Omnipotence in Medieval Philosophy*, Dordrecht 1985, 243-269. Finally, apart from many smaller case-studies which will be referred to in the following where necessary, there is an Italian volume of conference papers edited by A. Vetesse, *Sopra la volta del mundo*, Bergamo 1986.

[5] My arguments against the possibility of a "neutral" science as put forward in chapter 1

fend the thesis that one interpretation of the distinction between God's absolute and ordained power is legitimate from a Christian point of view, whereas another is not.[6] In the course of my argument I shall argue for this by pointing out the historical consequences and logical implications of the different interpretations.

The first clear specimen of a text which distinguishes between two ways of defining God's *potentia*[7] is the report of a diner conversation which bishop Peter Damian had with a friend of his, abbot Desiderius of the monastery at Monte-Cassino, probably in the year 1067.[8] In this conversation a difference of opinion had emerged on a word of Jerome in the latter's *Epistula ad Eustochium*. In recommending the state of virginity in this letter Jerome goes as far as claiming that even God, "although God can do all things, He cannot raise up a virgin after she has fallen."[9] Damian confesses that he has never been able to accept this particular claim of Jerome's. Jerome must have been unduly carried away by his religious devotion in writing this.[10]

Contrary to Damian, Desiderius has no difficulties in approving of Jerome's utterance. For Desiderius defines omnipotence, as is clear from Damian's report of their discussion, as the power to do whatever one wills. If it is said that God cannot do something, what is meant is that He does not *want* to do that particular thing. In this connection, Desiderius paraphrases the word of Augustine, that God is called omnipotent for no other reason than that He is able to do what He wills. To put it succinctly: *non potuit = noluit*. But Damian cannot accept this move, because he fears misuse on the part of malignant dialecticians. They could interpret a parallelism in extension between God's power and God's will in this sense, that God's power is apparently circumscribed by His will. "God cannot do whatever he wills; he can *only* do what he wills."[11] In this way, the dialecticians

---

pertain to historiography as well.

[6] For a very similar appraisal, the more remarkable since by that time the particulars of the distinction were less known than they are now, see Barth, *Church Dogmatics* II 1 (German original ed. 1940), 539-542.

[7] Since the distinction differentiates between two definitions of what God *can* do, rather than of what God actually does in ruling or sustaining the universe, it can best be conceived of as a distinction between two conceptions of divine C-power. Thus, if we use the word *potentia* in what follows, it should be taken as equivalent to what we labelled C-power before.

[8] See on this especially Oakley, *Omnipotence*, 42-44; Courtenay, "Dialectic," 244.

[9] "Audenter loquor: cum omnia Deus possit, suscitare virginem non potest post ruinam." Jerome, *Epistula* 22, 5 (CSEL 54, 150); cf. F.A. Wright (ed.), *Select Letters of St. Jerome* (LCL), London 1963, 62.

[10] P. Damian, *Disputatio super quaestione qua quaeritur, si deus omnipotens est, quomodo potest agere ut quae facta sunt facta non fuerint*, in: A. Cantin, *Pierre Damien: Lettre sur la toute-puissance divine* (SC 191), Paris 1972, 406; Damian's writing is better known under the name of its older edition *De divina omnipotentia* (PL 145, 595-622).

[11] Courtenay, "Dialectic," 244.

ascribed a lack of power to God, which Damian considered to be a derogation of God's freedom and perfection.

Hence, Damian defends the opposite point of view. God can do more than merely the things He in fact wants to do. The realm of possibilities open to God does not coincide with and, in consequence, is not limited by, what God has chosen to do. To put it in the later terminology: we should not conceive of God's power only as *potentia ordinata*, i.e. from the point of view of what He has willed and ordained to do, but also as *potentia absoluta*, i.e. in an absolute sense. In his disputation on divine omnipotence Damian elaborates this principle primarily in the direction of the power which God has in relation to past events. If God is able to change the customary laws of nature, as in the deliverance of the three friends of Daniel out of the fiery furnace, why should it be impossible for Him to restore the virginity of a fallen woman? In general, why should we deny that He is able to make past events undone, so that these must be considered as not having happened? If it is complained that this clashes with the principle of non-contradiction, then this seems to be all the worse for that principle.[12] Even if God usually refrains from doing x because He does not want x, that does not imply that He is unable to do x. In such a case, God certainly can do x, but He simply does not want to do x (*potuit, sed noluit*).

In this discussion between Desiderius and Damian the relevant later positions are already prefigured. Both Anselm (in his *Proslogion*) and Abelard opt for the view of Desiderius, that there are things which God is unable to do. Anselm tries to reconcile this view with the divine omnipotence by means of a semantic analysis of the modal verb "can," and points to what he alleges to be an ambiguity in the use of this verb. According to Anselm, in the sentence "I can lie" the word "can" is used improperly, because it is prefixed to the concept of an act resulting from weakness instead of power.[13] Thus, the claim that God cannot lie is a confirmation of God's omnipotence rather than a denial of it. The same

---

[12] Contrary to what is sometimes suggested, however, Damian is conceptually somewhat unclear at this point. Cf. Cantin, *Pierre Damien*, 174-176. Possibly, Damian could be interpreted as willing to undermine Greek necessitarianism, but lacking the conceptual and logical tools to present a consistent alternative. As a result, Damian is rather loose in some of his utterances. An interpretation along these lines is suggested by Knuuttila, "Time and Modality," 200-202 and explicitly defended by Lawrence Moonan, "Impossibility and Peter Damian," *AGP* 62 (1980), 146-163. On the other hand, Irvin Michael Resnick maintains that Damian in some contexts intentionally advocated the "outrageous view" that God can do even that which constitutes a contradiction. See his *Divine Power and Possibility in St. Peter Damian's* De Divina Omnipotentia, Leiden 1992, 98-111.

[13] We will argue later on, that this argument as it stands is incorrect. Actions of lying, sinning etc. do not ensue from weakness in the sense of a lack of abilities, but from moral weakness or imperfection. Surely they presuppose the ability (i.e. the power) to perform the required types of action.

argument applies to making past events undone, for this means making false what is true, which is of course an act of weakness as well.[14]

As to Abelard, it is interesting that he himself notices that he has inherited his view from Platonism. The fact that God cannot do things which are not in accordance with His nature means to Abelard, that what doesn't happen *could not* have happened. Since it is contrary to God's will, even God would not have been able to bring it about. In this way, an optimistic necessitarianism plays a role at the background of Abelard's theology.[15] In this way Abelard belongs to the dialecticians feared by Damian, because in a sense he makes God the prisoner of His own nature. God could not possibly have acted otherwise than He did, viz. in accordance with His own nature.

During the first half of the 12th century, however, this position is more and more considered to be incompatible with genuine Christian belief. A good illustration of this development is Anselm's later dissociation from his earlier view that God's will and power are equally extensive. In his *Cur Deus Homo?* - i.e. in his Christology, the *locus* in which the difference between Greek and Christian thought traditionally became most sharply manifest - Anselm was forced to adopt another approach to the problem than that which he had taken in his *Proslogion*. For if Christ was to be fully human (*vere homo*), He must have had the ability to sin. And since according to the doctrine of the *communicatio idiomatum* the properties of His human nature are shared by His divine nature, this ability should also be ascribed to God in Christ. So there is something which God can do, although He does not will to do it - namely to sin. Yet, according to Anselm, although Christ had the ability to sin, He lacked the ability to *will* to sin. Thus, it remains absolutely impossible to imagine Him really sinning. If we ask further why Christ (and God) lack the ability to will to sin, Anselm at one place gives the remarkable answer that this lack is not caused by any external necessity, but by an internal, self-imposed necessity. In other words: the ultimate reason why God doesn't sin and cannot will to sin is, that He limits Himself in this respect. In this way Desiderius' "non potuit = noluit" is replaced by "potuit, sed noluit," and the foundation for the later *absoluta/ordinata* distinction is laid.[16]

This way of solving the problem subsequently received wide acceptance. The school of Anselm of Laon, the Victorines (especially Hugh

---

[14] Anselm, *Proslogion* VII; cf. already Augustine, *Sermo de symbolo* 1, 2 (CCL 46, 185): "Quam multa non potest, et omnipotens est: et ideo omnipotens est, quia ista non potest." ("Although it is true that He cannot do many things, still He is omnipotent: precisely therefore He is omnipotent, because He cannot do those things").

[15] See his *Introductio ad theologiam* 3, 4-5 (PL 178, 1092-1101; the reference to Plato on 1094), and cf. the comments of A.O. Lovejoy, *The Great Chain of Being*, New York 1960, 70-73.

[16] See W.J. Courtenay, "Necessity and Freedom in Anselm's Concept of God," in his *Covenant and Causality in Medieval Thought*, London 1984, ch.I, 39-64; and id., "The Dialectic," 245, 260. The relevant places in *Cur Deus Homo?* are 2, 5; 2, 10; and 2, 17.

of St. Victor, in a vigorous attack on Abelard) and the Cistercians (cf. Bernard's contribution to Abelard's condemnation in 1140, partially on account of the latter's determinism) all took the line of the later Anselm. As a result, Peter Lombard was able to turn this approach into near dogma in his treatment of divine omnipotence in the first book of his *Liber sententiarum* (1154).[17]

Nevertheless, it still took half a century before the differentiation between the things God *can* do and the things God *wills* to do took the terminological form of the *absoluta/ordinata* distinction. In an anonymous commentary on the Pauline Epistles dating from ca. 1200, the author argues that we can speak of God's power not only according to what God has actually chosen to do, but also *without* regard to this divine choosing. To indicate this latter way he uses the term "absolutely" (*absolute*).[18] Some ten years later, Godfrey of Poitiers seems to have been the first who changed the adverb into an adjective, and phrases the distinction in the way that was to become standard[19] (although he writes *de potentia conditionali* for the later *de potentia ordinata*). Other theologians develop their own terminology in expressing the distinction, but in the course of some decades the terms *potentia absoluta* and *potentia ordinata* become standard.

It is important to realize the precise function of the distinction in its original setting. None of the theologians who employ it think of God as having two powers, acting now by means of the one, then again by means of the other. Rather, what is at stake in the distinction is that there are two ways to conceive and speak of the single power of God, viz. in an abstract sense, without regard to God's concrete revealed will, or rather from the point of view of this will as revealed in the actual orders of nature and grace. Since it cannòt occur that God does anything which He does not will to do (although God has the *ability* to do things which He does not will to do), it is similarly excluded that He would act at any time *de potentia absoluta*! The only reason for distinguishing a *potentia absoluta* in God is to conceptualize the conviction that the realm of God's potentialities did not coincide with the number of possibilities in fact realized by Him. Thus, the term *potentia absoluta* points to divine counterfactuals: "If God would have chosen q instead of p, q would have been the case." In this way, the distinction (apart from glossing authoritative statements on divine inability) seeks to counteract the classical Aristotelean necessitarianism, which was rapidly gaining ground as a result of the Aristotle-renaissance and the rise of Latin Averroism. Thus, Francis Oakley is right in emphasizing that the *potentia absoluta - ordinata* dialectics forms the Christian counterpart of the

---

[17] Courtenay, "Dialectic," 246; Oakley, *Omnipotence*, 45. See also D.E. Luscombe, *The School of Peter Abelard*, Cambridge 1970, 134-136; 189-191 (on Hugh of St. Victor).

[18] *Quaestiones in epistolam ad Romanos* q.91 (PL 175, 457); cf. Courtenay, "Dialectic," 261.

[19] Thus, Alexander of Hales (using the distinction in his *Summa*, written before 1245) was not the first one, as was thought for a long time.

classical principle of plenitude.[20] For contrary to the principle of plenitude, the *potentia*-distinction clearly acknowledges (and even articulates) the existence of possibilities which are and will always remain unrealized.[21]

As we saw in § 2.2, it had been one of the hallmarks of early Christian theology to describe created reality as from its genesis onwards dependent on the all-dominating and all-sustaining power of God. These notions we expressed in the concepts of A-power and B-power. In the struggle with Graeco-Arabic necessitarianism, however, the need was felt to explicate another element in God's power, which up till then was only implicitly present in the notion of C-power. In claiming that creation is dependent on the power of God, it became important to specify the precise character of this divine power. It was this further specification of the divine power which came to be expressed in the *potentia*-distinction. For this distinction makes clear that God's power in creating and upholding the universe is a power of alternativity rather than only a power of spontaneity. Creation is grounded in the free choice of God, a choice in which all opposite possibilities are excluded. Accordingly, creation is not necessary but contingent. Now the concept of *potentia absoluta* describes God's power irrespective of this choice. Later scholastics give a precise definition of its scope: it contains all entities which are not in themselves impossible (*per se impossibile*). The concept of *potentia ordinata*, on the other hand, indicates, that God has bound Himself to actualize His power henceforth only in a way which fits the order He has chosen to create.

In thinking of the order God has chosen to actualize one had of course primarily the order of creation in mind, as reflected for example in the laws and regularities of nature. Apart from this order, however, other orders came to play an important role alongside it, for example the moral order, the order of the history of salvation and the order of grace. All these orders were freely instituted by God, and in all these orders God had bound Himself to act in particular ways. To put it somewhat anachronistically: the distinction was used as a tool to relate God's election and covenant[22] to each other in a well-balanced way.

A representative treatment of the distinction we find in Thomas Aquinas. Aquinas is very reticent in his use of the distinction; in the earlier stages of his work (for example in his commentary on the omnipotence-sections of the *Sentences*) he even refrains from utilizing the distinction at

---

[20] Oakley, *Omnipotence*, 40 and passim; contrariwise A. Funkenstein, *Theology and the Scientific Imagination*, Princeton 1986, 123 n.22. Perhaps Funkenstein correctly points to the principle of economy (or 'Ockham's razor') as the real counterpart of the principle of plenitude, since it holds that the *least* possible number of possibilities should be conceived of as realized. But even in that case, it remains true that also the *potentia*-distinction in its original setting implies a straightforward denial of the principle of plenitude.

[21] See on the principle of plenitude Lovejoy, *The Great Chain*, and cf. the critical examinations and elaborations in S. Knuuttila (ed.), *Reforging*.

[22] Both Courtenay and Oakley underline the 'covenantal character' of God's *potentia ordinata*.

all. But where he refers to it,[23] he identifies God's ordained power with the whole of God's plan for creation. This plan is not co-extensive with God's wisdom, because God's wisdom is inexhaustible. It is solely based upon the choice of God's will. As to God's absolute power, this functions as a sort of "dialectical standby ... to underline the contingency of creation, ... the fact that it does not have either to be what it is or even to be at all."[24] It is a purely hypothetical abstraction of the power God has apart from His will. In an apt formulation:

> Accordingly we should state that by his absolute power God can do other things than those he foresaw that he would do and pre-ordained to do. Nevertheless nothing can come to pass that he has not foreseen and pre-ordained.[25]

So although God *can* do p *de potentia absoluta* (p being any logically possible act), it is not possible that He *does* p *de potentia absoluta*.[26] If he does p, this can only be *de potentia ordinata*.

For a long time the *potentia*-distinction has been disparaged by historians of doctrine as the expression of an extreme scepticism, according to which God could at any moment capriciously and inordinately intervene in the existing order.[27] We can now conclude that this interpretation is mistaken with regard to the original, authentic use of the distinction. *Potentia absoluta* is nothing more (and, for that matter, nothing less) than a transcendental concept, which "over against all that is real upholds the logical possibility of its being otherwise."[28]

2.3.2 *Complicating factors*
In spite of the clarity of its original intention, soon all kinds of varieties, misunderstandings and problems arose in the use and interpretation of the

---

[23] Aquinas, *Quaestiones disputatae de potentia Dei* 1, 5; *Summa Theologiae* I 25, 5.

[24] Oakley, *Omnipotence*, 50f.

[25] *Summa Theologiae* I 25, 5: "Secundum hoc ergo dicendum est quod Deus potest alia facere de potentia absoluta quam quae praescivit et praeordinavit se facturum. Non tamen potest esse quod aliqua faciat quae non praesciverit et praeordinaverit se facturum"; text and translation in Thomas Gilby, *St. Thomas Aquinas. Summa Theologiae* (Blackfriars edition) vol.5, London 1967, 173.

[26] It is worth noting that in this context at least Aquinas accepts the existence of unrealized possibilities, and thus implicitly denies the principle of plenitude. This point is acknowledged (but subsequently qualified) by Knuuttila, "Time and Modality," 215.

[27] See for this scepticist interpretation of the distinction elder historians of doctrine like A. Koyré, E. Gilson, E. Iserloh and G. Leff. The latter has abandoned this position in his later study *William of Ockham*, Manchester 1975.

[28] "Der Gedanke der *potentia absoluta* ... bezeichnet nur eine abstrakte Möglichkeit. Seine Bedeutung ist daher eigentlich bloss eine kritische, denn er hält allem Wirklichen gegenüber die logische Möglichkeit des Andersseins aufrecht." R. Seeberg, *Lehrbuch der Dogmengeschichte* Vol.3, Leipzig 1930[4], 654. But this judgment can no more be applied to Duns Scotus, as Seeberg does; see §2.3.4 below.

distinction. As it seems to me, this was primarily caused by the following five complications.

1. The interpretation of the distinction as sketched above clearly presupposes that categories of time can be applied to God. If God's *potentia absoluta* is to be equated, in an oft quoted definition of Courtenay, to "the total possibilities *initially* open to God, some of which were realized by creating the established order,"[29] then a time prior to God's choosing is assumed. Concomitant with this is the assumption of a sort of process of deliberation in God, which also precedes His creative choice. This ascription of time and deliberation to God conflicts with a number of classical divine attributes such as timelessness, immutability and omniscience (God need not deliberate between different options, since He knows which option is the best one).

Of course these conflicts were not insoluble. It could be argued for instance that this talk of time and deliberation in connection with God is anthropomorphic or metaphorical, and should therefore not be taken literally. But this usual move in turn evoked the attempt to formulate how things really are, i.e. how they are from the point of view of God. And then it is clear that for God there is no lapse of time, so neither past nor future. In the light of this argument, the proposition:

P1:   God *de potentia absoluta* could have done p, but He did not choose to do it and will not choose to do it

should be replaced by a present-tense proposition like:

P2:   God *de potentia absoluta* can do p.

For God lives, as it is sometimes called, in an "eternal now." But P2 as it stands seems to imply that it is possible that God interferes with the created order even in (what is to us) the present. Thus, here we have a first tendency towards "operationalization" (to use a phrase of Oberman) of the *potentia absoluta*.[30] Usually this tendency remained under the surface, since we of course have to conceptualize things as they are from our temporal point of view, and not from God's eternal standpoint (as Damian already insisted[31]).

---

[29] W.J. Courtenay, "Nominalism and Late Medieval Religion," now in: id., *Covenant and Causality*, Ch.XI, 39. The italicization of the word "initially" is Courtenay's, who further adds: "... the unrealized possibilities are now only hypothetically possible", ibid.

[30] Courtenay, "Dialectic," points to the problem of the temporal categories (249), but unfortunately does not show this inherent tendency towards operationalization. For the latter term, see H.A. Oberman, "*Via Antiqua* and *Via Moderna*: Late Medieval Prolegomena to Early Reformation Thought," in: A. Hudson & M. Wilks (eds.), *From Ockham to Wyclif*, Oxford 1987, 462.

[31] Damian, *De divina omnipotentia* (PL 145, 619).

2. The substitution of the earlier, somewhat more prolix descriptions of the distinction by the standard pair *potentia absoluta* and *potentia ordinata*, was in itself already a source of possible confusion. Earlier allusions to the *potentia absoluta*, like *potentia pure considerata* and *potentia accipi absolute*, unambiguously referred to power in an abstract, purely theoretical sense. They pointed to a certain way of conceiving the single power of God. But as soon as the terms *potentia absoluta* and *potentia ordinata* were generally accepted, there was always the risk of taking them as two different powers, both of which could be actualized by God. So in fact "the gain in brevity was more than offset by a loss in clarity."[32]

3. This risk of taking *potentia absoluta* and *potentia ordinata* as two distinct powers was aggravated by the permeating influence of the principle of plenitude. Although seldom openly professed, this principle exerted a constant pressure upon the shape of Western thought in that unrealized possibilities were always conceived of as inevitably becoming realized at some time. Even if the principle did not as such imply that also all *evil* possibilities would be realized along with the good ones, from Plotinus onwards evil was often considered as the unavoidable side-effect of the good. As a result, the notion of God's *potentia absoluta* became more and more a dark and threatening one. It became very hard to think of evil possibilities of which one could nevertheless be confident that they would not at any time become realized. For if God is able to act *de potentia absoluta*, there is always a chance that He will decide to do so at some time. If it is not the case that all His possibilities are realized deterministically, then at least He can realize some of them arbitrarily. The middle course between determinism and arbitrariness which was captured in the covenantal idea of God's *potentia ordinata* gradually disappeared.

4. In the original setting of the distinction miracles form a tricky problem. Officially miracles of course belong to what God does *de potentia ordinata*, for otherwise they could not actually take place. But the nature of God's *potentia ordinata* was often illustrated (as we did above) by referring to all kinds of regularities in natural and spiritual life. Miraculous over-turnings of these orders could hardly be given a place in this framework. What was needed was a distinction *within* the *potentia ordinata* between regular and irregular events, both of which happened in accordance with God's foreordained will. Since such a distinction failed to appear (or at least to become generally accepted), the impression arose that miracles should be taken as acts of God *de potentia absoluta*, interfering with the natural regularities as imposed by God's *potentia ordinata*. In this way, the rise of a slightly modified version of the distinction is explicable, which uses the ordinary or extraordinary character of an event as a discriminating principle.

---

[32] Courtenay, "Dialectic," 251.

In this variation, events following the common course of nature are associated with God's *potentia ordinaria* (instead of His *potentia ordinata*), whereas miraculous interventions in the existing order count as divine acts *de potentia extraordinaria*. This latter concept of replaces the traditional concept of *potentia absoluta*. But God's *potentia extraordinaria* is of course power which is fully "operational"!

This later application of the distinction became dominant in later scholasticism. Suarez for example prefers the term *potentia ordinaria* to *potentia ordinata*, and notices that the corresponding apprehension of the distinction had become the most usual ("magis usitatus") one in his time.[33] It was not until the Puritan theologians of the 17th century, that a coherent interpretation of miracles was offered within the original setting of the distinction. William Ames for example first explains the distinction in its authentic purport, and then goes on to distinguish within the realm of God's *potentia ordinata* between what he calls God's ordinary and extraordinary providence.[34]

5. A similar shift in meaning, also contributing to the operationalization of the concept of *potentia absoluta*, was facilitated by analogies drawn with interhuman balances of power. One of the most influential of these analogies arose when canon lawyers in the late thirteenth century deployed the distinction as a means to relate the papal power to the ecclesiastical law.[35] In the same way as God had bound Himself voluntarily to the existing order, the pope had committed himself freely to act in conformity with the existing ecclesiastical law. At the background of this rule was the principle of Roman law, that the prince is bound by the law out of benevolence, rather than constrained to it by some external necessity. Thus, although the pope is above the law *de potentia absoluta*, *de potentia ordinata* and in reality he is bound to act according to the law.

However, it might on occasion be required that the pope, for the greater good of the church, alters or suspends a particular law. To cite an example Courtenay[36] found somewhere, it could be necessary that a monk was released by the pope from his vows of chastity and poverty, and yet be allowed to remain a monk. Normally (i.e., *de potestate ordinata*), the pope of course lacks the authority to do this. But perhaps he is able to do it by means of an absolute authority, *de potestate absoluta*. In this way, the *potentia* or in this case rather the *potestas absoluta* was conceived of as a

---

[33] F. Suarez, *Disputationes Metaphysicae* 30, sect.17; quoted by F. Oakley, *The Western Church in the Later Middle Ages*, Ithaca 1985², 145.

[34] W. Ames, *Medulla Theologiae* I 6, 18-20; I 9, 8-13 (cf. J.D. Eusden, *The Marrow of Theology*, translated from the third Latin ed., 1629, Philadelphia 1968, 93, 107f.).

[35] Important material has recently been brought to light on the use of the distinction in legal contexts, and on the influence of this upon the theological use. See Courtenay, "The Dialectic," 251f., 264f.; Oakley, *Omnipotence*, 93-118; and Oakley, "Jacobean Political Theology: The Absolute and Ordinary Powers of the King," *JHI* 29 (1964), 323-346.

[36] Courtenay, "The Dialectic," 252.

power which could really be actualized. This juridical application of the distinction was to have a dramatic impact on subsequent theological developments.

2.3.3 *Scotus and Ockham on the potentia-distinction*

Remarkably, it is especially thinkers from the Augustinian-Franciscan tradition like Bonaventure and Henry of Ghent, who in reaction to its newer connotations come to a total rejection of the distinction. They fear a misinterpretation of the original theological use of the distinction, resulting in the ascription of arbitrary, extra-legal or even sinful activities to God.[37] But a strong impulse to further applications of the distinction is given by the Parisian condemnation of 1277, which repudiates any real or apparent curtailment of the divine omnipotence.[38]

The first appearance on the theological scene of the newer connotations of the distinction, including their tendency towards operationalization of the *potentia absoluta*, is brought about by John Duns Scotus. Like Aquinas before him, Scotus reviews the distinction in his treatment of the question of whether God is able to make other things than He has preordained to make. Again like that of Aquinas, Scotus' answer to this question is in the affirmative. But in contradistinction to Aquinas, Scotus appeals to the legal or juridical parallel in grounding his answer:[39]

> We should state that when an agent acts in conformity with a right law or rule he can, if he is not limited and bound by that law, but if that law is subordinate to his will, out of a *potentia absoluta* act otherwise... For example, supposing that someone (like a king) is free to make a law and change it, he can act apart from that law by means of his *potentia absoluta*, because he can change the law and institute another one... And so it is clear how it must be understood that God can make *de potentia absoluta* what He cannot make *de potentia ordinata*.[40]

---

[37] See on their arguments my "Absolute en geordineerde macht," 211f.

[38] Instructive on the repercussions of the 1277 condemnation upon the doctrine of divine omnipotence E. Grant, "The Condemnation of 1277, God's Absolute Power and Physical Thought in the Late Middle Ages," *Viator* 10 (1979), 210-244. Cf. H. Blumenberg, *Die kopernikanische Wende*, Frankfurt 1965, 35-37.

[39] This he does both in his *Ordinatio* I 44 and in his *Lectura* I 44; we quote from the more concise and crystal-clear exposition in the *Lectura*.

[40] J. Duns Scotus, *Lectura* I 44 q. un., n.3, 5 (*Opera omnia* XVII, ed. Vaticana, 535f.): "Dicendum quod quando est agens quod conformiter agit legi et rationi rectae, - si non limitetur et alligetur illi legi, sed illa lex subest voluntati suae, potest ex potentia absoluta aliter agere; ... sicut, ponatur quod aliquis esset ita liber (sicut rex) quod possit facere legem et eam mutare, tunc praeter illam legem de potentia sua absoluta aliter potest agere, quia potest legem mutare et aliam statuere... Et sic patet quomodo debet intelligi quod Deus potest facere de potentia absoluta quod non potest de potentia ordinata." Cf. Courtenay's conclusion, "The Dialectic," 254: "With Scotus the legal, constitutional definition entered theological discussion. ... not heeding the warnings of Henry of Ghent or Petrus de Trabibus, Scotus incorporated the analogy developed by the canon lawyers."

78

Thus, Scotus considers the distinction to be applicable to any personal agent who is in some way or another "above the law." In the *Ordinatio* he even goes as far as equating the distinction with that between what can be done "de facto" (which is the same as: *de potentia absoluta*), and "de jure" (*de potentia ordinata*). In comparison with its original intention, the distinction is turned completely upside down here. The concept of *potentia ordinata* functions merely as a sort of auxiliary hypothetical construction, indicating whether a particular action is lawful or not, whereas *potentia absoluta* is the really interesting concept, embracing all things which in fact ("de facto") can be the case. As to the effect of this move upon the theological discussion, clearly now the possibility should be conceded that God acts today or will act in the future by means of His *potentia absoluta*. In this respect, Scotus differs fundamentally from Aquinas.[41]

Scotus does, admittedly, incorporate some qualifications in his theory which warrant its continuity with the traditional interpretation of the distinction. Thus, he emphatically declares (like almost everybody commenting on the problem), that the distinction should not be understood as differentiating between two distinct powers in God, but only between two different aspects of one and the same divine power.[42] Moreover, he asserts that it is impossible for God to act *inordinate*.[43] For when God alters an existing law *de potentia absoluta*, the very act of this alteration constitutes again a new law. In the same way as it is by definition impossible for an absolute monarch to act illegally,[44] it is impossible for God to act inordinately. In this sense it is even unclear whether Scotus indeed considers God's suspending actions as actions *de potentia absoluta*,[45] or rather as introductions of a new dispensation within the single *potentia ordinata*. Scotus himself asserts, that in performing such actions the absolute power of God at least does not transcend His ordained power, because they are in accordance with a new order.[46] But however this may be, in any case Scotus does not regard God's

---

[41] See for comparative studies of Aquinas, Scotus and Ockham R.P. Desharnais, *History*, 73-167, who emphasizes the continuity between all three of them, and of scholastic thought on divine power in general; M.A. Pernoud, "The Theory of the *Potentia Dei* according to Aquinas, Scotus and Ockham," *Antonianum* 47 (1972), 69-95 (which to my mind does not quite get to the heart of the matter); and above all the thoroughgoing analysis of M.M. Adams in her monumental *William Ockham*, Notre Dame 1987, Vol.2, 1186-1207. Cf., however, the compelling criticism of H.G. Gelber in her review of precisely these pages in *F&P* 7 (1990), 246-252, esp. 250.

[42] J. Duns Scotus, *Ordinatio* I 44, q. un.; cf. the text and translation in A.B. Wolter, *Duns Scotus on the Will and Morality*, Washington 1986, 254-261.

[43] Ibid.

[44] See Funkenstein, *Theology*, 132f. for an illustration and formulation of this rule of Roman law: "Emperors, by definition, do not steal horses. Quod principi placuit, legis habet vigorem."

[45] In this vein W. Pannenberg, *Die Prädestinationslehre des Duns Skotus*, Göttingen 1954, 136. O. Miethke, *Ockhams Weg zur Sozialphilosophie*, Berlin 1969, 149, on the contrary, holds that Scotus used the concept of *potentia absoluta* not yet in the real mode ('realis'), but in the potential mode ('potentialis'), so no longer, like Aquinas, in the unreal mode ('irrealis').

[46] Scotus, *Ordinatio* I 44 q. un., n.5.

freedom to suspend the order previously established by Him as only an hypothetical possibility. Thus, he prepared the way for a more scepticist interpretation of the distinction.[47]

Moreover, Scotus extends the distinction's range of employment more than any scholastic theologian before him. It plays an essential role in his doctrine of justification, his doctrine of the sacraments and his moral theory. In other words, to Scotus the distinction has in general become an important theological tool. Almost every dogmatic *locus* he examines not only from the point of view of God's *potentia ordinata*, but also from the perspective of God's *potentia absoluta*. In this way, many things which seem to be fixed and necessary when considered from God's *potentia ordinata*, turn out to be contingent when addressed from the alternative perspective. Clearly, Scotus' predilection for the distinction is closely bound up with his theory of contingency,[48] and in general with what has been called "the widening of realm of possibilities"[49] which took place in the late Middle Ages.

In the light of this development, it is the more remarkable that Ockham is much more hesitant in his definition of the distinction than Scotus.[50] In Ockham's approach of the theme, the diverse influences of Aquinas, Scotus and others seem to merge into each other in a way which is difficult to unravel, and it is no wonder that his use of the distinction has been the subject of much research.[51]

On the one hand, this research has shown that Ockham elaborates on the original intention of the distinction. More plainly than Aquinas (and in the same way as Scotus) he defines the range of God's *potentia absoluta* as embracing all which does not imply a contradiction. God can bring about *de potentia absoluta* all entities which are logically possible. The *potentia ordinata*, however, has nothing to do with what is logically possible, but with what is *factually* possible, from the perspective of God's decrees. Thus, the meaning of *posse* in both components of the distinction is not the same. A comparison of Scripture texts proves, that here already the verb "can" is used ambiguously, sometimes referring to what is logically possible, some-

---

[47] Cf. F. Copleston, *A History of Philosophy* Vol.II, New York 1962², 550, in the context of a discussion of Scotus' moral theory.

[48] On this theory, see Antonie Vos, *Kennis en noodzakelijkheid*, Kampen 1981, 68-87, and now also A. Vos e.a. (eds.), *Johannes Duns Scotus: Contingentie en vrijheid. Lectura I 39*, Zoetermeer 1992; the innovative character of this theory leads both Vos and Knuuttila to a much more positive evaluation of Scotus' contribution to the history of ideas than I can subscribe to from the perspective of this theory's effect on, the interpretation of the *potentia*-distinction.

[49] J. Hintikka, "Gaps in the Great Chain of Being," in: S. Knuuttila, *Reforging*, 7. According to Hintikka, this phenomenon is "one of the most interesting overall features of the history of Western thought," *ibid*.

[50] Cf. Oakley, *Omnipotence*, 52: "... hesitations in some of Ockham's formulations of this ... distinction."

[51] See apart from the studies already mentioned (above, n.41) e.g. K. Bannach, *Die Lehre von der doppelten Macht Gottes bei Wilhelm von Ockham*, Wiesbaden 1975.

times to what is possible in terms of what God has decided to do. In any case, it cannot occur that God acts *de potentia absoluta in re*, since the *posse* which is implicit in this *potentia* indicates the non-necessity of our reality, rather than the actual possibility of things which God did not preordain with respect to this reality.

Ockham most clearly operates along these traditional lines in his political writings *Opus Nonaginta Dierum* and *Contra Benedictum*. In the latter work he even states: "God can do certain things *de potentia absoluta*, which He will never do *de potentia ordinata*, that is, *de facto* he will never do them."[52] Here, he identifies precisely the other *potentia*-concept than Scotus does with what God can do *de facto*! As to the former work, this is directed against pope John XXII, who denied the legitimacy of the distinction in the doctrine of God (not in ecclesiastical law!).[53] Ockham shows that this denial implicitly leads the pope to the endorsement of Abelard's heresy, because logically he cannot escape from an Abelardian determinism. Thus, it appears that according to Ockham the function of the distinction is only to counteract this heresy, by articulating God's freedom over all kinds of seeming necessities. As such, then, the distinction belongs to "the most basic of Ockham's theological tools."[54]

On the other hand, however, Ockham can comment almost simultaneously on the distinction in a much more Scotian tone. In the same *Opus Nonaginta*, for example, he at once refers to the legal analogy, and compares God's *potentia ordinata* with the human *posse de jure*.[55] And in his most well-known treatment of the distinction, Ockham defines the *potentia ordinata* in terms of laws instituted by God ("leges ordinatas et institutas a Deo").[56] A few lines further down he even draws the analogy with papal power: "In the same way, the pope cannot do certain things according to the law instituted by him, which he can do in an absolute sense."[57]

---

[52] W. Ockham, *Tractatus contra Benedictum* III 3, in: *Opera Politica* III (ed. H.S. Offler, Manchester 1956), 233: "Deus aliqua potest de potentia absoluta, quae tamen nunquam faciet de potentia ordinata, hoc est de facto numquam faciet"; quoted by Miethke, *Ockhams Weg*, 156.

[53] Understandably, the papal party suspected the theological use of the distinction, because it could easily be utilized to underline the non-necessity of the church and the sacraments (as seen from the perspective of God's absolute power). On the debate between Ockham and John XXII, see E. Randi, "Ockham, John XXII and the absolute power of God," *FS* 46 (1986), 205-216.

[54] S. Ozment, *The Age of Reform 1250-1550*, New Haven 1980, 38.

[55] W. Ockham, *Opus Nonaginta Dierum*, in: *Opera Politica* II (eds. R.F Bernnett, H.S. Offler, Manchester 1963), 726. Cf. Adams, *William Ockham*, 1202. The inevitable suggestion is of course, that the human *posse de facto* parallels God's *potentia absoluta*.

[56] W. Ockham, *Quodlibeta Septem* VI q.1, in: *Opera Theologica* IX (ed. J.C. Wey, St. Bonaventure [N.Y.] 1980), 586.

[57] Ibid.: "Sicut papa aliqua non potest secundum iura statuta ab eo, quae tamen absolute potest." According to E. Randi, "A Scotist Way of Distinguishing between God's Absolute and Ordained Powers," in: Hudson & Wilks (eds.), *From Ockham to Wyclif*, 43-50 this is probably the only place in Ockham's writings where he applies the distinction to a creature (46, n.7); but cf. above, n.55.

Moreover, in a way which is more unequivocal than Scotus, Ockham illustrates the distinction by applying it to the transition towards a new dispensation in the history of salvation. When it is stated in John 3:5 that "unless someone is born out of water and the Spirit, he cannot enter the Kingdom of God," this "cannot" is meant *de potentia ordinata. De potentia absoluta* it is very well possible for God to allow people to enter into His Kingdom who aren't born out of water and the Spirit, as is clear from the fact that people under the old dispensation were saved without being baptized (i.e., without being born out of water). In the same way, *de potentia absoluta* it is possible for God in the present to save people without having infused into them the *gratia creata*. For all things which He can do by means of secondary causes, He can also do directly.[58] *De potentia ordinata*, however, God is not able to omit the use of the ordinary secondary causes. So obviously, when such omissions took place in the past (as happened under the old dispensation), this occurred *de potentia absoluta*!

Finally, the way in which Ockham applies the distinction to God's election of Jacob and reprobation of Esau is interesting in this context. According to Ockham, if two persons have exactly the same natural and supernatural features it is possible for God to accept the one and reject the other, but only *de potentia absoluta*. This, he claims, is clear from the case of Jacob and Esau. So we may conclude that either the election of the one or the reprobation of the other must have taken place *de potentia absoluta*. But then, despite all assurances to the contrary, the distinction obviously does refer to two distinct powers in God, both of which can be actualized at any time!

However this may be, as it seems to me Ockham's discussions of the distinction are more strongly influenced by Scotus c.s. than many so-called revisionist[59] interpreters take for granted. In the light of the passages cited above, it is hard to credit the opinion of Courtenay that "Ockham's repeated and lengthy insistence on the proper meaning of the distinction was directed ... at Scotus' juridical formulation."[60] Oakley is more to the point in concluding that Ockham's use of the distinction is generally in line with that of Aquinas, but that Ockham from time to time slips into descriptions which represent much more the later Scotian connotations, "even though Ockham possibly did not so intend."[61] And even the revisionist interpreter Oberman

---

[58] *Quodlibeta septem* VI, 1 and 6; Blumenberg, *Kopernikanische Wende*, 37f. has coined the apt term "postulate of immediacy" ("Unmittelbarkeitspostulat") for this rule, which was also adhered to by Scotus. Cf. also Pernoud, "Theory of *Potentia Dei*," 90f.

[59] See for the technical meaning of this term in late medieval studies Courtenay, "Nominalism," 26, 32, 50 etc.

[60] Courtenay, "Dialectic," 254; unfortunately, precisely here in his otherwise excellently documented study Courtenay gives no references.

[61] Oakley, *Omnipotence*, 52f.; cf. the formulation of Adams, *William Ockham*, 1207: "His [viz. Ockham's] documented vacillation between the two accounts of ordered power, sometimes within the space of a few columns or pages, cannot be explained away..."

must admit that in Ockham we are confronted with a "predilection for exceptions to the established rules *de potentia ordinata*."[62]

Even so, the traditional view, which charges Ockham's view of divine omnipotence with engendering a radical scepticism, separating faith from reason, presenting God as an arbitrary tyrant who abuses His power, destroying all order and intelligibility in the world etc.[63] is equally untenable, and surely cannot be supported (as was usually suggested) by an appeal to Ockham's use of the *potentia*-distinction. The frequent use Ockham makes of the distinction is not meant to call into question the regularities of nature, the reliability of human knowledge, the order of salvation, the trustworthiness of God's revelation, and so on. Rather, in Ockham's *oeuvre* "the invocation of the divine omnipotence, *potentia Dei absoluta*, allows the dialectical proof that separates the accidental from the essential in the object of an investigation."[64]

Thus, if we are prepared to interpet the Ockham's use of the distinction *in bonam partem* (and there seems no reason not to do so), it can be seen to function as an heuristic instrument for detecting and articulating the radical contingency of created reality. In this way, the threat of the still pervasive Graeco-Arabic necessitarianism was not merely criticized verbally, but effectively overcome. Thus interpreted, Ockham's accentuation of the divine *potentia absoluta* is to be understood as a return to the Jewish-Christian conception of God,[65] to whom not only A- and B-, but also C-power (in the sense of freedom as alternativity) is due.

2.3.4 *God's absolute power and late medieval extremism*
As we saw above, in spite of certain inherent frictions and anomalies, Ockham's use of the classical distinction between God's absolute and ordained power can be aligned with the tradition of Peter Damian and Thomas Aquinas. With regard to the developments after Ockham, however, such a positive assessment becomes more and more problematic. Instead of a means, the distinction increasingly becomes a goal in itself. The critical,

---

[62] Oberman, *Harvest*, 192; later on (255-258) he adduces a famous example: God in his absolute power would have been able to incarnate Himself in a stone or an ass rather than in a man... Funkenstein, *Theology*, 58 n.3, however, points to the fact that the work this example stems from (the *Centiloquium theologicum*) is possibly an unauthentic writing of Ockham.

[63] See for these and other invectives accumulated from the elder literature M.A. Pernoud, "Innovation in William of Ockham's References to the <<*Potentia Dei*>>," *Antonianum* 45 (1970), 65; id., "Theory," 69-71; cf. Oberman, *Harvest*, 30-34; Ozment, *Age of Reform*, 38f., and Courtenay, "Nominalism," 27-31.

[64] P. Vignaux, *Philosophy in the Middle Ages*, New York 1959, 173.

[65] Cf. Courtenay, "Nominalism," 58: "The stress on omnipotence and divine power, the stress on the covenantal nature of man's relation with God ... mark a re-emphasis on the Judeo-Christian conception of God in contrast with the more distant and more mechanistic deity of Latin Averroism as influenced by Aristotle's Prime Mover."

transcendental concept of *potentia absoluta* is misunderstood as referring to a resource of power which is actualized from time to time in the real world.

Oberman attempts to bring the use made of the distinction by the Ockhamist Gabriel Biel (ca. 1410-1495) in line with that of his master. But he fails to convince here, since he only compares Biel with the Ockham of the *Quodlibeta*, and not with the Ockham of, for example, the *Tractatus contra Benedictum*.[66] That Biel indeed pursues the juridical and "interventional" lines in Ockham's work on the distinction is shown in a number of illustrative examples recently collected by Leonard Kennedy. According to Biel, God could *de potentia absoluta* without injustice annihilate someone who loves Him, produce an act of hatred of Himself in His creatures, lie to us, annihilate grace in the soul of the just, and last but not least assume a human nature and then set it aside, so that this nature, belonging again to a human person, could admit of sin.[67] Indeed, Ockham also considered some of these menacing events to be possible. However, here examples like these threaten to become detached from the context in which they were originally raised: not only the concept of God is made bizarre, but also the original purpose of the distinction is entirely misunderstood.

That the latter really is the case can be derived from the fact that Biel in his expositions of the distinction particularly follows Pierre d'Ailly (Peter of Aliaco, 1350-1420). For in the preceding century it had precisely been d'Ailly who had very consciously and explicitly opted against the original and for the derivative function of the distinction. In his commentary on the *Sentences* Peter distinguishes between the following two meanings that can be assigned to the term *potentia ordinata*:

1. God's power to bring about those things which He has preordained to occur.
2. God's power to do all things which do not conflict with some established law or with Holy Scripture.[68]

---

[66] Oberman, *Harvest*, 37f.; Oberman observes only a "slight change" in Biel in the direction of an operationalization of the *potentia absoluta*. His source references (37, n.27f.) reveal, however, that after all Biel simply sees God's *potentia ordinata* as *potentia ordinaria*, which can be continually suspended by miracles performed *de potentia absoluta*. When Biel nevertheless declares that the distinction should not be understood as referring to two distinct powers in God, and that God never acts *inordinate* (ibid.), this has little significance. As we saw above, these were commonplace statements.

[67] L.A. Kennedy, "The Fifteenth Century and Divine Absolute Power," *Vivarium* 27 (1989), 125-152; see for the examples respectively 127, 132, 135, 137, and 145.

[68] Peter d'Ailly, *Quaestiones super libros sententiarum cum quibusdam in fine adjunctis* (Lyon 1618; repr. Minerva 1964) I 13, 1 D. See for text and context Courtenay, "Nominalism," 41 n.1; cf. Oakley, *Omnipotence*, 56f. How Courtenay later ("Dialectic," 255) can speak of "Ockham's approach being *repeated* by ... Pierre d'Ailly and Gabriel Biel" (my italics) is in the light of his earlier d'Ailly-quotation unclear. Cf. in this connection the interesting criticisms of Courtenay's assessment in L.A. Kennedy, *Peter of Ailly and the Harvest of Fourteenth-Century Philosophy*, Queenston 1986, 27-29, 197-199, and Kennedy's own conclusion that Peter's obsession ("Peter

D'Ailly turns out to be aware of the difference between these definitions - the second is much wider ("magis large") than the first, he comments -, and makes his choice for the second definition, which he considers to be more appropriate ("magis proprius"). As a result, d'Ailly is entirely consistent in adducing miracles as instances of suspensions of God's *potentia ordinata*. For although in general the second definition is more comprehensive, at this point it is smaller in scope: miracles are covered by definition 1, but not by definition 2. Hence, from the perspective of definition 2 of *potentia ordinata*, if miracles happen (which is indubitable), they must be classified as divine actions *de potentia absoluta*. Thus God's *potentia absoluta* is reinterpreted as *potentia extraordinaria*.

It is precisely the combination of this qualitative shift of meaning on the one hand and the quantitative increase in speculations on what God *de potentia absoluta* could possibly do on the other hand, which radically changes the spiritual climate in which the distinction is discussed. Instead of *underlining* the stability of the present order and the reliability of God's relation with human beings and the world, as the distinction originally did, it now functions in a way which *undermines* these ideas. Of course, this was not the intention of those who went along with the new interpretation of the distinction. Their intention may have been laudable: exalting the power of God! But in doing so, they forgot that it was the power of *God* which had to be exalted, and that this power should not be isolated from God's goodness and trustworthiness.

One of the most intriguing illustrations of this upheaval is the history of the so-called hypothesis of the divine lie.[69] Arising round 1330 in radically Ockhamist circles at Oxford, it was especially popular there as support for certain libertarian views. The usual argumentation can be summarized as follows:

1. God can *de potentia absoluta* speak falsehoods.
2. When God's *potentia absoluta* is taken as *potentia extraordinaria*, it is possible that God actualizes, has actualized and/or will actualize this possibility to speak falsehoods.
3. If 2. is correct, then it is possible that God has spoken falsehoods in the Scriptures.
4. If 3. is correct, it is possible that these falsehoods occur also in certain up to now unfulfilled prophecies uttered in the Scriptures.

---

is *obsessed* with the notion of God's absolute power" 193-5), in spite of modern-day denials, leads him to scepticism (213).

[69] On this history two papers have recently been published, of which the second is especially instructive: T. Gregory, "La tromperie divine," in: Z. Kaluza, P. Vignaux (eds.), *Preuve et Raisons à l'Université de Paris*, Paris 1984, 187-195; J.-F. Genest, "Pierre de Ceffons et l'hypothèse du Dieu trompeur," in: ibid., 197-214.

5. If 4. is correct, it is possible that all biblical prophesies on what human beings are going to do in the future are false.
6. If 5 is correct, then it is possible that human action is significantly free, instead of determined by divine decrees.

This application of the distinction, however, was vigorously combatted in Oxford by Thomas Bradwardine[70] and in Paris by Gregory of Rimini. As a result, the thesis that it is possible *de potentia absoluta* that God actually speaks falsehoods seems to have been officially condemned in Paris in 1347 (in connection with the condemnation of John of Mirecourt in that year), and disappeared. At the end of the century, however, the thesis re-emerged in the writings of Peter of Ailly and subsequently in those of Biel. But these theologians were no longer condemned for it. Thus, it could happen that Descartes still had to struggle with the impact of the hypothesis in his proof of the existence of God in the *Meditationes*. Ockham had taken care not to suggest that it was really possible that God should lie - for to lie is to do evil, and to do evil is to act *inordinate*. However, his radical successors in England (especially Adam Woodham and Robert Holcot, and to some extent Richard Fitzralph), and probably also in France (Nicholas of Autrecourt and John of Mirecourt), were less scrupulous. They distinguish between "mentiri" (which God cannot do, for this presupposes an inordinate intention) and "decipere" (which God can do, because it does not presuppose such an intention, but simply means: speaking falsehood). Therefore, it is up to me, or so Holcot argues,[71] to make a prediction about my future actions true or false, and in consequence the one who uttered it into a true or a false prophet.

In the case of biblical predictions, the situation is in principle the same. For when God predicts something, it cannot be the case that His omnipotence is subsequently bound by this prediction in this sense, that He could no longer bring about the opposite of the predicted state of affairs or event. Consequently, it remains possible that the Bible contains untrue predictions, for example about the last judgment, the resurrection of the dead etc.[72] Here, the over-accentuation of God's omnipotence, or rather its separation from God's ordained will clearly leads to a rigorous scepticism.[73] God's actions *de potentia ordinata* have become completely unreliable,

---

[70] J.-F. Genest, "Le *De Futuris contingentibus* de Thomas Bradwardine," *RA* 14 (1979), 249-336, esp. 258-260, 263-265.

[71] Robert Holcot, *In Secundum Sententiarum*, Lyons 1518, q.2 a.8; quoted by Genest, "Pierre de Ceffons," 203, 212.

[72] H.A. Oberman, *Archbishop Thomas Bradwardine*, Utrecht 1957, 45f.; cf. also Oberman's characterization of Holcot and Woodham (two of Bradwardine's most important opponents) as 'pelagii moderni', ibid., 43-48.

[73] Cf. G. Leff, who transferred his initial negative appraisal of Ockham in this respect ("it is here, in the use of the *potentia absoluta*, that the full impact of skepticism is to be met"; *Medieval Thought from Augustine to Ockham*, St. Albans 1958, 289) to Ockham's radical successors.

because of the risk that they are overruled by intrusions *de potentia absoluta*.

A similar illustration of the later medieval developments could be adduced from the history of the epistemological conception of *cognitio intuitiva*.[74] Again, Ockham turns out to have built in a crucial proviso in order to avoid scepticist consequences,[75] which was consciously ignored by his radical followers. Even without pursuing this theme here,[76] we have assembled sufficient material to warrant the conclusion that in the 14th and 15th centuries speculations on what God actually can do by His absolute power became very popular. Further, we observed a strong tendency to equate this *potentia absoluta* with God's capacity to miraculously intervene in the *communis cursus rerum*.[77]

Since not everybody was fully aware of these modifications, in the late Middle Ages the *potentia*-distinction "was not a theory, but rather a set of problems, that almost everyone had to face."[78] All kinds of hypothetical possibilities which were considered to be impossible in earlier centuries, were now freely tested upon their implications. Scepticist consequences were sometimes explicitly accepted. Radicalizing developments took place in both Scotist and Ockhamist circles; Thomists were usually more reticent.[79] But in general Kennedy's conclusion is justified: "On the eve of the Reformation many philosophers and theologians were making extensive applications of the notion of divine absolute power."[80]

2.3.5 *Reformed protest and correction*
As the Reformation initially reacted violently against many parts of traditional theology, this was also the case with regard to the *potentia*-distinction. Luther, for example, initially dismissed the distinction as a piece of scholastic sophistry. Later, however, he took it up again, and used it in the newer meaning of *potentia ordinaria* and *potentia extraordinaria*.[81] When God performs miracles without using secondary causes, this happens *de potentia absoluta*.[82] Still, this is not all that can be said about Luther's use

---

[74] See on this point R. Wood, "Intuitive Cognition and Divine Omnipotence," in: Hudson & Wilks (eds.), *From Ockham to Wyclif*, 51-61.

[75] W. Ockham, *Quodlibeta* V 5; cf. P. Vignaux, "Nominalisme," in: *Dictionnaire de Théologie Catholique* XI, Paris 1930, 768f., and Gregory, "Tromperie divine," 190.

[76] But see Van den Brink, "Absolute en geordineerde macht," 219f.

[77] This tendency is reflected in Holcot's use of the term *ex privilegio speciali* as synonymous with *de potentia absoluta*, as well as in Marsilius van Inghen's preference for the phrase *de lege absoluta* to express the same idea (cf. Courtenay, "Dialectic," 257).

[78] Randi, "Scotist Way," 50.

[79] Kennedy, "Fifteenth Century," 152.

[80] Ibid.

[81] Oakley, *Omnipotence*, 57, 138.

[82] I. Ludolphy, "Zu einer fraglichen Verwendung des Begriffes 'potentia absoluta' bei Luther," in: M. Hager e.a., *Ruf und Antwort*, Leipzig n.d., 540-543 shows that even the prayer of a

of the distinction.[83] Oberman has recently pointed to the important link in Luther's thought between the God who acts *de potentia absoluta* and the *Deus absconditus*.[84] Just like the *Deus absconditus*, the God who acts *de potentia absoluta* should not concern us. Surely sometimes God acts *de potentia absoluta*, i.e. outside the fixed laws of nature and salvation, for instance when He saves unbaptized children. But it is His explicit will that we stick to what is in accordance with His actions *de potentia ordinata*.[85]

And as to the way in which God *de potentia ordinata* saves people, Luther is perfectly clear: "God's ordained power is His incarnate Son, we shall embrace Him."[86] In this way, Luther's use of the distinction is at the same time the sharpest possible criticism of its distortion, that is, of the unlimited speculations about God's *potentia absoluta* which led to the undermining of the trustworthiness of God's ordained power. It is precisely to this *potentia ordinata* that Luther calls us back.

As to Calvin, he resolutely and unambiguously rejected the distinction. Both in his *Institutes*, in his monograph on predestination, and in his sermons Calvin gives expression to his abhorrence of this "chimera of the absolute power."[87] Roman Catholic theologians such as Bellarminus in turn accused Calvin of limiting and thereby denying God's omnipotence.[88] Some scholars find it difficult to explain Calvin's rejection of the distinction. Especially for those who are inclined to assimilate Calvin's conception of God with the extreme-nominalistic picture of God as an arbitrary tyrant, it continues to be an anomaly.

However, when we start from the fact that in Calvin's theology God's power wholly coincides with His will, and that God's will in turn coincides with His goodness, wisdom and righteousness, it becomes clear that Calvin had to discard the late medieval speculations about God's *potentia absoluta* as improper.[89] Calvin refused to speak of divine power

---

believer can operate as a *causa secunda*; that is why according to Luther God's stopping the sun at Gibeon in answer to Joshua's prayer was an action *de potentia ordinata*.

[83] As Oakley, *Omnipotence*, 57 suggests.

[84] H.A. Oberman, "*Via Antiqua* and *Via Moderna*," 454 n.27, cf. 457 n.42. See for some distinct interpretations of this link also J. Dillenberger, *God Hidden and Revealed*, Philadelphia 1953, 43-47, 109f., 139-141.

[85] *WA* 43.71, 28: "Vult enim nos facere secundum ordinatam potentiam"; quoted by Oberman, "*Via Antiqua*," 457.

[86] *WA* 43.73, 3: "Ordinatam potentiam, hoc est, filium incarnatum amplectemur."

[87] Calvin, *Institutes* III 23, 2 ("commentum absolutae potentiae"). Cf. his *De aeterna Dei praedestinatione* (1552), *CO* 8, 361 (where Calvin points to "papales theologastri" from the Sorbonne as the culprits), and R. Stauffer, *Dieu, la création et la providence dans la prédication de Calvin*, Bern 1978, 113-116 for a survey of the many denouncings of the *potentia absoluta* in Calvin's sermons.

[88] Bellarminus, *De gratia et liberum arbitrium* III, 15; cited in H. Bavinck, *Gereformeerde Dogmatiek* Vol.II, Kampen 1928[4], 218.

[89] Case-Winters, *God's Power*, 45: "His reason for doing so [viz., rejecting the notion of *potentia absoluta*] seems to have been his concern to maintain that God's power is not indepen-

apart from divine willing, i.e. apart from divine goodness. As Case-Winters argues:

> For Calvin, God's power is coterminous with God's will. The freedom (power) of that will is freedom to act *in congruency with the divine nature*. The divine will, it should be remembered, is not being understood in some abstract sense but in a *personal* mode. It is not a neutral, blind force of nature; it is a personal will, and, like the will of any person, it is, to an extent, *determined*. It has a certain character. In God's case, it has the character of goodness and justice which are part of the divine nature.[90]

F. Wendel was probably right in assuming that Calvin's repudiation of the distinction was directed against "the arbitrary speculations and the exaggerations of certain nominalists at the end of the Middle Ages."[91] That at the same time Calvin's attitude reflects his hostility to the distinction as introduced by Duns Scotus,[92] does not necessarily conflict with this. Calvin opposes himself to the only interpretation of the distinction which was apparently known to him, and that was the interpretation which found its basis in Scotus and its most extreme representatives in certain late medieval nominalists.

All this is not to deny that the primacy of the divine will in Calvin, apart from the influence of Augustinianism in this regard, is also in part a Scotistic legacy. There is no doubt that important traces of nominalistic voluntarism remain extant in Calvin and Calvinism. The threatening idea of a dark side of arbitrary agency in God is never completely overcome (one only has to refer to the role of the doctrine of predestination, including the *decretum horribile* of eternal repudiation, in Calvin's theology[93]). Calvin's rejection of the notion of absolute power, however, should warn us not to overstate this issue. To my mind, in contemporary Calvin-research this warning all too often goes unheeded. Stephen Strehle, for example, is at best one-sided and at worst (viz. if he intends to include Calvin himself, which is not clear from the context) simply wrong in stating: "The Calvin-

---

dent of God's moral character; rather it expresses it." Cf. already B.B. Warfield, "Calvin's Doctrine of God," in: id., *Calvin and Calvinism*, New York 1931, 161 n.61: "Calvin is not denying that God can do more than He actually does, but only opposing such a *potentia absoluta* as is not connected with His Being or Virtues...".

[90] Case-Winters, *God's Power*, 43.

[91] F. Wendel, *Calvin. Sources et évolution de sa pensée religieuse*, Paris 1950, 94: "...les spéculations arbitraires et les exagérations de certains nominalistes de la fin du moyen âge." It is difficult to specify which particular nominalists Calvin concretely meant. Stauffer, *Dieu, la création*, points to Peter Aureol, but one could think equally well of Peter of Ailly or Gabriel Biel.

[92] Wendel, *Calvin*, 94: "... hostilité à l'égard de la distinction introduite par Duns Scot lui-même..."; but Wendel's conviction that the distinction was introduced by Duns Scotus is of course false.

[93] Cf. C. Graafland, *Van Calvijn tot Barth*, 's Gravenhage 1987, 5-46.

ists continue this tradition of searching out the God of *potentia absoluta* and his many possibilities..."[94]

An interesting question in this connection is whether Calvin would have disapproved of the distinction's authentic meaning as it functioned in Aquinas. From the perspective of Calvin's general view of divine action this seems highly doubtful. For Calvin acknowledges that God has the abilities to operate outside the established order; he did not deny that God can do more than He actually does. Therefore, he certainly would agree - as later Reformed theologians explicitly do - with the distinction's original intention to articulate that the present order is contingent rather than necessary.[95] In this connection Oberman points to the fact that, "Calvin utilizes the full potential of the realm which before d'Ailly used to be the *potentia absoluta*," and speaks of Calvin's "steady look beyond the officially ordained institutions and vessels of grace."[96] Indeed, Calvin holds (as Luther did), that God sometimes actually operates outside the fixed order. That does not mean to him, however, that God does do other things than He has preordained to do. Here Calvin, despite his fierce polemic against the "scholastics," entirely concurs with, for example, Aquinas.[97]

We conclude that Calvin in a sense implicitly uses the distinction in its later operationalized interpretation, but then as on a par with the distinction between *providentia ordinaria* and *extraordinaria*. Contrary to the later medievals and like the earlier ones, he neither plays off God's *potentia absoluta* against His *potentia ordinata*, nor isolates it in any way from God's goodness. Because of these qualifications Oberman can argue that Calvin provides an excellent counterexample against the thesis that the operationalization of the *potentia absoluta* should merely be regarded as detrimental.[98] Calvin accepts the operationalization, but transforms it in such a way that it is freed from its negative pastoral consequences.

---

[94] Stephen Strehle, "Calvinism, Augustinianism, and the Will of God," *TZ* 47 (1992), 233. To give one other example: In a paper mainly dedicated to Calvin's theology ("La toute-puissance du Dieu du theisme dans le champ de la perversion," *LThP* 47 (1991), 3-11), Jean Ansaldi, completely overlooking Calvin's rejection of the notion of divine absolute power, comes to a radically negative appraisal of Calvin's doctrine of God.

[95] See H. Bavinck's short but insightful discussion of the issue in his *The Doctrine of God*, Edinburgh 1977², 243-245; in the Dutch original, *Gereformeerde Dogmatiek* Vol.2, 218f. Bavinck refers to Polanus, Alsted, Heidegger and Mastricht as later Reformed theologians who accepted the distinction in the sense in which it was understood by Thomas. Cf. also in this connection Heinrich Heppe, *Reformed Dogmatics. Set Out and Illustrated from the Sources* (ed. E. Bizer), repr. Grand Rapids 1978, 103f.

[96] Oberman, "*Via Antiqua*," 462.

[97] Cf. the general conclusion of Arvin Vos, *Aquinas, Calvin, and Contemporary Protestant Thought*, Grand Rapids 1985, that in many cases Calvin's polemic against "the scholastics" was directed at late-nominalist contemporaries rather than at classical theologians like Aquinas, with whom Calvin had more views in common than is often acknowledged. Cf. L.J. Elders & C.A. Tukker, *Thomas van Aquino*, Leiden 1992, 213f.

[98] Oberman, "*Via Antiqua*," 462.

In this connection, Oberman's remark that the transition to the operational interpretation of God's *potentia absoluta* must be characterized not only as risky, but also as useful, is in general worthy of consideration. His thesis runs as follows:

> Once God's miraculous intervention was squarely placed outside the *lex statuta*, "secular" research could focus on the *common* course of nature by means of (practical) reason and (sense) experience.[99]

Oberman does not argue further for this thesis, but he could have pointed to the way in which the distinction is taken up in the "physico-theological" thinking of scientists like Francis Bacon, Robert Boyle and Isaac Newton.[100] As is clear from these examples, it is indeed precisely when miracles are considered to be extraordinary (in the literal sense of that word), that it is possible to demarcate the order which they overturn as an independent field of inquiry. In this sense, the shift in the interpretation and functioning of the distinction as documented for the first time in Scotus might be positively evaluated from the perspective of the history of science.

2.3.6 *Conclusion*
Here we break off our investigation of the history of the *potentia*-distinction, not because this history stops here, but because we have gathered enough material to draw some main conclusions.

First, we observed two different interpretations of the distinction between God's absolute and ordained powers. The difference between these interpretations may best be summarized by comparing two statements concerning the concept of *potentia absoluta*. Briefly stated, these are as follows:

S1   God is capable *de potentia absoluta* to change the established order.
S2   It is factually possible that God *de potentia absoluta* changes the established order.

Clearly, it is a logical mistake to assume a necessary implicative relation between these two statements. For although S2 implies S1, the reverse is not true. This being the case, the original interpretation claims that S1 is true but S2 is false, since God does not will to change the order previously established by Him, i.e., since it is not in accordance with His will and nature to change His mind about what kind of things He should bring about. The second interpretation, however, traceable from Scotus onwards, overlooks the key-position of God's stable will and faithfulness, and concludes from S1 to S2. Along with this difference, there is of course a different

---

[99] Oberman, "*Via Antiqua*," 451f.
[100] See on them Oakley, *Omnipotence*, 67-92, especially 88f.

interpretation of the *potentia ordinata*. In its original setting, God's *potentia ordinata* includes all specific things which are to be actualized and all events which are to happen in accordance with God's will. In the second interpretation, the *potentia ordinata* is expressed in terms of general laws which indicate only the general will of God, and which allow for exceptions.

Secondly, we discovered that such exceptions became to play an increasingly important role in discussions about God's power. Especially in the later Middle Ages, these discussions gradually evoked, as a net result of over-emphasizing the divine power, the image of God as a capricious agent who cannot be relied upon. We found reason to evaluate this line in the history of the distinction's interpretation as unfaithful to both its original intention and the Christian concept of God in general.

Thirdly, we suggested that the transition from the original to what we called the operational use of the distinction should not be judged as exclusively negative. When God's power is not isolated from His essential goodness or represented in a way which threatens the reliability of the divinely established order, the distinction simply coincides with that between God's ordinary and extraordinary providence. And despite eventual modern problems with *that* distinction, the covenantal character of God's relationship with human beings and the world is not endangered by it. Moreover, from the perspective of the history of science, the operationalization of the *potentia*-distinction has even had some very stimulating and fruitful consequences for the development of empirical scientific enterprise.

Fourthly, from a philosophical point of view the most important merit of the distinction in its original mode has been to provide a conceptual tool for counteracting any form of Graeco-Arabic necessitarianism by expressing the contingency of creation. According to the Christian doctrine of God, God does not only possess the power of dominating and sustaining the universe, but also the power of alternativity, i.e, the power to freely choose and decide about which things are to be created, respectively to be kept into being. In our terminology: God not only has A- and B-power, but also C-power in the specific connotation of being able to freely actualize or refrain from actualizing all possibilities. Thus not only is it the case that "nothing is impossible to God," but also that nothing is necessary to God, in the sense that all real possibilities necessarily should have to be actualized at some time, as is claimed in the principle of plenitude. The primary function of the distinction is to articulate precisely this intuition, which is deeply embedded in the Judaeo-Christian tradition.

Fifthly, we have seen that the major source of differences and quarrels about the proper interpretation of the distinction consisted in an underlying confusion about the relation between God's power and the being God is, i.e. the other properties which make up His character. It is therefore especially to this problem that we have to return in the systematic parts of our inquiry.

2.4 GOD'S POWER AND THE STATUS OF THE ETERNAL TRUTHS

2.4.1 *Abstract objects and eternal truths*

In the previous sections we have distinguished between three different constitutive characteristics of God's power as understood in classical Christian conceptions of the divine omnipotence. According to the Christian tradition, to say that God is omnipotent means to ascribe to Him the power of domination, the power actualized in the preservation of the universe, and the ability of unconstrained actualization of all possible states of affairs. Having elaborated on all of these three notions, however, we may ask whether by doing this we have exhaustively explicated the Christian conception of omnipotence. Does our tripartite elaboration of the concept of God's omnipotence form a complete description of this concept?

There is one important reason for doubt here. If God's power is really infinite, as the Christian tradition claims it is, then this seems to mean at least that it ranges over all and everything. Now the created universe as we experience it presents no problem in this respect. We can imagine what it means for mountains, seas, planets, electrons and human beings to depend in many ways upon God's power. But what about the whole realm of abstract objects? What about, as Plantinga calls it, "the Platonic pantheon of universals, properties, kinds, propositions, numbers, sets, states of affairs and possible worlds"?[1] These sorts of things are usually thought of as having neither beginning nor end, and therefore as existing eternally. Moreover, they are usually considered to exist *necessarily*. Can we specify any plausible way in which these things nevertheless may be considered subject to God's power?

The most natural reply to this question is to deny that universals, properties, kinds etc. are *things* which *exist*. Only concrete objects (which, by the way, do not necessarily include only material objects) can be said to exist. If it is held in the Christian tradition that there are abstract objects which exist in their own right as distinct entities, then this is due to the deplorable influence of the Platonic heritage. Usually, this reply is connected with *nominalism*: universals, properties etc. are only names which human beings give to things in ordering their experience. Since it is misleading to assign some form of separate existence to these names, it is equally misleading to ask whether they are dependent upon God's power. God's infinite power ranges over all *things*, but since names and concepts are no things, it is a category mistake to regard them as forming part of the sphere in which talk of God's power is meaningful.

This nominalist answer, however, although in line with certain modern views of modality,[2] shifts the problem rather than solving it. This can

---

[1] A. Plantinga, *Does God Have a Nature?*, Milwaukee 1980, 3.

[2] Cf. e.g. Georg Henrik von Wright, *Truth, Knowledge and Modality* (*Philosophical Papers*, Vol.3), Oxford 1984, 104-116; cf. Lilli Alanen, "Descartes, Omnipotence, and Kinds of Modal-

be shown as follows. Let us grant that numbers, propositions, universals etc. are concepts rather than abstract objects. Certainly, this does not alter the fact that what is expressed by means of these concepts in human thought and language may either be true or false. We use numbers, propositions, universals etc. to make claims which may even be *necessarily* true or false. For example, given the usual definitions of the involved concepts, the proposition that "three is less than five" is necessarily true; its truth can be known solely in virtue of the meanings of the concepts. And the same applies to the claim that "something which is red is also coloured." Thus, the abstract objects of the Platonic pantheon find themselves on the nominalist view translated into the rules of analyticity and logic. Here, abstract objects take the form of "eternal truths," to use the Augustinian expression for necessary truths.[3]

But then, we may ask the same questions with regard to these truths as we asked under the realist view with regard to abstract objects. Are such truths in any way dependent upon God's power? Does the claim that God is omnipotent according to the Christian tradition imply that even the rules of logic are subject to His power, so that God can make it the case that for example 5 is less than 3, or things may be red without being coloured? Clearly, such claims would be wildly counterintuitive. But the alternative seems to be that there are necessary truths (and, of course, necessary falsehoods) which limit God in His possibilities for action. And isn't it equally counterintuitive to the Christian understanding of God that God's power and actions would be entirely dependent upon the form necessary truths and falsehoods happen to have? In short, we seem to find ourselves involved in a dilemma: either necessary truths and falsehoods depend upon God's power, or God's power is in a relevant sense constrained by necessary truths and falsehoods.

One of the most intriguing solutions to this dilemma has been developed by René Descartes. Unlike contemporary philosophers such as Spinoza and Leibniz, who elaborated more traditional alternative theories,[4] Descartes held that necessary truths and falsehoods are no less dependent on God's power than contingent ones.[5] The details of Descartes' theory, however, are still a matter of academic debate. In what follows, I will join this debate in order to facilitate a fair evaluation of the Cartesian solution of our problem. After having presented Descartes' theory and indicated why its most natural

---

ity," in: P.H. Hare (ed.), *Doing Philosophy Historically*, Buffalo (N.Y) 1988, 196 n.40.

[3] Accordingly, it should be kept in mind that when I use the term "eternal truths" in what follows (for historical reasons), this should be read as "necessary truths."

[4] For a succinct comparison of the three great rationalist philosophers' theories on this point, see H.G. Hubbeling, *Principles of the Philosophy of Religion*, Assen 1987, 51, 132, 148.

[5] One might be inclined to think of Peter Damian as a precursor of Descartes in this respect; however, on the most plausible interpretation Damian mainly wanted to counter the intellectualist trend of his time, without intending to formulate a coherent theory of the relation between God's power and the laws of logic. Cf. §2.3.1 esp. n.12.

interpretation is problematic (§2.4.2), I will try to formulate a more satisfactory interpretation, thus assessing what exactly Descartes' view regarding the eternal truths amounts to (§ 2.4.3). Then, I will try to answer the question of Descartes' relation to the Christian tradition preceding him. Was Descartes the first to state explicitly an important point of view which was latently present in the heart of the Christian tradition before him, or is this tradition in fact committed to some other solution than the one advocated by Descartes (§2.4.4)?

2.4.2 *Descartes on the creation of the eternal truths*
The doctrine of the creation of the eternal truths does not form a substantial part of the argument in any of Descartes' philosophical works. Rather, his treatment of it is scattered over some eight letters which Descartes wrote to various persons and his *Replies* to two sets of *Objections* against his *Meditations*. All of these passages were written over a period of nineteen years, from 1630 to 1649, and there is no reason to suppose that Descartes changed his mind afterwards.[6] Although an unequivocal interpretation of them is impeded by the absence of an overall systematic exposition in Descartes' writings, it is generally accepted that together the passages do form a coherent whole. Its first account occurs in a letter to Mersenne, dated 15 April 1630. Descartes' formulation seems rather straightforward here:

> The mathematical truths which you call eternal have been laid down by God and depend on him entirely no less than the rest of his creatures. Indeed to say that these truths are independent of God is to talk of him as if he were Jupiter or Saturn and to subject him to the Styx and Fates. Please do not hesitate to assert and proclaim everywhere that it is God who has laid down these laws in nature just as a king lays down laws in his kingdom. There is no single one that we cannot understand if our mind turns to consider it. They are all inborn in our minds, just as a king would imprint his laws on the hearts of all his subjects if he had enough power to do so.[7]

Descartes' final remark on the eternal truths is in a letter to Henry More, written on 5 February 1649, where he answers the question whether God can create a vacuum as follows:

> For my part, I know that my intellect is finite and God's power is infinite, and so I set no bounds to it; I consider only what I can conceive and what I cannot conceive... And so I boldly assert that God can do everything which I conceive to be possible, but I am not so bold as to deny that he can do whatever conflicts with my

---

[6] As has been suggested by A. Koyré, *Essai sur l'idée de Dieu et les preuves de son existence chez Descartes*, Paris 1922, 19-21.

[7] I quote from the standard English translation of Descartes' philosophically relevant correspondence: Anthony Kenny (ed.), *Descartes. Philosophical Letters*, Oxford 1970, 11 (I will subsequently cite this work as "K").

understanding - I merely say that it involves a contradiction.[8]

Apart from the continuity in Descartes' thought, two things are clear from these quotations. First, as appears from the letter to More, eternal truths do not only include mathematical ones, but also fundamental physical intuitions. Other passages show that Descartes further considers logical, metaphysical and even moral principles as instances of eternal truths.[9] In general, the notion of "eternal truths", although never explicitly defined, corresponds to every truth the denial of which is supposed to form a logical contradiction.[10] Secondly, the most natural conclusion from both statements is that God, being the creator or rather legislator of the eternal truths, is able to do anything whatsoever, no matter whether it is self-contradictory and therefore inconceivable to our human minds. According to Descartes, we should not say that God is unable to bring it about that the lines drawn from the centre of a circle to its circumference are unequal, that twice four is something other than eight, that the three angles of a triangle are unequal to two right angles, that there exists a mountain without a valley, or that atoms (conceived as indivisible particles) exist.[11]

Indeed, one interpretation of the doctrine carries its extremely harsh and perplexing character to the maximum. According to this reading, Descartes' God is "a being for whom the logically impossible is possible."[12] This entails of course a very special view of modality, the most noteworthy feature of which is that there are neither necessary truths nor logical impossibilities. Although there are things and propositions which seem to be necessarily true to our minds, God is always able to make the opposites of these things and propositions true. Thus, these truths are not necessary in

---

[8] K 240f.

[9] For a useful survey, see J.-L. Marion, *Sur la théologie blanche de Descartes*, Paris 1981, 270f.

[10] Obviously, many of Descartes' eternal truths can hardly be considered as analytical in the modern sense; however, Descartes, being a heir of Scholasticism in this respect, was not an exception in lacking a clear view on the distinction between "truths of reason" and "truths of fact." Cf. on this point Amos Funkenstein, "Descartes, Eternal Truths, and the Divine Omnipotence," *SHPS* 6 (1975), 185-199, 196f. (re-edited in id., *Theology*, 179-192, 190f.); and Lilli Alanen, "Descartes, Duns Scotus and Ockham on Omnipotence and Possibility," *FS* 45 (1985), 186-188. Both authors argue convincingly that Descartes' eternal truths are best interpreted not as analytical but as intuitive, i.e., as "clearly and distinctly" perceived ideas.

[11] Descartes adduces these examples in respectively another letter to Mersenne (27 May 1630; K 15); the *Reply to Objections VI* against the *Meditations* (cf. E.S. Haldane & G.R.T. Ross, *The Philosophical Works of Descartes*, Vol.2, London 1955, 251; in agreement with a common use, I will subsequently quote this work as HR); a letter to Mesland (2 May 1644; K 151), to Arnauld (29 July 1648; K 236), and to More (5 February 1649; K 241).

[12] As Harry G. Frankfurt put it in his seminal article "Descartes and the Creation of the Eternal Truths," *PR* 86 (1977), 44. This essay, along with some of the others we will dicuss subsequently, has recently been included in a useful anthology: W. Doney (ed.), *Eternal Truths and the Cartesian Circle*, New York 1987, 222-243.

an absolute sense. Similarly, take any logical impossibility or contradiction you like - in view of the fact that "the power of God cannot have any limits,[13]" God can make it not only possible but even true (and, for all we know, might do so at any time). We may summarize this view of modality briefly as follows: for any proposition p, p is logically possible. It follows from this definition, that the p's truth-value may change at any time.

Since there is some quarrel about the question whether this interpretation should be labelled the "standard reading,[14]" let us call it the "extreme reading." Alvin Plantinga has argued that this reading, which he characterizes as "universal possibilism," represents "the fundamental thrust of Descartes' thought."[15] However, there are a number of considerations, emerging from a broader examination of Descartes' thinking, which make the extreme reading highly implausible. Therefore, many interpreters have put forward an attenuated version of it, ascribing some weaker position to Descartes. In what follows I will first indicate some general reasons why the extreme reading is problematic, and then in the next subsection discuss three of the weaker interpretations. I will argue that the first of these qualifying proposals is possibly true but irrelevant, the second one simply false, and the third one both true and relevantly different from the extreme reading. It is this last interpretation which renders the most credible conceptualization of the conviction that God's power ranges over the eternal truths.

Clearly, the idea that God may make any proposition p true is at odds with major strands of Descartes' philosophy. First, Descartes' version of the ontological argument does not only presuppose that there are truths which are, though not necessary, eternal and immutable (e.g. that the three angles of a triangle are equal to two right angles),[16] but also that the existence of God is a necessary truth independent of the contingent nature of the human mind.[17] Second, a universal possibilism would force Descartes to give up

---

[13] Letter to Mesland, 2 May 1644, K 151.

[14] See Alanen, "Descartes, Omnipotence," 185. It is not clear to Alanen who the proponents of this interpretation are (ibid., 194, n.16). But her argument in exonerating Harry Frankfurt from adopting this position (195, n.32), is unconvincing. Some other commentators who at least have not explicitly or implicitly distanced themselves from this reading are summed up by Alanen herself (192, n.1). Moreover, it is manifestly present in an earlier paper of Frankfurt, "The Logic of Omnipotence", *PR* 73 (1964), 262f., where he suggests that the Cartesian God is able to perform self-contradictory tasks, to the extent that he e.g. "can handle situations which he cannot handle" (263). Alanen is right, however, if she means that this interpretation is seldom explicitly defended *over against alternative readings*.

[15] Plantinga, *Does God Have a Nature?*, 112.

[16] *Meditations* V; HR 1, 180. Cf. E.M. Curley, "Descartes on the Creation of the Eternal Truths," *PR* 93 (1984), 572.

[17] Ibid.; HR 1, 181. "While from the fact that I cannot conceive God without existence, it follows that existence is inseparable from him, and hence that He really exists; not that my thought can bring this to pass, or impose any necessity on things, but, on the contrary, because the necessity which lies in the thing itself, i.e. the necessity of the existence of God determines me to think in this way."

central tenets of his very philosophical enterprise. Thus, universal possibilism would allow for the truth of the following proposition: "I think, but
nevertheless I am not." In similar ways, the validity of every link in the
application of Descartes' deductive method from the *cogito* towards the
science of physics might be questioned. But the initial reason which Descartes gave for his doctrine of the creation of eternal truths was precisely that
it formed the *foundation* of his physics![18] The denial of necessary truths,
however, would be detrimental to his methodology and philosophy of
science, since it would have lead him to a doubt far more radical than he
could make use of (for example, it would have lead him to methodical doubt
of the "ergo" in "cogito ergo sum"). Descartes himself was conscious of the
necessity of necessary truths for his physics, as appears from his repeated
remark that even if God had created other worlds, the most basic laws of
nature would be true in all of them.[19]

Apart from such general systematic reasons,[20] there are textual considerations in the passages on the eternal truths themselves which count
heavily against the extreme interpretation. We shall mention them hereafter,
in the course of dealing with the weaker readings of Descartes' doctrine.

2.4.3 *Three attempts at clarification*

The first qualification of the extreme reading of Descartes' theory simply
excludes a limited number of truths, which are necessarily true in the sense
that they cannot be changed even by God, from a majority of truths which
are only epistemically necessary, i.e. necessary given the conditions of our
human mind but not from the divine perspective. In contrast to the latter
class, the first set of necessary truths is conceived by Descartes as uncreated. The reverse side of this theory is of course, that there is an equal
number of absolute impossibilities.[21] The most likely candidates for the

---

[18] Letter to Mersenne, 15 April 1630; K 10f. Cf. Anthony Kenny, "The Cartesian Circle and
the Eternal Truths," *JP* 67 (1970), 698. Id., *The God of the Philosophers*, Oxford 1979, 21.

[19] In his unpublished *Le Monde*, see Charles Adam & Paul Tannery (eds.), *Oeuvres de
Descartes*, Vol.XI, Paris 1911, 47 (this edition of Adam & Tannery will subsequently be cited
as AT, followed by a volume number and page number); and in his *Discourse on Method*, HR
1, 108; Both texts are quoted by Curley, "Descartes and the Creation," 573, who points to the fact
that Descartes is anticipating here Leibniz' definition of "necessary" as "true in all possible
worlds."

[20] Curley, "Descartes and the Creation," 572 mentions still another one: if there are no necessary truths, Descartes has to give up his principle that everything which we perceive clearly and
distinctly is necessarily true. Since there are some complicated questions of interpretation here
(Descartes himself suggests that this principle is at least not self-evidently true, but requires
external warrant in the veracity of God), however, we leave this consideration aside.

[21] See for a rather extensive list of those M. Gueroult, *Descartes selon l'ordre des raisons*
Vol.2, Paris 1953, 26-29. Gueroult has been criticized on this point by Frankfurt, "Descartes on
the Creation," 47-50, and more recently by J. Bouveresse, "La théorie du possible chez Descartes," *RIP* 37 (1983), 304-309. For a richly documented discussion of the issue, to a large extent
validating Frankfurt's point of view, see J.-L. Marion, *Sur la théologie blanche*, 296-303.

privilege of being absolutely necessary are truths about God Himself, particularly the truth that God exists. Indeed, there are some indications in Descartes' wording of the theory which suggest that he assigns a special modality to truths concerning the nature and existence of God. Most notably, in his second letter to Mersenne on the topic of eternal truths he has it that "the existence of God is the first and most eternal of all the truths which can be, and the one from which alone all the others derive."[22]

On the other hand, Descartes emphatically declares that nothing is excluded from the realm of things which can be brought about by God.[23] Of course there are many things of which we cannot conceive that God brings them about. But the very point of Descartes' theory is, that our conceptual abilities do not form a valid criterion for measuring the scope of God's power. For this reason, Margaret Wilson is right in arguing that it would be rather arbitrary to exempt theological truths from the body of created eternal truths. "If what we cannot conceive in the realm of mathematics is no guide to strict or absolute impossibility and necessity in that realm, why should our mental constraints be any surer guide in the realm of theology?"[24]

Even if this qualification would be right, it is irrelevant in the sense that it does not at all contribute to the illumination of Descartes' view. For if the extreme interpretation holds for logical truths, so that God could make it the case that e.g. "2+2=5," or "2+2=5 and at the same time 2+2=4," then what precisely is achieved by subsequently denying that God could make it the case that "God is omnipotent and at the same time God is not omnipotent"? At any rate, the suggestion which is implicit in, for example, Gueroult, that the acknowledgement of uncreated truths makes Descartes' theory more intelligible, is simply false. On the contrary, it makes Descartes' theory to some degree internally inconsistent, since it postulates truths which set bounds to the power of God. Thus, even if we grant, as many commentators do,[25] and as we ourselves implicitly did above, that Descar-

---

[22] Letter to Mersenne, 6 May 1630; K 13. Perhaps apart from the letter to More, in which Descartes distinguishes between two kinds of impossibility (K 241), as far as I can see all other textual evidence is weaker than this statement. A somewhat ambiguous remark in the letter to Mesland (K 151) is, contrary to Curley's proposal ("Descartes," 594f.), most naturally interpreted as *not* supporting the hypothesis that Descartes distinguishes between two kinds of necessary truths, since the context is one in which Descartes defends that there are no necessarily necessary truths. Cf. on this point Frankfurt, "Descartes," 48.

[23] See the letter to Arnauld, K 236f.; and remember our previous quotation from the letter to More, K 240: "For my part, I know that my intellect is finite and God's power is infinite, and so I set no bounds to it." Given this statement, it would seem that any attempt to single out some uncreated truths would be experienced by Descartes as doing just that: setting bounds to the omnipotence of God. Cf. also *Reply to Objections VI*, HR 2, 250: "... it is clear that nothing at all can exist which does not depend on him. This is true not only of everything that subsists, but of all order, of every law, and of every reason of truth and goodness."

[24] M.D. Wilson, *Descartes*, London 1978, 124.

[25] Apart from Gueroult, the thesis that there are absolute theological necessities in Descartes

tes holds at least some truths (e.g. the existence of God, and possibly His omnipotence) to be absolutely unquestionable, this fact does not moderate the extreme interpretation in a relevant sense. We conclude that this first qualification, though probably providing a more correct reading of Descartes, is irrelevant in this sense that it leaves his theory equally bizarre.

A second alternative to the extreme interpretation was first proposed somewhat loosely by Peter Geach, then spelled out in more detail but rejected by Alvin Plantinga, and more recently formalized and advocated as the "most charitable" way of reading Descartes by Edwin Curley.[26] According to this interpretation, Descartes does not deny that there are necessary truths, but only that those which are necessary are necessarily necessary. The textual evidence for this suggestion is found above all in Descartes' letter to Mesland, where he argues that

> ... even if God has willed that some truths should be necessary, this does not mean that he willed them necessarily; for it is one thing to will that they be necessary, and quite another to will them necessarily, or to be necessitated to will them.[27]

Following this indication, Curley formulates Descartes' thoughts on the eternal truths in terms of "iterated modalities." According to him, Descartes did not hold that for any proposition p, p is possible, but that for any proposition p, p is *possibly* possible. Take any proposition you can think of - God could have made it possible. If p is a necessary proposition, then God could have made it the case that p is possible, i.e. that p is only contingently true. And if p is logically impossible, God could have made it the case that p is possible.

That this reading has some odd consequences is shown by Plantinga, who discusses it under the name "limited possibilism." In contrast to universal possibilism, this weaker version only allows that the modal status of all propositions are within God's control, while denying that their truth values depend upon God as well. Thus, God could only have made it the case that the proposition "2x4=8" is possibly false. That is: God could have made it

---

is supported by Curley ("Descartes," 592-594), by Alanen ("Descartes, Scotus and Ockham," 164), with some reservations by J.-M. Beyssade, "Création des vérités éternelles et doute métaphysique," in: *Studia Cartesiana* 2 (1981), 104f., and by J. Bouveresse, "Théorie du possible," 309 ("Il est probable que Descartes, sous peine de mettre en péril son propre système, a dû soustraire certaines vérités éternelles à la doctrine de la libre création, en particulier certaines vérités concernant Dieu lui-même").

[26] Geach, *Providence and Evil*, 9f.; Plantinga, *Does God Have a Nature?*, 103-114; Curley, "Descartes on the Creation," 576-583, 597.

[27] K 151. See also a comparable passage in the *Reply to Objections VI*: "Thus, to illustrate, God did not will ... the three angles of a triangle to be equal to two right angles because he knew that they could not be otherwise. On the contrary, ... it is because he willed the three angles of a triangle to be necessarily equal to two right angles that this is true and cannot be otherwise; and so on in other cases"; HR 2, 248.

the case that "2x4=8" could be false. But He could not have brought it about the "2x4=8" is in fact false.[28] Similarly, God could have made it the case that "2x4=9" is possibly true, but not that it is in fact true. The most puzzling feature of this interpretation is, that it implies the possibility of logically possible actions which the super-omnipotent Cartesian God cannot perform. For as soon as God has made it the case that "2+2=5" is possibly true, instantiating this possibility is no longer logically impossible. But precisely the latter ability is denied to God. This would really seem to be a limitation of God's power![29]

Of course one might hold that Descartes' theory of the creation of eternal truths is incoherent on *any* serious interpretation. At least, the fact that a proposed interpretation of it has some strange consequences does not necessarily count against its credibility as a sound description of Descartes' views. But apart from its perplexity, the iterated modality reading is in conflict with several explicit claims of Descartes to the extent that God *could* indeed have made necessary truths false. Descartes insists, for instance, that God could have made it false that all the lines from the centre of a circle to its circumference are equal, or that the three angles of a triangle are equal to two right angles.[30] Moreover, these claims are quite compatible with the forementioned passage from the letter to Mesland, appealed to by the proponents of the iterated modality reading. Therefore, we conclude that this interpretation hardly does more justice to the whole of Descartes' claims on eternal truths than the extreme interpretation.

Nevertheless, the iterated modality reading, at least in the version presented by Curley, has one important advantage in comparison to the extreme interpretation. For it does not only take seriously the fact that the eternal truths are *created* by God, but also the fact that they are created as *eternal*, i.e. necessary truths. All of Descartes' statements concur in the assumption that it is not in any way possible for God to abrogate the truth and necessity of the eternal truths *now*. This fact provides an important clue to the only reading of Descartes' theory which is both at first sight less bizarre than its alternatives, and does maximal justice to the totality of Descartes' statements on the theme. Leaving aside a discussion of some other mitigating readings,[31] let us now turn to this interpretation.

---

[28] For a slightly different version of this example, see Plantinga, *Does God Have a Nature?*, 112. Instead of his "he could only have made it the case that he could have made it false" I prefer to read: "he could only have made it the case that it is possibly false."

[29] Remarkably, as far as I know this consequence has not previously been noted in the literature.

[30] See respectively his letter to Mersenne of 27 May 1630 (K 15; cf. *Reply to Objections VI*, HR 2, 151), and to Mesland (2 May 1644; K 151). Significantly, at all these places Descartes uses perfect tenses in describing God's power. Thus, it is somewhat misleading when Alanen, "Descartes, Omnipotence," 186 refers to these texts as containing instances of what God "could make" true rather than of what he could *have made* true.

[31] Such as the one proposed by Hide Ishiguro, "The Status of Necessity and Impossibility in

A crucial passage, throwing light upon the question whether according to Descartes it is possible for God to change the eternal truths, occurs in his very first letter on the question to Mersenne. Imagining an objection which Mersenne would be confronted with when explaining Descartes' theory, Descartes constructs the following fictitious dialogue:

> They will tell you that, if God had established these truths, he could change them, as a king does his laws; to which one must reply yes, if his will can change. - But I understand them as eternal and immutable. - And I judge the same concerning God. - But his will is free. - Yes, but his power is incomprehensible. In general we can assert that God can do everything that we can comprehend but not that he cannot do what we cannot comprehend. It would be rash to think that our imagination reaches as far as his power.[32]

Several things are important to note here. First, the eternal truths are really eternal to Descartes in the sense that it is not possible that God will change them. Although God may be able to change them, there is not the slightest chance that He will change them, because His will does not change. Here, we meet with the same argument as the older medievals used in defending the view that God, though able to act *de potentia absoluta*, will never actually do so. As in Descartes' famous search for a new foundation of the sciences in his *Meditations*, here also it is the veracity of God which guarantees the reliability of our knowledge of the created order.

Second, the real problem concerns the nature of the divine will. How can God's will be both immutable and free? It would be too easy to respond that God's freedom entails the freedom to will things immutably. For if God did freely decide to will the eternal truths immutably, then He had the possibility to choose otherwise. But if God could have decided not to will the eternal truths immutably, then the eternal truths are not really immutable, since up to the moment of God's decision it was possible that they were changed by God. Moreover, since God continues to be *able* to change them, the eternal truths continue to be able to be changed, i.e. to be mutable. The problem is, in other words, how can the eternal truths on the one hand be necessary, and on the other hand contingent upon God's will? We will return to this problem in due course.

Third, it is characteristic that at this point Descartes invokes the incomprehensibility of God's power. Although we can not conceive what it

---

Descartes," in: A.O. Rorty (ed.), *Essays on Descartes' Meditations*, Berkeley 1986, 459-471, hinging on an alleged asymmetry between necessary truths (which God could make false) and necessary falsehoods, i.e. contradictions (which God could not make true) in Descartes. For a useful evaluation of the pros and cons of this reading, see Alanen, "Descartes, Omnipotence," 186-189.

[32] Letter to Mersenne, 15 April 1630; K 11. Valuable discussions of this section are in J.-M. Beyssade, *La philosophie première de Descartes*, Paris 1979, 112, and David E. Schrader, "Frankfurt and Descartes: God and Logical Truth," *Sophia* 25 (1986), 6f.

means that God might *make* truths *necessary*, we should not deny that God can do so, because God's power transcends our conceptual capacities. Significantly, Descartes hesitates to spell out precisely what this means. On the one hand, he often uses double negations when indicating the absolute power of God, as he does at the end of the passage just quoted. He seldom flatly says that God can make contradictions true,[33] but rather that we cannot say that God cannot make contradictions true. Thus, Descartes suggests an agnostic answer to the question whether or not God can do such things; since God's power transcends our conception, we simply don't know.[34] On the other hand, however, it is inherent in Descartes' doctrine of the creation of eternal truths that God could have made contradictions true, and this is precisely what Descartes *implies* in many statements. For example, in the letter to Mesland he formulates as follows:

> I turn to the difficulty of conceiving how it was free and indifferent for God to make it not be true that the three angles of a triangle were equal to two right angles, or in general that contradictories could not be true together. It is easy to dispel this difficulty by considering that the power of God cannot have any limits, and that our mind is finite and so created as to be able to conceive as possible things which God has wished to be in fact possible, but not to be able to conceive as possible things which God could have made possible, but which he has in fact wished to make impossible.[35]

So although we cannot *conceive how* God was free to make contradictories true together or things which are now impossible possible, we do *know that* God was free to do such things.[36]

As it seems to me, we should take very seriously Descartes' warning that we cannot conceive of the way in which God acts. Many of the attenuating readings of Descartes' theory try to make the nature of God's power conceivable to our human understanding. It is part of what Descartes intends his theory to express, however, that God's power cannot be elucidated in such a way that we may grasp it. According to Descartes, the incomprehensibility of God's power functions as a kind of great-making prop-

---

[33] This point is not sufficiently taken into account by Alanen, who claims that Descartes "says, repeatedly, that God can make contradictories true together" ("Descartes, Omnipotence," 184). In all of the three texts which she quotes for support Descartes uses double negations. Cf. R.R. la Croix, "Descartes on God's Ability to Do the Logically Impossible," *CJP* 14 (1984), 471: "In fact, the claim that God can violate the law of contradiction or do what human reason judges to be logically impossible or contradictory is conspicuous by its very absence."

[34] In this vein, Marion, *Sur la théologie*, 302 concludes from the letter to More that according to Descartes whether or not everything is possible to God is undecidable to us.

[35] K 150f.

[36] For the significance of this distinction between conceiving or comprehending (concevoir, comprendre, comprehendere) and knowing (savoir, connaître, intelligere) in Descartes' doctrine of God, see J.-M. Beyssade, "Création des vérités éternelles," 89ff. Although a statement like "God could have made contradictions true" is inconceivable, it is not unintelligible.

erty.[37] Therefore, as Frankfurt has seen, it is a mistake to seek a logically coherent explication of Descartes' assertions on God's ability to make contradictions true or to change the eternal truths.[38] For this would mean to try to comprehend the incomprehensible, which is not only impossible and unnecessary, but even impious.[39]

At one point, however, and here we part company with Frankfurt and Alanen, we should not make the Cartesian God more incomprehensible than He is. For clearly, Descartes is not committed to the view that God can make contradictories true or necessary truths false *at any moment in time*. On the contrary, Descartes explicitly rejects this view, for example when he argues that the mathematical truths are unchangeable and eternal because God so willed it.[40] Instead, Descartes believes that God has created the eternal truths *from all eternity*, and La Croix is right in concluding that they are for that reason coeternal with God.[41] He creates them by means of one single eternal act of continuously willing and conserving them.[42] Rather than *being* determined by external substances, God "determines Himself" to what He creates.[43]

---

[37] "The greatness of God ... is something which we cannot comprehend even though we know it. But the very fact that we judge it incomprehensible makes us esteem it the more greatly; just as a king has more majesty when he is less familiarly known by his subjects, provided of course that they do not get the idea that they have no king." Letter to Mersenne, 15 April 1630; K 11.

[38] Frankfurt, "Descartes on the Creation," 44; cf. Alanen, "Descartes, Omnipotence," 189.

[39] Cf. a striking passage in the letter to Mersenne from 6 May 1630: "It is easy to be mistaken about this [i.e., about the fact that the eternal truths depend upon God, GvdB] because most men do not regard God as an infinite and incomprehensible being, the sole author on whom all things depend; they stick to the syllables of his name and think it is sufficient knowledge of Him to know that 'God' means what is meant by 'Deus' in Latin and what is adored by men. Those who have no higher thoughts than these can easily become atheists."! K 14.

[40] *Reply to Objections V*; HR 2, 226. "... yet I think because God so wished it and brought it to pass, they *are* immutable and eternal" (Descartes seems to emphasize the word *esse* indeed). Cf. id., 250 ("It is because he willed the three angles of a triangle to be necessarily equal to two right angles that *this* is true *and cannot be otherwise*," italics added), and the interesting dialogue in the apocryphal *Conversation with Burman* on the ockhamist issue of the *odium Dei*, where Burman asks: "But does it follow from this that God could have commanded a creature to hate him, and thereby made this a good thing to do?" Reply of Descartes: "God could not now do this: but we simply do not know what he could have done. In any case, why should he not have been able to give this command to one of his creatures?" (AT V, 160; cf. John Cottingham, *Descartes' Conversation with Burman*, Oxford 1976, 22).

[41] See the Letter to Mersenne from 27 May 1630, the *Conversation with Burman*, (Cottingham, *Descartes' Conversation*, 15f.), and La Croix, "Descartes," 462. In general, the papers of La Croix and Schrader ("Frankfurt and Descartes"), though hardly noticed up to now, are convincing in emphasizing this point. Apart from them, the interpretation we advocate is also shared by Bouveresse, "Théorie du possible," esp. 305f.

[42] See on this special Cartesian concept of creation the *Meditations* 3 (HR 1, 168); Alanen, "Descartes, Duns Scotus and Ockham," 167; and Curley, "Descartes on the Creation," 577-579, who claims that we should not take Descartes' temporal expressions at face value, since Descartes conceives God's creative act as timelessly eternal.

[43] *Reply to Objections VI*; HR 2, 250.

Finally, let us return to the question how this conception of an eternal act of creation can be reconciled with Descartes' view of the absolute freedom of the divine will. Doesn't our reading of Descartes' enigmatic claims on the eternal truths simply "trade one paradox for another," as Curley[44] has it? Although on this interpretation we are not required to ascribe to Descartes the paradoxical view that there are no necessary truths, we are now faced with the dilemma that there are necessary truths which are at the same time not necessary, while dependent upon the free creative choice of God. For however eternal God's choice to create the eternal truths may be, Descartes will stick to his conviction that it is a *free* choice.

Perhaps some modal distinctions recently developed by Thomas Morris might help us to solve this dilemma. According to Morris, there are more modalities which might be utilized in the doctrine of God than only the usual ones of necessity and contingency, essentiality and accidence.[45] Concentrating upon entities of any sort, there may be entities which cannot cease to exist, as well as entities which cannot have begun to exist. Morris characterizes entities which belong to the first category as "enduring," entities belonging to the second category as "immemorial," and entities which belong to both categories as "immutable." Given this matrix, an immutable entity is not the same as a necessary entity. This can be seen as follows. Consider a being which (1) in fact exists, (2) could not have begun to exist, (3) cannot cease to exist, but (4) could have failed to exist at all. Clearly, such a being exists immutably (in virtue of 1 to 3) but not necessarily (since it fulfills condition 4 as well).[46]

As it seems to me, what Descartes wants to claim with regard to necessary truths is that they are immutably existing entities in the technical sense developed by Morris. First, Descartes considers the eternal truths as identical with *things* or *entities*, particularly with essences, as is clear from the following quotation:

> ... it is certain that God is no less the author of creatures' essence than he is of their existence; and this essence is nothing other than the eternal truths. I do not conceive them as emanating from God like rays from the sun; but I know that God is the author of everything and that these truths are something and consequently that he is their author.[47]

---

[44] Curley, "Descartes on the Creation," 577.

[45] T.V. Morris, "Properties, Modalities, and God," *PR* 93 (1984), 35f. (cf. his *Anselmian Explorations*, Notre Dame 1987, 77). Morris expounds his modal distinctions in terms of properties which can be exemplified by individuals or objects, but this feature can easily be left out.

[46] Ibid., 40. A. Vos et al., *Contingentie en vrijheid*, 35, show how the same distinctions can be made without introducing new modalities; it is enough to combine the existing modalities of neccesity and contingence with temporal categories.

[47] Letter to Mersenne, 27 May 1630; K 14. Apparently, the fact that Descartes presents his theory in terms of eternal truths rather than in terms of (abstract) things does not imply that he holds a nominalist view on the nature of those truths. But as we showed in § 2.4.1 above, this point does not make a relevant difference to the present discussion.

Second, let us consider the standard example of an eternal truth, "2+2=4,"[48] and assume like Descartes that it is an entity. On most interpretations of Descartes' theory, it is an entity which in fact exists. Moreover, on our reading of Descartes' theory, when this truth is an entity, it is certainly an enduring entity. For whether Descartes might have conceived of it as a temporal or a timeless entity, since he claims that God created it as an *eternal* truth, which cannot be changed even by God Himself, it is clear that this truth cannot cease to exist. Further, since Descartes claims that God created the eternal truths from all eternity, there cannot have been a time when it began to exist, and therefore it is also an immemorial entity in Morris's sense. Thus, "2+2=4" fulfills all three of Morris's conditions for an entity that exists immutably. But note that nevertheless it is not a necessary entity, since it also fulfills the fourth condition. It could have failed to exist at all, viz. if God had not wished to create "2+2=4," but perhaps some other truth instead of it (such as "2+2=5"), or no comparable truth at all. In this way, the status of eternal truths according to Descartes could "most charitably" be interpreted as immutable but not necessary truths.[49]

2.4.4 *Descartes' relation to the tradition*
However one might prefer to interpret Descartes' theory of the creation of eternal truths, it is generally agreed that it forms a novelty in comparison with the scholastic tradition preceding Descartes. In this section, I want to find out how this scholastic tradition used to deal with the problem which led Descartes to the development of his theory. Putting off till the next chapter the question whether anything can be said in favour of Descartes' theory from considerations of coherence and consistency, we first want to examine whether Descartes' position logically follows from motives which are implicit in the traditional Christian doctrine of divine omnipotence.

One reason to think so is the following. During the period of scholasticism, Christian theology had, in a fierce struggle with Aristotelianism, in the end won the debate concerning the eternity of matter. It was precisely the doctrine of divine omnipotence which had made a major contribution to this victory, in that it had become more and more generally accepted that one of the implications of this doctrine is, that matter cannot be co-eternal with God. Now what about abstract rather than material entities? Was Descartes right in his intuition that a proper understanding of the omnipotence-

---

[48] One may wonder whether this standard example is the best one, since it presupposes the context of a specific arithmetical system. We may bracket this context for present purposes, however, or otherwise take some basic principle of logic (such as *modus ponens*) as a better example.

[49] There is one statement of Descartes which at first sight seems to defy this interpretation, *viz.* Descartes' claim that there are laws of nature which would also be true if God had created other worlds (cf. note 17); see Schrader, "Frankfurt," 9f. In my "Descartes, Modalities, and God," *IJPR* 33 (1993), 10, I show how this claim nevertheless fits in with the interpretation defended here.

doctrine required a theory of the creation of the eternal truths as it required a doctrine of the creation of matter? This is an interesting question, since if so, *mirabile dictu* René Descartes was the first one to take God's omnipotence with sufficient seriousness. In what follows, however, I will argue that this is not the case, and that it was for philosophical reasons connected with his own programme that Descartes refused to accept the traditional solution to his problem, which was in fact much easier.

To start with, it has become clear from recent research that Descartes formulated his theory in opposition to the view defended by Suarez, that the eternal truths are necessarily true independently of God's will and intellect.[50] Particularly, a sentence in the second letter to Mersenne on the subject alludes to Suarez almost to the extent of quoting him:

> As for the eternal truths, I say again that *they are true or possible because God knows them to be true or possible, but not that they are known by God as if they were true independently of him*... One must not say, then, that *if God did not exist, nevertheless those truths would still be true*.[51]

Here as elsewhere, Descartes suggests that there are only two alternatives: either the eternal truths depend upon God, or God is dependent upon the eternal truths in the sense that they eternally exist outside His control.

Both from a historical and from a systematic point of view, however, this is a false dilemma. Traditional theism on the one hand did not accept a realm of entities distinct from God which was not created by God. On the other hand, it neither considered mathematical truths, universals etc. as resulting from the free creative choice of God and thus within His control. Rather, the eternal truths were conceived by, for example, Augustine, Anselm and Aquinas as existing in the mind of God. The mathematical essences and universals originate in the divine intellect, and, since there can be no parts or divisions in God, are even identical with Him.[52] According to Aquinas,

> If no intellect were eternal, no truth would be eternal. But because the divine intellect is eternal, truth has eternity in it alone. Nor does it follow from this that anything other than God is eternal; because truth in the intellect is God himself.[53]

As we will see in the systematic part of our study (§3.5.6), this traditional

---

[50] See Curley, "Descartes on the Creation," 583-588; Alanen, "Descartes, Duns Scotus and Ockham," 159f.; Marion, *Sur la théologie blanche*, 28-32 and passim.

[51] Letter to Mersenne, 6 May 1630; K 13. The italicized phrases were originally written in Latin, the rest of the letter in French. Cf. F. Suarez, *Disputationes Metaphysicae* XIII 13, 40.

[52] This is part of what the scholastics expressed in the doctrine of divine simplicity. See Plantinga, *Does God Have a Nature?*, 26-61, and the critical study of this work in F.G. Immink, *Divine Simplicity*, Kampen 1987, especially ch.3 and 4.

[53] *Summa Theologiae* I 16, 7. Cf. *Summa Contra Gentiles* II 25.

view of the eternal truths as existing in the divine mind can be unfolded in a coherent way, and therefore in essence shows us the way out of Descartes' dilemma. According to this view, the eternal truths certainly depend upon God (if God did not exist, they would not exist either), but this does not mean that they are freely created by God. If they were, this would imply that God had created Himself, which is not only incoherent, but also counterintuitive to the traditional Christian understanding of God.[54]

Why did Descartes neither accept nor even discuss the scholastic solution? According to Frankfurt,[55] Descartes himself suggests an answer when he insists that knowing and willing in God should be considered as one and the same thing.[56] There can not be any things which God knows without creatively willing them. Now it is clear that this principle can be directed against Suarez' theory that the necessary truths are from all eternity *known* by God, but not *willed* and *caused* by Him. Additionally, a case can be made for the view that Suarez's theory can also be found in Duns Scotus and Ockham, both of whom also held that things are possible or impossible or necessary ultimately in and of themselves, rather than in virtue of some act of divine causation.[57] Like Suarez, they even conceived of the eternal truths as logically (though not temporally, of course) antecedent to God's knowledge.

But surely Aquinas can neither be charged of advocating such an antecedence nor of disconnecting the divine faculties. For when the eternal truths reside in the divine mind to the extent of being identical with God, they are not conceived of as logically antecedent to God's knowledge. And since God's mind is identical with God's essence as well as with God's will, there is no priority of God's knowing them over His willing them. Rather, there is a logical equivalence between God's knowing and willing the eternal truths and the eternal truths being eternally true. Therefore, Descartes' insistence on the unity of God's faculties can hardly be interpreted as being opposed to Aquinas.[58] Why then did Descartes reject

---

[54] As is neatly pointed out by Immink, ibid., 83f.

[55] "Descartes on the Creation," 39-41.

[56] "If men understood properly the meaning of their words, they could never say without blasphemy that the truth of a thing precedes the knowledge God has of it, for in God willing and knowing are one, in such a way that from the very fact that he wills something, he thereby knows it, and on that account only such a thing is true." To Mersenne, 6 May 1630; K 13f. Cf. the next letter to Mersenne, 27 May 1630 (K 15).

[57] Cf. Alanen, "Descartes, Duns Scotus and Ockham," 172-182.

[58] Unless, of course, we should take Descartes as defending not the unity of God's faculties, but the priority of God's will over his knowledge. Indeed, there are some texts which appear to make God's intellect subordinate to God's will (most notably in the *Reply to Objections VI*; HR 2, 248); but both Marion (*Sur la théologie*, 293f.; cf. the whole of 282-294) and Alanen ("Descartes, Duns Scotus and Ockham," 183f.; cf. her "Descartes, Omnipotence," 191) warn that such statements should not be taken at face value, and make clear that Descartes did not endorse an extreme voluntarism.

Aquinas' solution, even though Aquinas appealed to the very notion of divine simplicity which Descartes was so anxious to uphold?[59]

Another answer to this question is proposed by Curley. According to him, Descartes "neglects Thomas's alternative theory ... because he tacitly accepts the validity of Suarez's criticism of Thomas."[60] In a rather intricate discussion, Suarez had criticized Aquinas for the fact that he does not identify the foundation of the necessity of necessary truths. To say, as Aquinas does, that this necessity is enclosed in God's idea of them will not do, since part of what Suarez wants to know is *why* God's idea of them represents them as necessary, whereas it represents other truths as contingent. According to Suarez, Thomas begged the question here. Now since there are no indications in Descartes that he agrees with Suarez's sophisticated argument, it is rather speculative to suppose that Descartes rejected the Thomistic answer for this reason. But let us grant that he did. Even in that case we may ask why? For surely Aquinas would have responded to Suarez's charge by saying that he asked the wrong question. Since necessary truths are identical with the divine ideas, it is mistaken to ask for a foundation of their necessity either in themselves as abstracted from God, or in God as if He were isolated from them. Thus, we may ask again: since Aquinas' position is not at first sight incoherent, why did Descartes ignore it?

Instead of speculating any longer about what Descartes may have thought, let us start by taking seriously what he explicitly tells us. What Descartes explicitly tells us is, that he developed his alternative theory on the status of the eternal truths to provide a foundation for his physics.

> Your question of theology is ... a metaphysical question which is to be examined by human reason ... That is the task with which I began my studies; and I can say that I would not have been able to discover the foundation of Physics if I had not looked for them along that road. It is the topic which I have studied more than anything and in which, thank God, I have not altogether wasted my time.[61]

Anthony Kenny[62] interprets this claim as follows. The prime novelty of Descartes' physical system consisted in the rejection of Aristotelianism. More specifically, Descartes rejected the Aristotelian apparatus of forms, essences, and qualities as explanatory principles for the duration and alterations of material and immaterial entities, forms and essences being responsible for the duration of these entities, qualities for their fluctuation.

---

[59] This is not to say that Aquinas did not allow for distinctions between different sorts of knowledge and will in God, and different ways in which God knows and wills things. But, as Kenny (*God of the Philosophers*, 19) states, such distinctions were also frequently drawn by Descartes.

[60] Curley, "Descartes on the Creation," 584f. See for the following ibid., 585, 587f.

[61] K 10f.; cf. note 18 above and AT I, 135. What follows is a summary of Descartes' theory of the creation of the eternal truths.

[62] See for the following Kenny, *God of the Philosophers*, 21f.

Apart from the essences, which he reinterpreted as eternal truths, he saw these elements as chimerical entities which were a hindrance rather than a help in physics.

In the Aristotelian system, however, it was precisely these ingredients which guaranteed the element of stability and order in the otherwise chaotic flux of phenomena. In turn, it was the stability and order in the world which formed a necessary condition for the acquisition of universally valid scientific knowledge. As a result of his rejection of them, Descartes was forced to provide himself with an alternative foundation for the permanent and indubitable validity of the physics he wished to establish. For that reason, Descartes reinterpreted the Aristotelian essences as eternal truths, i.e. as instantiations of the immutable will of God. As we saw above, Descartes considered the eternal truths to include not only the laws of mathematics but also the most basic physical laws. The stability of nature as governed by these laws was now guaranteed, since they were established by the immutable will of God. As Kenny summarizes the solution which he ascribes to Descartes: "The physics is immutable, because God's will is immutable."[63]

Despite its clarity, however, I cannot find Kenny's reconstruction entirely convincing for two reasons. First, even if we interpret the Cartesian eternal truths (as Kenny does and as we advocated above) as immutable and therefore as providing an element of stability, we must admit that some of Descartes' claims concerning them give the impression of utter *instability* in the world. If we cannot even say that God cannot make it the case that 2+2=5, or that "2+2=5 and at the same time 2+2=3," how should it be possible for us to establish a firm mathematical foundation of indubitable knowledge? Although we have found the extreme reading wanting, its popularity can certainly be explained as stemming at least partially from the textual support it has in some of Descartes' utterances. If Descartes intended his doctrine as conferring stability on his system, it is not clear why he did not avoid the opposite impression! Second, and more importantly, Kenny's theory still does not give us an answer to the question why Descartes departed from mainstream scholasticism by neglecting the classical Thomistic position. For it cannot be doubted that this position would have given Descartes' physics an equally or even more stable flavour than his own doctrine does. When the eternal truths are in the mind of the necessarily existing God, there is not the slightest chance that they would change or have to give way under the pressures of our precarious reality. Unlike Descartes himself, Aquinas does not need an auxiliary hypothesis concerning God's veracity in order to establish the stability of the eternal truths.

It seems to me that the reason why Descartes prefers his own theory to the one of Aquinas is not that on his view the eternal truths are more *stable*, but rather that they are *distinct from God*. Kenny has rightly pointed

---

[63] Ibid., 22.

to the fact that Descartes' theory of the creation of the eternal truths must somehow be related to his concern for the construction of a new, entirely trustworthy philosophical method. Kenny's failure to give a satisfactory account of the precise nature of this relation, however, shows how difficult this is, but a more plausible way in which the relation might be clarified is as follows. According to classical scholasticism, the multiplicity and diversity of essences is only apparent, since in the divine mind they form a complete unity.[64] The diverse essences as we know them only weakly reflect their true nature in God. This implies, however, that it is impossible for human beings to have full knowledge of the essences, since such knowledge would be knowledge of their unity as God's essence - and it would of course be preposterous to claim to possess perfect knowledge of God's essence, since God's essence is incomprehensible.

Descartes, on the other hand, had based his philosophy on a perception of truths which is not only clear but also *distinct*. According to this principle, it is only the distinctness of objects which can make us certain of their existence. For that reason, Descartes could not accept the Thomistic view that the distinctness of essences is in a sense only apparent, whereas their real nature cannot be comprehended by us because of their being identical with God. Thus, Descartes was drawn to the conviction that the eternal truths must be viewed as separate from God. Keenly seeing that Suarez' attempt to consider them as independent of God led to the heretical assumption that God's intellect is somehow on a par with our finite intellect, only one alternative was left to him, namely to affirm the creation of the eternal truths by God. In this way, Descartes could secure the reliability of human knowledge of the eternal truths which determine the created order. At the same time, Descartes could do full justice to the fact that the nature and power of God are incomprehensible to us, and we have seen him emphasizing this fact over and over again. Since science aims at the perfect knowledge of necessary truths, however, the nature of the eternal truths *should* be comprehensible, and therefore these truths must be thought of as distinct from God.[65]

Possibly, there are other ways in which Descartes' theory of eternal truths contributed to his programme of liberating philosophy and science from theology. For example, Marion identifies Descartes' rupture with tradition as the rejection of scholastic theories of analogy and univocity.[66] According to Descartes, it is rash to think that God is subject to the same

---

[64] Aquinas, *Summa Contra Gentiles* I, 54; here, Aquinas seems to repeat the familiar neoplatonic theme that diversity marks a defect or fall from unity.

[65] The preceding two paragraphs elaborate on an argument first put forward by E. Bréhier, "The Creation of the Eternal Truths in Descartes's System," in: W. Doney (ed.), *Descartes*, London 1968, 196f.; Bréhier's article was originally published in French in 1937.

[66] Marion, *Sur la théologie*, passim; cf. Alanen, "Descartes, Duns Scotus and Ockham," 171 n.26.

standards of rationality as we are, or that He can be known by some simple adaptations of our human concepts. Thus, he extends the range of God's power still wider than the most radical Ockhamists had dared to do,[67] denying that God is bound even by the laws of logic. In this way, he emphasizes the absolute transcendence of God to such an extent, that his doctrine was taken over in mysticism.[68] At the same time, however, Descartes neutralizes the threatening consequences of the radical ockhamist views by drawing heavily upon God's immutability and veracity.

According to Descartes, this divine immutability is primarily shown in the creation of the natural world, rather than in biblical revelation. From this point of view, Frankfurt attempts to trace yet another way in which Descartes used his theory of eternal truths to separate philosophy from theology. According to Frankfurt, in the intriguing final part of his paper,[69] Descartes views the biblical revelation as enabling us to share the perspective of God. In virtue of this fact, however, the contents of revelation at the same time share God's incomprehensibility. Therefore, they are of little help for the foundation of the sciences. Though ontologically more profound, revelation is irrelevant to our human rational interests. Human reason should submit to its own rationalities. Aided by the attainability of a perfect knowledge of necessary truths, it should content itself with the examination of the created order, rather than mixing rational considerations with claims stemming from God's revelation. In this way, Descartes' doctrine of the eternal truths might be interpreted as an attempt to support Galileo's position in his conflict with the church!

Surely, Frankfurt's account is highly speculative here. Moreover, it is marred by the fact that at that time he ascribed a coherence theory of truth to Descartes.[70] It also seems that Frankfurt fails to take Descartes' pious commitments with sufficient seriousness. On the other hand, his hypothesis would offer us a good explanation of the fact that Descartes was anxious to propagate his theory in public. Apparently, Descartes considered his theory to be "so dubiously orthodox as to lead him to ask Mersenne to try it out on people without mentioning the name of its inventor."[71] However this may be, although we should not too easily suspect Descartes' piety (his rejection of Suarez is as sincere as that of Aquinas), we cannot escape the conclusion of Bréhier:

As for the creation of the eternal truths, it is the reverse side of the autonomy of

---

[67] Cf. § 2.3.4 of this study.

[68] Especially by P. Poiret; cf. Bréhier, "Eternal Truths," 202-204.

[69] Frankfurt, "Descartes on the Creation," 54-57.

[70] In a later article, "Descartes on the Consistency of Reason," in: M. Hooker (ed.), *Descartes*, Baltimore 1978, 37, Frankfurt acknowledges that Descartes adheres to a correspondence theory of truth. Accordingly, the truth of something consists in its correspondence with reality even from the perspective of God, rather than only in some condition of the human mind.

[71] Kenny, "Cartesian Circle," 697; cf. K 12.

reason, seeking not to rise toward a divine model of which it would be a trace, but to progress toward new truths.[72]

2.4.5 *Conclusion and Transition*
We conclude that from a historical point of view the position that God's power ranges over the eternal truths as well as over created reality marks the first step of the secularization of the European mind, rather than being part and parcel of the Christian tradition. No doubt, the Christian tradition is divided on the question how the eternal truths relate to the power of God. It cannot be held, however, that it is a authentically Christian view to consider them as subject to the control of God's omnipotence. Rather, in determining the authentically Christian view of divine power we should hold to our tripartite definition of the doctrine of divine omnipotence. According to the Christian tradition, to say that God is omnipotent means to ascribe to Him universal dominion and authority, the continuous caring preservation of the world, and the ability of unconstrained actualization of all possible states of affairs. As to the latter, this ability should be kept in balance with what God has in fact decided to do, i.e. God's *potentia absoluta* should not be isolated from His *potentia ordinata*. Historically, ascribing omnipotence to God does not include, however, ascribing to Him the power to create or change the laws of logic or other eternal truths, universals, numbers, propositions, or abstract objects of any other sort.

Nevertheless, answering historical questions is different from answering systematic questions. The preceding discussion at least shows, that the relation between the divine omnipotence and abstract objects or the laws of logic calls for careful conceptual analysis. From a conceptual point of view, the common view that God's omnipotence stands apart from the distinctions of modal logic appears to be self-contradictory. For surely, power cannot be *omni*potence if it is limited by what according to the laws of logic are necessary truths and logical impossibilities? Thus, it seems that if we don't want to mitigate the doctrine of omnipotence, we should grant that Descartes was right after all! In short, what is at stake here from a systematic point of view is the problem of the *scope* of omnipotence: what does it mean to say that God's power is infinite in scope? So again we are ending up with a systematic question which requires further reflection.

In concluding the historical part of this study, let me finally sum up its main results in terms of an agenda for further conceptual analysis. First, in §2.2 we experienced how important it is to have a clear conception of the *nature* of power and the relations between different kinds of power. In contemporary discussions on God's power, one of the confusing factors is

---

[72] Bréhier, "Eternal Truths," 208. Cf. the conclusion of Bouveresse, "La théorie," 310, who asserts that despite his deviating conception on the nature of God's power in relation to the eternal truths "Descartes est et reste incontestablement un représentant du rationalisme le plus classique."

113

that such a clear and generally accepted conception is still lacking. As a result, wrong-headed interpretations and evaluations of the doctrine of God's omnipotence are still influential. For example, if it is argued that the doctrine of divine omnipotence makes God into a capricious tyrant who elicits fear and anxiety rather than love, this is at least partly due to a misinterpretation of power as necessarily conflictual and coercive in character. Therefore, we will start our analysis with examining the concept of power, in order to find out how we should describe the phenomenon of power, how it fits in with various power-related concepts, and how different kinds of power relate to each other. This is what I plan to do in §3.2.

Second, in §2.3 we met with another cluster of problems that must be sorted out. Our discussion of the distinction between God's *potentia ordinata* and *potentia absoluta*, and particularly of the different interpretations of the latter notion, showed what kind of conceptual difficulties may arise in relation to the *being* to whom power is ascribed. These difficulties are of two sorts. First, there are the problems connected with the ascription of all power to one and the same being; and second, additional problems come about when the omnipotent being has other properties apart from its power which have to be taken into account. The development of the distinction between God's absolute and ordained power can be seen as an attempt to solve these problems, or at least to prevent them from becoming manifest. That both sorts of difficulties are real rather than due to some deplorable state of underdevelopment of the medieval mind, is confirmed by the numerous present-day philosophical discussions which still centre around the same questions. As to the ascription of all power to one and the same being, the main question is now whether "omnipotence" is a coherent concept at all! And as to the relation between an omnipotent being's power and its other attributes, the main question in contemporary philosophical theology has become what it means to claim that *God* is omnipotent. In this way, studying the doctrine of omnipotence brings us right into the heart of the doctrine of God. In what follows, I will join both fields of contemporary debate. In §3.3 I take up the conceptual problems concerning the definition of "omnipotence," whereas in §3.4 I set about examining the meaning and role of this concept in a properly Christian doctrine of God.

Third, in the present section, §2.4, we encountered still another set of conceptual questions, pertaining not to the nature of power nor to the being who possesses all power, but to the *scope* of this being's power. The problem that worried Descartes was how to avoid the idea that God's omnipotence is to some extent limited and therefore not really *omni*potence. Again, if we look around us it occurs to us that also this question is by no means obsolete. Nowadays, a number of mainly Christian philosophers who are occasionally referred to as the "neo-Cartesian school" share Descartes' concern for an adequate view of the relation between God's power and the status of logical and mathematical truths. They respond to this concern by developing theories which have close similarities to Descartes' doctrine of the creation of the eternal truths. In §3.5 I will discuss some of their views (alongside those of others), and try to solve the conceptual problems concerning the infinite scope of God's power in a way which avoids the bizarre consequences of both Cartesian and neo-Cartesian theories.

3

Conceptual Analysis

Wir haben keine klare Vorstellung davon, was wir meinen, wenn wir von Gottes Macht sprechen.

Hans Asmussen[1]

3.1 INTRODUCTION

In much contemporary discourse concerning the credibility of the Christian view of life, the concept of divine omnipotence plays a very significant role. It is often contended that the endorsement of some reasonable claim or option leads the Christian believer into great difficulties, since that particular claim or option is incompatible with God's omnipotence. On closer examination, however, it turns out that the concept of omnipotence which is presupposed is a rather crude and rudimentary one. Paul Davies's best seller on the relationship of science and religion is a case in point here.[2] Among the many antinomies construed by Davies between God's omnipotence and other things,[3] there is one which regards God's personhood. According to Davies, either God is timeless, and then He cannot be a personal God who thinks, converses, feels, plans, and so on, or God is in time, and then He cannot be omnipotent because of His being "subject to the physics of time." Thus, God cannot be at the same time omnipotent and personal.[4]

This way of opposing omnipotence to one of the other traditional divine qualities discloses a low degree of reflection concerning the conceptuality which is involved in the ascription of attributes to God. On the one hand, the ascription of personhood to God has never been meant to imply that *all* aspects of what it means to be a person are applicable to God. For example, certain characteristics of human personhood (e.g. mortality) have

---

[1] H. Asmussen, *Über die Macht*, Stuttgart 1960, 8.

[2] Paul Davies, *God and the New Physics*, London 1983.

[3] God's omnipotence is claimed to be incompatible, e.g., with the universe being indeterministic (142), with God's benevolence (143), with his performing miracles (195), but remarkably enough also with his not performing miracles, i.e. with his alleged inability to act outside the laws of physics (209). Notably, in his recent *The Mind of God*, London 1992, 172, Davies is much more friendly to the doctrine of divine omnipotence.

[4] Ibid., 133f. For a critique of Davies's concept of omnipotence, see A. van den Beukel, *More Between Heaven and Earth*, London 1992, 88-104, esp. 96.

always been denied in the case of God. Moreover, in Christian trinitarian theology it has always been held that God is not a person, but three persons. Thus, it has to be sorted out in each single case separately whether or not it makes sense to use a particular characteristic feature of human personal being in speaking of God. In fact, to call God a person or personal means to highlight those aspects of the way in which God is related to the universe and to human beings which resemble human personal relationships. Whether or not these aspects are in some way compatible with timelessness is a matter which cannot be decided without argument.[5]

On the other hand, as the historical survey in the previous chapter learned us, the ascription of omnipotence to God has never been simply meant to say that "God can do all things" in an absolute, context-free sense. As we saw in §2.2, in the context of Christian belief it is easy to sum up a number of things which the omnipotent God cannot do. Most of such things can be done perfectly well by human beings, as they often demonstrate. Contrary to human beings, for example, God cannot deny Himself (in the sense of becoming unfaithful to His promises). Of course the precise meaning of "cannot" in this claim should be sorted out. But in any case, the believer will claim that in this respect God is neither "personal" nor literally omnipotent! Accordingly, the logic of omnipotence in the context of faith is much more refined and sophisticated than authors like Davies suggest.

The Davies-example may suffice to remind us of the fact how important it is not only to carefully analyse the concept of omnipotence, but also to be aware of the special character of the language and logic of faith in which it has its proper place. In the present chapter, I both want to analyse the concept, and try to find out what happens to it when it is used in the language of faith, more particularly in the doctrine of God. First, in §3.2 I concentrate on the main locution of the concept by discussing the notion of power and some of its cognates. In this way, I follow up the task which emerged from our study of early Christian thought on divine power. Second, in §3.3 I examine the conceptual complications which occur when the concept of power (or "potence") is preceded by the qualifier "omni," and consider whether the concept of omnipotence is meaningful in itself, irrespective of any theological connotations. A further question which is also raised in the course of this section, however, is whether omnipotence is compatible with other classical divine attributes such as omniscience and impeccability. Third, in §3.4 I attempt to trace the differences and similarities between the philosophical concept of omnipotence discussed so far and the theological notion of God's almightiness which functions in a specifically Christian doctrine of God based upon the biblical revelation. In doing this I attempt to illuminate the relation between omnipotence and the character of the

---

[5] Suffice it to mention only one of the many recent studies on this theme: Paul Helm, *Eternal God*, Oxford 1988, in which it is argued that timelessness *is* compatible with the other classical divine attributes.

Being who possesses it, a theme which was prompted by our historical study of the distinction between God's abolute and ordained power. Fourth, in §3.5 I recur to the question of the scope of God's power, which we considered as the legacy of our discussion of Descartes' theory concerning the eternal truths.

One additional remark in defence of my procedure may be helpful in advance. To follow the outlined route may seem to presuppose a rather straightforward theory of analogical predication, since it looks as if the meanings of "power" and "omnipotence" as used in ordinary language is simply conveyed and employed to explain its theological use. Explaining omnipotence in terms of power, as I plan to do, presupposes that God's omnipotence and natural or human powers are at least in some way or another on a par. Although we may of course differentiate between both in many respects, we still assume that there are enough similarities which justify the use of our ordinary concept of power in trying to grasp the nature of God's omnipotence.

This I admit. My approach is not meant, however, to prejudge the issue of the form of theological predication that underlies an adequate account of the doctrine of divine omnipotence. For surely, we must leave open the possibility that we entirely understand the meaning of a phrase like, say, "having all power" as a definition of omnipotence, but nevertheless are radically mistaken about what is involved in *God's* omnipotence. This is not simply a logical point (the concrete meaning of a particular property is always co-determined by the nature of its bearer), but more specifically a theological one: our ordinary human concept of omnipotence may be subverted by the encounter with God's revelation, in which we discover what it does really mean for God to be omnipotent. It is perhaps only from this insight that we may grasp the primary meaning of power, our common-sense notion of it representing only power in a secondary and impure sense.[6]

All this is granted, and I will return to the issue at a later stage. But even though it will then turn out that both our ordinary concept of power and its philosophical sophistication "omnipotence" are indeed transformed by the theological context of the term (as determined by the biblical account of God's powerful acts), it is nonetheless important to assess how these different concepts are related to one another. For only in this way it is possible to establish the precise ways in which our ordinary ideas and intel-

---

[6] This option is impressively worked out by Roger White with regard to the related theme of divine kingship; see his "Notes on Analogical Predication and Speaking about God," in: B. Hebblethwaite & S. Sutherland (eds.), *Philosophical Frontiers of Christian Theology*, Cambridge 1982, 208-221. Cf. for more or less comparable conceptions of God's omnipotence (as decisively qualified by the saving acts and loving nature of the God of Israel and Jesus Christ) Karl Barth, *Dogmatics in Outline*, London 1949, 46-49, and in Dutch theology e.g. K.H. Miskotte, *Bijbels ABC*, Amsterdam 1966[2], 39, 49f., 59-67; P.B. Suurmond, *God is machtig - maar hoe?*, Baarn 1984, esp.32-45; J.C. de Moor, *Gods macht en liefde*, Kampen 1988, passim.

lectual reconstructions of divine power deviate from and are transformed by God's revelation.[7] Therefore, we will proceed by offering a provisional analysis of God's omnipotence by means of the philosophical method of conceptual analysis of ordinary language.

3.2 THE NATURE OF POWER

3.2.1 *Power-over and power-to*
The most natural way to start the search for a definition of omnipotence is to take the locution "potence" as equivalent to "power," and thus to conceive of omnipotence as the quality of having all power. This in itself does not take us much further, however, since (as we already discovered in the historical part of our inquiry) the definition of power is notoriously contested.[1] Moreover, the uses of "power" are to such an extent multifarious and variegated, that it seems incorrect to look for one uniform definition of its "essence." Rather, we should try to analyze its manifold uses and determine in this way its central functions.[2] Thus, many studies on the concept of power simply set about quoting some dictionary-entry for "power" and discussing the various nuances of meaning listed there. Indeed, if we use the concept of power in defining omnipotence, we should be aware of its conceptual ramifications. An examination of the results of those studies which are generally interested in the phenomenon of power may help us to gain insight into these, and thus into which aspects of power might possibly be ascribed to God when He is called omnipotent.

This task, which is undertaken in the present section,[3] is not an easy one, however, since there is a huge and ever growing amount of especially sociological literature, which in itself testifies to the intangible and elusive nature of the concept of power. Indeed, "in sociopolitical sciences, there is no end to the disputes regarding the definition and usage of the term 'pow-

---

[7] See on this point further my "Almacht bij Anselmus en Abraham," *KETh* 43 (1992), esp. 218-224.

[1] Cf. S. Lukes, *Power: A Radical View*, London 1974, 9, who considers power as an "essentially contested concept." Cf. W.B. Gallie, "Essentially Contested Concepts," *PAS* 56 (1955-56), 167-198.

[2] Here I concur with S.R. Clegg, *Power, Rule and Domination*, London 1975, Ch.1; Clegg shows how this shift in method in general originates in Wittgenstein.

[3] Briefly, of course. We do not involve ourselves in discussions of the organizational and other typically social or political aspects of power, nor in rather technical issues such as the ways in which powers might be quantified, measured, compared etc. All this is at best of only indirect relevance to our specific interest in power. For a recent comprehensive and impressive survey of (and elaboration on) especially the social science literature on power, see Stewart R. Clegg, *Frameworks of Power*, London 1989. For a still useful review of some older sociological literature, see J.A.A. van Doorn, "Sociology and the Problem of Power," *SN* 1 (1963), 3-51.

er'."[4] A large part of the literature in question is not of much help to our objectives, however, since it is primarily inspired by and focused upon political theory. As a result, it is hopelessly biased in its choice of the *definiendum* in connection with power.[5] For power is generally conceived here as power over persons rather than as power to do (or bring about) things. What many social scientists since Weber[6] are exclusively interested in is power which has as its objective the subordination of other persons. As influential a power-specialist as Steven Lukes, for instance, recognizes the existence of the locution "power to." But he quickly dismisses it as irrelevant, arguing that it "indicates a 'capacity', a 'facility', an 'ability', not a relationship. Accordingly, the conflictual aspect of power - the fact that it is exercised *over* people - disappears altogether from view."[7]

In this way, Lukes makes precisely the opposite mistake: all forms of power which are *not* by definition conflictual disappear from view. Thus, the concept of power is vitiated with negative connotations from the beginning, before even the process of analyzing it has started. Certainly the possession and exercise of power often play a prominent role in interpersonal relationships. But this does not imply that power is essentially a relational concept. Since in many circles it is fashionable to suppose that intricate problems are solved by declaring some concept to be "relational" rather than "objective" or "ontological" or whatever, it may not be redundant to emphasize that power is *not* inherently a relational concept if this qualification is meant to reserve its use to interpersonal relationships.[8] The concept of power is also properly used, for example, to indicate the abilities people have with regard to the natural world surrounding them, or with regard to

---

[4] Case-Winters, *God's Power*, 29.

[5] Cf. K. Röttgers, *Spuren der Macht*, München 1990, 47: "Der ... Usus, gegen den ich mich wende und der zugleich jeden sinnvollen Zugang zur Tradition des macht-theoretischen Denkens versperrt, ist die Reduktion des Verständnisses des Begriffs der Macht auf den von *politischer Macht*."

[6] Weber's classical and influential definition runs as follows: "'Power' (*Macht*) is the probability that one actor *within a social relationship* [italics mine] will be in a position to carry out his own will despite resistance, regardless of the basis on which this probability rests"; M. Weber, *The Theory of Social and Economic Organization*, New York 1947 (ed. T. Parsons), 152.

[7] Lukes, *Power*, 31. For more examples, see Peter Morriss, *Power: A Philosophical Analysis*, Manchester 1987, 32-35. In general, I am highly indebted to Morriss's excellent study for my argument in the present section.

[8] That power is a relational concept is defended by e.g. Felix E. Oppenheim, *Political Concepts*, Oxford 1981, 6f., and (from a definitely sociological point of view) by Van Doorn, "Sociology," 8-10, 12. A specific elaboration of this thesis is offered by J. Ogilvy, "Understanding Power," *PSC* 1 (1978), 129-144 (see especially 138ff.), whose claim is taken over by Röttgers, *Spuren*, 30, 51, 335 (and passim). On the other hand, R. Harrison Wagner, "The Concept of Power and the Study of Politics," in: R. Bell, D.V. Edwards & R. Harrison Wagner (eds.), *Political Power: A Reader in Theory and Research*, New York 1969, 4, rightly states that "'power' does not mean a relationship," and goes on to explain how this misunderstanding could have come about.

their own bodies or characters, not to speak of the powers we may rightly attribute to *things* (such as the power of a stormy sea to wreck a ship; why should we reject this use of the word as anthropomorphic or even animistic?[9]).

Of course, one might also call these forms of power relational, since abilities are always related to the specific entities with regard to which they might be exercised.[10] But surely this move obscures things, since this general kind of relationality is quite different from the interpersonal or social relationality which is usually conveyed by the term.

More importantly, however, in so far as power is operative among people - i.e., in so far as it is a social phenomenon - it is misleading to qualify it exclusively as exercised *over* people. In fact, "to have power over" is a rather vague and unspecific expression, since it is not clear *in what respect* or *with regard to which actions or states of affairs* one has such power.[11] A teacher of philosophy may have power over her students with regard to their reading *Leviathan*,[12] but not with regard to their partner choice. The most natural way to indicate this is to say that she has the power to get her students reading *Leviathan*, but lacks the power to affect her students' partner choice. Thus, the power-*over* vocabulary is quite naturally translated in terms of power *to* accomplish things.[13]

In general, we can establish the relation between both locutions as follows. All forms of power which we usually exercise in order to obtain some *specified outcome* (other than the vague outcome "affecting other people") are more adequately formulated in terms of "power to." They indicate *abilities* to do things rather than possibilities for manipulating relations with other people. My power to drive a car for instance is certainly a relational and social phenomenon: I acquired it by taking driving lessons and I exercise it in constant interaction with other traffic participators. Nevertheless, it is hard to say over whom this power is exercised. On the other hand, if we state that A has power over B, we simply mean that there is a wide (but unspecified) range of things which A can get B to do. Clear-

---

[9] Cf. Paul Tillich, *Love, Power and Justice*, Oxford 1954, 7. Interestingly, the physicist Max Jammer, *Concepts of Force*, New York 1962, 264, wants to banish the concept of "force" from physics altogether because of its anthropomorphic character. Q. Gibson, "Power," *PSS* 1 (1971), 103f., however, argues that we should not confuse the origin of the concept with its nature. As it seems to me this is correct, provided that we realize this nature to be multifarious rather than uniform. In this vein also Morriss, *Power*, 26f.

[10] As is done, for example, in Oppenheim, *Political Concepts*, 7, 29.

[11] This dimension of power is sometimes called the "zone of acceptance"; cf. P.H. Partridge, "Some Notes on the Concept of Power," *Political Studies* 11 (1963), 118; Case-Winters, *God's Power*, 32.

[12] See for this example Oppenheim, *Political Concepts*, 6.

[13] Cf. Stephen T. Davis, *Logic and the Nature of God*, London 1983, 77: "To have power over x can surely be analyzed as having power to do certain things, e.g. to do certain things to x or to make x [d]o certain things."

ly, such power is only a subset of all forms of power A may possess. For example, A being a blackmailer and B his victim, A usually has more forms of power than only his power over B.

It may be argued against this that sometimes it is much easier to say *over* whom power is exercised than to specify this power over others in terms of power-to. If A has power over B, it is not always clear in advance what kind of states of affairs A can bring about by exercizing this power. Thus, the car-example can be countered by examples of situations in which the notion of power-over applies better than the notion of power-to. However, such counter-examples do not show that there are instances of power-over which are not translatable in terms of power-to. They only show that in practice it is often difficult to perform this translation, because of our lack of knowledge. It is for that reason that we sometimes prefer the vaguer term power-over to the more precise term power-to. On the conceptual level, however, power over people is reducible to power to bring about certain states of affairs, whereas the opposite reduction cannot always be made.

The recognition of the fact that "power to" is conceptually irreducible to "power over" is of more than academic relevance, as is pointed out by Peter Morriss in an instructive example concerning the slogan "Black Power":

> "Black Power" encapsulated a platform aimed at giving blacks the power to run their own lives; it represented a demand for autonomy. The originators of the movement never intended the slogan to imply that black people should have disproportionate power *over* non-blacks - should somehow dominate them. ... White supremacists, however, by equating power-to with power-over, were able to portray the legitimate demands of black people for equality as equivalent to a desire for black domination. It is regrettable that reputable, and liberal, academics, by considering power over others as the only sort of power, may have unwittingly encouraged such distortions.[14]

An extreme consequence of this conflictual theory of power, now rejected by most of the theory's adherents but in a sense laying bare its very oddity, is the so-called *zero-sum* explanation of power. This explanation hinges on alleged analogies between power and money, or power and the physical concept of energy. Basically, it amounts to the assumption that if I gain a certain amount of power, necessarily one or more other people thereby loose an equal amount of power, so that the sum total of power remains the same.[15] Now apart from the confusion between power and its

---

[14] Morriss, *Power*, 33f.

[15] A zero-sum conception of power is usually ascribed to C. Wright Mills, *The Power Elite*, London 1956. For a refutation, see the power-studies of Talcott Parsons, who, by the way, takes precisely the money-analogy as a basis for elucidating the nature of power; cf. esp. his "On the Concept of Political Power," *PAPS* 107 (1963), 232-262, repr. in S. Lukes (ed.), *Power*, Oxford 1986, 94-143, and his *Sociological Theory and Modern Society*, New York 1967.

exercise which plays a role here (see on this point below), it is easy to sum up counterexamples which falsify this assumption. If I exercise my power to walk, it is unclear why whoever else would loose any power. Even in relational and social forms of power, the assumption is hopelessly inadequate. To cite an example of Partridge,[16] the political process of appointing a leader is based upon the contrary assumption. In doing so we endow the leader with power, including power over ourselves, hoping that in this way we augment our own power to bring about our intentions. And actually, this is the way it often works. Only in conflictual situations exercises of power tend to be zero-sum. But certainly, this eventuality is peculiar and not typical for every instance of power.[17]

3.2.2 *Power-over and omnipotence*
Although we must be careful not to draw premature conclusions from our present discussion of "power" with respect to the concept of omnipotence, it might be illuminating to show already at this stage how the former can be seen to bear upon the latter. For this reason, while realizing that the full impact of our analysis of the concept of power can of course only become clear at a later stage, we nevertheless insert a small section on the relation between power and omnipotence here. For it is precisely at this juncture that a rather close connection between both can be brought to light.

The misunderstanding that power should exclusively be understood as power *over* seems to play a prominent role in the rather negative appraisal of the doctrine of omnipotence by contemporary philosophers and theologians.[18] A good example here is the recent study of Anna Case-Winters. Although Case-Winters denies that power must necessarily entail a conflict of interests,[19] she claims that the power which is implied in the assertion that God is omnipotent has traditionally been interpreted as power in the mode of domination and control.[20] In other words, she takes it that omnipotence is *conflictual* power which is exerted *over* people. But this is definitely incorrect both from a logical and from a historical point of view.

---

[16] Partridge, "Some Notes," 122f.

[17] Morriss, *Power*, 91.

[18] Of course, there are also other motives and considerations which may lead to the adoption of a power-over concept of omnipotence. Peter Geach e.g. thinks that it is logically incoherent to define omnipotence in terms of power-to (i.e., in terms of abilities), and that therefore we should reformulate the doctrine of omnipotence in terms of power-over. The result is a defence of what Geach calls the *almightiness* of God. Cf. his *Providence and Evil*, 3-28, §2.2 above, and §3.4 below.

[19] Case-Winters, *God's Power*, 33f.

[20] "Traditionally, the power implied here [viz. in the assertion that God is omnipotent, or all-powerful] has been interpreted as power *in the mode of domination and control* ... [italics by the author]. Moreover, as this notion becomes divinized the exercise of this kind of power in the realm of human affairs is legitimated and promoted - with obvious disastrous results in the form of oppression, exploitation, and violence." Ibid., 19.

First of all, power-over logically implies power-to, and therefore *omni-potence* must primarily denote the power to bring all things about. And secondly, as has been demonstrated in the previous chapter, the Christian tradition grasped this logical connection already at an early stage. For example, Augustine unambiguously construed omnipotence as primarily signifying God's infinite capacity to do things rather than His dominion over things (let alone any oppressing domination over people). So it is a gross caricature to interpret the classical doctrine of divine omnipotence in terms of a divinization of oppressing, exploiting and violating power.

The extreme limit of this misconception of omnipotence may become clear when the zero-sum view of power is applied to it. Then, the ascription of omnipotence to God would imply the ascription of absolute power-lessness to all other entities in the universe! If God is to have *all* power there is, no power is left over for anyone or anything else. But this is clear-ly at odds with what seems to be required, or in any case with what has usually been understood, by the concept of omnipotence. As John Lucas explains:

> Although God is able to do all things, we do not think He does do all things. Not only do we often ascribe events to human agencies or natural causes rather than to divine action, but we allow that some things happen against God's will. Al-though He could intervene to prevent the plans of the wicked from coming to fruition, often He does not.[21]

Furthermore, there is an important theological motive for concep-tualizing God's omnipotence in terms of power-to rather than in terms of power-over. Contemporary philosophical and phenomenological studies into the practical functioning of power in society have shown that the productive and repressive dimensions of power are always inexorably bound up with each other. Particularly the work of Michel Foucault is illuminating in this respect, not only because of its uncovering the all-pervasiveness and non-localizability of power, but also because of its disclosing the fact that the phenomenon of power is irreducible to either its repressive or its productive and creative aspects.[22] Now if we use the concept of power theologically in characterizing the nature of the unique Being who determines the mean-ing of our lives and who is worthy of our worship, it seems that we do not want to ascribe to Him this ambivalent character of mundane instances of power. Rather, it seems appropriate to associate God's power with His

---

[21] J.R. Lucas, *The Freedom of the Will*, Oxford 1970, p.75.

[22] For the rare explicit discussions of power in his work see M. Foucault, "The Subject and Power," afterword in: H.L. Dreyfus & P. Rabinow, *Michel Foucault: Beyond Structuralism and Hermeneutics*, Chicago 1983[2], 208-226, and C. Gordon (ed.), *Power/Knowledge: Selected Inter-views and Other Writings by Michel Foucault, 1972-1977*, New York 1980. Cf. Peter Jonkers, "God en macht," in: F. Vosman (ed.), *God en de obsessies van de twintigste eeuw*, Hilversum 1990, 12ff.

creative and sustaining activities. These activities are exemplifications of His infinite abilities to do things, and are therefore best conceived of in terms of power-to.

Notice that we can also interpret the other aspects of God's power which we distinguished above along these lines. Surely, God's authority over His creation and His preservation of the world are forms of power exercised *over* creaturely entities. Nevertheless, these forms of power (coined above respectively as "A-power" and "B-power") are exemplifications of power-to, in this case of the infinite divine creativity to fulfill His purposes. Thus, even these forms of power don't in themselves have conflictual or repressive characteristics - which is not to say that they might not occasionally be exercised in vigorous and conflictual ways, for example in God's wrathful confrontation with human sin and evil.

3.2.3 *Power as a dispositional concept*
In his recent conceptual history (*Begriffsgeschichte*) of power, Kurt Röttgers distinguishes between two alternative lines of thought which play a role in this history.[23] Broadly, these lines of thought can be referred to as the causal and the modal conception of power. According to the causal conception, we are justified to speak of power only in circumstances in which power is actualizing itself or has been actualized. There is no other way to assess whether we have to do with an instance of power than by means of studying its effects. According to the modal conception, however, the causal view confuses power with its exercise, and robs the description of power of its very essence since power disappears as soon as it becomes actualized. Therefore, power should rather be defined in terms of possibility.

The identification of power with cause has a long history,[24] culminating in Robert Dahl's famous behaviourist definition of power.[25] As Quentin Gibson eloquently argues, however, it is demonstrably false.

> It is simply not the case in any but the most idiosyncratic use of the word "power" that to have power to do something is the same as actually to cause it to happen. It is merely to be *able* to cause it to happen. Thus it is perfectly possible to have power without doing anything at all. The policeman on traffic duty ... has the power to direct the traffic not only when he is actually directing it, but also when there is not a vehicle in sight.[26]

---

[23] Röttgers, *Spuren*, 51, 55, 59, 69, 73, 76f., 86f., 93f. (the number of page-references shows that Röttgers's argument is not very well structured).

[24] Including, among others Hobbes ("Power and Cause are the same thing"; *De Corpore* 10, 1) and Hume. Cf. Gibson, "Power," 102f.

[25] "For the assertion 'C has power over R' one can substitute the assertion 'C's behaviour causes R's behaviour'"; R.A. Dahl, "Power," *International Encyclopedia of the Social Sciences*, New York 1968, Vol.12, 410; for his longer, "official" definition, see 407. The article is reprinted as "Power as the Control of Behaviour" in: S. Lukes (ed.), *Power*, 37-58.

[26] Gibson, "Power," 102.

On the other hand, if we define power in terms of *logical possibilities*, it largely becomes a useless concept, since upon this definition it is indeed impossible to determine whether we have to do with an instance of power *which is really actualizable* (except retrospectively from its concrete effects). This dilemma is solved, however, as soon as we realize that power is basically a *dispositional* concept, referring to *abilities or capacities*.[27] It is a peculiar feature of dispositional statements in general that although they do not refer to separate observable facts, they nevertheless are meaningful and can even be known to be true.[28] We may know that a cup is fragile, although it has never broken.

Röttgers objects to this move from a modal towards a dispositional description of power, suggesting that in doing this we reify the concept of power and presuppose an obsolete metaphysics of substances and attributes. According to him, power is wrongly conceived here as an attribute of an isolated subject.[29] But this is a strange kind of argument. For surely both in everyday language and in scientific discourse we do not only talk about observable things and events, but we also often find it necessary to go beyond the changing flux of events and refer to their relatively unchanging underlying conditions and liabilities.[30] These we may call dispositional properties, and if some specific metaphysical assumptions play a role in calling them so it is not clear a priori why these should be bad ones. If there is something wrong with talk about dispositions, we should either find another collective term for concepts like "soluble," "fragile," "prone to smoke" etc., or refrain from using such "unobservable concepts" at all. But we may talk perfectly well about the dispositional properties of objects without presupposing any invisible substantial substructures or "secret powers" inherent in them. For "to ask *why* a substance has a property ... is different from, and not necessary for, asserting that it *does* have this property."[31] We need not point to some secret force or metaphysical substance hidden in the cup which is responsible for its fragility in order to observe

---

[27] See, e.g. Dennis H. Wrong, *Power*, Oxford 1979, 6. Wrong differentiates between this dispositional concept of power and what he calls an *episodic* concept of power, thus applying a distinction made in Gilbert Ryle's classic *The Concept of Mind*, London 1966[11] (see esp. 116-153). Whereas the episodic concept of power approximates to Dahl's mistaken view of power as causal action, the dispositional concept is concerned with "recurrent tendencies of human beings to behave in certain ways" (Wrong, ibid). Both the use of the word "tendencies" and the restriction to human beings are disputable, however. Cf. also Clegg, *Frameworks*, 83f.

[28] Cf. Ryle, *Concept of Mind*, 124.

[29] Röttgers, *Spuren*, 51f., 61-63, 70 ("so dass man der Macht ... als eine materielle Fähigkeit reifiziert ..."). A similar suspicion is in Gibson, "Power," 111. Interestingly, Röttgers attempts to show that this metaphysical conception of power is *not* traceable to Aristotle (ibid., 69f.).

[30] Morriss, *Power*, 14.

[31] Ibid., 18. On "secret power" theories, cf. Röttgers, *Spuren*, 52 n.6. One of the realistic conceptions Röttgers has in mind, assuming an "intrinsic nature or constitution" of things and persons as principle of explanation for their powers, is expounded and defended in R. Harré & E.H. Madden, *Causal Powers*, Oxford 1975.

that the cup is fragile.

Meanwhile, it is important to note that abilities form a very special kind of dispositions. Usually, dispositions can be circumscribed in the form of conditionals: *if* zinc is dropped into sulphuric acid, it dissolves; *if* this cup falls to the ground, it will break, etc. If we try to describe abilities in this way, there is one antecedent clause to which our attention is inevitably directed, viz. a person's *choosing* or *deciding* or *trying* to do the thing in question. What it means for me to possess the ability to lift the stone which is lying at my feet can neatly be described as follows: if I choose to lift this stone at t, the stone will be lifted at t. For clearly, given my choice to lift the stone at t, the only possible reason why the stone is not lifted at t is that I lack the power, i.e. the ability to do so.[32] Thus, in speaking about the power of human beings, the occasioning condition is usually to be identified as their will or choice to activate this power.

Of course we should distinguish such a choice from a tendency to behave in a certain way. Here, we have to draw two crucial distinctions, viz. one between power and influence and another between intended and unintended power. In a sense, influence can be considered as a soft form of power. If we imagine a scale of power, it may be placed at one of the extremes, the other extreme referring to "hard" forms of power like physical force or domination.[33] This is not entirely adequate, however. For we also know instances of influence which we are definitely not prepared to classify as forms of power. For example, we may speak about Cézanne's influence on painting, but find it odd to substitute "power" for "influence" here, since we do not usually ascribe powers to the dead. In this case, influence may be seen as a tendency to affect others, in which no clear decision of the will is involved. In other words: influence is not necessarily intended.[34] Only if it is, (for example, if we *make use of* the influence we have), are we inclined to treat influence as an instance of power. Power, it seems, being the ability to *effect* outcomes, presupposes for its exercise a decision of the will, i.e an intention.[35]

This suggests a rather neat and clear-cut distinction between power and influence. Indeed, a good many theories of power include in their definition of power the notion of intentionality, following the example of Bertrand Russell in this respect.[36] There are some problems, however, regard-

---

[32] Provided, of course, that I am in the *opportunity* to lift the stone; but this is guaranteed by the clause that the stone is lying at my feet.

[33] For elaborations of this idea of a power-scale, see Partridge, "Some Notes," 107-125; S.I. Benn, "Power," in: P. Edwards (ed.), *Encyclopedia of Philosophy*, New York 1967, Vol.6, 424; Case-Winters, *God's Power*, 33f.

[34] Cf. the well-known case of a parent who has the unintended influence of stiffening her child's determination to be as different from her as possible.

[35] Cf. Morriss, *Power*, Ch.5.

[36] B. Russell, *Power: A New Social Analysis*, London 1938, p.35, defines power as "the production of intended effects," thus not only including intentionality in the definition of power,

ing the relation between power and intentionality. For certainly in ordinary language we distinguish forms of power the exercise of which does not require a conscious decision of the will. All powers we attribute to inanimate things rather than to persons must be mentioned here. The power of a stormy sea to wreck a ship can hardly be maintained to be intentional (perhaps that is why we are so eager to declare it anthropomorphic...). Moreover, although we would perhaps hesitate to say that he *uses* it, the careless smoker who causes fire in this way certainly *manifests* his power (i.e., his ability) to cause fire. These examples falsify the inclusion of intentionality in the description of power. Therefore it is wrong to argue that intention is part of the definition of power.[37]

Rather, we should consider human abilities which are exercised unintentionally to constitute a special form of power, which is related to the classical category of *passive* power.[38] To understand a language, for example, is an example of a power or ability which does not involve an action. If I know French, I do not intentionally choose or try to understand a French discussion which happens to be held within earshot; or compare the ability of male adults to grow a beard. As to the careless smoker, surely the throwing away of a cigarette does involve an action, but if we assume that unintended consequences are not necessarily included in the description of an action, setting the forest on fire is not an (intentional) action of the careless smoker. Rather, it is comparable in this respect to the exercise of a passive power. If he is held responsible for it, this is because he *refrained* from acting intentionally. In the same way, I might be held responsible for overhearing a French conversation taking place within earshot.

Thus, although intentionality is involved in many manifestations of power, it is not necessarily bound up with it. In fact, this is also the case with many other power-related concepts. There is no "hard core" of power, but only a "family of ability concepts," displaying a number of features which often but not always play a role in the phenomenon of power in diverse and complex ways.[39] Let us finally illustrate this by considering the concept of *authority* in its relation to power.

---

but also equating power with its exercise.

[37] Here I part company with Morriss; see his *Power*, 27. Cf. on the example of the careless smoker ibid., 20f., a passage correcting a mistake of Gibson, "Power," 103, who nevertheless is right in his argument that the careless smoker offers an example of unintentionally exercised power. The example stems from Benn, "Power," 426.

[38] For the reintroduction of this concept in the contemporary debate (albeit in a modified sense), and for the difference between a passive ability and a liability, see Morriss, *Power*, ch.13.

[39] For this method of analyzing "power," see Benn, "Power," 424. Benn enumerates five features of power, acknowledging that not every feature is present in every instance in which we properly speak of power.

3.2.4 *Power and authority*

Authority differs from power in that it is an unambiguously relational and social phenomenon. This being widely agreed upon, there is no further consensus about their mutual relation. As a result, we are faced with many questions. Is authority a special form of power, as some writers claim,[40] or is power rather a special form of authority, as others hold?[41] Or are power and authority distinct and mutually exclusive concepts? And if the latter is the case, should we consider power to be the most desirable property,[42] or rather authority?[43] As often, the confusion on these matters is a result of the fact that the concept of authority, like that of power, has been employed to fulfill different tasks. Thus, in order to solve the problems we have to draw some distinctions which make us aware of the variety of meanings which are attached to the concept of authority.

To begin with, "authority" can be employed both in a *de jure* and in a *de facto* sense. When we state that a particular person has authority, we may mean by this that this person has the right to issue commands of a particular kind and enforce obedience to them. This right is not necessarily acknowledged by those who are subject to the person's authority (who may even try to resist it), but is due to the person in accordance with the set of rules or legal conventions - including, presumably, some method of entitlement - which is prevalent in that particular society.[44] In so far as this *de jure* authority consists in the right not only to issue commands but also to enforce their execution, it is a special type of power, viz. *legitimate* power, which can be exercized by means of physical force. This corresponds to the classical Weberian definition of authority,[45] and at the same time explains

---

[40] E.g. Van Doorn, "Sociology," 22: "... 'authority' is in fact a type of power."

[41] Barry Barnes, "On Authority and its Relationship to Power," in: J. Law (ed.), *Power, Action and Belief*, London 1986, 182: "Whereas a power directs a routine with discretion, an authority directs it without discretion. ... Authority, then, is power minus discretion." Although Barnes is not completely clear on this point, the latter statement might be translated as: power is authority plus discretion.

[42] As e.g. Hannah Arendt, *On Violence*, London 1970, 44f., who defines "power" harmoniously as "the human ability not just to act but to act in concert," whereas she determines the hallmark of authority in much more negative terms as "unquestioning recognition by those who are asked to obey." Thus, whereas power implies equality, authority essentially points to inequality.

[43] As e.g. Richard S. Peters, "Authority," in: Richard E. Flathman (ed.), *Concepts in Social & Political Philosophy*, New York 1973, 154: "It is only when a system of authority breaks down or a given individual loses his authority that there must be recourse to power if conformity is to be ensured. The concept of 'authority' is necessary to bring out the ways in which behaviour is regulated *without* recourse to power...".

[44] Cf. Richard B. Friedman, "On the Concept of Authority in Political Philosophy," in: Flathman (ed.), *Concepts*, 125f., and S. Lukes, "Power and Authority," in: T. Bottomore & R. Nisbet (eds.), *A History of Sociological Analysis*, London 1978, 640. Lukes, whose concise remarks are more to the point here than the lengthier formulations of Friedman, rightly indicates that the concepts of both *de jure* and *de facto* authority reflect a descriptive as opposed to a normative approach of authority.

[45] Weber, *Theory*, 157 characterizes authority as the "legitimate use of physical force." See

why those who seize power find it advantageous to transform their "naked power" into authority.[46] So in this sense, the concept of authority overlaps with that of power, and even with that of violence. Its function here is to distinguish between legitimate and illegitimate forms of coercive power.

Sometimes, however, when we state that someone has authority we mean this in a *de facto* sense, viz. as a report of our observation that those subject to the person who has authority acknowledge his right to issue commands of a special type. Here, the acknowledgement of the ruler's authority by those under his control is a necessary condition for its very existence![47] This use of the concept of authority elucidates how it is possible to claim that authority relations may imply the *absence* of power. Since the person who exerts authority is recognized by those under his control as having the right to do so, he need neither use violence to implement his commands nor threaten to do so, nor (in the extreme case) offer any arguments in support of his commands. Thus, if we take authority in this *de facto* sense, talk of power seems out of place.

Now in a sense this conclusion as it stands is not completely correct. For although the exercise of *de facto* authority is not accompanied by the use of physical or psychical force, it certainly originates in an ability to bring things about, i.e. in some form of power.[48] Bearing this in mind, we can summarize the difference between power and both meanings of authority by saying that whereas power, taken as "force," coerces, authority obliges. In the case of *de facto* authority the obligation is acknowledged, in the case of *de jure* authority this is not necessarily the case, in spite of the authority's legal right to oblige. Accordingly, the concept of authority points to two different sorts of situations: the situation of coerced obedience (*de jure* authority) and non-coerced deferential obedience (*de facto* authority).[49] In contrast to the concept of power, both concepts of authority presuppose *legitimation*.

This does not imply, however, that power in its general meaning as "ability to bring about" and authority are mutually exclusive concepts. For certainly the *de facto* authoritative person does hold power; only, the person does not exercise it by using separate means (neither external ones, such as violence, threats, rewards etc., nor internal ones such as rational arguments),

---

also Talcott Parsons's description of authority as the institutionalized legitimation which underlies power (in his *Sociological Theory*; cf. the discussion in Clegg, *Frameworks*, 130-137).

[46] For some qualifications of this formulation, see Barry Barnes, *The Nature of Power*, Oxford 1988, 121ff.

[47] Cf. Evans, *The Logic of Self-Involvement*, 170-173.

[48] Cf. M.D. Bayles, "The Functions and Limits of Political Authority," in: R. Baine Harris (ed.), *Authority: A Philosophical Analysis*, Alabama 1976, 102, where a distinction is drawn between a social science concept of power, covering all abilities of X to make Y perform some action, and an ordinary concept of power, covering only the instances in which X uses external means (like coercion) to make Y perform that action.

[49] Cf. Friedman, "On the Concept," 127.

130

but in virtue of the formal position he finds himself in, or in virtue of the kind of person he is. In order to clarify this latter point in more detail, let us develop another distinction. If someone exerts *de facto* authority, it may be that people simply acknowledge this authority because of his authoritative position, i.e. because of the fact that he is *in* authority. (This is the sense in which, for example, Dutch citizens usually acknowledge "the Dutch authorities.") But this need not necessarily be so. It may also be the case, that the person who has authority does not at all possess such an official position, but derives his authority from some personal quality of his. In that case, we say that such a person is *an* authority.[50] Four explanatory comments are fitting here.

First, the personal qualities which function as *grounds* for someone's being an authority may vary considerably, but they are always bound up with some special insight the authority is claimed to have on a particular field. This insight may be of a religious, a scientific, a political nature etc. Second, to be an authority is in a sense to possess the most desirable form of authority, since not only power but even a formal legitimation is unnecessary for the exercise of this form of authority. Although people who are authorities in a certain branch sometimes have related formal appointments that underline their authority, this is not necessarily the case. Third, if someone is in authority, although it may be that he has subsequently grown into an authority as well, the system of authority is *logically prior* to the person. On the other hand, if someone is an authority, even if (perhaps as a result; cf., for example, Vaclav Havel in Czechoslovakia) he would also become a person in authority, his personality is logically prior to the system. Fourth, to be *in* authority is often connected with the ability to influence the *conduct* of other people, and to be *an* authority with the ability to influence their *beliefs*. We should keep in mind, however, that belief and action are to a larger degree interdependent than this distinction suggests. For example, if I am a diabetic, someone who is an authority on diabetes may influence not only my beliefs but also my eating behaviour. Conversely, someone who is in authority may influence my beliefs, for example by stimulating the ideological distortion of history.

Interestingly, both kinds of *de facto* authority share two important features. First, they are constituted by "that special and distinctive kind of dependence on the will or judgment of another so well conveyed by the

---

[50] See on this distinction, for example, Friedman, "On the Concept," 139-146; Peters, "Authority," 149-151. The distinction between "in authority" and "an authority" roughly coincides with Weber's distinction between traditional and charismatic authority, cf. his *Theory*, 301. It is also basic in J.M. Bocheński, *Was ist Autorität?*, Freiburg i.Br. 1974, who puts it in yet another (and more precise) terminology by differentiating between epistemic and deontic authority (49-56). In general, I want to refer to Bocheński's instructive study as a whole for a more extensive analysis of the logic of authority than I can provide here. Cf. also his "An Analysis of Authority," in: F.J. Adelmann (ed.), *Authority*, The Hague 1974, 56-85.

notion of a 'surrender of private judgment'."[51] In the case of *an* authority, to accept authority is to take a shortcut to the place where reason is presumed to lead. If I believe something on authority, I do so without questioning the reasons my authority has for his utterances, because I trust that these will be good reasons. In the case of people who are *in* authority, however, my compliance with authoritative commands does not imply my personal agreement with them. But even if I don't agree with the person in authority on a particular utterance of his, I surrender my private judgment in order to follow the decision the authority has taken.[52]

Secondly, the authority relation involves "a certain kind of recognition that the person to whom one defers is entitled to this sort of submission."[53] As indicated above, a person *in* authority derives this entitlement from his position, whereas someone who is *an* authority owes his entitlement to his personal qualities. In both cases, to accept someone as being entitled to speak authoritatively is basically an act of *belief.* Either I believe that some institutional structure is sufficiently justified for me to act in accordance with it, or I believe that some person is sufficiently qualified for me to rely upon his judgment.

Now both this act of belief as well as the surrender of private judgment may suggest that to believe or act upon authority is essentially irrational. Such a suggestion may in turn lead to a negative appraisal of the whole phenomenon of authority, as is in fact the case in much post-Enlightenment discourse. It is important to note, however, that this is incorrect. For I may have perfectly good reasons not to rely and act upon my own judgment. In the case of *an* authority such reasons correspond to the superior personal qualities I know someone to have. For example, the forementioned diabetic does not require a comprehensive rational argumentation before being prepared to use some medicine recommended by his consultant. In the case of someone *in* authority my reasons not to act upon my own judgment correspond to my second-order judgment that acting upon my own judgment will lead to a less desirable overall state of affairs. For example, I may judge it a wrong decision of those in authority to raise taxes, but nevertheless pay the raised taxes since my refusing to do so would promote anarchism, which I consider to be a less desirable overall state of affairs. In practice, all of us believe and act upon authority in myriads of situations.

In all forms of authority discussed above - *de jure* and *de facto*, "in authority" and "an authority" - we have to do with abilities or capacities to

---

[51] Friedman, "On the Concept," 131; for an elaboration of the two "dimensions" of all *de facto* authority, see ibid., 127-134, and Lukes, "Power and Authority," 639-641. As both writers observe, the phrase "surrender of private judgment" must be qualified in cases in which people simply lack such a private judgment, because they have never been in the opportunity to develop one.

[52] For a useful discussion of this point, see Friedman, "On the Concept," 132, 141.

[53] Ibid., 131.

bring things about, i.e. with power. There is one use of the term "authority," however, which points to a *lack* of power. This is when we apply the term, as we sometimes do, to representatives of people who are in authority, and focus upon the relation between the authority and his representative. In this sense, one might argue that policemen have authority but lack power. They are simply the representatives of the authorities who must see to the execution of their laws, but lack the power to bring about things in accordance with their own will.

Barry Barnes even goes as far as arguing that *all* forms of authority should be described in this way, and defines authority as "power minus discretion,"[54] so as something less than power. But this is rather odd, and certainly incompatible with most of the normal functions of "authority." Moreover, even in the case of representatives it can be questioned whether they indeed lack power. After all, even when they act under orders they exercise their abilities to bring things about. But let us grant that in fact they do not exercise their own power in such cases, but only extend and execute the powers of their superiors. At least, a case can be made for this point of view. We may conclude, then, that here in the end we have come across a function of the concept of authority which might entail the absence of power. On the other hand, there are forms of power which have nothing to do at all with authority. This is true, for example, for my power to lift my arm (which surely will not make me "an authority on arm-lifting," since most people possess this power).

3.2.5 *Conclusion*
Let us now, finally, summarize the results of our examination of "the logic of power." It is difficult if not impossible to offer a clear-cut definition of "power," going beyond the statement that power is the ability to effect or bring about things.[55] Its nature is clarified to a larger degree, however, by analyzing its relations to kindred notions belonging to "the family of ability concepts." In doing so, we came to the conclusion that in many but not all cases the presence and exercise of power coincides with a conflict of interests, with a relationship between people, with influence, with intentional action, and with the possession and recognition of authority. The proviso "but not all," however, is of crucial importance to the logic of power.

In conceptualizing omnipotence in terms of power, it will turn out that this proviso is both a hindrance and a help. It is a hindrance, because

---

[54] See above, note 41.

[55] Cf. Lukes, "Introduction," in: id. (ed.), *Power*, 4f.: "It is more likely that the very search for such a definition [of power] is a mistake. For the variations in what interests us when we are interested in power run deep ... and what unites the various views of power is too thin and formal to provide a generally satisfying definition, applicable to all cases." Lukes goes on, then, to propose the following "thin" description which roughly agrees with the one we give here: "to have power is to be able to make a difference to the world" (5).

if we are unaware of this "but not all" it can easily happen that we convey certain aspects of power to omnipotence which are definitely out of order. For example, this may be the case (as we saw in §3.2.2) when the conflictual aspect of power is included in our conception of omnipotence.

It is a help, however, as soon as we become conscious of the large variety of ways in which the concept of power is used. For then we are in a position to specify which aspects of power are to be ascribed to God when He is called omnipotent and which are not. For example, as to God's power in His relationship to human beings, we might specify this aspect of the divine omnipotence as a form of coercion, so that God's will is in itself a sufficient condition to bring something about. Or alternatively, we might consider God's omnipotence over people as a form of *de facto* authority, so that God's will is a necessary but not a sufficient condition to bring something about, since the *recognition* of God's authority is also required. Whereas the former option leads to a description of the relationship between God and human beings in causal terms, the latter views this relationship in covenantal terms.

In this section, we have undertaken the task to spell out what it means to have power. In doing this we have concentrated upon the phrase "potence" as part of the concept of omnipotence. Traditionally, however, the other part of the term, the qualifier "omni," has caused more conceptual problems in defining omnipotence, and accordingly received more attention. It is to these problems that we turn next.

3.3 THE ANALYSIS OF OMNIPOTENCE

3.3.1 *The problem of omnipotence*
In recent Anglo-Saxon analytical philosophy there has been a considerable amount of interest in questions regarding the concept of omnipotence. Between 1955 and 1990 over one hundred journal articles and chapters, contributions or sections in books were in some way or another devoted to problems concerning the concept of omnipotence. In what follows, I join this field of debate in order to examine the conceptual implications of connecting the quantifier "omni" to the concept of power. I will not, however, discuss or even quote all of these contributions, but make a reasonable choice in the light of this singular interest. Thus, I will focus on studies dealing with the definition and conceptual analysis of omnipotence, rather than with metaphysical[1] or epistemological[2] questions concerning omnipotence.[3] Before developing my own position, it seems helpful first to trace

---

[1] Such as, e.g., the discussion between Paul Kuntz, Donald Dunbar, and Leonard Eslick in *NS* 42 (1968), 270-292.

[2] Cf., e.g., D. Lackey, "The Epistemology of Omnipotence," *RS* 15 (1979), 25-30.

[3] For a collection of summaries of contemporary literature dealing with omnipotence up until

the main thrust of the relevant literature in order to set out the parameters within which my own discussion will have to be conducted.

However, my intentions in this section are not merely descriptive. What I hope to show in rendering the contemporary discussions is that what I will call the literal concept of omnipotence, especially when it comes to be applied in the doctrine of God, is so heavily fraught with highly complicated conceptual difficulties, that the prospects for offering a coherent account of it are very bleak indeed. In particular, I hope to show three things. First, that the general effort to produce a correct all-embracing *definition* of omnipotence is in a sense misplaced; second, that the source of many of the conceptual problems concerning omnipotence have to do with what we may by now call the "Cartesian problem," viz. the relation between omnipotence and modal logic; and third, that most of the debates on the definition of omnipotence are characterized by a profound tension between two alternative conceptions of omnipotence, viz. a literal or philosophical and a theological one. I will suggest that the situation becomes much more hopeful, however, if we found sufficient reason for making the clear choice here of unambiguously rejecting the literal conception and embracing its theologically qualified alternative. In the next section, I hope to show that there is independent and sufficient reason for this choice indeed.

3.3.2 *The paradox of omnipotence*

The philosopher who is often rightly credited as initiator of the post-war philosophical debates on omnipotence is J.L. Mackie. In his seminal article "Evil and Omnipotence," Mackie claims that the traditional problem of evil as formulated in the classical "trilemma," shows that religious beliefs "are positively irrational, that the several parts of the essential theological doctrine are inconsistent with one another, so that the theologian can maintain his position as a whole only by a[n] ... extreme rejection of reason."[4] Next, Mackie discusses several theistic responses intended to escape this conclusion, one of which assumes that God has made men so free that He *cannot* control their wills. This leads Mackie to what he calls the "Paradox of Omnipotence": can an omnipotent being make things which he cannot subsequently control? Mackie observes that "the answers 'Yes' and 'No' are equally irreconcilable with God's omnipotence,"[5] then proposes a kind of

---

1977, see William J. Wainwright, *Philosophy of Religion: An Annotated Bibliography of Twentieth-Century Writings in English*, New York 1978, 61-85. A useful anthology which covers work up until approximately the same year (including many classic texts from earlier centuries) is Linwood Urban & Douglas N. Walton (eds.), *The Power of God: Readings on Omnipotence and Evil*, New York 1978. Bibliographic references to more recent titles are included in Frank Blaakmeer, Pieter J. Huiser & Nelleke van der Plas (eds.), *Philosophy of Religion. A Select Bibliography 1974-1986*, Groningen 1988 (cf. 99f.).

[4] "Evil and Omnipotence" originally appeared in *Mind* 64 (1955), 200-212; I quote from the reprint in Urban & Walton, *Power of God*, 17.

[5] Ibid., 29.

solution, but nevertheless sees himself forced to the conclusion that "... what the paradox shows is that we cannot consistently ascribe to any continuing being omnipotence in an inclusive sense."[6]

It is interesting to note that Mackie focused mainly on one aspect of the traditional doctrine of divine omnipotence as outlined in chapter 2, viz. on God's ability to make things or bring about states of affairs. By concentrating on what we labelled "C-power," Mackie seemed to be insensitive to the dimensions of A- and B-power, i.e. to the original religious connotations of the property of omnipotence. Apart from the many reactions provoked by Mackie's atheistic argument from evil,[7] his presentation of the omnipotence-paradox lead to a separate series of subsequent papers as well. In the light of our observation, the very first reply in this series was at the same time one of the most interesting ones: Ian Ramsey argued that the paradox of omnipotence, based as it is on a misunderstanding of the true nature of religious language, is in fact a pseudo-problem. According to Ramsey, the theological meaning of "omnipotence" cannot adequately be grasped by simply extrapolating from the meaning of "power" in everyday language.[8] Although Ramsey illustrates this point by interpreting omnipotence as power-over rather than power-to (or as A-power rather than C-power), by attacking Mackie he suggests that this criticism is applicable to a power-to conception of omnipotence as well.

Other, more straightforwardly philosophical contributions, however, tried to rebut the charge that omnipotence is an inconsistent concept by proposing alternative solutions to Mackie's paradox and similar riddles ("Can an omnipotent being make an unliftable stone?"; "Can it make a being it cannot destroy?," etc.). In the course of the discussion three different types of response to such paradoxes crystallized. Some authors argued that what Mackie's paradox actually states is simply that if an omnipotent being can make a thing, then by definition it can control it.[9] Others emphasized that, given the assumption that God is omnipotent, the task of "making a

---

[6] Ibid., 30.

[7] The most well-known of these are no doubt Alvin Plantinga's publications on the free will defence, the first of which was "The Free Will Defence," in: Max Black (ed.), *Philosophy in America*, London 1965, 204-220; cf. further his *God, Freedom, and Evil*, Grand Rapids 1974, 12-24, 32f., and §4.4.2 below.

[8] Ian T. Ramsey, "The Paradox of Omnipotence," *Mind* 65 (1956), 263-266. Unfortunately, Ramsey does not offer us a positive clue as to what the theological meaning of omnipotence does consist of. For some attempts to give such a clue, see Jerome Gellman, "The Paradox of Omnipotence, and Perfection," *Sophia* 14.3 (1975), 31-39; Philip E. Devenish, "Omnipotence, Creation, Perfection: Kenny and Aquinas on the Power and Action of God," *MTh* 1 (1985), 114-116.

[9] G.B. Keene, "A Simpler Solution to the Paradox of Omnipotence," *Mind* 69 (1960), 74f.; id., "Capacity Limiting Statements," *Mind* 70 (1961), 251f.; C. Wade Savage, "The Paradox of the Stone," *PR* 76 (1967), 74-79 (also included in Urban & Walton, *Power of God*, 138-143); M. McLean, "The Unmakable-Because-Unliftable Stone," *CJP* 4 (1975), 717-721. This last article is a clear piece of writing, which would have deserved a better fortune than being practically neglected in subsequent discussion.

being which God cannot control" and phrases such as "a stone too heavy for God to lift" are self-contradictory. Thus the paradoxes demand from an omnipotent God to do things which are logically impossible for Him to do. And either an omnipotent God can even do what is logically impossible,[10] or the fact that He cannot do what is logically impossible does not count against His omnipotence.[11] A third group of philosophers objected against the method of presupposing that God is omnipotent in the first place, and considered the paradox as an elegant demonstration of the fact that it is logically inconsistent to ascribe all abilities (omni-potence) to one and the same subject. These authors usually shared Mackie's conclusion that omnipotence cannot be attributed to God, so that (if God exists) God's power must necessarily be limited in one way or another.[12]

3.3.3 *The definition of omnipotence*

In order to clarify the paradox of omnipotence it is necessary to have a clear understanding of what omnipotence is. Therefore, it was an important shift in the direction which the discussion took when Peter Geach, especially in the first of his two articles on omnipotence, started the search for a sound *definition* of omnipotence. In this article, which we discussed before (§2.2), Geach tried to show inductively that an adequate definition of the concept of "omnipotence" is not only philosophically impossible, but also religiously superfluous, since what really matters is God's almightiness rather than His alleged omnipotence.[13] Although this claim turned out to be highly controversial, the result of Geach's approach was that subsequent attention began to shift from the search for a satisfactory solution of the paradox towards the quest for an adequate definition of the very concept of (divine) omnipotence. Although separate discussions of the paradox, not preceded by some specific definition-proposal, continued to appear,[14] most writers now

---

[10] Frankfurt, "Logic of Omnipotence"; also in Urban & Walton, *Power of God*, 135-137. Cf. the "standard-reading" of Descartes' doctrine of omnipotence as described in §2.4.2 above.

[11] B. Mayo, "Mr. Keene on Omnipotence," *Mind* 70 (1961), 249f.; George I. Mavrodes, "Some Puzzles Concerning Omnipotence," *PR* 72 (1963), 221-223 (also in Urban & Walton, *Power of God*, 131-134); Alvin Plantinga, *God and Other Minds*, 168-173; Terence Penelhum, *Religion and Rationality*, New York 1971, 231.

[12] A.F. Bonifacio, "On Capacity Limiting Statements," *Mind* 74 (1965), 87f.; J.L. Cowan, "The Paradox of Omnipotence," *Analysis*, Supplement to Vol. 25 (1964/1965), 102-108 (= Urban & Walton, *Power of God*, 144-152); id., "The Paradox of Omnipotence Revisited," *CJP* 3 (1974), 435-445; S. Gendin, "Omnidoing," *Sophia* 6.3 (1967), 17-22; George Englebretsen, "The Incompatibility of God's Existence and Omnipotence," *Sophia* 10.1 (1971), 28-31. Julian Wolfe, "Omnipotence," *CJP* 1 (1971), 245-247, on the other hand, argues that although God lacks the ability to do certain non-contradictory things (such as creating a stone which its maker cannot lift), He might nevertheless be omnipotent.

[13] Geach, "Omnipotence." Regardless of whether Geach utters a sound intuition here (which is what I hope to show later on), the merits of his argument are sometimes overestimated; for a convincing refutation of one of its crucial steps, see Murray MacBeath, "Geach on Omnipotence and Virginity," *Philosophy* 63 (1988), 395-400.

[14] Such as Douglas Walton, "The Omnipotence Paradox," *CJP* 4 (1975), 705-715 (included

accommodated their response to the paradox to the outcome of their discussion of the definition of omnipotence.

In an earlier stage Mackie had already proposed a definition of omnipotence in a second paper of his, but this contribution, though equally innovative, proved much less influential than his first one.[15] Furthermore, Plantinga had attempted to develop a sound definition of omnipotence in order to solve the paradox, but he had given up rather quickly, switching to a solution of the paradox independent of any particular definition of omnipotence.[16]

In the same year as Geach's first article, Richard Swinburne published an important paper on omnipotence which also concentrated upon the project of defining the concept. In contrast to Geach, however, Swinburne not only claimed that a sound definition of omnipotence is possible, but also developed one himself. In the course of doing this, Swinburne was the first one to make explicit a point to which Plantinga and Cargile had only alluded,[17] namely that omnipotence need not be a *necessary* property of an omnipotent being. If omnipotence is considered as a *contingent* attribute, all capacity limiting statements (and "power curtailing actions" or "essentially reflexive tasks"), including those of the omnipotence paradox, lose their problematic character. Under this assumption God is certainly able to make a thing which He cannot subsequently control, and thus to abandon His omnipotence. But this does not at all endanger His omnipotence as long as He freely refrains from making such a thing. "A being may remain omnipotent for ever because he never exercises his power to create stones too heavy to lift, forces too strong to resist, or universes too wayward to control."[18]

As a result of both Geach's and Swinburne's contributions, subsequent discussion centred more and more on the question whether it is possible to develop a tenable definition of omnipotence, and if so what such a definition looks like. In a couple of short papers Richard R. La Croix tried to show deductively what Geach had attempted to show inductively, viz.

---

in Urban & Walton, *Power of God*, 153-174).

[15] Mackie, "Omnipotence," *Sophia* 1.2 (1962), 13-25; a slightly revised version is in Urban & Walton, *Power of God*, 73-88. Here, the definition occurs on 78: ".. God's omnipotence includes only the power to make it to be that X in all cases where X, and making-it-to-be-that-X, are logically possible and where God's-making-it-to-be-that-X is neither paradoxical nor incompatible with logically necessary aspects of God's nature." Mackie acknowledges that on this definition the paradox of omnipotence as put forward in his earlier paper can be solved (83f.).

[16] Plantinga, *God and Other Minds*, 169ff.; James Cargile, "On Omnipotence," *Noûs* 1 (1967), 201-205, continued where Plantinga had made a halt; the result, however, was a highly complicated definition intended to solve only one self-construed (pseudo-)problem. See for telling criticism Wainwright, *Philosophy of Religion*, 62f.

[17] Plantinga, *God and Other Minds*, 171; Cargile, "On Omnipotence," 202.

[18] Richard Swinburne, "Omnipotence," *APQ* 10 (1973), 236; a revised version of this article is included as chapter 9 in Swinburne's *The Coherence of Theism*, Oxford 1977.

"the impossibility of defining 'omnipotence'."[19] Challenged by this contention, Mavrodes put forward a definition which he claimed to be immune to La Croix's criticisms, but which in turn was attacked by La Croix as well as by others.[20] Nevertheless, attempts to define omnipotence continued, and criticisms against them gradually took the form of rejections of the analysis of a particular author or issue, rather than denying in general the very possibility of defining omnipotence. If we neglect details and technicalities, the standard strategy in this phase came to be as follows:

1. Start with an intuitively appealing candidate for a definition of (divine) omnipotence, e.g., "God can do all things."
2. Proceed to refine this provisional definition by offering counterexamples against this and subsequent candidates, taking into account the work of other authors.
3. Declare the fourth or fifth candidate to be immune of any possible further flaw you can imagine, and thus take this candidate to express the "real" meaning of omnipotence.
4. Test your final definition by confronting it with some notorious (and usually rather strange) puzzles, such as those specified by the paradoxes of omnipotence. Show how all difficulties and objections involved in these puzzles can satisfactorily be solved given your definition.[21]

Many recent studies on omnipotence still follow basically the same inductive method.[22] A chronological reading of this group of texts leads one to notice two interesting developments.

First, a sort of consensus seems to have come about as to how the

---

[19] As is the title of his most noted article, published in *PS* 32 (1977), 181-190; other contributions of La Croix include "Swinburne on Omnipotence," *IJPR* 6 (1975), 251-255, and "Failing to Define Omnipotence," *PS* 34 (1978), 219-222. See also note 50 below.

[20] G.I. Mavrodes, "Defining Omnipotence," *PS* 32 (1977), 191-202; La Croix, "Failing to Define Omnipotence"; Joshua Hoffman, "Mavrodes on Defining Omnipotence," *PS* 35 (1979), 311-313; B.R. Reichenbach, "Mavrodes on Omnipotence," *PS* 37 (1980), 211-214.

[21] As far as I know the first author following this procedure was James F. Ross, *Philosophical Theology*, Indianapolis 1969 (1980²), 195-221, though rudimentary features of it are already present in Plantinga, *God and Other Minds*, 168-173, and Mackie, "Omnipotence," 15ff. Others who structured their argument in this way include Swinburne (cf. his article cited in note 18 above); Robert Young, *Freedom, Responsibility and God*, London 1975, 186-201; Rebecca D. Pentz, *Formal Adequacy of Saint Thomas Aquinas' Analysis of Omnipotence*; David E. Schrader, "A Solution to the Stone Paradox," *Synthese* 42 (1979), 255-264; Gary Rosenkrantz & Joshua Hoffman, "What an Omnipotent Agent Can Do," *IJPR* 11 (1980), 1-19; and Stephen T. Davis in an admirably clear exposition in his *Logic*, 68-85.

[22] Cf. most recently Edward Wierenga, *The Nature of God*, Notre Dame 1989, 12-35. In a footnote which might be seen as a predecessor of the present section Wierenga also indicates some broad areas of agreement and disagreement in current literature on defining omnipotence (14f., n.9).

paradox(es) of omnipotence should be dealt with. Although attempts to defend one particular solution over against others continue to be undertaken,[23] it is increasingly recognized that there is not just one and only one solution to the paradox. Rather, what may count as the solution depends upon the sort of omnipotence one has in mind. If we assume that a being is *essentially* omnipotent, then making beings which it cannot control, stones which it cannot lift etc. are self-contradictory tasks. Thus, the fact that an omnipotent being cannot perform them does not count against its omnipotence, since self-contradictory tasks *logically* cannot be performed, and are in fact no tasks at all. It is presupposed here that what is logically impossible does not fall under the realm of omnipotence. On the other hand, if a being is *accidentally* or contingently omnipotent, there is no reason to suppose that it is unable to perform the tasks specified by the paradoxes. In this way, both the Mayo-Mavrodes solution and Swinburne's solution are correct, but they apply to different situations.[24] It seems to me that this concensus is to be accepted, and that therefore we have reached the point where we may stop quarrelling about the paradox of omnipotence.

Second, unlike solutions to the paradoxes, proposals to *define* omnipotence (although proliferating) do not seem to develop in the direction of a consensus. Rather, they tend to get entangled in different ways in a mass of technicalities. In recent literature we encounter many divergent definitions, most of which are less than elegant as a result of various kinds of complicated *ad hoc* restrictions. Consequently, the very claim that an unambiguous definition of the concept of omnipotence is possible is in danger of dying the death of a thousand qualifications. The most striking

---

[23] Thus, Loren Meierding, "The Impossibility of Necessary Omnitemporal Omnipotence," *IJPR* 11 (1980), 21-26 claims to provide a formal proof that verifies Swinburne's solution of the paradox. On the other hand, C. Anthony Anderson, "Divine Omnipotence and Impossible Tasks: An Intentional Analysis," *IJPR* 15 (1984), 109-124 tries to illustrate "the relevance and utility of logic for rational theology" (110) by invoking intensional logic to prove just the opposite position, i.e., to show that only the Mayo-Mavrodes analysis indicates the proper solution of the paradox. The fact that Meierding's and Anderson's formalizations contradict each other (as a result of their slightly different presuppositions) shows that formal logic has no decisive influence on philosophical theology.

[24] This double solution was already suggested by Plantinga, *God and Other Minds*, 168ff.; it is explicitly expounded in E.J. Khamara, "In Defence of Omnipotence," *PQ* 28 (1978), 215-228. Other pleas for the double solution (though in varying conceptualities and with minor differences) include Schrader, "A Solution to the Stone Paradox"; Rosenkrantz & Hoffman, "The Omnipotence Paradox, Modality, and Time," *SJP* 18 (1980), 473-479; Thomas P. Flint & Alfred J. Freddoso, "Maximal Power," in: A.J. Freddoso (ed.), *The Existence & Nature of God*, Notre Dame 1983, 99f. (also included in T.V. Morris (ed.), *The Concept of God*, Notre Dame 1987, 134-167); Wierenga, *Nature of God*, 29-33. Pentz, *Formal Adequacy*, 93-119, also puts forward the double solution, but she further distinguishes between an essentially omnipotent being which is only accidentally eternal (this being is able to perform the paradox-tasks, but would put itself out of existence if it did so), and one which is essentially eternal (so that its inability to perform the paradox-tasks does not count against its omnipotence).

140

example in this respect is offered by C. Anthony Anderson. According to him, what we mean (or should mean) when we use the word omnipotence might best be formally expressed as follows:

(D2) Maxomnip(x)=df (F)[Tsk(F)⊃.◊F(x)⊃Can(x,F)].
·◊ [∃y)((F)[Tsk(F)⊃.Shr(F)⊃.Can(x,F)⊃Can(y,F)).
(∃G)(Tsk(G).Shr(G).Can(y,G).·Can(x,G))].
(D3) Shr(F)=df◊(∃x)(∃y)[x ≠ y.F(x).F(y)].[25]

Hardly less astonishing is W.S. Anglin's policy. After having blamed "traditionally minded philosophers" for the fact that their definitions of omnipotence are "rather long and clumsy,"[26] Anglin goes on to produce his own definition. Here is the result:

x is omnipotent if and only if

(i)   x is a person (with libertarian free will) who has the power knowingly to create or destroy any contingent thing; and

(ii)   it is not logically possible that there be some person who has all of x's nonrelative powers and also some other nonrelative power whose possession is compatible with x's being necessarily omniscient and necessarily good; and

(iii)   there is no limitation on the exercise of x's powers that does not have its source in an exercise of x's libertarian free will.[27]

Now it may well be that this definition avoids some of the pitfalls of its competitors; it does not, however, earn a prize for elegance, simplicity or direct intelligibility. Moreover, although some conceptual problems are taken into account by this definition, other questions and aspects are neglected. For example, is it enough for an omnipotent being to have the power to create or destroy any contingent thing? Should we not expect such a being also to possess the power to keep any contingent thing in existence, or in general: the power to control every entity? Or, suppose that it is logically possible that there be some person who has all of x's powers and also some other nonrelative power whose possession is compatible with x being, say, necessarily wise or necessarily just. Then, clearly, if x is God (and Anglin's second clause is obviously intended to let x be God), God is not omnipotent. Other recent definitions similarly continue to provoke questions and refutations, as is clear from published reactions.[28]

---

[25] Anderson, "Divine Omnipotence," 121; to give him his due, Anderson explains most of his symbols.

[26] W.S. Anglin, *Free Will and the Christian Faith*, Oxford 1990, 48.

[27] Ibid., 64.

[28] In this way Flint & Freddoso, "Maximal Power" is criticized by Gellman, "The Limits of Maximal Power," *PS* 55 (1989), 329-336; and by Rosenkrantz & Hoffman, "Omnipotence Redux," *PPR* 49 (1988), 283-301, in which article they also defend their own work against Wierenga's initial attempt to define omnipotence in E. Wierenga, "Omnipotence Defined," *PPR* 43 (1983),

It is here that my first systematic point comes in. Before producing definitions of omnipotence we should recognize the *function* of presenting a definition. It is the function of a definition either to capture our pre-analytical notion of a concept (descriptive definition) or to summarize the analysis of the way in which a concept should be used (prescriptive definition). In both cases, definitions should be as succinct as possible and intelligible without much additional information. In the latter case, what is really interesting is not the definition of a concept in itself - sometimes it is very difficult to give a definition which is completely satisfying in these respects - but rather the analysis which yields the definition. Accordingly, apart from comprehensive attempts to define the concept of omnipotence, there are also numerous inquiries that limit themselves to the examination of one or more particular aspects which play a role in the *analysis* of omnipotence. Usually, these inquiries concentrate on issues concerning the relation between omnipotence and (1) logic, (2) time, (3) essentialism, (4) the possibility of other omnipotent beings, (5) omniscience, (6) impeccability and (7) human freedom. Analyses of omnipotence which purport to be comprehensive and to lead to an adequate definition of the concept usually discuss some but not all of these areas. In order to find out how to analyse omnipotence let us now briefly explore the problems and give an outline of the main solutions which are discussed under each of these headings.

3.3.4 *Issues under discussion in analysing omnipotence*
First, the question whether an omnipotent being has the power (or should be required to have the power) to bring about logically impossible states of affairs is generally answered in the negative. The same applies to the power to bring about states of affairs which are logically necessary. Nevertheless, from time to time dissident opinions are expressed, urging, for example, that "Descartes was right. God could make a contradiction true."[29] Moreover, some of those who are not dissidents in this extreme sense, try to portray the relation between God and necessarily existing abstract objects (or "eternal truths") in such a way that the latter can in some way or another be said to be dependent upon God. According to them, God is responsible for the existence of abstract objects or necessary truths, since these are created by Him.[30] This amounts to saying that God is responsible for the fact that the

---

363-375. Again, Wierenga's revised edition of his earlier paper in his *Nature of God* is attacked in reviews of this book by Rosenkrantz, *PPR* 51 (1991), 725-728 (see esp. 726), and by Flint, *F&P* 9 (1992), 392-397, esp. 392-394. Of course, the fact that there is no consensus on defining omnipotence does not in itself count against the correctness of any of the proposed definitions.

[29] D. Goldstick, "Could God Make a Contradiction True?," *RS* 26 (1990), 387.

[30] Alvin Plantinga first tentatively suggested this point of view in his *Does God Have a Nature?*, 145f.; two years later, he restated it more self-confidently in "How to Be an Anti-Realist?," *Proceedings and Addresses of the APA* 56 (1982), 70.; his claim was elaborated by T.V. Morris & C. Menzel in their "Absolute Creation," *APQ* 23 (1986), 353-362 (also included

rules of modal logic are as they are. Others, however, deny that a coherent account can be given of what such responsibility consists in, if — as is usually acknowledged by the proponents of this view — it was impossible for God to create them otherwise (or to refrain from creating them at all).[31]

Second, the relation between omnipotence and time is considered in two closely connected questions: Should an adequate definition of omnipotence be time-indexed? And: Does omnipotence entail the power to change or bring about the past? Although there are exceptions also here,[32] the latter question is usually answered in the negative.[33] If it is not, then the first question can be answered in the negative since in that case considerations of time do not pose a particular problem to omnipotent agency anyway. If it is, then the answer to the first question depends upon the argumentation of that to the second. If an omnipotent being lacks the power to bring about the past simply because it is logically impossible to do so, then according to some authors considerations of time need not be included in the definition of omnipotence either.[34] Others, however, hold (but hardly argue) that in spite of the logical impossibility of bringing about the past time-indices are indispensable to an adequate definition of omnipotence.[35]

---

in Morris's *Anselmian Explorations*, 161-178). Similar positions are held within the so-called philosophy of the cosmonomic idea, cf. e.g. Hendrik Hart, "On the Distinction between Creator and Creature," *PRef* 44 (1979), 183-193. Hart's article is directed against N. Wolterstorff's *On Universals*, Chicago 1970, which makes a case for the view that the laws of logic are independent of and co-eternal with God. Cf. also Roy Clouser, "Religious Language: A New Look at an Old Problem," in: H. Hart e.a. (eds.), *Rationality in the Calvinian Tradition*, Lanham (Md.) 1983, 395-401.

[31] Scott A. Davison, "Could Abstract Objects Depend upon God?," *RS* 27 (1991), 485-497. Davison's main charge (ibid., 490-492) against Morris & Menzel had already been rebutted in an ingenious article not mentioned by him: Brian Leftow, "God and Abstract Entities," *F&P* 7 (1990), 194-198. Leftow points to other difficulties in the argument of Morris & Menzel, however, which according to him cannot be overcome without abandoning their position.

[32] An implicitly affirmative answer can be found in, for example, Michael Dummett, "On Bringing About the Past," *PR* 73 (1964), 338-359, and David Lewis, "The Paradoxes of Time Travel," *APQ* 13 (1976), 145-152. An affirmative answer is explicitly defended by Anglin, *Free Will*, 60f., who argues that an omnipotent being has the power but simply lacks the opportunity to change the past. Anglin attributes this idea to Kenny, *God of the Philosophers*, 96f., but Kenny is clearly not prepared to apply his distinction between power and opportunity to the question of power over the past (cf. his chapter 8).

[33] Alan Brinton, "Omnipotence, Timelessness, and the Restoration of the Virgins," *Dialogos* 45 (1985), 149-156. See also Ronald H. Nash, *The Concept of God*, Grand Rapids 1983, 46f., who distils from Kenny's discussion (*God of the Philosophers*, 107f.) three arguments in support of the contention that no sense can be made of the claim that an omnipotent being or anyone else is able to bring about the past.

[34] Cf., e.g., Khamara, "In Defence," 222f.; John Zeis & Jonathan Jacobs, "Omnipotence and Concurrence," *IJPR* 14 (1983), 21f.

[35] E.g. Wierenga, "Omnipotence Defined," 365f.; *Nature of God*, 16f. Although they are not explicit about this, it seems that Rosenkrantz & Hoffman, "Omnipotent Agent," (the first contribution to introduce time-indices in the definition of omnipotence) also assume that it is *logically*

Finally, a temporally relativized concept of omnipotence is also advocated by those who think that it is not logically but "temporally" impossible to have power over the past, and that an omnipotent being should not be required to have such power.[36]

Another way in which the concept of omnipotence is sometimes associated with temporal conditions is by asking what happens when omnipotence is ascribed to a timeless (or atemporal) being. Of course many conceptual puzzles are tied to the idea of a being which is not "in time," but the question is whether the ascription of omnipotence to such a being adds another one. A natural candidate is provided by the following argument: If an omnipotent being cannot bring about the past, then its abilities clearly change through time. For example, in June 1962 such a being was able to prevent me from being born, but in June 1963 it had lost this ability, since I was born in May 1963. Now if a being is atemporal it seems that its abilities cannot change through time. Wierenga is one of the few philosophers who explicitly addresses this problem; it leads him to include an additional condition in his definition of omnipotence which makes it applicable to timeless beings too.[37]

Third, one of the most intractable problems in defining omnipotence is formed by what I would like to refer to as the issue of essentialism. In order to grasp what is at stake here, consider the following proposition:

(1)   There is a table which has not been made by an omnipotent being.

Some philosophers argue that (1), although indicating a logically possible state of affairs, cannot be brought about by an omnipotent being.[38] Others, however, hold that it does belong to the power of an omnipotent being to bring about (1), since to say that the table *was not* made by an omnipotent being is not the same as to say that an omnipotent being *could not* have made it.[39] But even if the latter are right (and it is clear that they are), in any case an omnipotent being lacks the ability to actualize the following logically possible states of affairs:

---

impossible to have power over the past. Since this article, which is almost exclusively focused upon the time-problem in relation to the definition of omnipotence, many subsequent authors provide their omnipotence-definitions with temporal indices. Unfortunately, Rosenkrantz and Hoffman ignore the point that if it is logically impossible to bring about the past, then there seems to be no need to introduce temporal conditions in the definition of omnipotence at all.

[36] As e.g. Flint & Freddoso do, cf. their "Maximal Power," 88. On this special kind of temporal (or: accidental) necessity, see more extensively Freddoso, "Accidental Necessity and Power over the Past," *PPQ* 63 (1982), 54-68.

[37] Wierenga, *Nature of God*, 33-35. Cf. Paul Helm's argument in favour of divine timeless agency in his *Eternal God*, 67-72.

[38] E.g. Plantinga, *God and Other Minds*, 169f.; La Croix, "Impossibility," 181f.

[39] E.g. Mavrodes, "Defining Omnipotence," 194f.; Pentz, *Defense*, 37f.

144

(1')   There is a table which *essentially* has not been made by an omnipotent being.

Given (1'), it is *logically* impossible that this table would have been made by an omnipotent being. Thus, any omnipotent being lacks the ability to make this table. One response to the problem posed by (1') is to claim that entities such as the table specified by it are simply nonsensical.[40] Although it is not immediately clear that this is indeed the case, one can easily grant this point, since the argument does not apply in other situations.

Consider, for example, the following state of affairs, which is no doubt logically possible:

(2)   Jones freely decides to buy a car.

On a common-sense contra-causal understanding of freedom, (2) describes a state of affairs which it is logically impossible to bring about for any being other than Jones. We will return to the special status of propositions about human free actions later on, but for now it suffices to observe that here at last we seem to have a logically possible state of affairs which an omnipotent being is unable to bring about. If that is true, however, then an omnipotent being is not *omni*potent! The most usual move to avoid this embarrassment is to stipulate that an omnipotent being should only be required to be able to bring about states of affairs which are logically possible *for it* to bring about.[41] In this way, we need not ascribe to an omnipotent being the ability to bring about some state of affairs the description of which entails that it logically cannot be brought about by an omnipotent agent.[42]

This stipulation, however, has the unpalatable consequence that also clearly non-omnipotent beings must be regarded as omnipotent. The most notorious example here is the so-called Mr. McEar, a being which is *essentially* unable to do anything else than scratching its own ear (and all things included in this activity).[43] Since Mr. McEar is able to do all things which are logically possible for him to do, he should be considered as omnipotent. Recent contributions show numerous attempts to avoid this conclusion, but few of them are entirely convincing.[44] We will not pursue the issue further

---

[40] This response is suggested by Davis, *Logic*, 79, 159 n.29 ("It seems to be a peculiar temptation of contemporary philosophers to use the notion of essential predication to generate hypothetical entities which a moment's reflection will show cannot possibly exist").

[41] E.g. Pentz, *Defense*, 39f.; Wierenga, *Nature of God*, 16.

[42] Cf. Swinburne, *Coherence*, 152.

[43] McEar was invented by Plantinga, *God and Other Minds*, 170, baptized by La Croix, "Impossibility," 183, and refined by Reichenbach, "Mavrodes on Omnipotence," 213. In his "Failing to Define" La Croix shows that the definition proposed in Mavrodes' "Defining Omnipotence" succumbs to the McEar-objection.

[44] The most promising line of approach is indicated by Charles Taliaferro, "The Magnitude

here, but postpone an examination of various proposed resolutions of the essentialism-issue to our own discussion.

Fourth, suppose that we succeed in specifying the conditions for being omnipotent in a way which unambiguously prevents the ascription of omnipotence to obviously non-omnipotent beings (such as McEar). Then is omnipotence a predicate which can properly be attributed to one and only one being? Or, alternatively, is it possible that two or more beings are simultaneously omnipotent? In other words: is omnipotence necessarily a unique attribute, which can be exemplified by maximally one being, or does it possibly have a wider denotation? The most natural answer to this question is that there can be only one omnipotent being. For surely, the will of an omnipotent being is unthwartable. But if there are two omnipotent beings, their wills are far from unthwartable, since the will of the one might be frustrated by the conflicting will of the other (and vice versa). Thus, if there are two omnipotent beings it is possible to think of a being having more power than each of them, viz. an omnipotent being not co-existing with another one. Only this being could properly bear the title "omnipotent," since its scope of power would exceed that of the other ones.[45]

In an interesting essay, however, Louis Werner has advocated the idea that a plurality of omnipotent beings is very well possible. For suppose that one of two omnipotent beings wants to bring about p whereas the other wants to bring about q, which is incompatible with p. Then both want to bring about logically impossible things. For no doubt it is logically impossible to bring about p when an omnipotent being wants to bring about q, and vice versa. Now it is generally accepted that the scope of omnipotence is restricted to logically possible states of affairs; but then neither the inability of the one omnipotent being to bring about p, nor the inability of the other to bring about q counts against the omnipotence of either of them! Therefore, there can be more than one omnipotent being.[46]

Assuming the possibility of two simultaneously existing omnipotent beings, George Mavrodes has pointed out in a thought-provoking parable that it is extremely difficult to tell what happens when the wills of the two contradict each other.[47] For this reason, Werner had contended that it is "logically impossible for there to be two [omnipotent beings] with contra-

---

of Omnipotence," *IJPR* 14 (1983), 99-106, who seeks the solution in comparing beings of different powers, such as McEar and an ostensibly omnipotent being, and maximizing the amount of abilities an omnipotent being should be required to have. A similar condition is proposed by Flint & Freddoso, "Maximal Power," 98, who are nevertheless criticized precisely on this point by Gellman, "The Limits of Maximal Power."

[45] So Taliaferro, "Magnitude," 105f. (taking up an argument of Scotus). Cf. Anglin, *Free Will*, 70f.

[46] L. Werner, "Some Omnipotent Beings," *Critica* 5 (1971), 55-69 (included in Urban & Walton, *Power of God*, 94-106).

[47] G.I. Mavrodes, "Necessity, Possibility and the Stone which Cannot be Moved," *F&P* 2 (1985), 265-271.

dictory wills."[48] But others have recently sought another way out of this stalemate by invoking the to my mind highly implausible notion of uncaused events, arguing that in case of a conflict between two omnipotent wills either will can be actualized provided that this happens uncaused.[49] If the will of the one is realized by an uncaused event, it is logically impossible for the other to have his contradictory will realized, and therefore this does not count against its omnipotence.

Fifth, there is the relation between omnipotence and omniscience. This relation can be constructed so as to resemble the paradoxes of omnipotence discussed above. One can ask, for example, whether an omnipotent being can make a being which performs an act only known to itself and to no other being. If so, then according to La Croix the omnipotent being is not omniscient, or at least, as he corrects himself later on, not essentially omniscient.[50] If not, then the omnipotent being clearly is not omnipotent after all. In a similar way, Aleksandar Pražić argues for the incompatibility of omnipotence and omniscience. According to him, either God is able to tempt people (e.g., Abraham), and in that case He is not omniscient since "ignorance is a necessary condition for temptation," or God is unable to tempt people, and in that case He is not omnipotent. And again: either God has the power to forget things, and then He is not omniscient since "forgetfulness contradicts omniscience," or He lacks the power to forget things, in which case He is not omnipotent.[51]

Obviously, these dilemmas are all varieties of the paradoxes of omnipotence,[52] and if one or more of the above-mentioned solutions to these paradoxes are sound, then these are equally applicable here. An at first sight somewhat more sophisticated argument (but possibly after all another parallel to the paradoxes) has been put forward by David Blumenfeld. Blumenfeld argues, that omniscience requires experiences of a type which an omnipotent being could not possibly have, such as fear, frustration and despair.[53] Thus, omniscience and omnipotence mutually exclude each other,

---

[48] Werner, "Some Omnipotent Beings," in: Urban & Walton, *Power of God*, 100; Werner distinguishes between contrary and contradictory wills (only the latter of which pertain to mutually exclusive alternatives), allowing for the logical possibility of there being two omnipotent beings with contrary wills.

[49] Alfred R. Mele & M.P. Smith, "The New Paradox of the Stone," *F&P* 5 (1988), 283-290.

[50] See La Croix, "The Incompatibility of Omnipotence and Omniscience," *Analysis* 33 (1972/1973), 176, and id, "Omnipotence, Omniscience and Necessity," *Analysis* 34 (1973/1974), 63f. respectively (instead of "essentially omniscient" La Croix has "immutably omniscient"). The flaw in La Croix's previous argument was pointed out by John W. Godbey, "On the Incompatibility of Omnipotence and Omniscience," *Analysis* 34 (1973/1974), 62.

[51] A. Pražić, "An Argument against Theism," in: A. Pavković (ed.), *Contemporary Yugoslav Philosophy: The Analytical Approach*, Dordrecht 1988, 251-262 (quotations are from 260).

[52] As is the one briefly discussed by G.B. Keene, "Omnipotence and Logical Omniscience," *Philosophy* 62 (1987), 527f.: Can an omnipotent being who is omniscient complete the task of setting himself a task which he cannot complete?

[53] D. Blumenfeld, "On the Compossibility of the Divine Attributes," *PS* 34 (1978), 93, 95;

and God cannot simultaneously possess both properties. Others, however, have countered this conclusion by pointing to the fact that God might have the relevant experiences (or the basic-experiences of which they are composed) in other contexts, in which they are not incompatible with any of His attributes.[54]

It should be noted here that we have started to exchange talk of "an omnipotent being" for talk about God. It is not accidental that this happens just here. For considering the relation between omnipotence and omniscience is not usually inspired by the wish to analyse the concept of omnipotence for its own sake, i.e., for purely philosophical reasons. Rather, it is the theistic conception of God which prompts the question of whether omnipotence and omniscience can be ascribed to one and the same being. Thus, many studies in this category have a distinctly theological background.[55] The same holds to an even higher degree for the fields of inquiry to be discussed below. The question which arises in all of these cases is, of course, whether the *sort of omnipotence* ascribed to God can be, or need to be, qualified in any sense by the divine nature or not. It is remarkable that this question has hardly been deemed worthy of separate discussion in the literature under review.[56]

Sixth, an issue which has definitely been deemed worthy of separate and extensive discussion concerns the relation between omnipotence and goodness. Often this relation is dealt with under the more precise heading "omnipotence and impeccability." Does omnipotence imply the ability to sin, in the sense of: to do evil? That is the main question here, raised for the first time in Nelson Pike's distinguished paper on "Omnipotence and God's Ability to Sin."[57] In this paper Pike argues that if a being lacked the ability to do evil, it would not be omnipotent. Therefore, if God is omnipotent, the claim that He is also impeccable should be understood in some other way than as straightforwardly expressing a divine inability to do evil. Instead, Pike provides two alternative ways in which divine impeccability

---

also in Morris (ed.), *Concept of God*, 204, 206.

[54] See Marcel Sarot, "Omniscience and Experience," *IJPR* 30 (1991), 96, 102 n.26.

[55] The theological motive is quite explicitly present in Frederick Sontag, "Omnipotence Need not Entail Omniscience," *Sophia* 29.3 (1990), 35-39, who argues that we should "start with the requirements of salvation and work backward to conceive of God in ways that make this possible, since no one metaphysics is forced upon us. ... The Gospels ... are documents which for Christians set the kind of metaphysics they need..." (36). These assumptions lead Sontag to conclude that we need not ascribe omniscience to God, since God's omnipotence is enough to warrant final salvation. Richard Francks goes even further when he argues in "Omniscience, Omnipotence and Pantheism," *Philosophy* 54 (1979), 395-399, that if God is both omnipotent and omniscient, Spinoza's pantheism is vindicated because "there is no difference between him and the universe" (399).

[56] The above-mentioned articles of Jerome Gellman are the only exceptions I know of; see further (for references to some non-analytical literature) §3.1 above.

[57] *APQ* 6 (1969), 208-216.

might be understood, which according to Pike together guarantee God's steadfast goodness as well as His moral praiseworthiness.

One commentator has expressed his doubts about the sufficiency of Pike's account for assuring God's steadfast goodness, and offered additional considerations in order to strengthen it.[58] On the other hand, another critic has objected that Pike's interpretation of divine impeccability constrains God's freedom and thus jeopardizes His moral praiseworthiness. In his attempt to repair this defect, this author weakens Pike's account of impeccability to the extent of abandoning not only the claim that God is *unable* to do evil, but also the claim that He is by (His) nature *unwilling* to do evil. Only in that case, he claims, we have reason to praise God for His refraining from evil actions.[59]

It is clear that notwithstanding their differences, all these authors nevertheless share a basic presupposition, namely that the apparent conflict between omnipotence and impeccability should be removed by modifying the latter, in denying that God lacks the power or ability to do evil.[60] This position has only two alternatives, both of which are also advanced and defended in current literature.

The first is to choose the opposite line of argument and to maintain God's inability to do evil at the cost of a modifying interpretation of His omnipotence. A consequence of this option seems to be the denial of God's omnipotence, since "modified omnipotence" or "limited omnipotence" are clearly contradictions in terms. Anyone who is omnipotent can do all things, but anyone who cannot do evil cannot do all things and is therefore not *omni*potent (though he might still be very powerful). Therefore, if God is unable to do evil He is not omnipotent.[61] The only way to escape this conclusion is to stipulate the definition of omnipotence in such a way that the ability to do evil is excluded. Following this procedure, some authors reject or trivialize the literal conception of omnipotence and contend that the

---

[58] Vincent Brümmer, "Divine Impeccability," *RS* 20 (1984), 203-214; cf. Paul Helm, "God and the Approval of Sin," ibid., 215-222, and Brümmer's rejoinder "Paul Helm on God and the Approval of Sin," ibid., 223-226.

[59] Robert F. Brown, "God's Ability to Will Moral Evil," *F&P* 8 (1991), 3-20; for an application of a similar line of thought (i.e., of the denial of divine impeccancy) in the field of theodicy, see Van de Beek, *Why?*, esp. ch.18.

[60] As do B. Gibbs, "Can God Do Evil?," *Philosophy* 50 (1979), 466-469; Jonathan Harrison, "Geach on God's Alleged Ability to do Evil," *Philosophy* 51 (1976), 208-215; id., "Geach on Harrison on Geach on God," *Philosophy* 52 (1977), 223-226; Pentz, *Defense*, 55-61; B.R. Reichenbach, *Evil and a Good God*, New York 1982, ch.7; S.T. Davis, *Logic*, 94; T.V. Morris, "Perfection and Power," *IJPR* 20 (1986), 165-168, re-edited in his *Anselmian Explorations*, 70-75; I.U. Dalferth, "Gott und Sünde," *NZSTh* 33 (1991), 1-22.

[61] This is one of the reasons why Geach rejects the doctrine of divine omnipotence; see his *Providence and Evil*, 15, 19f.; cf. also his "Can God Fail to Keep Promises?," *Philosophy* 52 (1977), 93-95 (although Geach is reluctant to deduce his negative answer to this question from a divine inability to do evil). See further W.R. Carter, "Omnipotence and Sin," *Analysis* 42 (1982), 102-105; id., "Impeccability Revisited," *Analysis* 45 (1985), 52-55.

historically authentic or really interesting or religiously relevant concept of omnipotence must be understood from the context of divine metaphysical and moral perfection.[62]

The second alternative to Pike's position is to argue that omnipotence and impeccability are not mutually exclusive properties at all, since if an essentially omnipotent being is at the same time impeccable, then it is logically impossible for it to do evil.[63] And since a being's inability to do things which are logically impossible for it to do does not count against its omnipotence, it can be both omnipotent and impeccable. This is the so-called "Anselmian position," in our times first adopted by Hoffman[64] and further endorsed by philosophers from the Plantinga-school such as Wierenga and Flint & Freddoso (although the latter themselves have their doubts about the successfulness of their intricate underpinning of it).[65] Given this position, God is clearly not praiseworthy for His refraining from evil. But this is not an unacceptable conclusion to its defenders, since they usually hold that God is praiseworthy for His acts of supererogatory goodness.

Before exploring our last field of debate concerning the definition of omnipotence, I want to point to a second remarkable omission in the literature. Parallel to the vexed relations between omnipotence and omniscience and between omnipotence and impeccability other essential properties which one might be willing to ascribe to an omnipotent being would cause similar conceptual troubles. For example, we human beings can go to places where we have never been before. An essentially omnipresent being, however,

---

[62] See Jerome Gellman, "Omnipotence and Impeccability," *NS* 51 (1977), 21-37 for a definition of omnipotence as the power to do everything which it is logically possible for an essentially perfect being to do. His proposal is accepted by Nash, *Concept of God*, 43. A variant of this definition (with God's omnipotence qualified not by his impeccability as such but by his perfect freedom and knowledge as the ground for his inability to do evil) is advocated by Swinburne, *Coherence*, 158-161. Cf. further, e.g., Anglin, *Free Will*, 62f.

[63] In effect, this alternative is only slightly different from the last mentioned option. The difference is important, however, since here a literal conception of omnipotence is preserved, whereas in the former case a theistically modified conception of omnipotence is adopted instead; this difference is overlooked by Thomas Morris, "The Necessity of God's Goodness," now in his *Anselmian Explorations*, 47f., 245 n.8,9, but not by Flint & Freddoso, who explicitly criticize Gellman's solution ("Maximal Power," 109 n.3). In general, Morris leaves us at a loss as to how he considers the relation between omnipotence and impeccability (or essential goodness), suggesting divergent points of view in several of his essays.

[64] "Can God Do Evil?," *SJP* 17 (1979), 213-220. The tenability of this solution was already granted by Mackie, "Omnipotence," 18; cf. also Khamara, "In Defence," 227f. Whether this is historically St. Anselm's position remains to be seen; Gellman makes the same claim with regard to the position he defends, supplying us with textual evidence for it.

[65] "Maximal Power," 101-108 (section III), 109 n.2; Wierenga has less problems here (*Nature of God*, 18, 26), since he has contented himself with a more intuitive grasp of which states of affairs belong to the unchangeable past of a possible world (ibid., 18-20, see esp. n.19). A defence of the compatibility of essential omnipotence and essential moral perfection along somewhat different lines is provided by Laura L. Garcia, "The Essential Moral Perfection of God," *RS* 23 (1987), 137-144.

lacks this ability.[66] Thus it seems that an omnipresent being cannot at the same time be omnipotent, whereas an omnipotent being cannot at the same time be omnipresent, since omnipotence should include the ability to go to places where one has never been before. Or consider an essentially immutable being, which is unable to change; such a being lacks an ability we human beings quite naturally have, and thus cannot, or so it seems, be judged omnipotent in a literal sense. All such apparent conflicts can of course be solved in ways analogous to those raising in relation to omniscience and impeccability, but what kind of solution one favours may vary from property to property. All depends here on what we hold to be the essential attributes of God, i.e. on what we may claim to know about God's *nature*. As I hope to show in the next section, we can only get any further here by answering the question how such knowledge of God's nature can be *received*.

Seventh, some philosophers construe their definitions of omnipotence in such a manner as to take explicitly account of the way in which free actions of other beings are related to it. Others don't include this relation in their definition, but their proposed definitions are certainly of consequence with respect to the issue. The dividing lines are relatively easy to draw here; we can broadly distinguish three positions.

Most of the philosophers referred to above adhere to a libertarian account of freedom. They hold that God cannot determine the free actions of His creatures. More accurately: they hold that it is logically impossible for God (or anyone else) to bring about free actions of other agents in a strong sense. Some of them, however, distinguish a weak sense of "bringing about" in which it is logically and even actually possible for an agent to bring about the free actions of other agents. As Flint & Freddoso explain:

> In such cases the agent in question, by his actions or omissions, strongly brings it about that another agent S is in a situation C, where it is true that if S were in C, then S would freely act in a specified way. For instance, a mother might actualize her child's freely choosing to have Rice Krispies for breakfast by limiting his choices to Rice Krispies and the hated Raisin Bran.[67]

Now some of those libertarians unfold their definitions in such a way that an omnipotent being is required to have the power to weakly actualize the free actions of other agents.[68] Others, however, argue that even an omnipotent being might be unable to weakly actualize particular counterfactuals of freedom since there might be simply no "situation C" in which such counterfactuals become true; consequently, they let their definitions capture

---

[66] This example is mentioned in passing by Morris, "Perfection and Power," 70f.

[67] "Maximal Power," 86; the distinction between strong and weak actualization was introduced by Alvin Plantinga, *The Nature of Necessity*, Oxford 1974, 172f.; cf. also R.M. Chisholm, *Person and Object*, London 1976, 67-69.

[68] Flint & Freddoso, "Maximal Power," 86.

strong actualizations only.[69]

However this may be, both groups of philosophers agree that an omnipotent being is unable, and (since this inability is a logical one) should not be required to be able, to strongly actualize the free actions of other agents. It is precisely this conviction, however, which makes them vulnerable to the criticism of atheistic philosophers. Sticking to the traditional conception of omnipotence, and not being prepared to compromise the *omni*, these thinkers argue that if there really is an omnipotent being, its power should be unlimited in every respect. Thus, it should have the power with respect to *any* contingent event to determine whether the event occurs or not. It would be inconsistent with the very meaning of the concept of omnipotence to exclude human free actions from the realm of events that an omnipotent being should be able to bring about. But then, given the libertarian assumption that it is impossible for A's free action to be brought about by B, if there is an omnipotent God there can be no free actions of other agents! Moreover, as Antony Flew shows, those in search of an atheological argument need only one additional assumption to finish their task: since we know (e.g., from everyday experience) that there are human free actions - and Flew suggests we do know this - there cannot be an omnipotent God.[70]

An implication of this way of thinking is that an omnipotent God not only can actualize everything but also does actualize everything. Now to give Flew his due, Flew does not claim that this implication is inherent in the concept or doctrine of omnipotence in itself. Rather, he thinks that it is entailed by the Christian doctrine of creation. "As Creator he [God] must be the first cause, prime mover, supporter, and controller of every thought and action throughout his utterly dependent universe. In short: if creation is in, autonomy is out."[71] Others, however, go further and claim that there is an intrinsic entailment between the ability to do everything and the actuality of doing everything. They claim, that is, that omnipotence entails omnificence. Again, Mackie seems to have been the first one to develop an argument to that end. Assuming that God is omnipotent, he argues as follows:

---

[69] Wierenga, *Nature of God*, 24.

[70] Antony Flew, *God and Philosophy*, 47.

[71] Ibid. Although Flew thinks the real problem emerges from God's creatorship rather than from his omnipotence, he closely connects both notions; cf. ibid., 46 ("The problem really begins with omnipotence."), 48 ("... to creative omnipotence there are no obstacles."), and Flew's earlier essay "Divine Omnipotence and Human Freedom," in: A. Flew & A. MacIntyre (eds.), *New Essays in Philosophical Theology*, London 1955, 164-168. As we shall see in a moment, however, Flew recognizes another sense of freedom which *is* compatible with both omnipotence and creation.

If God can make it to be that X, but it is that not-X, he has chosen to let it be that not-X, and therefore, he has made it to be that not-X. Anything that God could have made otherwise, but leaves as it is, he in effect makes as it is. Therefore, for all things that are in God's power, whichever way they are he has made them so. ... This need not be taken to mean that because God does everything no-one else, and nothing else, does anything. There is nothing in the argument to deny that a man does what we ordinarily take him as doing; it only adds that God also does these same individual acts.[72]

Another way of making the same point is to say that if there exists an omnipotent being, that being "exhausts *all* the power in the universe, leaving no room for other centres of power."[73] In fact, although this quotation does not stem from a process-thinker, it is a neat formulation of what may be called a basic assumption of process-theism - in combination, of course, with the conviction that there is no such being. According to David Basinger's critique of the process view of divine power, here we encounter "the most crucial difference" between process theology and classical Christian theism.[74] In the first full-length process theodicy David Griffin argues that if there is an omnipotent being in the traditional sense, then any other actual beings must be totally devoid of power, and this, he says, is quite incompatible with a manifest metaphysical truth, namely that there are beings other than God that freely exercise power.[75] Rather than denying the existence of an omnipotent God, however, process thinkers are usually inclined to reinterpret the concept of omnipotence as it is ascribed to God.[76]

The third way of construing the relation between omnipotence and

---

[72] Mackie, "Omnipotence," 22, 23. Some years later Frederic B. Fitch, "A Logical Analysis of Some Value Concepts," *JSL* 2 (1963) 135-142 (see esp. 138) claimed to provide a formal proof of the same thesis, which was validated by Douglas Walton, "Some Theorems of Fitch on Omnipotence," *Sophia* 15.1 (1976), 20-27 (repr. in Urban & Walton, *Power of God*, 182-191).

[73] Linwood Urban & Douglas Walton, "Freedom within Omnipotence," in: Urban & Walton, *Power of God*, 193 (italics by the authors). The argument of this paper is critically examined and rebutted by Nelson Pike, "Over-Power and God's Responsibility for Sin," in: Freddoso (ed.), *Existence and Nature*, 11-35.

[74] Basinger, *Divine Power in Process Theism*, 5; in addition, Basinger holds "the process conception of divine power to be the most fundamental and important component in the process system" (19). Indeed, the denial of divine omnipotence (as traditionally understood) is essential to process thinking, as e.g. appears from one of Hartshorne's latest book titles, in which from six classical theological mistakes only omnipotence deserves explicit mention: *Omnipotence and other Theological Mistakes*.

[75] D.R. Griffin, *God, Power and Evil*, Lanham 1991², ch.17, 18. See also Hartshorne, "Omnipotence," in: Vergilius Ferm (ed.), *An Encyclopedia of Religion*, New York 1945, 545f.; id., *Divine Relativity*, ch.1, 2. For a critique of this view of power (remarkably ignored by Basinger), see Nelson Pike, "Process Theodicy and the Concept of Power," *PrS* 12 (1982), 148-167.

[76] Either maintaining the term "omnipotence," as Griffin (*God, Power and Evil*, 269) and Case-Winters (in her "process-feminist synthesis"; *God's Power*, 212-214) do, or substituting it by other ones such as "all-powerful," as Hartshorne now prefers (*Omnipotence*, 26).

creaturely freedom partially agrees and partially disagrees with both of its alternatives. It agrees with libertarianism (and disagrees with the process-view and its atheistic variant) in holding that the existence of an omnipotent being does not preclude meaningful talk of creaturely freedom. It disagrees with libertarianism (and agrees with its rival), on the other hand, in that it believes omnipotence to be incompatible with the libertarian account of such freedom. Rather, its proponents opt for another, weaker conception of freedom, which according to them *is* compatible with the traditional conception of omnipotence and at the same time upholds the possibility of human activity that is free in a relevant sense. This third view derives its most common name from this compatibility-claim: compatibilism.[77]

According to compatibilism, an action is free if it satisfies only one criterion: it should be performed voluntarily, i.e., without the agent being forced to perform it against its will. Libertarians usually agree with this criterion, but emphasize that another one is much more important, viz. that the agent could have acted otherwise (or could have refrained from acting at all): only if the agent had a genuine *choice* his action can be called free in a relevant sense. Now some compatibilists are prepared to grant this point, and agree that it belongs to the definition of a free action that the agent could have chosen and done otherwise; for clearly, the agent always had the physical abilities to will and to do otherwise. But they insist that these undeniable facts of action and choice do not conflict with important deterministic presuppositions. As Flew has it:

> ... there can be no ultimate and fundamental contradiction in suggesting that another man, or God, might, by direct physiological manipulations, ensure that someone performs whatever actions that other man, or God, determines; and that the actions of this creature would nevertheless be genuine actions, such that it could always be truly said that he could have done otherwise than he did.[78]

For to say that a person could have done otherwise than he did is not to say that what he did was in principle unpredictable or that there were no sufficient causes which determined his actions. "It is to say that *if* he had chosen otherwise he would have been able to do so; that there were alternatives, within the capacities of one of his physical strength, of his I.Q., with his knowledge, and open to a person in his situation."[79]

---

[77] Like the term "free will defence," as far as I can see the name "compatibilism" was invented by Antony Flew. For the former, see his "Divine Omnipotence," 145; for the latter his "Compatibilism, Free Will and God," *Philosophy* 48 (1973), 233.

[78] "Compatibilism," 244. Cf. Flew's highly partial account of "freewill and determinism" in his *A Dictionary of Philosophy*, London 1983², 125f. Later, however, Flew appears to have qualified his compatibilism at least in this respect, that he now, in an article directed against behaviourism, denies the compatibility of *physical* determinism and human (free) action; cf. his "Freedom and Human Nature," *Philosophy* 66 (1991), 61.

[79] "Divine Omnipotence," 150. For discussions of this so-called hypothetical interpretation of "can," see Gary Watson (ed.), *Free Will*, Oxford 1982, esp. Watson's "Introduction" and the

Indeed, Flew not only claims that this is the way in which we use the concept of freedom in ordinary, non-technical language, but he also shows that many classical Christian theists subscribed to such a compatibilist view. In this respect, Luther and Calvin only stated "with harsh clarity and without equivocation" what was implicit in Aquinas as well as in Roman Catholic conciliar pronouncements.[80] According to Flew, traditional theism has been so anxious to uphold the conceptual and theological implications of the doctrine of divine omnipotence, that it could only conceive of human individual actions as being specifically directed and determined by God. Yet this position does not simply amount to the positive affirmation of the view that Urban & Walton, process thinkers and others so vehemently reject,[81] because it also ascribes to human activity a type of freedom (viz., freedom as voluntariness)[82] which it considers to be strong enough to entail moral responsibility. Contemporary proposals for compatibilist accounts of omnipotence along these lines have been advanced by James Ross[83] and, more hesitatingly, by Robert Young.[84]

3.3.5 Conclusion

Our exploration of the contexts in which the concept of omnipotence can be and has been analyzed is by no means exhaustive. Other fields of analysis could be examined, such as the precise phraseology in terms of which omnipotence should be defined,[85] and the implications of definitions of om-

---

contributions of A.J. Ayer, R.M. Chisholm, B. Aune/K. Lehrer and Peter van Inwagen (chapters I-IV).

[80] Ibid., 163 n.26; cf. "Compatibilism," 240f., where Flew reckons the compatibilist position among "the agreed essentials of theism" (240).

[81] As Pike holds, cf. his "Over-Power," 21.

[82] See e.g. Aquinas, *Summa contra Gentiles* III 67: "God alone can move the will, as an agent, without doing violence to it ... God can cause a movement of our will in us without prejudicing the freedom of the will ...".

[83] *Philosophical Theology*, chapter 5; "Creation," *JP* 77 (1980), 614-629; "Creation II," in: Freddoso (ed.), *Existence and Nature*, 115-141. For a critique of Ross's definition as formulated in his *Philosophical Theology*, uncovering as one of its consequences that God is the prisoner of His own power since He cannot refrain from actualizing either p or non-p (p being any contingent state of affairs), see W.E. Mann, "Ross on Omnipotence," *IJPR* 8 (1979), 142-147. Other critical discussions of Ross' definition can be found in Young, *Freedom, Responsibility*, 189-194, and in Anglin, *Free Will*, 56-59.

[84] *Freedom, Responsibility*, chapters 11 and 14; "Omnipotence and Compatibilism," *Philosophia* 6 (1976), 49-65.

[85] Most of the authors referred to above define omnipotence in terms of the power or ability to do or bring about or actualize things or states of affairs or situations, or to "make it the case that a sentence is true" (Schrader), to "make it be that X" (Mackie 1962) etc.; only some of them briefly argue for this choice (Swinburne, Davis, Flint & Freddoso, Wierenga). Others prefer to develop their definitions in terms of the capability to do or perform actions (Plantinga, Cargile, Gellman 1975) or tasks (Savage, McLean, Anderson), in terms of the number of powers or scope of power an omnipotent being possesses (Wolfe, Kenny, Anglin, Taliaferro), or in terms of the omnipotent being's effective choices (Ross, Zeis/Jacobs). I suspect that on closer scrutiny most

nipotence for the problem of evil (how is the existence of an omnipotent and wholly good God compatible with the existence of evil?). As to the first issue, I did not include it in my survey because in the literature there are no separate discussions explicitly dedicated to it. As to the second, I ignored it because it is not usually discussed in connection with the search for an adequate *definition* of omnipotence, and because the available options largely reflect the multifarious options advocated in the copious recent literature on theodicy; moreover, I will give special attention to the question of theodicy in relation to the ascription of omnipotence to God in §4.4 below. At the present stage we are in a position to draw some conclusions. I will cast these in the form of suggestions for the direction which further inquiry might take.

First, there is something odd in the ardent search for an exact definition of omnipotence. Current definitions tend to get more and more remote from our pre-analytical intuitions of omnipotence, which they are intended to capture. Therefore, over against all existing "long and clumsy" definitions, I cut the Gordian knot by proposing a very simple one which does capture our pre-analytical intuitions:

Def.: x is omnipotent = x has the power to do all things.

Of course, prior to a good many conceptual clarifications it is not at all clear what this crude and unsophisticated definition precisely implies.[86] But this is equally the case with its more intricate fellow-definitions. The more complicated a definition is, the more its intelligibility depends upon a clarification of its (technical) terms. This points to the fact that what is really interesting is not so much the *definition* of omnipotence as its *analysis*. Surely it may be useful if an analysis of omnipotence can retrospectively be summarized in one formula (however long and clumsy). But this is not strictly necessary. What is necessary is a comprehensive analysis of omnipotence in relation to all such issues as those discussed above, in order to discover the conceptual network within which it functions, its conceptual implications, presuppositions etc.[87] It is to this task that we will give priority in what follows; the condensation of such an analysis in a stipulated

---

of these phrases turn out to be mutually translatable, so that a rational choice for one of them should only be made on pedagogical grounds. The same goes for the use of possible world language in definitions of omnipotence.

[86] As Case-Winters demonstrates, different doctrines of omnipotence within the Christian tradition can be classified according to the way in which they interpret and qualify each of the concepts which make up the proposition "God can do all things"; cf. her *God's Power*, 21-24.

[87] For a discussion of differences between the definition of words and the analysis of concepts, see V. Brümmer, *Wijsgerige Begripsanalyse*, Kampen 1989[3], 83f.; cf. ibid., 72 (= *Theology*, 73f.), where Brümmer points to some inadequate impressions which might be conveyed by the term "analysis" as a metaphor for philosophical conceptual inquiry, but also indicates how these can be avoided.

definition is a task of only secondary importance.

Second, our exploration of this conceptual network brought to light that many of the issues involved in analyzing omnipotence shows can be approached in parallel ways. The way one construes omnipotence in relation to one of them has consequences for the way one should account for others. This is especially clear in the case of the relation between omnipotence and modal logic. Once we have decided that omnipotence should only quantify over states of affairs which it is logically possible to actualize (or over actions which it is logically possible to perform), many possible solutions to further problems are predetermined. For example, the paradoxes of omnipotence can now be dealt with by claiming that actions such as creating an object which its maker cannot destroy are logically impossible for an omnipotent agent to perform, and that hence its inability to perform them does not entail that the agent is not omnipotent. For the same reason, an omnipotent being's inability to bring about states of affairs as specified in our third category (in connection with the issue of essentialism) does not count against its omnipotence. Moreover, if we assume that an essentially omnipotent being is at the same time essentially omnipresent, omniscient, omnibenevolent (i.e., impeccable) etc., there are many additional states of affairs which, although perfectly conceivable, cannot be brought about by that particular omnipotent agent. Again, it can be argued that these restrictions are compatible with omnipotence, since in all such cases it is logically possible for an omnipotent being to bring about the states of affairs in question.

Where this principle of exclusion of logically impossible actions leaves us can best be illustrated with reference to our fourth category. If we assume that there are more (say, two; but why not: two hundred?) omnipotent beings, all of them can correctly claim to be omnipotent, since for none of them it is logically possible to bring about states of affairs the actualization of which is prevented by an(other) omnipotent being. At the same time, however, all of them seem to have thwartable wills, and may in fact turn out to possess only highly limited powers! I conclude that the relation between omnipotence and modal logic is apparently a crucial one, and that therefore it should be examined very carefully. It is both significant and promising that some of the most recent work on the doctrine of divine omnipotence and sovereignty gives special attention to this area.[88] In agreement with this development, I will concentrate below upon rethinking the relation between the doctrine of God and the status of the laws of logic, abstract entities, universals, etc.

Third, as already pointed to above, our survey of issues revealed an ongoing tension between two alternative conceptions of omnipotence, which could perhaps be described as a strictly philosophical or literal one on the

---

[88] Cf. the studies of Plantinga, Morris, Menzel, Leftow and others quoted in notes 30 and 31 (as to Morris, cf. in general his *Anselmian Explorations*).

one hand, and a theologically qualified one on the other. Some authors discussed above focus exclusively on the analysis of omnipotence as a bare concept. In doing so, some of them encounter problems which are to such a degree intractable, that they are led to affirm the internal inconsistency of omnipotence as a concept, and by extension the wrong-headedness of any theological application of the concept in the doctrine of God. Others, however, argue that the meaning of omnipotence in the theistic ascription of omnipotence to God cannot be derived from the literal conception of omnipotence, but should rather be tied to and determined by the nature of the divine being. In this way, it appears that many of the conceptual puzzles involved in the literal conception of omnipotence can quite easily be overcome or bypassed, and a perfectly coherent definition of divine omnipotence can be formulated.[89] But what about the price to be paid for this procedure?

In any case, the relation between the literal and the theologically qualified conception of omnipotence deserves explicit discussion. Too many studies confuse both conceptions, using logical and theological arguments indiscriminately,[90] and often aiming to provide an analysis of the bare concept of omnipotence, while in fact merely explaining what could be meant by the notion of divine omnipotence. More specifically, we should ask how important it is for theistic concerns to maintain a literal conception of omnipotence. What precisely is lost when it is conceded that God's omnipotence does not imply that He is able to actualize all logically possible states of affairs, but only those which are compatible with His existence and nature, as well as with His bringing them about? Or is this an unnecessary, and perhaps even religiously damaging concession, which in effect leaves us with a limited, finite God? Is it possible to give a self-consistent and coherent description of such a non-literal conception of omnipotence? For clearly, even if we prefer to interpret the notion of omnipotence theologically, conceptual consistency remains a necessary condition for religious adequacy.[91] If we cannot spell out unambiguously what it means that God is omnipotent, how should we be able to know what attitude we should adopt to an omnipotent God? It is to topics like these that we turn next.

---

[89] In addition to literature already mentioned, see for an example of a strictly theological definition of omnipotence Richard L. Purtill, *Thinking about Religion*, Englewood Cliffs (N.J.) 1978, 30f.: "... by saying that God is all-powerful or omnipotent we mean that God can bring about any state of affairs, S, such that S is 1) consistently describable, 2) not inconsistent with the existence of God, and 3) not inconsistent with God's bringing it about" (31). Whether this definition "involves no *real* limitation on the power of God" (ibid.), however, can be doubted (especially if God is conceived as essentially impeccable etc.).

[90] For a recent example see Anglin, *Free Will*, 48-71; a good exception is Flint & Freddoso, "Maximal Power."

[91] William J. Wainwright, "Divine Omnipotence: A Reply to Professors Kuntz and Macquarrie," *Proceedings of the Seventh Inter-American Congress of Philosophy*, Vol.1, Quebec 1967, 147.

3.4 OMNIPOTENCE AND ALMIGHTINESS

Every meaningful statement about God's omnipotence must be able to base itself on God's Word. If it cannot do this, it is directed against God and is a denial of His omnipotence, even if, as far as its content goes, it seeks to say the most tremendous and wonderful things about the infinity of His power.

K. Barth[1]

3.4.1 *Introduction*

Having analyzed both components of the term "omnipotence" in the preceding sections, it seems that we are now in a position to combine the results and give a precise description of the meaning of "omnipotence" as a bare concept. Let us therefore recapitulate what has been established so far in the present chapter. In section 3.2 we came to the conclusion that power is basically the ability to effect things or bring things about. To have power is to be able to make a difference to the world (Lukes). In section 3.3 we concluded that, despite its simplicity, "x is omnipotent = x can do all things" should be preferred as a definition to more intricate alternatives. Combining these two conclusions, we can now see that the "can" in "x can do all things" should be interpreted as an ability concept, and that omnipotence consists in the ability to bring about all things, or to make a maximal difference to the universe.

At the same time, however, both in analyzing "power" and in examining the "omni"-phrase, we came across some questions which could not be resolved immediately at that stage of our inquiry. The concept of power turned out to have a number of aspects and conceptual relations within the family of ability concepts which play a role in *some but not all* instantiations of power, and it was not clear in advance which of these (if any) were bearing upon the notion of omnipotence. More specifically, it was unclear which of these aspects and conceptual relations had to be conveyed to the context of *divine* omnipotence. Our examination of the qualifier "omni" in "omnipotence" ended in a similar deadlock, since again we were faced with the intractable problem of how to transfer the outcome of our conceptual inquiry into the theological context. Apart from the remaining problem of its relation to logic, we reached a rather clear and relatively simple account of the concept of omnipotence; its theological relevance, however, remained uncertain.

All in all, the results reached thus far in the present chapter may strike us as rather meagre - but precisely that fact is revealing. For apparently the most crucial questions cannot be settled by means of a context-free analysis of the involved concepts alone. On the contrary, the concept of omnipotence can only be adequately examined from the context (or "language game") in which it functions, viz. the religio-theological context.[2]

---

[1] Barth, *Church Dogmatics* II.1, 537.
[2] It may be objected that the concept of omnipotence does not function in religion at all, but

Therefore, in order to make some progress, we will now approach the matter from the other side, i.e. from the theological perspective. Rather than proceeding from the bare concept of omnipotence in order to illuminate the nature and range of God's power, we will now take our starting-point unambiguously in the nature of the theistic (and more specifically Christian) belief in God. For it is only by asking why we do or should call God omnipotent in the first place that we can get a clear idea of what is involved in the affirmation of divine omnipotence. Only after thus having clarified the concept of divine omnipotence theologically, will we be in a good position to tackle the questions which we came across previously.

3.4.2 *Omnipotence and the concept of God*
What does it mean to hold that God is omnipotent? That is the key question we have come to now. It is a question which in a sense[3] presupposes belief in God, but we will omit a discussion of this presupposition here, since in chapter 1 we have argued in some detail for its rationality. Here, we try to find an answer to this question by looking for the *reasons* we could have for calling God omnipotent. Although this point is seldom made explicit in current discussions about omnipotence, it seems to me that the Western tradition of philosophical theology contains two different reasons for ascribing omnipotence to God, both of which are competitively lurking in the background of the contemporary debate.

It is of crucial importance to achieve clarity here, because it is precisely the differences between these two reasons which are responsible for the confusions, uncertainties and mutual disagreements with respect to the specific nature of God's omnipotence. In order to resolve these difficulties, we should therefore make up our mind with regard to the reason we have to ascribe omnipotence to God in the first place. When we have decided upon that issue, an answer to the question whether God's omnipotence is literally omni-potence or a form of (divinely) qualified omnipotence follows almost automatically. Let us therefore make the two possible reasons for ascribing omnipotence to God explicit.[4]

The first reason believers may have for calling God omnipotent is simply that they consider omnipotence to be included in the concept of God. We may call God omnipotent, because what it is to be omnipotent is included in what it is to be God. If God were not omnipotent, He would not

---

precisely in the context of philosophical theism where we discussed it before; this may be true, but even so this philosophical use of the concept is derivative, and parasytic on the concept's origin in the religio-theological notion of God's almightiness.

[3] Indeed, this is only the case in a sense. In another sense, it remains entirely possible for those who do not believe in God to ask the same question, viz. hypothetically: "Imagine that God exists, and that He is omnipotent - what could that possibly mean?".

[4] I have worked out this distinction in a slightly different context in my article "Almacht bij Anselmus en Abraham," *KETh* (1992), 205-225.

be God. This claim, in turn, can be substantiated in two different ways, viz. inductively and deductively. In this subsection I will trace the inductive way, in the next the deductive way.

The inductive way starts by pointing to the phenomenological fact that there seems to be no religion in the world which does not consider power to be the most fundamental property of the divine.[5] Thus, Gerardus van der Leeuw opens his *Phänomenologie der Religion* with an extensive discussion of the concept of power as basic to every form of religion:

> Thus the first affirmation we can make about the Object of Religion is that it is a *highly exceptional* and *extremely impressive "Other".* ... There arises and persists an experience which connects or unites itself to the "Other" that thus obtrudes. ... this Object is a departure from all that is usual and familiar; and this again is the consequence of the *Power* it generates.[6]

Van der Leeuw further attests to the centrality of power as a divine attribute by arguing that religion in its essence and manifestation consists in "being touched by Power," "being affected by Power," "conducting oneself in relation to Power," etc.[7] According to Van der Leeuw, "worship always depends on the substantiation of power."[8] From the earliest accounts of religion on, power has been the central property ascribed to the divine. Power as a divine attribute seems structurally to precede other attributes such as will, goodness, wisdom, personality etc.[9] Whether we consider animism, dynamism, polytheism or monotheism, in each type of religion the divine is primarily conceived of as powerful, although understandings of the nature and operation of its power vary.

As to monotheism, it can additionally be argued that here the divine, since it is one, is seen as the unique bearer of all the power there is. This concentration of all power in the divine entity can even be considered as the essential characteristic of monotheism. Thus, Van der Leeuw contends that the monotheism of Islam was not a protest against polytheism, but an enthusiastic belief in God's omnipotence.[10] However this may be, with monotheism unmistakably the conception of (an) omnipotence comes to the fore.

---

[5] Cf. for the following Case-Winters, *God's Power*, 24-27.

[6] I quote from the ET: G. van der Leeuw, *Religion in Essence and Manifestation*, Princeton, N.J. 1986 (repr. of J.E. Turner's translation, London 1938, 1964[2]; the original German edition appeared at Tübingen in 1933), 23; Cf. Ninian Smart's comment on Van der Leeuw's approach in his "Foreword" added to the 1986-edition: "Rather for him the central phenomenon of religion is Power" (ibid., xvi).

[7] Ibid., 191.

[8] Ibid., 85.

[9] Cf. apart from Van der Leeuw also Lewis R. Farnell, *The Attributes of God*, Oxford 1925, 224: "The gods and the spirits are imagined as powerful before they are recognized as beneficent or just."

[10] Van der Leeuw, *Religion*, 180; cf. 642: "In Islam, then, the concept of Power reaches its lofties peak."

As we have already observed,[11] the Judaeo-Christian tradition also considers power as an essential characteristic of God. With regard to Judaism Grundmann asserts, that the very divine essence was located in power.[12] And that Christianity to a large extent adopted the Jewish view of divine power is clear from the Apostles' Creed, where omnipotence is the only attribute explicitly ascribed to God the Father. In conclusion, while power is the central divine phenomenon in religions that are not monotheistic, in monotheistic belief systems all the power becomes concentrated in the divine being, who in consequence is conceived as omnipotent.

In this way, it may be inferred inductively from the empirical reality of the phenomenon of religion, that wherever people speak of the divine, this divine is conceived as powerful; wherever they speak of God, God is conceived as omnipotent. H.M. Kuitert seems to be to such a degree impressed by this universality of power as a central feature in all kinds of religious veneration, that he considers "exercising power over all things" as part of the very meaning of the concept of God. According to him, besides being person-like, exercising power over all things is one of the necessary, religion-independent conditions for being truly God.[13]

As it seems to me, however, this view is highly questionable. It is doubtful whether it can be empirically shown that anyone saying "God" implicitly says "exercising power over all things." Consider the following counter-examples. First deism, with its characteristic emphasis on the *absence* of actual divine power-wielding. And second, those streams in modern Judaism and Christianity which stress God's vulnerability, weakness and even powerlessness rather than His power.[14] One only has to recall the oft-quoted words of Dietrich Bonhoeffer:

---

[11] See §2.2.1 above.

[12] W. Grundmann, "dynamai/dynamis," in: Kittel (ed.), *ThDNT* Vol.2, 297.

[13] H.M. Kuitert, *Wat heet geloven?*, Baarn 1977, 145; id., "Het geloven waard," in: M.A. Maurice & S.J. Noorda (eds.), *De onzekere zekerheid des geloofs*, Zoetermeer 1991, 113-115: "Ik besluit: een persoon-achtige God die macht over alles uitoefent - twee (niet tot de christelijke godsdienst beperkte) criteria die beslissen over God/niet God" (115). In his *Het algemeen betwijfeld christelijk geloof*, Baarn 1992 (ET: *I Have My Doubts: Christian Belief Today*, forthcoming London 1993), 54-56, on the other hand, Kuitert much more correctly in my view derives God's power from the Bible, especially the Old Testament. The a priori equation between "God" and "all determining power" also characterizes the theology of W. Pannenberg; see e.g. his *Basic Questions* Vol.1, 1: "The word 'God' is used meaningfully only if one means by it the power that determines everything that exists," and §1.1.1 n.9 above; cf. M.E. Brinkman, *Het Gods- en mensbegrip in de theologie van Wolfhart Pannenberg*, Kampen 1980², 32-34; Van Egmond, *Lijdende God*, 236f. n.13 shows how Pannenberg in later publications qualified his definition so as to include divine suffering and powerlessness as well.

[14] Suffice it to give one example from both the recent Jewish and Christian literature, Hans Jonas, "The Concept of God after Auschwitz: A Jewish Voice," *JR* 67 (1987), 1-13 ("... we come to what is perhaps the most critical point in our speculative, theological venture: this is not an omnipotent God," 8); Howard R. Burkle, *God, Suffering & Belief*, Nashville 1977, esp.118-121 (on "divine impotence").

God allows himself to be edged out of the world on to the cross. God is weak and powerless in the world, and that is exactly the way, the only way, in which he can be with us and help us. Matthew 8.17 makes it crystal clear that it is not by his omnipotence that Christ helps us, but by his weakness and suffering.[15]

Even if this statement should be interpreted as bringing the divine omnipotence in a polar relationship with His purported weakness, powerlessness etc. rather than as straightforwardly denying God's omnipotence, it still has not been established that the latter is religiously impossible. Similarly, even if it could be established that under closer scrutiny also in deism God is seen as having power over all things, it always remains possible that somewhere in the future a type of religious belief emerges which does not depict the divine as powerful at all. One such instance would be enough to falsify the thesis that the concept of power (let alone the concept of omnipotence) is always empirically implied in the concept of God. Perhaps, in the end, despite overwhelming evidence suggesting the contrary, there are some religions or viable types of religious belief which succeed in *not* associating the divine with power. At any rate, if we do not stipulate the definition of God in such a way that God is (all-) powerful by definition this possibility cannot be excluded.

In fact, here we encounter a well-known limitation which is inherent in the inductive method. As Karl Popper has made clear, "no rule can ever guarantee that a generalization inferred from true observations, however often repeated, is true. ... Induction, i.e. inference based on many observations, is a myth."[16] This is so simply because in principle at any time a contrary observation might be made, which falsifies the theory based upon the earlier ones. For this reason, the second way to substantiate the theory that the concept of God implies the concept of omnipotence, is far more interesting. For since it is deductive, it is not plagued by the perennial possibility of future falsification. Let us therefore now have a look at the deductive way.

The first one to develop the deductive way in a consistent manner was Anselm. Let us, in addition to what has been said about Anselm in §2.3.1 above, expand for a moment on the structure of his doctrine of divine omnipotence. After having concluded from his famous definition of God as *id quo maius nihil cogitari potest* to the existence of God,[17] Anselm goes on to show that this same definition also implicitly contains all the attributes which we believe God to have. For if God really is the being than

---

15 D. Bonhoeffer, *Letters and Papers*, 122.

16 K.R. Popper, *Conjectures and Refutations*, New York 1965², 53.

17 Some commentators on the *Proslogion*, such as Richard Campbell, *From Belief to Understanding*, Canberra 1976 have argued that this traditional rendering of Anselm's procedure is inadequate in that Anselm does not start from a definition of God, but from a speech-act which uses the words "something than which nothing greater can be thought," which he *shows* to be a proper definition of God. Whether they are right or not does not affect my argument, however.

which nothing greater can be thought, and if the "greater" in this formula must be explained, as Anselm does, in terms of perfection, then God is the most perfect being we can conceive of.[18] Now this means, as Anselm observes, that God is "whatever it is better to be than not to be."[19] In other words: God has all those properties which it is intrinsically better to possess than not to possess. Moreover, since nothing more perfect than God can be thought, God possesses all of these great-making properties in the highest possible degree.

At this stage only one additional premise is needed to complete the deductive way, viz. that it is better to possess power than not to possess power. Controversial though this assumption may be in contemporary philosophy and theology, to Anselm it is true beyond all doubt; in the *Proslogion* its truth is taken for granted without argument. Thus, as the most perfect being God must be maximally powerful, i.e. omnipotent.[20] That is: God is able to bring about all logically possible states of affairs - for the "omni" should be taken as seriously as possible. Otherwise, He would not be the most perfect conceivable being, and therefore not worthy of our worship, briefly: otherwise He would not be God.

Furthermore, like His other great-making properties, omnipotence must be a *necessary* attribute of God, in the sense that it is impossible for Him to lose it, or to have lacked it at some time in the past. For if God could possibly lose His omnipotence, or if there could possibly have been a time in the past in which He lacked it, we would clearly be able to conceive of a being more perfect than God, viz. a *necessarily* omnipotent being. Since it is impossible, however, that there should exist a being more perfect than God, God is this necessarily omnipotent being. To be sure, Anselm does not make this last step explicitly; but it logically follows from his argument for the necessary existence of God.[21] For since the concept of God analytically entails the concept of omnipotence, if God exists then the only way for Him to lose His omnipotence would be by ceasing to exist. This, however, is logically impossible if God exists necessarily. Hence, contemporary Anselmians are right in claiming explicitly that God, being IQM, possesses His omnipotence, like the other properties contributing to His perfection, in an essential and necessary way.[22]

---

[18] In fact, this loose way of rendering Anselm's formula is misleading, since it suggests that God is conceivable, which is precisely what Anselm will deny later on in his *Proslogion* (Ch. XV). According to Anselm, God transcends the human conceptual capacities. The Latin idiom of IQM is so peculiarly fit for Anselm's purposes because it expresses both the superlative and the transcending aspects of the divine being. Cf. Carlos Steel's comments in his Dutch translation, *Proslogion gevolgd door de discussie met Gaunilo*, Bussum 1981, 48, 50; M.J. Charlesworth, *St. Anselm's Proslogion*, Oxford 1965, 54-72.

[19] Anselm, *Proslogion* V (Charlesworth, *St. Anselm's*, 120f.).

[20] *Proslogion* VI.

[21] Ibid. III. The fact that Anselm sees God as both timeless and immutable may explain that there was no need for him to explicate the necessary character of God's omnipotence anyhow.

[22] Morris, "Introduction," in: id., *Concept of God*, 12; id, *Anselmian Explorations*, 12. For the

Developed along these lines, the deductive way gives us a clear image not only of the way in which omnipotence is implied by the concept of God, but also of the *sort* of omnipotence which is involved here. Omnipotence is an essential, necessary, and therefore immutable property of the God who in His necessary existence possesses ontological priority over the whole of creaturely reality. The phrase "omni" should be taken literally as quantifying over all logically possible states of affairs. Obviuisly, it is this conception of omnipotence that gives rise to the famous paradoxes concerning omnipotence (most notably the paradox of the stone) which we discussed in the previous section.

To summarize: the first answer which might be given to the question why we should ascribe omnipotence to God is, that omnipotence is semantically included in the concept of God. This can be demonstrated by means of the inductive method, as it is done sometimes in religious studies, but more convincingly along deductive lines as it is done in Anselmian theology. The latter way leads us to the affirmation of a very specific sort of divine omnipotence. But is this the only conception of divine omnipotence we can reasonably adhere to? In order to answer that question we will now discuss the second reason we might have for calling God omnipotent.

3.4.3 *God's power in the history of salvation*

A second reason for ascribing omnipotence to God would simply be that God has revealed Himself as omnipotent. Since long times there have been people who experienced God as a powerful, indeed an all-powerful, agent in their lives. In one way or another some of them had come into contact with what they experienced as the powerful divine, or more specifically as a personal God whom they came to know as all-powerful from His words and deeds. It is from such special experiences of God's self-revelation, and from their being shared with others and handed down to later generations, that the tradition's knowledge of God as (among other things) omnipotent stems.

This second reason for calling God omnipotent presupposes a different theory of reference, according to which we do not know in advance to what kind of entity we refer in using the word "God." We do not derive God's omnipotence a priori from a clear-cut *description* that uniquely picks out God, such as, for example, "the absolutely perfect being". Rather, we start with a being presented to us in individual and communal experience. On this "direct reference approach," as William Alston labels it, "we are pretty much exclusively thrown back on our experience of God, including His messages to us, to determine what God is like, though we can, of course, proceed to reason from that."[23] We learn to refer to God not by

---

difference between essential and necessary properties, see A. Vos, "De theorie van de eigenschappen en de leer van de eigenschappen van God," *Bijdragen* 42 (1981), 75-102, esp. 80f., 95f.

[23] W.P. Alston, "Referring to God," in his: *Divine Nature*, 116; in this essay Alston applies

correctly employing a particular description, but by being initiated into the religious practice of prayer, worship, confession, and so on, and by learning in this way what it is like to come into contact and communion with God.[24]

According to the Judaeo-Christian tradition, the person with whom this chain of transmission of God's revelation started was Abraham. Interestingly enough, as to God's omnipotence, the first place in the Bible where the word "almighty" occurs is in Gen.17:1, where God appears to Abraham and addresses him with the words: "I am God the Almighty."[25] Now we should be careful of course in establishing the meaning of "almighty" in such a proposition. We cannot take it for granted that we should interpret it as synonymous with what we have come to understand by omnipotence in the tradition of Anselm. It may be that a different *reason* for ascribing omnipotence to God results in a somewhat different concept of omnipotence! The Hebrew text of Gen.17:1 reads *El Shaddai* for "God the Almighty," and what that means is not entirely clear (like most of the Hebrew names of God it probably connotes some form of power),[26] but it definitely does not mean "being able to bring about all logically possible states of affairs." As we saw in chapter 2, the latter definition could only develop via the Latin rendering (*omnipotens*) of the Greek translation (*pantokrator*) of Old Testament names of God like *El Shaddai* and *YHWH Sebaoth*.

The only way to establish the meaning of "Almighty" here is to give up the atomistic approach of the term in favour of a contextual approach, which takes into account the context in which it functions.[27] Abram is ninety-nine years old, his wife Sarai ninety. Even in terms of Genesis such ages are too high to receive offspring. In this situation God addresses Himself to them, and promises them that they will become the progenitors of many people. It is obviously in order to underline His ability to realise this one particular promise of salvation that YHWH presents Himself as *El Shaddai*. When the story continues it turns out that Sarai becomes pregnant, gives birth to a child etc., in other words that God is indeed the *El Shaddai* in the sense in which He had presented Himself.

This enables us to formulate the second reason for ascribing omnipotence to God more adequately: God's omnipotence appears from His *actions*. In the same way as Abraham also Isaac, Jacob, Israel and the Chris-

---

Kripke's famous non-descriptivist theory of reference (according to which reference is secured by an "initial baptism" which uniquely identifies some object) to talk about God. Cf. Saul A. Kripke, *Naming and Necessity*, Oxford 1980[2], esp. 91-97.

[24] Alston, "Referring to God," 109.

[25] Cf. on "El Shaddai" e.g. Joh. de Groot & A.R. Hulst, *Macht en wil*, Nijkerk n.d., 110-118.

[26] See §2.2.1 above. Cf. on the power of God in the Old Testament in general De Groot & Hulst, *Macht en wil*, 178-181.

[27] Cf. B. Wentsel, *God en mens verzoend*, Kampen 1987, 473-475: "De contekst onthult de betekenis van El Sjaddai" (473). Wentsel's doctrine of God's power is a good example of a piece of biblical as distinct from Anselmian thinking.

tian community have experienced in the course of history that God is able to realize His particular promises, and it is for that reason that they came to call Him omnipotent (or came to assent to His self-revelation as the Omnipotent one). As Newbigin says:

> The Christian tradition of rationality takes as its starting point not any alleged self-evident truths. Its starting point is events in which God made himself known to men and women in particular circumstances - to Abraham and Moses, to the long succession of prophets, and to the first apostles and witnesses who saw and heard and touched the incarnate Word of God himself, Jesus of Nazareth.[28]

Thus, the concept of divine action is of central significance here in justifying the ascription of omnipotence to God. "What it will make sense to say a divine being can do depends on what it makes sense to say a divine being does."[29] In His actions, God shows Himself to possess the capacities to do the things He wants to do - that is the biblical portrayal of what His omnipotence amounts to. As we found it in Augustine: God is called omnipotent for no other reason than that He can do what He apparently wants to do.[30] God is never "naked power," His power is always conceptualized as His ability to fulfill His purposes.

Although this procedure leads, as we shall see in a moment, to a distorted view of the real situation[31], it is instructive to distinguish this "Abrahamite" conception of omnipotence as sharply as possible from the Anselmian one. Anselm derived the divine omnipotence from his rational faculties, Abraham from his experience of God's revelation. As a result, for Anselm God's omnipotence is a priori beyond all doubt; it does not need experiential confirmation, neither can it be falsified experientially. The special charm and significance of the ontological argument for Anselm had precisely been the fact that it proved the divine existence without appealing to any form of human experience whatsoever. As for Abraham, on the other hand, it is clear that he can only uphold his belief in the divine omnipotence when, in the long term at least, this belief is vindicated by God's concrete actions in life and history. Anselm's God is necessarily omnipotent; whether Abraham's God is omnipotent at all (let alone necessarily omnipotent) remains to be seen.

"Remains to be seen" is not quite the right expression, however. The strange God who had called Abraham out of Ur had not asked him to adopt an attitude of waiting, but an attitude of faith. He had asked him to leave

---

[28] Lesslie Newbigin, *The Gospel in a Pluralist Society*, London 1991³, 63.

[29] Philip E. Devenish, "Omnipotence, Creation, Perfection," 115. It does not follow necessarily, as Devenish seems to suggest, that God's omnipotence can therefore only be defined in terms of powers rather than in terms of states of affairs.

[30] Augustine, *Enchiridion* 24, 96; cf. §2.2.4, n.77.

[31] In what follows I am giving a one-sided account of Anselm's theology, which will be qualified and balanced in §3.4.4.

his own country without knowing where he was going, trusting God to keep His promise.[32] Anselm's God, on the other hand, necessarily existing and necessarily omnipotent, in no way requires such an act of faith. It is possible in principle to believe in this God and His omnipotence, while at the same time adopting an "existentially neutral" attitude towards Him.[33] Of course, in Anselm's own life this is not the case, but later on in the history of Western thought (specifically in the age of the Enlightenment) it turns out how easily arguments like those of Anselm can be abstracted from their religious context.[34] For Abraham it is in a sense a bold venture to believe in God's omnipotence, since his entire way of life is at stake. Accordingly, it is a matter of pure delight and intense joy when God fulfills His promises and thus turns out to be omnipotent indeed.

Here we meet with the old opposition between the God of the philosophers and the God of the Bible. The God of the Bible is the God who reveals Himself to people and requires their unconditional trust. He is the God who acts in history, but not in an empirically verifiable way: His acts are unpredictable, sometimes even giving the impression of sheer capriciousness. At one time they are conspicuous by their very absence, suggesting an utterly powerless God, for example at the oppression of Israel from Egypt to Auschwitz, and at the crucifixion of Jesus. But then again they gloriously attest to God's unambiguous and steadfast love, for example when Israel is brought out of Egypt "with a mighty hand" (Deut.26:8), and when Jesus is raised from the dead.[35] Abraham's God is the God whom Pascal came to know in the night of Monday 23 to Tuesday 24 November in the year 1654: "Certainty, certainty, heartfelt, joy, peace. God of Jesus Christ."[36] Anselm's God, on the contrary, is the God of the philosophers: cold and unaffected, immutable and apathetic, in His necessary being and omnipotence elevated far above the everyday experiences of common human life.

In this way, it is possible to set out both reasons for calling God omnipotent sharply over against each other. The two reasons are not only mutually exclusive, but also seem to convey two different meanings or even concepts of omnipotence. Thus, the dilemma may strike us as inescapable: shall we serve the necessarily omnipotent but at the same time lofty, ab-

---

[32] Cf. Hebr.11:8, 11.

[33] On existential neutrality, see Brümmer, *Personal God*, 59.

[34] See on this point Theo de Boer, *De God van de filosofen en de God van Pascal*, 's Gravenhage 1989, esp. 16-31, and cf. the paragraph on philosphical theism in §1.2.1 above.

[35] For discussions of the biblical witness to God's power in this vein, see Migliore, *Power of God*, ch. 3; Berkhof, *Christian Faith*, Grand Rapids 1986², §21; Van Gennep, *Terugkeer*, ch.24.

[36] Blaise Pascal, *Pensées*, tr. A.J. Krailsheimer, New York 1966, 309. The repeated "certainty" is noteworthy; the original has "certitude" here (cf. the edition of L. Brunschvicq, *Blaise Pascal. Pensées et opuscules*, Paris 1951, 142). Apparently the God of the Bible does give certainty, but it is the unique certainty (*certitudo*) of faith, not the mathematical certainty (*securitas*) with which we can be sure of the existence and nature of the God of the philosophers.

solutely transcendent God of the philosophers, or the God of the Bible, who has involved Himself in history, and asks for our faith in His continuously challenged power to realize His purposes in overcoming sin and evil? Some radically cut the knot here indeed, following as they say such thinkers as Pascal, Kierkegaard, Buber, Levinas etc. in choosing unequivocally for the God of Abraham, Isaac and Jacob as opposed to the God of the philosophers.[37]

Others, however, stand out against being forced into a dilemma here, claiming that "the God of the philosophers is not different from the God of Abraham, Isaac and Jacob."[38] In what follows I will argue that, at least from the perspective of the ascription of omnipotence, both solutions are wrong because they obscure either the similarities or the differences between the God of the philosophers and the God of the Bible. As it seems to me, the issue can only be satisfactorily solved by carefully analyzing both the aspects in which all or some philosophers concur with the biblical tradition as well as those in which they differ from it. In the next two sections I attempt to provide such an analysis with regard to the doctrine of divine omnipotence.[39]

3.4.4 *Greek influence?*

From the perspective of the history of philosophy, there are at least three considerations which force us to qualify the oversimplified way in which the God of the philosophers is sometimes opposed to the God of Abraham, Isaac and Jacob. Together they call into question the easy, undifferentiated characterization of the doctrine of divine omnipotence as simply a piece of "philosophical" or "Greek" thought. On the other hand, if we start from the biblical perspective it turns out that many questions which traditionally play a role in connection with the God of the philosophers also pertain to the God of the Bible. Thus, there are important converging tendencies from both perspectives. In what follows I will first approach the issue from the philosophical "Anselmian" perspective, stating my three considerations in what seems to me the order of increasing significance;[40] then I will take the inverse route by proceeding from the biblical "Abrahamite" perspective.

---

[37] E.g. De Boer, *God van de filosofen*. For a more extensive discussion of De Boer's views from the perspective developed in the present section, see my "Almacht bij Anselmus en Abraham." Another clear example of this strategy, but without sufficient analysis of the philosophical tradition, is De Moor, *Gods macht en liefde*.

[38] Keith Ward, *Divine Action*, 7. Eventually, I do not know of many contemporary philosophers or theologians who opt for the God of the philosophers as opposed to the God of the Bible, but in the age of the Enlightenment there were many of them, of course.

[39] I do not exclude the possibility that analyses of other attributes or aspects playing a role in the doctrine of God might lead to other results; but a general evaluation of the issue should at least include a comparison of the sorts of power which characterizes the God of the philosophers and the God of the Bible.

[40] For this reason the length of my discussion of each of them increases accordingly.

Firstly, let us consider Anselm himself once more. What should make us suspicious of portraying Anselm as the champion of the philosophers' God, is the literary form of his *Proslogion*. As is already more or less implicit in its name, the *Proslogion* is composed in the form of a prayer. Now the significance of this fact can be and has been overstated. We need not uncritically adopt the Barthian interpretation of the *Proslogion*-argument[41] in its extreme form, however, in order to be justified in drawing at least the following conclusion from the stylistic form of the *Proslogion*. Since Anselm directly addresses himself to God in prayer, clearly he must have known of this God antecedently to the development of his ontological argument. Thus, what Anselm is doing in this argument may not be so abstracted from every experience and purely grounded in rational reflection (*sola ratione*) after all. If this is correct, then the ontological argument may indeed be interpreted as a paradigmatic instantiation of the principle *fides quaerens intellectum*, with faith as the proper response to God's revelation preceding and enabling a full-fledged rational understanding of its conceptual implications. In any case, the discussion prompted by Barth on this issue is not yet closed.

Secondly, however this may be, in unfolding his argument Anselm consciously proceeds without any reference to the categories of revelation and divine action in the world. He had been so passionately searching for his ontological argument precisely because of the fact that his earlier arguments, as presented in his *Monologion*, were dependent upon premises pertaining to forms of contingent, i.e. changeable and non-universal, human experience.[42] Being dissatisfied with them for this reason, Anselm wanted to have what Abraham did not ask for: more conclusive evidence for God's existence, established with the help of necessary reasons (*rationibus necessariis*) rather than derived from contingent experience.

Not all classical Christian philosophers followed Anselm in this respect, however. For example, Thomas Aquinas, usually regarded as the greatest of them, explicitly rejected the ontological argument and replaced it by his own *quinque viae*.[43] What is interesting here is not the question whether Aquinas' five ways are more convincing than Anselm's ontological

---

[41] Karl Barth, *Anselm: Fides Quaerens Intellectum*, London 1960 (orig. ed. 1931); for current criticism of Barth, see e.g. Charlesworth, *St. Anselm's*, 40-46; others, however, (such as Steel, *Proslogion*, 54; cf.22f.; Campbell, *From Belief*, 3f., 17), have expressed a more favourable opinion on at least parts of Barth's exegesis, or even seem to echo it (e.g. De Boer, *God van de filosofen*, 42-50).

[42] On the relation between *Monologion* and *Proslogion*, see Steel, *Proslogion*, 20-24; G.R. Evans, *Anselm*, London 1989, 49f.; and, smothering the differences, Charlesworth, *St Anselm's*, 49-52.

[43] Aquinas, *Summa Theologiae* I 2, 3. For the rejection of the ontological argument see *ibid.*, I 2, 1 and *Summa contra Gentiles* I 10. A useful discussion of the reasons for this rejection and its philosophical merits is provided by Alvin Plantinga, "Aquinas on Anselm," in: C. Orlebeke & Lewis B. Smedes (eds.), *God and the Good*, Grand Rapids 1975, 122-139.

170

argument or not, but the different structure of Aquinas' argumentation on the one hand and Anselm's on the other. Aquinas does not attempt to infer his knowledge of God's existence a priori from necessary reasons, but a posteriori from the effects of God's actions in the world.[44] To spell out only one example: in his third way (the cosmological argument *e contingentia mundi*) Aquinas takes his point of departure in the experiential datum of contingent existence. We observe that there are entities in the world which exist at some times but do not exist at other times, and therefore do not exist necessarily. On the basis of this observation Aquinas tries to show that only a non-contingent, uncaused and necessary being can be credited for the existence of all contingent entities. This is the being we call God.

By thus deriving his knowledge of God from the human recognition of God's actions in creation and history, Aquinas in a sense sides with Abraham as opposed to Anselm. Even Aristotle, in whose sphere of influence Aquinas finds himself here, in principle shares Abraham's receptivity to revealing experience (although in practice it is often overshadowed by his metaphysical assumptions). One might object that this agreement is a purely formal one, which does not in any way bridge the gap between religious believers like Abraham on the one hand and the philosophers on the other. In the case of Aristotle this is of course correct.[45] But in the case of Aquinas the objection is not very convincing, since this thinking *ex effectibus* rather than in terms of self-evidence is fundamental to the very structure of his theology, and beyond him to the structure of later Catholic and Protestant thinking about God in general.

In Calvin's doctrine of God, for example, we can recognize the same structure in a very pointed way.[46] Calvin is remarkably unwilling to speak of God apart from the way in which God has revealed Himself in His words and deeds. Applied to the divine attributes this means that separate discussions of them are lacking in Calvin's systematic theology.[47] Calvin es-

---

[44] *Summa Theologiae* I 2, 2, ad 3: "Et sic ex effectibus Dei potest demonstrari Deum esse ..."; see on this point e.g. L.M. de Rijk, *Middeleeuwse wijsbegeerte*, Assen 1981², 161-166.

[45] Cf. on the relation between Aristotle and Christian thought Colin Brown, *Christianity and Western Thought*, Vol.I, Leicester 1990, 47: "If the idea of a unique personal Creator who is both the agent and goal of creation is lacking in Aristotle, there are nevertheless aspects of his thought which are compatible with Christian thought and capable of adaptation, as Thomas Aquinas was to show centuries later. Not the least of these is Aristotle's method of reflection on questions posed by our experience of the world ...".

[46] This is a confirmation of our hypothesis, adopted from Arvin Vos, *Aquinas, Calvin*, that there are more similarities between the theologies of Aquinas and Calvin than has often been recognized; cf. the historical part above, esp. § 2.3.5 n.97.

[47] Cf. John T. McNeill's comment in his edition of Calvin's *Institutes* Vol.I, Philadelphia 1960, 120 n.1: "A systematically presented list of divine attributes ..., characteristic of both medieval theologians and Reformed orthodoxy, is notably absent from Calvin." Thus, in a sense Calvin is much more modest in his claims about our human knowledge of God than many other classical theologians. God not only transcends our experiences of Him, but also is more than He has revealed of himself (here we meet a crucial difference between Calvin and Barth!). Never-

chews metaphysical speculation abstracted from the actual and existential experience of the believer in his relationship with God. There is no place for existential neutrality in his theology. With regard to the doctrine of God's omnipotence, this leads to a refusal on the part of Calvin to speak of it in terms of potential abilities. Calvin only discusses it as a function of the divine providential agency in creation and history.[48] As a result, "the best vantage point from which to view Calvin's concept of divine omnipotence is from the perspective of his doctrine of providence."[49] In brief, the concentration on an Abrahamite relationship of faith springing from the divine effects in the world, rather than on cognitive knowledge acquired *sola ratione* in the Anselmian way, is of more than trivial importance for the central thrust of mainstream Western theology.

Thirdly, it could be countered that the very conviction that God is omnipotent and absolutely sovereign is suspect in itself. Irrespective of whether this conviction is derived from any alleged experience of God's effective actions in the world or from reason alone, as part of the classical doctrine of the divine attributes it seems to originate in our philosophical heritage rather than in the biblical tradition. And clearly this conviction, whether explicitly discussed or not, is the basic axiom of Calvin's theology and, though less tangible, of the Western theological tradition as a whole.

Now unmistakably, a great deal of philosophical "Greek" thought about God was integrated in Christian theology. In the course of this process, early Christian and medieval theologians came to ascribe a number of properties which were current in Greek thought as indications of the loftiness of the divine to their biblical God.[50] What is not so clear, however, is whether by doing this they, as is often claimed, betrayed their authentic Christian belief. For Greek and Christian thought are at least not *necessarily* mutually exclusive and incompatible. The easy principle "Greek, therefore not authentically Christian" is far too simple to do justice to the issues at stake. Another simplification which is responsible for much confusion here, is in the thesis that the classical doctrine of the divine attributes *as a whole* can be subsumed under the heading "Greek thought." What often happens is that some conclusions are drawn from an examination of one or two of the most contested attributes (such as immutability, impassibility or time-lessness), which are then without further inquiry extended and uncritically

---

theless, what God has revealed is sufficient for our salvation, so that we have no excuse for existential neutrality.

[48] Calvin, *Institutes* I 14-16; see esp. I 16, 3.

[49] Case-Winters, *God's Power*, 54; cf. her preliminary definition of how Calvin conceived divine omnipotence: "For Calvin, omnipotence means *the effectual exercise of the divine personal will in accomplishing divine purposes.* ... It is exercised in the context of a relationship, and the relationship is of the personal sort." (ibid., 40; italics by the author).

[50] See, to mention only one important study on this issue, Wolfhart Pannenberg, "The Appropriation of the Philosophical Concept of God as a Dogmatic Problem of Early Christian Theology," in: *Basic Questions* Vol.II, London 1971, 119-183.

applied to the other attributes, and thus to the doctrine of God as a whole.

Immutability, impassibility and timelessness are no doubt proper qualifications of the divine in the most influential strands of Greek ontology, such as Platonism, Aristotelianism and Neoplatonism. Their impact on Christian thought must at least partly[51] be explained by the fact that they were firmly rooted in these strands of Greek philosophical thinking.[52] According to some, the same holds even for a less typically transcendent, "communicable" property like goodness.[53] Although Plato's highest Idea was that of the Good, and the eternally emanating divine in neoplatonic ontology was equated with goodness, this nevertheless does not settle the issue, since also in the (Jewish) Bible goodness is seen as one of God's most outstanding characteristics.[54]

However this may be, the thesis I want to defend here is that *the concept of omnipotence in any case does not belong to this series.* The idea that God is omnipotent does not owe its enduring popularity in Christian theology to the influence of Greek thought, since omnipotence is simply not a Greek category. Let me explain this thesis by considering the different main strands of thought in the Greek tradition. The gods of Greek mythology, to start with them, were too numerous to be omnipotent. Of course in a more or less monolatric practice all power was sometimes ascribed to one godhead, especially to Zeus.[55] In general, however, the mythological de-

---

[51] On the other hand, however, also qualities such as immutability, impassibility and timelessness can be ascribed to God wholly independent of Greek influence, viz. as corollaries of God's absolute independence (or "unconditionedness," as Marcel Sarot, *God, Possibility and Corporeality*, Kampen 1992, 48f. calls it), which is a central characteristic of the Judaeo-Christian conception of God. For recent defences of immutability, impassibility etc. in this vein, see e.g. R.A. Muller, "Incarnation, Immutability and the Case for Classical Theism," *WThJ* 45 (1983), 22-40. Brian Davies, *Thinking about God*, London 1985, 148-172; Herbert McCabe, "The Involvement of God," in his: *God Matters*, London 1987, 39-51. For a discussion see Sarot, ibid., 43-57.

[52] This is emphasized with regard to these three properties respectively by e.g. W. Maas, *Unveränderlichkeit Gottes*, Paderborn 1974 (the main purpose of which study is to show that the notion of divine immutability stems from Greek-philosophical thought, 165); J. Moltmann, *The Crucified God*, London 1977³, 267-270; N. Wolterstorff, "God Everlasting," in: Orlebeke & Smedes, *God and the Good*, 181-203.

[53] See e.g. H.M. Vroom, "God and Goodness," in: Van den Brink et al. (eds.), *Christian Faith*, 240-257. "The idea of necessary goodness has arisen under influence of Greek philosophical thought" (257).

[54] In his "Gods goedheid en het menselijk tasten," in: Maurice & Noorda (eds.), *Onzekere zekerheid*, 57, 61 Vroom criticizes the traditional metaphor of the "fountain of goodness," apparently for its neoplatonic reminiscences. He overlooks that this metaphor also has a biblical background, cf. e.g. Rev.21:6, 22:1. It does not indicate here that the divine goodness is a matter of course, but just the opposite, viz. that it evokes surprise for its unexpected abundance. Cf. also Psalms like 118.

[55] E.g. by the tragic poets and in orphic circles; the textual evidence, however, attests to pantheistic forms of worship rather than to the ascription of omnipotence to a fully personal God. See Van der Leeuw, *Religion*, 185-187 (the reference to Orphicism is only in the German orig-

ities are clearly depicted as limiting the range of each other's power. It is only since the first century A.D. that we find an "increasing emphasis on absolute divine power"[56] in the amalgamation of Jewish, Christian and pagan religious thinking. In this atmosphere, the second-century rhetorician Aelius Aristides, for example, could in his *Orations* ascribe every power to Zeus Asclepius, a god whom he believed to be personally involved in history and human life. However, if such utterances are not simply due to Jewish-Christian influence, then at least it is the congenial environment which permitted theology both Christian and pagan at that time to develop along similar lines.[57]

Next, as to the Platonic Forms including the Form of the Good, we do not get the impression that they exercise much power. Rather, they are conceived in such an impersonal and inert way that it is doubtful whether they can properly be said to wield any power at all. In Plato's *Timaeus* it is not the most divine entity, the Form of the Good, which is held responsible for the making of the physical world, but the figure of the Demiurge. When it comes to the metaphysical status of the Demiurge much is obscure; we are not sure, for example, whether Plato believed such a being as the Demiurge to exist in reality or not. What we are sure about, however, is that the Demiurge was not conceived as omnipotent. In producing the physical world the Demiurge not only had to take into account the model of the Forms, but also was limited and hampered by the pre-existent sphere of unformed, chaotic matter.[58]

Aristotle's Unmoved Mover certainly functions as the causal explanation of the universe and its history (though as its *causa finalis* rather than its *causa efficiens*). As the self-sufficient, living source of all life and energy it is a being of a different order than other beings.[59] Nevertheless, it is not omnipotent. Rather, it is the exemplary model of the deistic type of deity, which has no need (if not no power) to intervene actively in the world apart from its functioning as the first cause of all being. "If there is one thing that is clear in Aristotelian theology, ... it is that Aristotle denies his transcendent deity any form of practical activity. In his view the entire credibility of a sound theology is at stake here!."[60]

Plotinus' "One," finally, almost has powerlessness as a mark of its divinity. It is not able to do anything else than to emanate, and even that is

---

inal, Tübingen 1956[2], 207). Cf. R.M. Grant, *Gods and the One God*, Philadelphia 1986, 77f.

[56] Grant, *Gods*, 84.

[57] Ibid., 123; cf. on Aristides 116-119.

[58] See Plato, *Timaeus* 27-30, 48A-B, and compare for this and the following any good manual of the history of Western (classical) thought; especially on classical philosophical thinking about divine omnipotence, see Redmond, *Omnipotence of God*, 39-51, and Griffin, *God, Power, and Evil*, 38-53.

[59] Brown, *Christianity*, 47; cf. in general 43-48.

[60] A.P. Bos, "World-Views in Collision," in: D.T. Runia (ed.), *Plotinus amid Gnostics and Christians*, Amsterdam 1984, 18.

something which it can hardly be said to do freely. Since it is immutable, it is necessarily involved in the eternally emanating flow of *exitus* and *reditus*. As absolutely transcendent to the physical reality it is not capable of action - let alone of omnipotent action - within it.[61] In a sense, however, it is quite improper to say that the One is *not able* to do anything else than to emanate, or *incapable* of action. For since it would be demeaning to the One if it had to act in any way, its incapacity to act is not at all an imperfection. On the contrary, the divine has no need of power! Neoplatonism is the culmination point of Greek thought in many respects, one of these being its carrying to extremes the idea that the intellectual life is superior to the practical life. It is hard to overestimate the impact of this idea on, for example, the Greek doctrine of God. Whereas the Aristotelian divine being is still supposed to be eternally involved in the activity of thinking himself (*noèsis noèseoos*), the Neoplatonic One is even exempted from this "labour." It is here, in the identification of divine perfection with a life of totally self-contained inertia that the most crucial difference between Greek metaphysics and the Judaeo-Christian tradition lies.[62]

These admittedly very general remarks on the main currents in Greek thought may suffice to demonstrate that the Christian ascription of omnipotence to God should not be considered as a Greek heritage. One might object that in most of these Greek traditions the divine certainly is omnipotent, but that its almighty power is manifested in other ways than those I have in mind. For instance, in Plato, Aristotle and Plotinus the divine, itself being absolutely self-sufficient and transcendent, exercises universal power in that all things are utterly dependent upon it for their existence. Further, there is an important deterministic line of thought in Greek philosophy as a whole,[63] according to which all events unfold themselves with absolute necessity from the divine first cause. Thus, it seems that this first cause exercises its power by determining everything which happens.

This objection can easily be rebutted, however. As to its latter part, we saw already (in §2.3 above), that Greek necessitarianism compromises God's omnipotence rather than articulating it.[64] The notion of God's *potentia absoluta* was introduced precisely as a conceptual tool for counteracting it. And as to its former part, concerning the divine self-sufficiency and transcendence as well as the radical dependence of all existing reality upon it, these notions have certainly influenced the shape of Christian theology. However, apart from the fact that it is far from clear that all of these no-

---

[61] That the Neoplatonic One is unable to act is explicitly affirmed in Plotinus' *Enneads* I 7, 1.

[62] Cf. Muller, "Incarnation," 27-29.

[63] Cf. Vos, *Kennis en noodzakelijkheid*, 1-38, 245-247.

[64] Again, the background for this lies in the specifically Greek idea of perfection: To have potentiality and choice implies to have failed to determine oneself timely, and therefore to be imperfect.

tions are incompatible with the Judaeo-Christian doctrine of God, they obviously express something different from what is comprised in the notion of divine omnipotence. What is involved in the notion of divine omnipotence is the unlimited power or ability to bring things about by acting in the world.

It is with regard to this notion that I claim to have shown that it does not stem from Greek sources. In general, the Greek considered it to be unworthy for their deities to act and to bring about things, for acting means that something is lacking and has to be brought about. The gods, however, don't lack anything, and therefore they don't need a property like omnipotence. Thus, the ascription of omnipotence to God can only be explained from the perspective of the biblical, monotheistic tradition with its personal conception of God. Let us now consider somewhat more closely the way in which the notion of divine omnipotence arises from this tradition, in order to come to a final comparison with the way in which it arises from the Anselmian tradition.

3.4.5 *Omnipotence as a biblical concept*

Since this is a study in philosophical rather than in biblical theology, I will not attempt to give detailed exegeses of biblical passages in which God's power plays a prominent role. Nevertheless, it is important for my purposes to indicate some of the most conspicuous aspects of the biblical conception of God's power. I have argued above that the omnipotence of the God of Abraham, Isaac and Jacob is primarily located in His ability to realize His promises in concrete, often unexpected, salvific actions in history. It is the power by means of which He calls Isaac out of the barren womb of Sara, Israel out of its womb Egypt, and his Son Jesus out of the darkness of the tomb, which also turns out to be a womb of new life. At the same time, it is the power by means of which He conquers in various ways the forces of evil which try or are employed to obstruct these salvific actions: the military forces of Abimelech (Gen.20), of Pharaoh at the Red Sea and of Pilate at the tomb. In other words: the way in which God shows His omnipotence to Abraham exemplifies the way in which He manifests it throughout the whole of the biblical history.

Now since the God of the Bible is a God who acts in history, the question arises as to how far His possibilities for action reach. For example, when we say that God realizes His promise by letting Isaac be born, we imply that His power is not constrained by the laws of nature. For clearly it is a biological law of nature that a woman after her change of life is no longer fertile. In the present context it does not matter whether God violates these laws of nature by suspending them in the case of Sara, or whether He only makes use of their structural openness,[65] for instance (to mention only

---

[65] For a defence of this approach of direct divine action, see William P. Alston, "God's Action in the World," in: id., *Divine Nature and Human Language*, Ithaca 1989, 197-222, esp.2-

one conceivable scenario) by arranging that an accidentally surviving germ-cell became fertilized. In both cases the laws of nature do not set bounds to the realm of the divine possibilities for action. That means, in turn, that we can hardly if at all conceive of anything which it is beyond God's power to bring about. The only cases which may come to mind are those in which "God brings about x" involves a contradiction. However, the view that contradictory statements do not specify things but nonentities, as C.S. Lewis once pointedly put it, is at the very least prima facie reasonable.[66]

We will return to this issue later, but here it is important to state that precisely the same conclusion is drawn in the biblical literature. From their experience of God's mighty acts people come to the conclusion that nothing could be impossible for this God. Already in Gen.18 it is asked as a rhetorical question, aimed at underlining the sincerity of the promise concerning Isaac's birth, whether anything would be too hard for the Lord to do. The same or virtually the same question is repeated, often in the form of an affirmative statement, in many strands of the biblical literature: "Nothing is impossible with God!"[67] Of course we should not misconstrue such utterances as downright factual propositions. The exclamation mark already indicates that we have to do here with exclamations and acclamations rather than with factual statements. As I have argued in §2.2.4, however, although the explicitly asserted illocution of the speech act in question is either an expressive (when uttered by the addressee of the promise) or a commissive (when uttered by or on behalf of the promising God), the assertion of a constative is undeniably implied in it. For it would be logically incoherent to exclaim or promise: "Nothing is impossible for God!," and at the same time to contend that there are of course in fact many things which God is unable to do. Thus, if God's promises are in any way relevant to our concrete physical and biological reality, then His possibilities for action should be conceived as extending to this same reality. And if God's promises are to be unconditionally trusted, we cannot avoid the ascription of unrestricted possibilities for action to God.[68]

In this way, we seem to have returned to the literal meaning of omni-

---

12f. Cf. also C.S. Lewis, *Miracles*, New York 1947, chapter 8.

[66] "... meaningless combinations of words do not suddenly acquire meaning simply because we prefix to them the two other words 'God can'. It remains true that all *things* are possible with God: the intrinsic impossibilities are not things but nonentities." C.S. Lewis, *The Problem of Pain*, London 1946[17], 16. Incidentally, Peter Geach, *Providence*, 13, rightly points out that in this quotation Lewis conflates syntactically incoherent combinations of words and self-contradictory statements.

[67] Cf. on the scope of God's power apart from Gen.18:14, Jer.32:27, Job 42:2, Mat.28:18, Mark 10:27 p.p., Luke 1:37. See also the list in §2.2.4 above, in connection with n.90.

[68] As is attempted by e.g. F.O. van Gennep, *Terugkeer*, 416-427, 452-458. Van Gennep on the one hand encourages his readers to lead a life in the light of God's promises, and on the other hand denies that God is able to act physically in the world. Peter Geach, *Providence*, 5, is more consistent in this respect.

potence which the Anselmian philosophers are so keen to maintain.[69] Does this mean that, despite their different derivations, both conceptions of omnipotence distinguished in the present section are identical after all? Is Keith Ward vindicated in his equation of the God of the philosophers with the God of Abraham in the end, at least with respect to the nature of God's power? As it seems to me, this is not exactly what follows from our argument up to now. What does follow is that the omnipotence of both Abraham's and Anselm's God consists in His unrestricted possibilities for action, or His ability to bring about all logically possible states of affairs. Nevertheless, there are at least five differences between these conceptions, due to the different contexts in which they arise. Since it is of crucial importance not to overlook these differences, let us now briefly discuss them one by one.

Firstly, in Anselmian thought the statement "God is omnipotent" is first of all a constative, a factual claim, whereas in the Bible it is as we saw primarily an expressive or commissive, and only by implication a constative. In other words, in the Bible belief in God's omnipotence is never abstracted from the existential experience of God's actions in creation and history, as well as in the personal lives of people of flesh and blood. It has its home (i.e., both its context of discovery and its context of justification[70]) at the place where God's words and deeds are heard and experienced. It is significant that in the book of Revelation the predicate "omnipotent" is almost always ascribed to God in a liturgical setting, in the context of praise and worship: that is where it inalienably belongs. In Anselmian thinking, on the other hand, the context of prayer and worship can eventually be stripped off without affecting the argument, as becomes especially clear in the Enlightenment period.[71] The only thing which is needed here is sound logic.

Secondly, in the Bible the nature of God's omnipotence is disclosed in the realization of God's promises in his actions. It is not, as in Anselmian theology, derived from some preconceived concept of power with which we are acquainted from our common interpersonal power-relations. Therefore, we do not get a proper understanding of God's omnipotence by simply extrapolating our everyday notion of power infinitely.[72] In that case God would simply be a ruler of the human sort, admittedly much more powerful than all of us, but nevertheless not qualitatively different as a result of God's perfect character. Such a way of conceiving the divine omnipotence

---

[69] Cf. Flint & Freddoso, "Maximal Power," and Wierenga, *Nature of God*, chapter 1.

[70] For the use of these terms from the philosophy of science in theology, cf. Wentzel van Huyssteen, *Theology & the Justification of Faith*, Grand Rapids 1989, 7 and passim.

[71] De Boer, *God van de filosofen*, 16-31; cf. the discussion in H.M. Vroom (ed.), *De God van de filosofen en de God van de Bijbel*, Zoetermeer 1991, esp. the essays of B. Vedder and P. Jonkers, and De Boer's response (132, 140f.).

[72] See on this point I.T. Ramsey, "The Paradox of Omnipotence"; J. van Genderen & W.H. Velema, *Beknopte gereformeerde dogmatiek*, Kampen 1992, 177. For a biblical theological elaboration of the specific character of God's power, see e.g. Van Gennep, *Terugkeer*, 416-423.

would have disastrous consequences for theology, since the possession and use of power in the human realm is inextricably linked with sin and evil. But the biblical discourse of God's almightiness is not simply an extension of our own power-politics, precisely because its primary function is to accentuate the trustworthiness of God's promises of ultimate salvation over evil. Thus, the omnipotence of God is not an arbitrary power, causing both good and evil depending on the whims of its exerciser.

It is the systematic relevance of the notion of God's *potentia ordinata*, as we saw it functioning in Thomas Aquinas, to rule out this misunderstanding. Another way of avoiding this misconception would have been by an appeal to the doctrine of divine simplicity, which bars the way to separate God's attributes, such as His omnipotence and His goodness, from one another. In scholastic thinking, however, this doctrine was not usually employed theologically to emphasize the unity of God's attributes, but rather God's transcendence, aseity and otherness.[73] It could hardly be used for illuminating the nature of God's omnipotence, moreover, since if it were, God's omnipotence should not only have to be considered as qualified by His goodness, but also by His timelessness and immutability. And in that case a notion of omnipotence would have developed which excluded God's ability to relate to a temporally structured world of change at all. Accordingly, Christoph Schwöbel argues that "the traditional interpretation of God's omnipotence seems to confront us with the choice between an omnipotent God whose omnipotence excludes only the logically impossible, but not arbitrariness, and an omnipotent God who cannot relate to a temporal world subject to contingent change."[74] This dilemma was solved, however, by the classical distinction between God's *potentia absoluta* and *potentia ordinata*. The latter notion was introduced precisely to exclude from God's omnipotence the arbitrariness which is always involved in our human exercise of power.[75]

This is not to say that this classical reception of the biblical notion of omnipotence was not liable to human abuse. Certainly the Christian doctrine concerning God's power (as well as its Anselmian philosophical counterpart) could be and has been and indubitably still is abused for legitimating improper human claims to power and authority. For theologians or philosophers such as Sölle, Van Gennep en De Boer this fact offers sufficient reason to reject all forms of traditional talk about God's omni-

---

[73] As is shown by Immink, *Divine Simplicity*; see esp. 23-31.

[74] C. Schwöbel, "Exploring the Logic of Perfection," in: Van den Brink et al. (eds.), *Christian Faith*, 214.

[75] This crucial systematic value of the distinction was of course my main reason for paying so much attention to its development in my historical survey (§2.3). See also Luco J. van den Brom, "En is Hij niet een God voor filosofen?," in: H.M. Vroom (ed.), *God van de filosofen*, 109f., 168f. It is not the case that "the notion of *potentia absoluta* is rejected in Christian faith" (169), however; what is rejected (and this is what Van den Brom means to say) is any conception of *potentia absoluta* which is isolated from the notion of *potentia ordinata*.

potence.[76] As Ulrich Bach has pointed out, however, such a rejection is inadequate for two reasons. First, in principle there is no theological claim which is immune for abuse. Even if we substituted talk of God's omnipotence by talk of, for example, His humility (as is proposed by De Boer), this would hardly solve anything, since people in power could in that case require such praiseworthy humility from their subjects. The only way to prevent abuse of theological utterances is to stop speaking of God at all. But, second, precisely that would be to the advantage of those who exercise illegitimate power. For the biblical confirmation of God's existence and omnipotence implies the fundamental qualification and relativation of all human totalitarian power-claims. To God alone belongs the power and authority over my life, not to any boastful human being. If we refused to call God omnipotent after Hitler, we would after all have our theological agenda determined by Hitler in a disgraceful way! Theology can only be done by means of morally damaged and vulnerable concepts. What counts is in what *context* these concepts are used. Thus, it turns out again that the context in which our talk of God's omnipotence takes place is of crucial importance.[77]

Thirdly, unlike Anselmian theology the biblical tradition does not suggest that God is *necessarily* omnipotent, in the sense that if He were not omnipotent, He would not be God.[78] Nowhere in the Bible is the concept of God considered to be strictly equivalent to the concept of omnipotence. Abraham learns to know God as omnipotent, but he does not come to know Him as essentially omnipotent. On the contrary, as Abraham experienced and as is clear from both the Old and the New Testament, God's power is continuously challenged by counterforces which try to thwart His intentions. This does not mean that God is not omnipotent (as, for example, H. Berkhof argues[79]). As the Creator of heaven and earth He certainly is. It does mean, however, that since the time of creation God's omnipotence is no longer a matter of course, of absolute necessity. Therefore, omnipotence is not an essential attribute of God. It is not logically impossible for God to lose His power. Perhaps some find this a threatening view, since it seems to represent God's power as fleeting, unstable and precarious. But then consider that we are talking about a *voluntary* resignation here. In a way, one could argue that the possibility of such resignations is is even implied by God's

---

[76] D. Sölle, *Suffering*; "Vom Gott-über-uns zum Gott-in-uns," *EK* 23 (1990), 614f.; Van Gennep, *Terugkeer*, 427 (for the influence of Sölle, see 375f.); De Boer, *God van de filosofen*, 156.

[77] See for this line of thought Ulrich Bach's reply to Sölle's "Vom Gott über uns": "Schüttet das Kind nicht mit dem Bade aus!," *EK* 24 (1991), 289-292.

[78] Here I side with Davis, *Logic*, 73, 76: "Someone may object that necessary omnipotence is part of the concept of God, but ... I [do not] see any reason why it must be part of the *Christian* concept of God" (my italics).

[79] Berkhof, *Christian Faith*, 146, 451. Cf. L. van Driel, *Over het lijden en God*, Kampen 1988, 56f.

being really omnipotent, since omnipotence should include the ability to give up and so to lose (part of) one's power. As Karl Barth says, to deny God this ability would be to make Him the prisoner of His own power![80]

Interestingly, this biblical portrayal of God's power offers us an unambiguous solution to the paradoxes of omnipotence which we considered in the previous section. Let us illustrate this solution with regard to the paradox of the stone. The question whether God can make a stone which is of such a kind that He is unable to lift it afterwards should be answered in the affirmative.[81] If God made such a stone, He would thereby give up part of His power. But as long as He does not make such a stone because He does not want to, He continues to be omnipotent. Now of course from a theological perspective this is a rather trivial example. We have to inquire whether the non-necessary character of God's omnipotence has theologically more significant ramifications. For example, to what extent does God's creation of morally free human beings have similar consequences as His creation of the stone contemplated in the paradox of the stone? It is with questions like these that we will have to deal in the next chapter.

Fourthly, we must go one step further still. Not only does the Bible refrain from ascribing necessary omnipotence to God, it to some extent also qualifies the "omni" in a rather uncomplicated way. Especially in the later parts of the canonical literature a number of things are mentioned with respect to which it is stated that God cannot do them.[82] For example, it is said that God cannot swear by someone greater than Himself (Hebr.6:13), and that He cannot lie (Hebr.6:18). Further, God cannot deny Himself (2 Tim.2:13), and He cannot be tempted by evil (James 1:13). Clearly, in the first case we have to do with something which is logically impossible *for God* to do, since no one greater than God exists, in the other cases we have to do with things which are incompatible with God's character, especially with His moral perfection. All four examples, however, refer to states of affairs which are in themselves logically possible. Most if not all of us are able to swear by someone greater than ourselves, to lie, to deny ourselves, and to be tempted by evil. So it seems that the word "all" in the statement "all things are possible for God" should not be interpreted as a logical operator quantifying over literally all possible states of affairs. Here again the Anselmian conception of omnipotence differs from the biblical one.

It is noteworthy that also Thomas Aquinas quite unproblematically provides a list of things which God, though omnipotent, cannot do. According to me, it is not accidental that Aquinas' list consists of examples belonging to the same two categories as the examples we quoted from the

---

[80] Barth, *Church Dogmatics* II 1, 587.

[81] Here I concur with Swinburne, *Coherence of Theism*, 157f. In questioning the claim that God should be thought of as *essentially* or *necessarily* omnipotent, I follow Davis, *Logic*, 73, 76.

[82] Again, we are now systematically elaborating a point which we encountered already in the historical part of our inquiry: see §2.2.4 above.

Bible.[83] Anselm, on the other hand, had to devote a separate chapter of his *Proslogion* to the antinomies evoked by his deduction of the concept of omnipotence from the concept of God.[84] In present-day Anselmian theology, the relation between God's omnipotence and His nature, especially His goodness, is still highly problematic, as is clear from the complex discussion in Flint & Freddoso, issuing in what is only a tentative conclusion.[85]

Fifthly, the Bible not only ascribes power to God, but also weakness. According to Paul, the divine weakness is manifested particularly in the Cross of Christ (1 Cor.1). How does this Pauline emphasis affect the ascription of omnipotence to God? Of course it may be that the weakness of God is not quantitatively but qualitatively different from His power, indicating the sort of power which is involved in God's furthering His purposes. But even so, Anselmian theology with its focus on the upper logical limit of power has difficulties to capture this distinctive character of God's power. In this connection Paul Helm has a point when he observes: "A Christian account of divine power could hardly omit the Pauline emphasis, but it could well be omitted by perfect being theology; perhaps perfect being theology *must* discount it."[86]

If we substitute the Anselmian conception of omnipotence by the "Abrahamite" one, some of the conceptual difficulties we came across in the previous section can quite easily be solved. For there is no need to insist that God must possess a form of literal omnipotence unqualified by His character. An adequate analysis of God's omnipotence need not suggest that God in some way can do things which are logically impossible for Him to do or which are incompatible with His nature. Of course, God's omnipotence includes his being *able* to do evil, in the sense of having sufficient power and abilities to bring about evil states of affairs. It is even vital to uphold this, since this ability is constitutive for the moral character of God.[87] But that does not imply that God therefore *can* do evil, in the sense that it is a live option for Him to choose to do so. It is precisely the wish to maintain that it is possible for God to do literally everything, including

---

[83] Aquinas, *Summa contra Gentiles* II 25; cf. Brümmer, *What Are We Doing When We Pray?*, London 1985, 30-33.

[84] *Proslogion* VII; cf. §2.3.1 above.

[85] Flint & Freddoso, "Maximal Power," 101-108.

[86] P. Helm, "The Power and Weakness of God," unpublished paper; I am grateful to Prof. Helm for sending me a copy of this paper, the intentions of which are very similar to my own concern in the present section (although its strategy differs). Another study which tries to account for this aspect of weakness in the doctrine of God without abandoning the doctrine of divine almightiness John Timmer, *God of Weakness*, Grand Rapids 1988; E. David Cook, "Weak Church - Weak God," in: Nigel M. de S. Cameron (ed.), *The Power and Weakness of God*, Edinburgh 1990, 69-92, on the other hand, argues that talk of the weakness of God "omits the power of God to overcome sin and transform the sinner" (88), which in my view is not necessarily the case.

[87] Cf. the lucid argument of William Wainwright, "Christian Theism and the Free Will Defence," *IJPR* 6 (1975), 248-250.

what is contrary to His nature and perhaps even what seems logically impossible for Him to do, which gives rise to some of the antinomies and
hairsplitting discussions listed in the previous section. As soon as we see,
however, that we need not stick to a literal conception of divine omnipotence, we can easily solve, for example, the problem of impeccability. For
although God is able to do evil, given His perfectly good character He
cannot bring Himself to do so, and therefore there is not the slightest chance
that at any time He will perform evil.[89]

Can we apply a similar argument to the relation between God's
power and modal logic? Should we say that although God is able to change
the laws of logic, there is not the slightest chance that He does so, since He
cannot bring Himself to do so? Or should we construe the relation between
God and logic in some other way? That question is so complicated, that we
devote the final section of the present chapter to it.

3.4.6 Conclusion

In conclusion, my elaboration of a religiously adequate notion of divine
omnipotence has vindicated the Geach-thesis, that we should distinguish
between a philosophical and a properly Christian concept of omnipotence.
My way of distinguishing between these two concepts differs in some respects from Geach's, however. First, I have shown that it does not make
sense to define the philosophical concept as power to do all things and the
religious concept as power over all things. Instead, I have argued that both
concepts can be defined as power to do all things. Second, I have not been
able to confirm Geach's contention that it is impossible to give a sound
definition and analysis of the philosophical concept of omnipotence. Instead,
I have suggested that all of the conceptual problems which Geach raises
may in principle be overcome (though I have not seen an analysis which
does so in a completely convincing way). Third, I have questioned Geach's
suggestion that God's omnipotence does not imply the ability to do evil.
Instead, I have claimed that although God has the ability to do evil, He
cannot do evil because of His character.

Despite these differences, however, Geach is quite right in distinguishing between two concepts of omnipotence, a philosophical one and a
religious one, only the second of which is of use in philosophical theology.
In order to be able to distinguish between these concepts in an easy way
(for reasons of practice rather than of principle), I will accept Geach's
proposal, and henceforth call the first one omnipotence and the second
almightiness. Whereas belief in the almightiness of God belongs to the core
of Christian faith, "a Christian cannot belief in absolute, uncircumscribed
omnipotence."[90] The differences between both concepts have been expounded above, and I will not repeat them here. But in short, "omnipotence"

---

[89] Cf. Brümmer, "Divine Impeccability," as well as Pike's view rendered above (§ 3.3.4).
[90] Urban & Walton (eds.), *Power of God*, 11.

is a concept which we derive from our preconceived notions of God and of power, and which can simply be defined as the ability to do all logically possible things. Almightiness, on the other hand, is a concept we infer from our experience of God's revelatory actions, and which can be defined as God's ability to do all things which are compatible with His nature. Whether these things also in some way or other include logical impossibilities, is what we are going to examine next.

3.5 LOGIC AND THE LIMITS OF POWER

3.5.1 *Introduction*

In the previous section I have sketched the main lines of a religious, biblical conception of God's almightiness as distinguished from what I have alternately called the literal, philosophical, a priori, Anselmian or "bare" concept of omnipotence. I have shown that on the one hand this biblical conception of God's powerful activity is a far cry from the Greek idea of divine impotence and inertia, but that on the other hand it cannot simply be identified with our pre-conceived notion of literal omnipotence. It was this notion of literal omnipotence which had turned out to be problematic in many respects in the last section but one. There we met with a number of conceptual puzzles and riddles which proved not open to ready-made solutions. The question that naturally emerges now is, whether the biblical conception of God's almightiness as outlined in the previous section provides us with a vantage point which enables us to solve these conceptual problems convincingly. This is what I plan to examine now. First of all, I want to consider the relation between God's power and the laws of logic, since, as we saw above, the way we construe this relation has important implications for the doctrine of God's power as a whole.

Obviously, a biblical conception of divine power does not in itself settle the issue whether laws of logic, abstract entities such as numbers, properties and their relations, universals etc. are subject to God's power or not. When it is stated that "nothing is impossible for God," that "all things derive from God,"[1] or that God is the "maker of all things visible and invisible" (Nicene Creed) it is clear that what the writers have in mind is not such things as laws of logic (provided for a moment that these are "things").[2] What they do want to express is that God's intentions cannot be thwarted, since nothing falls outside the scope of God's control. But are the laws of logic like entities which can be controled? Are such analytical truths as "2+2=4" and "a circle is round" or "red is a colour" included in the things which do not fall outside God's control, and if so, what are the implications of this? Or is it coherent to maintain both that God's intentions are

---

[1] Romans 11:36.
[2] N. Wolterstorff, *On Universals*, Chicago 1970, ch.12.

inthwartable and that such analytical truths are independent of God's will?

Here, of course, we are back again with the questions which Descartes was so anxious to answer in a radical way in his discussions of the "eternal truths." Since as a result of new developments in the philosophy of religion interest in these issues has revived in recent times,[3] we will seriously discuss Descartes' view and its contemporary varieties as defended in what has come to be called the "neo-cartesian school."[4] As it seems to me, there are at least four possible positions with regard to the relation between God and logic which deserve attention. Using more or less common labels, let us refer to them respectively as universal possibilism, universal creationism, theistic activism and standard independentism. I will first briefly indicate the differences between these four positions, and then try to find out which of them offers the most adequate conceptualization of the relation between God's power and the laws of logic by comparing the relative advantages and disadvantages of each of them.

Universal possibilism takes the view that nothing is impossible for God to extremes, insisting that God is able to make logical contradictions true at any time He wants. This means that for every proposition p (whether logically coherent or not), p is possible. Universal creationism is the view that God is unable to change the modal status of propositions, but was free to determine the modal status as well as the truth value of every proposition in the moment of creation.[5] So at the time of creation God could have made logical contradictories either possibly or necessarily true, and necessary truths either possibly or necessarily false, but it is no longer possible for Him to do such things now. According to theistic activism, although necessary truths and falsehoods are precisely what they are called, viz. *necessarily* true and false, and thus independent of God's power and will even at the moment of creation, they nevertheless are created by God. According to standard independentism, finally, the necessary truths and falsehoods are completely independent of God, not even being created by Him.

3.5.2 *The irrefutability of universal possibilism*
The advantage of universal possibilism is, that it seems to do maximal justice to the sovereignty and almightiness of God. Necessary truths and necessary falsehoods may be necessary for us they are not so for God. They cannot be necessary for an almighty God, since if they were, they would be brute facts which limited God's possibilities for action in a way that detracted from His perfection. Moreover, if God cannot make it the case that "2+2=5," or that "human beings have freedom of choice and at the same

---

[3] Like so many new developments in the philosophy of religion, this one has been initiated by a publication of Alvin Plantinga, in this case his *Does God Have a Nature?*

[4] Charles Taliaferro, "The Limits of Power," *P&Th* 5 (1990), 116.

[5] For these two options, cf. the different interpretations of Descartes' doctrine of the creation of the eternal truths discussed in §2.4.

time their free actions are determined by God," it is simply false that "everything is possible for God." On the contrary, in that case God's power would be limited in numerous ways: He would (probably[6]) be unable to change the past, He would be unable to perform tasks as specified in the paradoxes of omnipotence, to bring about things which are incompatible with His own essential attributes (i.e., with His own nature), to create other omnipotent beings etc. If universal possibilism is true, however, God can do all such things, since the fact that they are contradictory (either in themselves, or conditionally upon some other state of affairs) does not make a difference for God: He is able to realize them anyway!

One or more of the following three objections are usually raised against this view. It has been urged against universal possibilism (1) that it is incoherent, (2) that it is unintelligible, and (3) that it is counter-intuitive, since it clashes with our ordinary linguistic form of life. I will argue that although all of these objections are sound, none of them succeeds in proving that universal possibilism is false. Objection (3), however, forces the universal possibilist to qualify his position to a considerable degree.

First, in order to substantiate the charge that universal possibilism is incoherent, look at the following proposition which expresses the universal possibilist's position:

(P)   God has power over all truths.

Now what about (P) itself? Either God has no power over (P), in which case (P) is false since there is at least one truth over which God has no power, or He does have power over (P). If He has, then it is possible that He decides P to be false. This, in turn, implies

(PP)   It is possible that God has no power over all truths.

Clearly, if both (P) and (PP) are true, then it is up to God to decide whether the possibility specified in (PP) becomes realized or not, i.e., to determine whether He has power over all truths or not. For otherwise (PP) would be a truth over which God has no power, in which case universal possibilism would be incoherent. If it is up to God to decide whether He has power over all truths, obviously the only way for Him to secure that He has no power over all truths would be by *limiting* His power so as to exclude one or more truths from the realm of truths falling under his power. But now consider (P'):

(P')   God has power over all truths unless He limits his power.

Clearly this is a necessary truth, since there is no way even for God to make

---

[6] I.e., if changing the past is logically impossible.

it the case that (P') is false. Therefore, either God has no power over (P) or God has no power over (P'). In either case there is a truth which falls outside God's power, so universal possibilism is incoherent on any account.[7]

However, the universal possibilist need not in any way be disturbed by the successfulness of this argument. Rather than trying to refute it, he may simply point to the fact that even if the charge of incoherence is correct this does not falsify his theory. For his theory precisely consists in the claim, that God can make incoherent propositions true, so that it is possible for a theory to be both incoherent and true. It may even be the case that God, inscrutable as His ways are, secures the realization of (PP) by enhancing His power rather than by limiting it. In this sense, universal possibilism is irrefutable by an appeal to the common resources of logical reasoning, since it questions the necessary validity of these resources.[8]

Second, it might be objected that universal possibilism is an unacceptable position because it is *unintelligible*. We simply cannot imagine what it would mean - to mention some of its implications - that 2 plus 2 may equal 5, or that the law of non-contradiction may from now on no longer hold, or that God can both make a stone which He cannot lift and lift that very stone, that He might even do so without Himself existing at that moment, etc. Or to stick to our previous point: if God's infinite power both entails that all truths are up to God and that there is at least one truth which is not up to God, then we cannot grasp the concept of God's infinite power. In short, if we claim such things we do not know what we are saying. So how could we hold that such claims are true if we do not even know what they amount to?

Like the first one, this objection can also rather easily be rebutted, however. For universal possibilism intentionally insists that there *are* things which we cannot possibly grasp and understand. Far from showing that some state of affairs cannot exist, the fact that we cannot imagine such a state of affairs duly reminds us of our human finitude, and more specifically: of the limitedness of our mental capacities. God's thoughts are higher than ours, however, and it would be preposterous to hold that God's power is bound by our humanly limited capacities for imagination. That would be creating a God in our own image! As Stephen Davis has a fictitious de-

---

[7] Of course, there seem to be easier ways to show the incoherence of universal possibilism, e.g. by showing that it has incoherent implications, such as (Q): "It is possibly true that both 2+2=5 and 2+2=4." But a defender of universal possibilism's coherence might counter that (Q), though false (and perhaps necessarily false) is not incoherent, since incoherence should be defined much more narrowly, such as to consist in e.g. "offering an argument of such a sort that in accepting one of the premises one is committed to denying the conclusions" (Plantinga, *Does God Have a Nature*, 120). Therefore, I have chosen a somewhat less elegant way of showing universal possibilism's incoherence in order to satisfy Plantinga's examples of incoherence. In doing so, I have summarized an argument put forward by Eleonore Stump in her review of Plantinga's book, in *The Thomist* 47 (1983), 617-620.

[8] Cf. Davies, *Thinking about God*, 175; Geach, *Providence and Evil*, 9; Stump, ibid., 620.

fender of universal possibilism saying:

> It is true that definition (A) [Davis's equivalent of universal possibilism] leads to *what we understand* as contradictions. But surely our minds are limited in comparison to God's infinite wisdom. Surely there are systems of logic God can understand but we can't in which what seem to us to be contradictions make perfectly good sense.[9]

And Davis rightly gives this universal possibilist her due, granting that our minds are limited indeed, so that there might be "a system of logic L' which God understands and we do not in which *Jones is a married bachelor* is not only coherent but true."[10] Since it is very difficult if not impossible for us to draw the boundary line between what is unintelligible to us simply as a result of our defective knowledge and insight, and what is unintelligible "in itself," we cannot with absolute certainty subsume certain statements under the latter category.

Third, however, it might be argued that nevertheless we still cannot have the vaguest idea how a system like L' would work, or what a proposition like *Jones is a married bachelor* (given the usual definition of a bachelor as an unmarried man) would mean. For what we can meaningfully say is determined by our common standards of rational discourse, which in turn rest upon our acceptance of the necessary validity of the laws of logic. We cannot circumvent this acceptance and at the same time claim that what we say is meaningful. One way to illustrate this point is as follows. According to the universal possibilist, it is possible for God to make contradictions true, since the laws of logic do not apply to Him. But in saying that it is *possible* for God to make contradictions true, i.e. to do the logically impossible, either we derive the meaning of "possible" from our standard framework of modal logic, in which case the claim is contradictory, or we equivocate upon the meaning of "possible," in which case it is unclear what we are saying. In both cases, we would be flouting our ordinary standards of speech and thought if we held that the claim is nonetheless true.

Again, this objection does not show that universal possibilism is false, since even though certain claims are not meaningful *to us* they may be true. We have little reason to assume that only utterances which are meaningful to us are true. This is why the usual form of criticism against universal possibilism is not decisive. Consider Richard Swinburne's formulation of this criticism: "A logically impossible action is not an action.

---

[9] Davis, *Logic*, 78.

[10] Ibid.; Stump, ibid., 621, overlooks this point. Oddly enough, Davis himself immediately goes on to add that we have no present grounds for affirming the claim about L'. But obviously the ground for the claim about L' is precisely the fact that it articulates the limitedness of our mental capacities and the absolute distinction in this respect between Creator and creature; both of these notions are deeply embedded in the Christian tradition (contrast Davis's reference to Scripture and Christian tradition in this connection, ibid.).

It is what is described by a form of words which purport to describe an action, but do not describe anything which it is coherent to suppose could be done."[11] Or take Thomas Morris's complaint that universal possibilism "comes out by simple argument to be either trivially false or conceptually malformed."[12] The tacit presupposition underlying such criticisms is that our ordinary conceptual and linguistic standards - determining among other things that actions can only be done if it is coherent to suppose that they can be done, and that only conceptually well-formed descriptions are possibly true - are necessarily true. But it is precisely this claim which universal possibilism calls into question! Therefore, our third objection is in no way a knock-down argument against universal possibilism.

What our third objection does show, however, is that universal possibilism is incompatible with the linguistic and conceptual forms of life in which all of us take part insofar as we are engaged in rational thinking and discourse. It is our linguistic practice which makes it impossible for us to trust the claim that contradictions might be true. Take for example advice such as: "If you want to come to my home it might be true that you should simultaneously take the right and the left side at the traffic lights." If universal possibilism is correct, this is a perfectly well-formed sentence, since God can make contradictions true, and for all we know might actually do so at any moment. Therefore, we should either give up universal possibilism, or our belief in the validity of our ordinary conceptual and linguistic practices, in short: our belief in the rationality of rationality. We would simply be at a loss about how to live our lives if universal possibilism were true.

But universal possibilism would not only have disastrous consequences for our participation in society, but also for our theology. For clearly, if God can make contradictions true, then everything that we say about Him (no matter how incoherent) might be or become true. For example, what the Bible tells us about God might be both completely true and completely false at the same time and in the same respects. The result of this would be a negative theology, according to which the negation of anything we assert about God is equally (possibly) true. This position, in turn, leads to agnosticism. As Geach puts it: "As we cannot say how a non-logical world would look, we cannot say how a supra-logical God would act or how he could communicate anything to us by way of revelation."[13]

It is for reasons such as these that we are justified in rejecting uni-

---

[11] Swinburne, *Coherence of Theism*, 149. Cf., among many others, Davies, *Thinking about God*, 176; Lewis, *Problem of Pain*, 16.

[12] Morris, *Anselmian Explorations*, 169. To be sure, Morris consciously makes this judgment from the perspective of his own (theological activist) standpoint. This enables him to derive universal possibilism's falsehood from its incoherence. The question how we should assess universal possibilism from a more neutral perspective remains unanswered.

[13] Geach, *Providence and Evil*, 11.

versal possibilism as highly counterintuitive, even though we cannot show irrefutably that it is false (in fact, our proofs seldom satisfy the strict demand of irrefutability).[14] At this point, however, while the philosophical notion of omnipotence leaves us at a loss, it is our intended reconstruction of the doctrine of omnipotence from the biblical tradition which helps us further. For universal possibilism does not allow us to structure the doctrine of omnipotence in a way which is compatible with the biblical tradition. Clearly, this tradition presupposes neither a negative theology nor its unavoidable counterpart, agnosticism. Most things which are said about God in the Bible are presented as definitely and immutably true, some others (e.g. the words of the impious) as definitely and immutably false. In the end, it is the *trustworthiness* of God which is at stake here. If universal possibilism were true, God could turn Himself into the devil, He could make Himself not to exist at all, or even both to exist and not exist. Such unthinkable implications rule out universal possibilism as part of a religiously adequate doctrine of omnipotence.

3.5.3 *Universal creationism: Clouser and Descartes*
Perhaps, however, it is possible to qualify universal possibilism in such a way that its negative consequences (both conceptually and theologically) can be avoided, without retreating to standard independentism. Since we have seen that we should not easily reject universal possibilism as completely false, it is important for us to find out whether its advantages can be retained without us having to accept its disadvantages. Fortunately, there have been some recent attempts to achieve this. The one which remains closest to universal possibilism is dubbed "universal creationism" by its inventor, Roy Clouser. Although only Clouser expounds this view and its ramifications in some detail, others have made suggestions which point in the same direction.[15] Moreover, it is basically the same position which I have tried to establish above as the "most charitable" way of interpreting Descartes' enigmatic utterances on the creation and status of the eternal truths. Let us therefore now examine this view from a systematic rather than a historical perspective, and find out whether it enables us to solve our problem.

According to Clouser, who presents his case as a new look at religious language, both in the Bible and in the theology of Luther and Calvin the distinction between Creator and creature is rightly regarded as exhaus-

---

[14] Cf. Plantinga, *Does God Have a Nature?*, 124f., who also argues for a substitution of the common claim that universal possibilism is false by the more modest claim that it is counterintuitive: "The most we can fairly say, here, is that his view [i.e. Descartes' view, interpreted as universal possibilism] is strongly counterintuitive - that we have a strong inclination to believe propositions from which its falsehood follows."

[15] E.g. D. Goldstick, "Could God Make A Contradiction True?"; J.F. Ross, "God, Creator of Kinds and Possibilities: *Requiescant universalia ante res*," in: Robert Audi & William J. Wainwright (eds.), *Rationality, Religious Belief & Moral Commitment*, Ithaca 1986, 315-335 (though some of Ross's remarks suggest that he adheres to universal possibilism; see esp. 319).

tive. That is to say, all things, including "properties, propositions, laws, and the so-called host of abstract animals in the great corral of Plato's Other World,[16]" should be seen as created by God. This claim that God has created everything other than Himself does not entail, however, that nothing is logically impossible or logically necessary. Neither does it imply that God can make contradictions true. Here, Clouser marks off his position from universal possibilism. It is absurd, he contends, to hold that all things are logically possible, including those things which are excluded by the laws of logic. There is no absurdity, however, "in holding that although there really is necessity, impossibility, and possibility for creation, the laws which determine those conditions also depend on God."[17]

We can summarize the difference between universal possibilism and universal creationism by stating that according to the former God can make contradictions true at any time, whereas according to the latter God *could have made* what are now contradictions true, if He had wished so at the moment of creation. Clouser is well aware of the fact that the phrase "could have made" in this claim presupposes that our ordinary modal distinctions apply to God, which is precisely what is denied by universal creationism. But he provides an interesting analogy in order to show that such talk, if qualified in a proper way, may nevertheless convey something true. As is well known, Augustine held that God, existing Himself in timeless eternity, created time before He created things in time. In his commentary on Genesis Augustine wrestles with the problem of how to express the fact that God existed before creating time. Since "before" is itself a temporal term, in the proposition "God existed before creating time" it cannot mean what it usually means. Nevertheless, if we qualify this proposition so as to mean that God existed outside time, or (to eliminate the spatial metaphor as well) that He existed although time did not exist, we succeed in conveying a meaningful assertion (although, of course, there is still a temporal element in the word "existed"). God existing before creating time is an example of what Clouser calls a "limiting idea," i.e. a use of language which points to the limits of our conceptual capacities, indicating a reality beyond them. Although talk expressing a limiting idea does not constitute a usual or common employment of language, neither does it "constitute a unique symbol-system, nor have a unique logic of its own, nor require an extensive analogy theory to understand its meaning."[18] As in the case of the Kantian unifying transcendental ideas of God, the soul and the world, we are driven to affirm the existence and validity of such limiting ideas, without being able or entitled to treat them as objects for scientific study, to make argumentative claims about them etc.

Similarly, the claim that God could have created another framework

---

[16] Clouser, "Religious Language", 386.

[17] Ibid., 398.

[18] Ibid., 393; cf. 400.

of modalities than the actual one may be meaningful and even true if interpreted as a limiting idea. The objection that there is "no Archimedean point outside the actual ... activity of God from which we could judge it to be possible that God conceive a framework different from the one which, in fact, ... gives us all possibility and all necessity"[19] does not hold against this interpretation. Surely it is a valid objection if we take "possible" in the ordinary sense. But then neither do we have an Archimedean point from which we could judge it to be *im*possible that God conceive a framework different from ours! Therefore, that God creates a framework different from ours, although not logically possible, is in a sense conceivable[20]; we do not only speak from within our framework of modalities, we can also speak *about* it, imagining that it is only one of the "possible" frameworks. In this context, the term "possible" should not be taken in the ordinary sense of logically possible, of course, since this conceptuality only applies *within* our modal framework. We are unable to spell out the content and implications of the possibility in question: we only have a *limiting* idea of what is involved in suggesting that God could have created a different modal framework of reality, in a similar way in which we have a limiting idea of what is involved in the claim that God existed before time.

Now what about the claim that God can still make contradictions true? Could we interpret this claim also as a limiting idea? Clouser ignores this question, but it seems that there are no reasons to answer it negatively. Since we are not entitled to draw any argumentative conclusions from it, we can now avoid the damaging conceptual and theological consequences which we came across in our discussion of universal possibilism. At the same time, we may add that there is not the slightest chance that God will make or does make or has made contradictions true,[21] since God's will does not change. As Descartes pointed out, it is in virtue of God's immutable, steadfast will that our modal framework of reality is immutable. Or to put it in the words of D. Goldstick: "God always *could* make a contradiction true; ... the only reason He does not - if existent - actually make a contradiction true is simply that He does not wish to do such a thing."[22]

So it seems that many of the problems which vitiated universal possibilism are solved by universal creationism as elaborated along these lines. There is, however, one problem which remains unsolved by universal creationism, and which makes it an inadequate construal of the relation between God and logic. This pertains to the nature of God. If God created (in

---

[19] Morris, "Absolute Creation," in: *Anselmian Explorations*, 170.

[20] Here I invoke a distinction between what is logically impossible and what is conceivable, introduced by Morris himself at several places in his *Anselmian Explorations*; cf. e.g. 22, 45f.

[21] The extreme point of view that from time to time God does make contradictions true has been defended by the Russian Christian convert Leo Shestov. See e.g. his *Athens and Jerusalem*, Athens, Ohio 1966, 309, quoted by Goldstick, "Could God Make," 378 (cf. 378-380).

[22] Goldstick, "Could God Make," 366, cf. the final sentences on 367.

the sense of *creatio ex nihilo*) all abstract entities, properties, propositions etc., then among other things He created His own properties. Since His properties are traditionally considered to be essential, this implies that God must have created His own nature! Clouser tries to avoid this awkward conclusion by making some exceptions with regard to the number and sorts of abstract entities created by God. Unlike, for example, God's wisdom and God's love, "God's divine being (his non-dependence) and his ability to bring everything else into existence are not themselves created properties,[23]" he stipulates. But this leads to a highly contestable conception of God, according to which some of God's essential attributes (such as His power) are more firmly rooted in reality than others (such as His goodness). In the end, Clouser's concept of God is highly voluntaristic, equating the uncreated core of God's being with arbitrary power and absolute independence. All the other attributes belonging to God, including His goodness, righteousness and love are created by Him as only the ways in which He relates to us.

Now Clouser emphasizes that despite the createdness of most of the divine characteristics, they nevertheless *really* apply to God. The position that the truths about God are all (with the exceptions noted) created truths does not make them any less true of God. There is no reason to suppose that behind the relations and properties which He has taken on He really has other properties, or is another sort of personality altogether. But if it is true that "'behind' what God has revealed our concepts simply do not apply at all," how are we able to rule out this possibility? As soon as we allow this kind of dichotomy between the *Deus in se* and the *Deus quoad nos* in our conception of God, we can no longer be sure that God indeed reveals *Himself* to us, rather than some range of characteristics assumed (for how long?) in His relation to us. Again, it is in the end God's trustworthiness which is at stake here. But the claim that God is trustworthy in His revelation is a basic presupposition of the biblical conception of God. Therefore, in looking for a biblical conception of God's power we cannot accept Clouser's proposal. In the next section we shall examine a proposal which avoids Clouser's questionable distinction between a range of created attributes and an uncreated core in the being of God.

3.5.4 *Theistic activism: Barth and Morris*
Let us start our discussion of theistic activism with quoting Barth's vivid presentation of it at some length.

> We have, indeed, to keep an inflexible grip on the truth that God is omnipotent in the fact that He and He alone and finally (because He is who He is) controls and

---

[23] Ibid., 392. Cf. the first weak interpretation of Descartes' doctrine on the creation of the eternal truths, discussed in §2.4.3 above, according to which some eternal truths, particularly those concerning the existence and omnipotence of God, are uncreated.

decides what is possible and impossible for Himself and therefore at all. ... God's omnipotence consists in the fact that in this sense His power and His will are *sola omnis possibilitatis fundamentum et radix*. They are not subordinate and responsible to any higher and independent idea of what is possible and impossible... Up to and including the statement that two and two make four, these [conceptions of what is creaturely possible] do not have their value and truth and validity in themselves or in a permanent metaphysical or logical or mathematical system which is "absolute" in itself, i.e. independently of God's freedom and will and decision. They have their value and truth and validity by the freedom and will and decision of God as the Creator of all creaturely powers.[24]

Up to these statements, it looks as if Barth is going to defend a universal creationism. But now notice the way he continues his argument, after having insisted that we can indeed rely upon the law of (non-)contradiction, not because of its necessity in itself but because God is reliable.

We not only have no cause, but, bound by faith in God, we have neither the permission nor the freedom to ascribe to God, in respect to the world He has created, other possibilities than those which He actually chose and actualised in the creation and preservation of the world. We are not summoned by God's Word to honour Him by ascribing to Him a capacity which He did not choose to use as a Creator... For example, we are not summoned by God's Word to assert that through God's omnipotence two and two could also be five.[25]

So it seems that Barth wants to say that although God's creative power is responsible for the validity of the laws of logic (and if he were a platonist with regard to abstract objects he would no doubt have added the existence of such things), this does not imply that He could also have created them otherwise, or other laws in their place. This is the gist of the position Thomas Morris and Chris Menzel have recently defended as "theistic activism."

Theistic activism tries to reconcile the apparent conflict between the platonic view of abstracta and the Judaeo-Christian ontology, according to which God is the sole source of everything in the universe. In keeping with the latter, the theistic activist holds that every entity, either concrete or abstract, derives its existence from God's creative activity (theistic activism even derives its name from this conviction). In keeping with the former, the theistic activist claims that abstract objects are really necessary entities, so that it was not in God's power to refrain from creating them or to create them otherwise. The view of theistic activism carefully distinguishes beween the issues of control and dependence. Although abstract objects and necessary truths are causally dependent upon God, they are not within His control. Morris and Menzel argue that "the most exalted claims possible are thus secured for the theistic God, while all the implausibilities and problems

---

[24] Barth, *Church Dogmatics* II.1, 535. The Latin formula is a quotation from J.H. Heidegger, *Corpus Theologiae* III, Zürich 1700, 107.

[25] Ibid., 536f.

of Descartes, of universal possibilism are avoided."[26]

Now what about God's nature on this view? Clearly, among the abstracta created by God from all eternity are the essential properties which make up His own nature. Therefore, according to theistic activism God also creates His own nature. Morris and Menzel try to mitigate the apparent absurdity of this claim by insisting that it should not be identified with the claim that God creates Himself. Since God cannot be identified with His nature, it does not follow from the fact that God creates His nature that He also creates and causes Himself. In this way they try to avoid the almost universally acknowledged absurdity of concepts like self-causation and self-creation. But this is unconvincing. For according to theistic activism God's activity is responsible for all necessary and contingent truths. Now whether the fact that God exists is a necessary or a contingent truth does not matter here (Anselmians like Morris and Menzel will claim that it is a necessary truth). In either case, theistic activism is committed to the claim that God's creative activity is responsible for the fact that God exists. This amounts to the claim that God creates Himself.[27] The only alternative is to grant that there is at least one truth which cannot be accounted for by referring to the divine activity (viz. the truth that God exists), but as Morris and Menzel argue themselves, such a move "would amount to scrapping the whole project of theistic activism and abandoning the view of absolute creation."[28]

Let us, however, for the sake of argument grant that theistic activists are right in distinguishing the claim that God creates Himself from the allegedly more modest claim that God creates His own nature. Then what about this latter claim? Is it in any way more plausible than the former? I think not. To be sure, in their elaboration of this claim Morris and Menzel are keen to avoid the assumption of a dichotomy in God as we found this in Clouser. They illustrate their view by drawing an ingenious analogy with what they call a "materialization machine," which in its most perfected form is "sitting on a table, continually producing all of its own parts, batteries included. ... The machine, like God, is creating that on which it depends for its ability to create and for its occurrent activity of creation."[29] As Brian Leftow has rightly pointed out, however, this analogy is misleading, since what it illustrates is a case of preservation rather than of creation.[30] What the materialization machine does is to warrant that all of its parts *continue* to exist. The materialization machine is not responsible for the fact that its

---

[26] "Absolute Creation," in: Morris, *Anselmian Explorations*, 171.

[27] See for a similar argument Brian Leftow, "God and Abstract Entities," 204f.

[28] "Absolute Creation," 172.

[29] Ibid., 175.

[30] Leftow, "God and Abstract Entities," 205-209, 216 n.22. Perhaps Leftow's criticism does not hold if "creation" is understood as *creatio continua* rather than as *creatio ex nihilo*; but there are no indications in Morris & Menzel that they take their key term creation as conveying something less than *creatio ex nihilo*.

this could be the case. Clearly, bringing the nature (i.e., the essential properties) of x into existence presupposes that x does not exist already. But if x does not exist already, it cannot bring into existence anything at all, let alone its own nature. So the very idea of creating one's own nature is flatly self-contradictory.[31]

But let us once again give theistic activism the benefit of the doubt, and suppose that it is able to solve the problem of God's relation to His own nature in a satisfactory way (though I do not see how this could be done within its parameters). Then we are still left with a more general difficulty which definitely cannot be repaired by means of a similar partial emendation, because it pertains to the very heart of the theistic activist's position. This difficulty concerns the *freedom* of creation. It is pivotal to the traditional view of creation, that God is a free Creator of our physical universe. As Morris and Menzel themselves declare: "He was free to create it or to refrain from creating it; he was free to create this universe, a different universe, or no such universe at all."[32] On theistic activist principles, however, God lacked such freedom in creating the realm of abstract objects. The modal framework of reality is both eternal and necessary: it never was, never will be, and never can be or could have been, other than it is.[33] So although God created the abstracta, His sovereignty over them is nevertheless highly compromised, since He *had to* create them, not being free to refrain from creating them. We may wonder what, after all, is won in comparison to standard independentism when theistic activism denies God's freedom to create abstract objects in such a categorical way.

Morris and Menzel have anticipated this objection, and defend themselves by claiming that in a sense God's creation of abstract objects *is* free. This is how they put it:

> It is an activity which is conscious, intentional, and neither constrained nor compelled by anything existing independent of God and his causally efficacious power. The necessity of his creating the framework is not imposed on him from without, but rather is a feature and result of the nature of his own activity itself, which is a function of what he is.[34]

Now the last claim is enigmatic, since according to theistic activism what God is is in turn a function of God's creative activity. But apart from this problem, which we now ignore, there is another one. What Morris and Menzel are suggesting in this passage is that God's freedom in creating abstract objects is a form of "liberty of spontaneity" rather than of "liberty of indifference" (to use the traditional terminology). In order to act in liber-

---

[31] Cf. for similar criticism of Barth's version of theistic activism Immink, *Divine Simplicity*, 83f.

[32] "Absolute Creation," 170.

[33] Ibid.

[34] Ibid., 170f.

ty of spontaneity it does not matter whether one is constrained by influences from without or from within. The critical point is that, although one can act voluntarily, there is no alternative; one has no free choice to act in another way than one does.

In the human case, such liberty of spontaneity is often considered as a form of freedom which is hardly worth that name. Especially libertarians - - and most Anselmians, including Morris, are libertarians[35] - are keen to insist that an act is performed freely only if its agent in some sense *could have done otherwise*. But we need not even deny that the notion of liberty of spontaneity can in some situations express a meaningful concept of freedom, in order to see that ascribing only this sort of freedom to God's creative activity with regard to abstract objects detracts from His perfection and sovereignty. Compatibilist thinkers, according to whom we have no reason to ascribe to human beings a stronger form of freedom than liberty of spontaneity, rightly consider this to be a deplorable predicament of the human being, subject as it is to external or internal causal factors which it cannot influence. If the possession of only liberty of spontaneity degrades and depersonalizes human beings, how much more does it detract from the perfection and sovereignty of God![36]

It is for these three reasons, all circling around its use of the concept of *creation*, that theistic activism's view of the relation between God and abstract objects is unsatisfactory from a biblical view of God's almighty power.

3.5.5 *Standard independentism: Ockham and Wittgenstein*
In the preceding subsections we have discussed three attempts to interpret the relationship between God and abstract objects or necessary truths as a relationship of dependence, and we have found all three of them wanting. The sort of dependence we assumed to exist between God and the abstracta became gradually weaker; first we had to drop the notion of permanent control, next the notion of initial control, and finally the notion of creative responsibility. It is therefore natural at this point to break off our quest for a convincing interpretation of the relationship between God and abstracta as a relationship of dependence. Why not cast the net on the other side of the ship, and grant that abstract objects are simply not the kind of things which God has control about, nor the kind of things which He is creatively responsible for? The advantage of such a strategy is clear: everything which God controls He *fully* controls, in the sense that if He does no longer want

---

[35] Cf. e.g. *Anselmian Explorations*, 27-32.

[36] Similar criticism has been put forward by Scott Davison, "Could Abstract Objects Depend upon God?," 494f., who concludes with the following perceptive observation: "It seems that M & M's account of the creation of abstract objects involves something like the neo-platonic notion of emanation, rather than the traditional theistic notion of creation (which is typically viewed as *free* in the strong sense that God could have created different things or nothing at all)" (495).

God controls He *fully* controls, in the sense that if He does no longer want it to exist it goes out of existence, or if He wants to change its nature its nature does change etc. And everything which God creates He creates freely, unconstrained by external or internal factors; for anything God creates, He could have created it otherwise, or refrained from creating it at all.

An obvious objection to this strategy, however, is that it seems to deprive God of His sovereignty, since there are things (viz. abstract objects) which exist independently of Him, and therefore affect and delimit His possibilities for action. As a result, God's sovereignty is even more in jeopardy than on the theistic activist view, which ascribed at least a weak form of creative responsibility for abstract objects to God! Whether this objection is valid, however, depends upon how we construe abstract objects. There is a very attractive alternative here, which consists in the consistent removal of every trace of Platonism from our conception of the modal framework of reality. One way to accomplish this task was adopted by medieval nominalism or conceptualism[37] (with Ockham as its most characteristic representative). Another was invented in modern times for very different reasons than safeguarding God's omnipotence, and has become popular as "conventionalism" under the influence of the philosophy of Wittgenstein. I will not go into details here, but concentrate on what the different versions of anti-Platonism have in common.

Basically, this alternative view amounts to the denial of the claim that abstract objects exist in reality. Instead, propositions, properties, numbers, sets etc. are thought of as only *names* (nomina) or, rather, *concepts* which we have invented in order to structure our manifold experience. As such, they are very useful and indeed indispensable; but they have no reality in themselves, and therefore (since they are not things at all) they are not the kind of things with regard to which the question whether or not they depend on God is meaningful. Consider the proposition "4+4=8." This proposition is not at all necessarily true. Whether it is true or not depends upon the system within which it is affirmed. In the decimal system with which we are acquainted it is certainly true. But nothing forbids us to base mathematics on another system than the one we have probably derived from the fact that most of us happen to have ten fingers. Take for instance an octonary system, working from 1 to 7, then continuing from 10 to 17, from 20 to 27 and so on. In this system the proposition "4+4=8" would be false, since 4 and 4 would make 10 (10 being the symbol for 1+1+1+1+1+1+1+1)! Or take another apparent necessary truth, such as "blue is a colour." On closer examination, that this proposition is necessarily true turns out to be far from self-evident. The Navaho-language, for example, does not distinguish blue as a separate colour, but rather has one concept corresponding simultaneously to our terms "blue" and "green." Therefore, in

---

[37] Cf. Diogenes Allen, *Philosophy for Understanding Theology*, London 1985, 156.

Navaho, in a sense blue is not a colour![38]

In short, analytical propositions express necessary truths only within a pre-conceived conceptual system which people have agreed to use. Such a system is not inferred from some objective external reality, but only from the practical conventions of those who use it. That the Navahos do not distinguish blue as a separate colour is not due to their suffering from a peculiar form of colour-blindness. Neither do English-speaking people suffer from colour-blindness because of the fact that they have only one word for "black," whereas the Navaho have two concepts expressing different aspects of our "black." Rather, given their natural environment it was simply a matter of practical interest for them to make some colour distinctions which we lack, and the other way round. Extending this line of argument, properties, numbers, propositions etc. are simply conceptual tools which we have found useful to employ in certain directions. To ask whether they exist or are true (or even necessarily true) apart from the language game within which they are used is to make a category mistake.

We can also make the same point in a slightly different way. To construe properties, propositions etc. as abstract *objects* is to fail to do justice to the illocutionary variety of our conceptual forms. Not all our propositions function as reality-depicting constatives. Analytic propositions, for example, clearly function as stipulations, indicating the way in which a certain conceptual system is correctly used. A constative function can only be ascribed to them in a very limited sense, viz. in so far as they describe a reality *within the system*. As a result, they are always (necessarily) true or false *given this particular system*, which in turn is based upon certain inter-human conventions. To ask for the existence of properties or the truth of propositions apart from any conceptual system or language game is meaningless; to ask whether such properties, propositions etc. depend upon God, even more so. So on this instrumentalist account of language and conceptual forms, our problem of relating God's power to abstracta simply disappears.

Nevertheless, this instrumentalist account of thought and language, according to which abstracta have a prescriptive or rule-governing rather than a descriptive character, cannot be extended to all our conceptual forms. The price of such a position would be a pragmatic theory of truth totally separating truth from objective reality. For whether a particular proposition is true or false (and necessarily so or not) could then only be determined within some particular system, and not with regard to reality itself. There are at least two problems bound up with such a position.

First, it is counterintuitive on its own terms. Consider for example the principle of non-contradiction. In Wittgensteinian circles this principle is usually seen not as stating a fact about reality, but as indicating a rule for

---

[38] Cf. Paul Henle, *Language, Thought and Culture*, Ann Arbor 1965, 7.

the proper use of language and concepts.[39] But clearly "If all men are mortal, and if Socrates is a man, than Socrates is mortal," and "A is A" are not only rules indicating a proper use of language, but also true in reality. As John Hospers in his instructive account of these matters has one of the partners in a fictitious discussion saying:

> The principles of logic, I hold, are very general truths. They can also be formulated, as you say, as inference-rules, and as rules they are not true or false but useful, in that they enable us to go from true propositions to other true propositions. But though they can be *stated* as inference-rules, I would remind you that any inference-rule still *presupposes* certain general truths, which Aristotle called 'laws of thought.' A is A - for example, an inference-rule is an inference-rule and not something else ... If these general principles didn't hold, we could not speak of inference-rules, or, indeed, of anything else. Facts of reality still underlie verbal conventions.[40]

Or again take some mathematical proposition, like "2+2=4." Despite the fact that it is couched in a particular system, it is clearly reality depicting. For whatever symbols we use, it is true in reality that $1+1+1+1 = 1+1+1+1$ (which is what the formula tells us). If mathematical formulae did not say something about the real world, "it would be an insoluble mystery why the tautologies of applied mathematics are so useful to us, even predictively useful."[41]

Second, the view that all abstracta are prescriptive rather than descriptive is also devastating for any theology aiming to say something about how things really are. For it obscures our possibilities of making truth-claims about the extra-linguistic reality. Since the biblical tradition clearly aims at saying something about how things are in the extra-linguistic reality, our search for a biblical conception of God's power will not be helped by adopting this position with regard to the relationship between God and abstracta. So we must conclude that at least some of our abstract concepts are rooted in reality rather than merely in our linguistic and conceptual conventions. This conclusion is corroborated by the fact that despite their differences human conceptual schemes are in principle translatable in terms of each other.[42] We can in principle understand an octonary mathematical system as well as the decimal one, and Navaho's can in principle teach us how we should distinguish between their different sorts of black, etc.

Given this conclusion, if we stick to standard independentism there

---

[39] See e.g. L. Wittgenstein, *Philosophical Investigations* 1, Oxford 1976³, §125; cf. Goldstick, "Could God Make," 380.

[40] John Hospers, *An Introduction to Philosophical Analysis*, London 1967², 225; although the discussion is open-ended, perhaps we are entitled to infer from the fact that the quotation forms the final word in the discussion that it reflects Hospers's own position.

[41] Goldstick, ibid., 384.

[42] See on this point Donald Davidson, "On the Very Idea of a Conceptual Scheme," in: id., *Inquiries into Truth and Interpretation*, Oxford 1984, 183-198.

is only one alternative left, viz. what we could call unqualified Platonism. According to this form of standard independentism, abstract objects exist without being in any way controlled or created or caused by God. They simply exist next to God, most of them[43] like God in a necessary way. Embracing this option has a number of unpalatable consequences for the theist, however. For obviously this platonist form of standard independentism is incompatible with the biblical intuition that the Creator-creation relationship is exhaustive, i.e. that anything that exists is either God the Creator or part of God's creation.[44] Moreover, it severely compromises God's sovereignty and almightiness, since like us God simply finds Himself in a situation which is given to Him by the modal framework of reality (as constituted by the necessary abstract objects), and which - as we saw above - limits His possibilities for action.[45] Finally, in the end it is again God's trustworthiness which is at stake. As Hendrik Hart lucidly puts it:

> ... a doctrine of entities which control God, over which He has no control, whose origin we do not know, ... which do not tell us about themselves and give us no grounds for their existence except themselves, such a doctrine does not augur well for rational man's belief in a sovereign God who can be trusted completely.[46]

3.5.6 *The Laws of Logic and the Divine Mind*
I conclude that none of the options reviewed thus far provide us with a completely satisfactory view of the relation between God's power and the abstracta. Since I do not know of other ways to interpret abstract objects as dependent upon God which avoid the failures we have discussed,[47] there seems to be little prospect in construing the relation between God and abstract objects as one of dependence. Further, since both conceivable versions of standard independentism proved deficient, the prospects for a satisfactory construal of the relation between God and abstract objects in terms of mutual *in*dependence seem equally remote. Let us refer to this situation briefly as the dependence-dilemma.

Fortunately, there is a rather easy way out of this dilemma, which is hinted at (but not straightforwardly worked out) by some of the authors

---

[43] An exception should be made for some abstract objects such as sets containing only contingent members, which do not exist necessarily; cf. Plantinga, *Does God Have a Nature?*, 66f.

[44] See for arguments supporting the thesis that this is indeed what the biblical tradition suggests e.g. Clouser, "Religious Language," 386-389; Morris, "Absolute Creation," 164.

[45] See §§ 3.3.5 and 3.5.2.

[46] Hart, "On the Distinction," 193.

[47] Brian Leftow has recently come up with yet another proposal, concentrating around the thomistic claim that God is purely actual. But as Leftow notes himself, it seems that this proposal cannot escape the charge of leading (like universal possibilism and universal creationism) to a negative theology; cf. Leftow, "God and Abstract Entities," 208-214, esp. 214. This being the case, it is clear in advance that Leftow's theory will not provide us the solution to our problem.

discussed in the preceding subsections, and which is in fact so well-known and well-founded in the classical tradition that it will suffice here to sketch out only its main lines. Let us start again with the maxim that from a biblical point of view the Creator-creation distinction should be regarded as exhaustive. Since this maxim forbids us to view abstract entities as existing independent of God, and since we were unable to construe them as parts of God's creation, why not try to consider them as participating in the life of God the Creator Himself? The attractiveness of this solution becomes clear as soon as we see that the dependence-dilemma only arises when we consider abstract entities as existing *distinct from God*. The dilemma disappears, however, when we start to consider abstract objects as *participating in the mind of God*. This position can in turn be elaborated along two different lines of thought.

First, there is the doctrine of divine simplicity, advocated in different versions by e.g. Augustine, Anselm, and Aquinas. According to this doctrine, God is identical with each of His properties, which in turn are identical to one another. In recent literature it is a hotly contested issue whether this doctrine can be given a coherent formulation.[48] We will not inquire into this issue, but take the forceful criticisms of (among others) Plantinga, Immink and Morris as a warning not to lean too heavily on it. Second, there is the view, also endorsed by classical theists such as Augustine, Anselm and Aquinas, as well as by later philosophers such as Spinoza[49], that the laws of logic should be seen as the ideas in the divine mind. It is this option which seems to me to be still the most promising one for a fully adequate interpretation of the relation between God and abstract objects, the laws of logic, necessary truths etc.

In my opinion, interpreting the whole Platonic realm as existing *within* the divine mind as divine concepts and thoughts offers us a way out of the dependence-dilemma, since it combines the advantages of each of the discussed alternatives while avoiding their deficiencies. Let me finally point this out in some detail. First, it is in harmony with the biblical maxim that the Creator-creation distinction is exhaustive.[50] Second, it satisfies the basic condition of universal possibilism, universal creationism and theistic activism that God's sovereignty and perfection should not be diminished by the existence of abstract entities. Since God's almightiness is traditionally related only to the divine activity *ad extra*, and never to a potential for change in God Himself,[51] the divine almightiness is not in any way af-

---

[48] Cf. e.g. Plantinga, *Does God Have a Nature?*, 26-61; William E. Mann, "Divine Simplicity," *RS* 18 (1982), 451-471; Immink, *Divine Simplicity*, esp. chapter 3; Thomas V. Morris, "On God and Mann: A View of Divine Simplicity," included in *Anselmian Explorations*, 98-123.

[49] Hubbeling, *Principles*, 51; cf. 132, 148.

[50] Cf. Ward, *Rational Theology*, 81: "There is nothing that exists that is not either part of God or created wholly by God."

[51] Cf. Richard A. Muller, *Dictionary of Latin and Greek Theological Terms*, Grand Rapids

fected by the abstract entities when these are conceived as divine thoughts. Third, this conception integrates the intuition of standard independentism that, for example, the laws of logic cannot be changed or abrogated by God at random; for clearly, they share the necessity of the divine being, existing essentially in the divine mind.

At the same time, it avoids the deficiency of portraying the relation between God and His nature (like the relationship between God and abstract objects in general) as a causal relationship. This is where not only Clouser, but also Morris and Menzel, who explicitly assert that they also consider the Platonic pantheon as existing within the divine mind, go wrong. God is neither the Creator of His own nature nor of His own thoughts. With regard to abstract objects, God essentially thinks the thoughts He thinks, and we cannot meaningfully ask whether He could have thought other thoughts than He actually thinks.[52] God Himself is the sole standard of rationality. Moreover, God possesses the properties which constitute His nature essentially. The fact that God did not create, for example, His omnipotence, is a matter of God's being subject to His own nature which is to say it is a matter of God being God, rather than a matter of God's being subject to some property existing apart from Him.[53] Finally, that God is essentially the perfect being He is guarantees His trustworthiness much more convincingly than any of the alternative views.

All this does not, on the other hand, entail that God is a static, immutable being. For there is no reason to deny that apart from God's essential properties God has contingent properties as well. Actually, above we have found some reason to suppose that God's omnipotence is a contingent property. This not only goes for God's properties, but also for His thoughts; it is only the thoughts concerning abstract objects c.q. the laws of logic which God necessarily thinks. There are many other thoughts, however, which God may influence Himself or perhaps even have influenced by outward events. Here again we should be careful not to present God as the prisoner of His own power.

1985, 208 (s.v. *omnipotentia*).

[52] Here, Clouser's use of the concept of a limiting idea has a point.

[53] Cf. the conclusive statements of Taliaferro, "Limits of Power," 123.

4

Systematic Evaluation

It is a special revelation of God's divine power that he is able to bring some good even out of evil. But his use of evil for good does not immediately sterilise it...

Austin Farrer[1]

4.1 INTRODUCTION

In order to see where our argument so far has left us, let us revert to our discussion of the criteria-problem in systematic theology, which issued in the outline of the present study's structure at the end of chapter 1. In that discussion, we distinguished three criteria for the formulation and evaluation of doctrine in systematic theology. First, a doctrinal proposal should be in harmony with the authoritative sources of the religious tradition within which it is advanced. For that reason, we examined the history of the doctrine of divine almightiness in chapter 2, sorting out its general purport and the main elements which it came to convey in the period of its formation. Second, a doctrinal proposal should be characterized by what we have called "comprehensive conceptual coherence." I have devoted chapter 3 to spelling out the doctrine of divine almightiness in such a way, that it satisfies this second criterion. Third, a doctrinal proposal must be adequate to the demands of life. It is to the application of this criterion to the doctrine of divine almightiness that we turn now, in order to find out whether our rendering of this doctrine in the previous parts can stand out the crucial test of adequacy to the demands of life. Can we (still) live with a doctrine of divine almightiness as outlined up to now?

We can also formulate the difference between this and the previous parts in the following way. Up to now we have been concerned with the "inner mechanics" of the doctrine of God's almightiness. We have developed these in such a way that an internally coherent conception of the doctrine resulted. Now, we must shift our attention to the question whether this conception is also "externally coherent," i.e. compatible with other beliefs we consider to be true either as Christians or more generally as rational beings. To be sure, it is especially such external considerations which have in recent times generated a crisis of credibility around the almightiness

---

[1] Austin Farrer, *Love Allmighty and Ills Unlimited*, London 1962, 168.

doctrine. We will therefore trace the main difficulties in this area, and examine whether they force us to reconceive or even to abandon the claim that God is almighty in the sense in which we unpacked this claim previously. In doing this it will be my contention that, although the credibility crisis has very serious backgrounds which should not be dismissed too easily, it is still entirely appropriate to conceive of God as almighty in the traditional sense.

To claim that holding fast to the doctrine of God's almightiness is *appropriate*, however, is ambiguous. It may mean either that maintaining God's almightiness is still a rationally acceptable position *among others*, or that there are compelling reasons to prefer this position *to others*. My defence of almightiness will take the latter form, which is of course the more far-reaching of the two. The task which I set myself is to show not only that the doctrine of God's almightiness is conceptually tolerable, but also that it is theologically compelling. The first mentioned, weaker form of defence would be sufficient to bolster the psychological security of those who want to keep the "plausibility structure" of their traditional Christian theism intact. Such a defence is certainly not completely worthless, the more so since all of us necessarily draw upon such plausibility structures at least to some degree.[2] We should not content ourselves with psychological considerations, however, since "psychological cosiness is an unreliable criterion of theological truth."[3] Rather, in order to gain theological integrity we must critically evaluate whether the doctrine under consideration can stand up to scrutiny better than its modern alternatives.

There are at least two[4] reasons which give rise to a considerable degree of suspicion here, and which prevent us from claiming too quickly that this is the case indeed. These reasons are in fact closely interrelated, but let us try to state them separately. First, there is the issue of human freedom and responsibility. It is often argued that the doctrine of divine almightiness destroys any viable conception of human freedom and responsibility. Second, there is the much-discussed problem of evil. It seems that if God is both almighty and perfectly good, there cannot be genuine evil in the world. Since we clearly experience that there *is* genuine evil in the

---

[2] Vernon White makes some similar points in the context of his discussion of another traditional Christian doctrine, viz. that of atonement; see his *Atonement and Incarnation*, Cambridge 1991, 5-7, 14.

[3] White, *Atonement*, 14.

[4] Cf. Case-Winters, *God's Power*, 9, 17-19, 228f. This is by no means to say that these are the only ones; we may also think e.g. of Sigmund Freud's objection that the omnipotence-doctrine is the result of subconscious processes of projecting upon God the attributes which in our childhood we ascribed to our father. Or take the feminist critique of the omnipotence-doctrine, circling around the connection between power and masculinity. The selected issues, however, are among the ones which play a prominent role in the contemporary debate on God's power in philosophical theology. Hopefully, their treatment here sets the scene for a fruitful discussion of other difficulties.

world, and since it belongs to the demands of life to cope with this experience, it seems that we must either reject the claim that God is perfectly good, or the claim that He is almighty. Confronted with this dilemma, many contemporary theologians recommend to give up the latter claim.

It is to these two problem-fields that I will pay attention in the present chapter. In section 4.2 I discuss the relation between divine almightiness and human freedom in general, whereas in section 4.3 I examine this relation more specifically with respect to the classical issue of predestination and free will. Section 4.4, finally, deals with the problem of evil.

It is perhaps helpful to make one further preliminary remark here, pertaining to both of these issues. As it seems to me, in a sense both of these issues belong to the perennial problems of theology, which have returned in different theological and cultural contexts throughout the centuries. The problem of evil, for example, has been a vexed question in theology ever since Marcion, or even, if you prefer, since Job. In another sense, however, the difficulties which the issues of human freedom, moral and natural evil, always posed to the doctrine of divine almightiness are felt to be strongly aggravated in the age of modernity. The Enlightenment emphasis on the human individual and its autonomy precipitated a shift from theological paradigms in which divine power and freedom were fundamental towards paradigms in which human freedom and autonomy had priority. Two World Wars and all the subsequent evils of which our century is so satiated, in combination with our rapidly growing ability of getting direct information about them by means of the mass media, have led to a severe aggravation of the problem of evil in our modern human experience. Moreover, the scope left for unambiguous divine actions - God's action being the mode in which His power becomes concrete and tangible - seems to have turned to naught as a result of the rise of modern science, which provided us with intramundane explanations for almost all natural phenomena.

It is for these reasons that we shall have to evaluate the doctrine of divine almightiness carefully in the light of the two mentioned challenges. For in any case, a simple, inconsiderate repetition of traditional answers will not suffice to do justice to them. Let us therefore discuss each of them in turn, and find out which strategies we should follow in order to cope with them in a conceptually satisfactory and theologically convincing way.

4.2 DIVINE ALMIGHTINESS AND HUMAN FREEDOM

4.2.1 *The problem*

There is a popular negro-spiritual which consists of only two lines:

> He's got the whole world in his hands
> He's got the whole wide world in his hands

Sometimes, for example when a favourite football club has won the game, a slightly different secularized version of this song is heard, which runs as follows:

We've got the whole world in our hands
We've got the whole wide world in our hands

Of course, the "He" who is referred to in the original version is God, whereas the "we" who are mentioned in the second version are human beings. Now despite the simplicity of these two song-texts, together they give expression to a *prima facie* dilemma which has deeply concerned many thoughtful believers as well as theological giants through the centuries.

Clearly, the claim made in the original version of the song reflects a traditional Christian commitment which is linked up with the doctrine of God's almightiness. As we discovered in the historical part of this study, one of the key elements implicit in the notion of God as *pantokrator* had to do with God's universal dominion over the world and His sovereign government of all that happens in its history. But if God indeed has the whole world in His hands by governing all events which take place in it in the course of history, including human actions, then what about the other basic Christian conviction that human beings are created as *persons* with a relevant degree of creaturely freedom and moral responsibility? Initially, the claim that God has the whole world in His hands - and those who endorse this claim will no doubt be prepared to extend its scope even to the whole universe - may sound comforting. When we consider its implications, however, the question arises whether it in fact leaves any room for genuine human freedom, and avoids to turn human beings into mere puppets in the hands of God.

On the other hand, if we start from the second version of the song, the contention that we as human beings have the whole world in our hands is of course hyperbole. But if we substitute it for the weaker and more realistic claim that we have at least *some* events in the world in our hands, in the sense that we can choose and decide freely with respect to their occurrence or non-occurrence, and that we are therefore *responsible* for those events etc., then the opposite problem arises. For if human freedom and responsibility have a relevant scope, rather than being restricted to regions of minor importance, then how can we hold that it is God who governs all that happens in world history, and determines the ultimate future of our universe? If human freedom and responsibility are real rather than merely illusory, then it is at least theoretically possible that God's will be thwarted and His intentions frustrated by human actions. Moreover, assuming a standard account of the Christian doctrine of sin, we must add that this theoretical possibility is actualized time and again, for the concept of sin implies that God's will *is* thwarted and His intentions *are* frustrated. In any case, since human beings determine at least *part* of what happens in the world, it seems clear that God cannot be said to govern the *whole* world, i.e. to have the whole world in His hands.

In order to enable ourselves to deal with this prima facie dilemma, let us try to express it somewhat more formally. In fact, the dilemma is produced by the combination of two claims, both of which form a central tenet not only of the Christian, but also of other theistic (e.g. Jewish and Islamic[1]) traditions. David and Randall Basinger state these tenets as follows:

T1:   God creates human agents such that they are free with respect to certain actions and, therefore, morally responsible for them.

T2:   God is omnipotent in the sense that he has (sovereign, providential) control over all existent states of affairs.[2]

Unfortunately, the Basinger brothers don't attempt to resolve the apparent conflict between T1 and T2; nor do they argue that one of them should be given up. They only show that theists frequently utilise T1 and T2 in an arbitrary way, appealing to T1 for clarification of some events (particularly evil ones) and to T2 for clarification of other (predominantly good) events, without offering an explanation for this selectivity. This may be true, but the pivotal question is of course whether T1 and T2 can be retained together, i.e. whether their conjuction can be shown to be consistent.

In the Christian tradition this general question has become especially acute in the realm of soteriology. Here it goes under the common label of the relationship between "freedom and grace." Why is it that some people come to faith after having heard the Gospel whereas others do not? The typically orthodox response to this question has always been twofold. On the one hand God and God alone is to be credited for faith; faith is a free gift of God, it is not to the slightest degree an achievement or merit of the believer; to presume that it is would amount to prideful self-assertion, incompatible with the very nature of faith. On the other hand, however, those who refrain from coming to faith upon hearing the Gospel are wholly responsible for this. It is they rather than God who are to be blamed for their unbelief, as well as for the fact that as a result of their unbelief they are excluded from eschatological salvation. In fact, it is precisely the same tension between T1 and T2 which we encounter here in a concrete form. And the twofold response to the question of the origin of faith is a striking example of the apparently arbitrary appeal to T1 and T2 for clarifying different situations. Again, the key question is whether both parts of this re-

---

[1] An exposition of the form which the dilemma takes in Islamic thought has been provided by F.L. Bakker, *De verhouding tusschen de almacht Gods en de zedelijke verantwoordelijkheid van den mensch in den Islam*, Amsterdam 1922.

[2] D. Basinger & R. Basinger, "In the Image of Man Create They God: A Challenge," *SJTh* 34 (1981), 97; I have omitted the authors' reference to God's omniscience and perfect goodness in their formulation of T2.

sponse are compatible with each other.

In our conceptual analysis of the doctrine of God's almightiness it proved of great help to us in solving a number of conceptual difficulties to start from a biblical conception of God's power. It is doubtful, however, whether this strategy will also help us in the present context. For the truth of both T1 and T2 seems to be presupposed throughout the Bible. Both the divine sovereignty over the whole of history as well as over every single human life and the responsibility of human beings for their own actions are maintained. The only difference seems to be that the biblical writers are less hesitant in ascribing the same situations both to God and to human beings, thus not displaying the arbitrariness signalled by the Basingers. Well-known examples are the hardening of Pharaoh's heart (cf. Exod.4:21, 8:15,32, 9:34f.; Rom. 9:17f.) and the betrayal of Judas (Matt.26:24 p.p.). But also positive events are often described as the work of both God and human beings. Salvation, for example, is sometimes seen as wholly dependent upon God's election (e.g. in Rom. 8:30), whereas at other times it seems to be - at least also - dependent on free human decision (e.g. in II Cor.5:20). In Phil.2:12f., both approaches are even combined: "Work your salvation ... because God works in you..." In short, also in the Bible divine sovereignty and human freedom seem to be inextricably interwoven.

Let us therefore assume that we are not prepared to give up either the divine almightiness and sovereignty or some form of human freedom and responsibility. The central question is now, whether it is possible to offer a systematic and conceptually coherent account of the relation between these two in a way which gives full credit to both instead of underplaying either of them (as happened in, for example, Pelagianism and Arminianism on the one hand, and in extreme predestinatianism on the other)? Or are we forced to uphold a "tension theology,"[3] in which we affirm both T1 and T2 fideistically, i.e. without trying to give a coherent account of their paradoxical relation at all?[4]

In the following subsections I shall first discuss one attempt to relate almightiness and freedom to each other in a coherent way; I shall conclude that it fails, since it draws upon an unsatisfactory notion of human freedom (§ 4.2.2). Next, I develop in some detail the notion of human freedom which to my mind should be adopted given the demands of life (§ 4.2.3). Then, after having rejected for various reasons some alternative proposals, I shall argue that this notion of freedom is compatible with all the commitments of the traditional doctrine of God's almightiness as set out in the preceding chapters (§ 4.2.4). Finally, in section 4.3 I hope to elaborate my argument in a way which shows that it is also soteriologically adequate.

---

[3] This term is proposed by D.A. Carson, *Divine Sovereignty and Human Responsibility*, London 1981, 218.

[4] This is argued by e.g. J.I. Packer, *Evangelism and the Sovereignty of God*, Downers Grove 1961, chap.2.

4.2.2 *Almightiness and omnidetermination*

In a thought-provoking essay William E. Mann argues that the classical ascription of omniscience, omnipotence and simplicity to God has a very specific entailment, in that these attributes together limit the divine freedom.[5] His argument can be summarized as follows. God's omniscience entails that God knows every situation which is the case (1). His omnipotence implies that His will is unimpedible: if God wills a state of affairs, He actualizes that state of affairs (2). God's simplicity involves that there is no plurality of activity in God, so that (among other things) God's knowing a situation is identical with His willing that situation (3). Therefore, from the fact that God knows every situation, it follows from (1) and (3) that God wills every situation. If God wills every situation, then it follows from (2) that He actualizes every situation. In conclusion, it follows that God is decisive with respect to every situation. But then, if omniscience, omnipotence and simplicity are conceived as *necessary* attributes of God,[6] there is one sort of thing which God is not free to do, viz. forbearing from being decisive about any possible situation! For any logically possible situation *s*, God necessarily actualizes *either s* or non-*s*.[7]

This consequence of the classical concept of God is rather unpalatable, since it implies that God is in a significant sense less free than we as human beings are. He cannot but be the exclusively determining cause of the occurrence of every event, as well as of the non-occurrence of every possible event which is not actualized. In this sense, He is "condemned to be free," as Mann concludes - but we could equally well say that, on this view, God is condemned to be all-determining. According to Mann, this should be seen not as a lack of ability but as a lack of limitation.[8] I take it that this claim is comparable to claims we encountered earlier in connection with, for example, the paradox of omnipotence and the problem of divine impeccability.[9] In both cases, we were also confronted with apparent limitations of God's power which are conditional upon His nature. But whereas it is reasonable to argue that God's inability to do evil and to make

---

[5] W.E. Mann, "God's Freedom, Human Freedom, and God's Responsibility for Sin," in: T.V. Morris (ed.), *Divine & Human Action*, Ithaca 1988, 182-210.

[6] Remarkably, Mann ignores this further requirement; it can easily be seen that it is needed, however, since if one of the three attributes in question were accidental rather than essential to God He could decide to drop this attribute, and the chain of argument would be broken.

[7] This paragraph summarizes Mann, "God's Freedom," 192-200; Mann's use of the term "decisive" is somewhat puzzling here. Suppose that five men are trying to push a car with their hands but do not succeed until a sixth man joins them. In this case, the action of the sixth man is decisive. Clearly, however, whether the car moves or not is not up to the sixth man only; in order to move the car he needs the help of his colleagues. The form of divine agency which Mann has in mind is not of this kind, but could better be described as *exclusively* determining with regard to every situation.

[8] "God's Freedom," 201.

[9] See above, §3.3.2 and 3.3.4.

210

a stone He cannot lift afterwards belong to the logical corollaries of His perfection, things are different with regard to God's inability to refrain from exclusively determining an event. In fact, the latter inability really seems to constitute an imperfection. As Kierkegaard lucidly argued:

> But if one will reflect on omnipotence, he will see that it also must contain the unique qualification of being able to withdraw itself again in a manifestation of omnipotence in such a way that precisely for this reason that which has been originated through omnipotence can be independent... All finite power makes [a being] dependent; only omnipotence can make [a being] independent, can form from nothing something which has its continuity in itself through the continual withdrawal of omnipotence... He to whom I owe absolutely everything, although he still absolutely controls everything, has in fact made me independent.[10]

Apart from the question whether God in fact made us independent, it would certainly be an imperfection, indeed a serious handicap, if He *could* not do so.

There is, however, still another objection which can be raised against Mann's conception of God, one which is of particular interest in the context of our discussion: If God cannot refrain from being decisively determining for every situation, there is no room left for the exercise of genuine freedom of His creatures. To use the example provided by Mann himself: If God unimpedibly wills every state of affairs, He unimpedibly willed you to read these words, so that you were not free with regard to reading them. Mann's refutation of this charge is worth considering in some detail.

First, Mann adopts the common retreat to a compatibilist notion of freedom. According to this notion, freedom is compatible with determination, because it does not consist in the possibility to act contrary to the determining causes,[11] but in the voluntariness of acting in accordance with those determining causes. Thus, acting voluntarily is not only a necessary, but a *sufficient* condition for acting freely. All cases in which I am not forced to act against my will offer good examples of free actions. Now clearly, the fact that God unimpedibly wills me to perform a certain action does not imply that He forces me to perform this action against my will. He may direct or persuade my will in such a way that I voluntarily (and perhaps even enthusiastically) perform the action which He has determined me to do. Clearly, in such a situation the freedom of my action is preserved. So it is quite easy to show that on a compatibilist view of freedom human freedom and divine all-determination are compatible.

Second, however, Mann makes the further case that God's all-decisiveness is also compatible with a libertarian account of freedom. On this account, acting voluntarily is a necessary, but not a sufficient condition of

---

[10] S. Kierkegaard, *Papirer* VII 1, A 181; ET from H.V. Hong & E.H. Hong (eds., tr.), *Søren Kierkegaard's Journals and Papers*, Vol.2, London 1970, 62f.

[11] In other words, it is no "contra-causal" freedom.

acting freely. Another necessary condition is that I could have acted otherwise than I did, in the contra-causal sense of "could."[12] No matter how many causes are pressing on me to perform a certain action, only if they leave me the choice of *not* performing it I am significantly free with regard to that action. This notion of freedom looks incompatible with divine determination, but consider Mann's argument to the contrary:

> There is nothing contradictory in the notion of God's willing both that you bring it about that *s* and that you have the power to refrain from bringing it about that *s*. What follows, if he does will both situations, is that you do not exercise your power to refrain. It does *not* follow that you *cannot* exercise your power to refrain.[13]

According to Mann, the latter consequence would only follow if God *necessarily* willed you to bring about that *s*, and Mann holds that there is nothing which forces us to accept such a strong assumption.

Is this a convincing argument? I think not. For despite Mann's claim to the contrary, on a libertarian account of freedom (or, in this connection, of power), the premise of his argument is contradictory. Of course, God may will both that you bring it about that *s* and that you have the power to refrain from bringing it about that *s* - but only in different senses of "willing." If God unimpedibly wills me (rather than merely wishing me) to bring it about that *s*, He cannot at the same time unimpedibly will me to have the power to refrain from bringing it about that *s*. Clearly, if I have the power to refrain from bringing it about that *s*, it is up to me whether *s* is brought about or not. Consequently, God is no longer exclusively determining with regard to *s*. Otherwise, I would not be free in the libertarian sense to bring about or to refrain from bringing about *s*.[14] Thus, if God grants me such freedom with regard to a certain action, He logically cannot at the same time guarantee the outcome. Therefore, Mann does not succeed in showing that his conception of God is compatible with a libertarian account of freedom.

I conclude with a twofold remark. First, Mann's concept of God (whether identical with "the classical concept of God" or not) leads to at least two substantial difficulties.[15] It derogates from God's almightiness

---

[12] The phrase "could have done otherwise" is vague as a result of the notorious ambiguity of the verb "can." The compatibilist John Feinberg distinguishes no less than seven possible meanings of "can," only one of which, viz. the contra-causal meaning, he argues to be at stake in the debate between compatibilism and libertarianism. See J. Feinberg, "God Ordains All Things," in: D. Basinger & R. Basinger (eds.), *Predestination & Free Will*, Downers Grove 1986, 27f.

[13] Mann, "God's Freedom," 204.

[14] Mann's mistake here is equivalent to the one Leibniz made in his theodicy, and which Alvin Plantinga has therefore aptly labelled as "Leibniz' Lapse." See (also for a more extensive refutation of the argument than I can provide here) Plantinga, *Nature of Necessity*, 169-184; *God, Freedom, and Evil*, 32-44.

[15] Mann himself discusses yet a third difficulty, viz. an aggravation of the problem of theo-

and it forces us to adopt a compatibilist account of freedom. Confronted with such difficulties, the most promising way out is simply to re-examine the assumptions which generated them. A fairly natural candidate for reinterpretation in this connection is the notion of simplicity which Mann ascribes to God. The claim that God's activities are identical with one another is highly implausible on its own terms.[16] Moreover, rejecting this part of the doctrine of divine simplicity has far less unwelcome implications than the position Mann opts for. Second, our discussion has shown that the claim that God decisively (or, rather, exclusively) determines every situation, conflicts with a libertarian account of freedom. If we want to speak of human freedom at all in combination with divine all-decisiveness, we should adopt a compatibilist notion of freedom. It is sometimes suggested, however, that there are good reasons to adopt such a notion of freedom anyway. In that case, the second consequence of Mann's concept of God would not be so damaging after all. So let us now compare these notions of freedom more closely.

4.2.3 *Freedom and responsibility*
The concept of freedom no doubt belongs to the most disputed concepts in the history of Western thought. We will by no means be able to offer a comprehensive discussion which takes into account all the issues here. Even if we would limit ourselves to the contemporary philosophical debate, this would leave us at a loss, since studies proliferate which put forward alternative solutions in the freedom-determinism debate.[17] I will not enter into this discussion as such, but concentrate upon the aspects which are relevant from our theological perspective.

There is a remarkable congruence between the traditional theological debate on "freedom and grace" and the contemporary state of the philosophical free will-debate, in that the key questions and dividing lines are still largely the same. To these belong the following. Is the assumption that human beings have freedom of choice plausible in the light of the pressures exerted by the fixed patterns of either the laws of nature or the "law of sin"? If not, is it possible to specify an alternative sense in which human beings can be considered as free, a sense which is substantial enough to satisfy at least one important and generally acknowledged requirement of freedom, viz. that it allows the ascription of moral responsibility? Contemporary compatibilist philosophers such as Frankfurt and Berofsky not only

---

dicy. Since I will turn to this problem in the next section, however, I refrain from discussing it here.

[16] As is shown by Immink, *Divine Simplicity*, 95.

[17] Recent defences of compatibilism include e.g. Bernard Berofsky, *Freedom from Necessity*, London 1987; Richard Double, *The Non-Reality of Free Will*, Oxford 1991; among recent defences of libertarianism are e.g. Peter van Inwagen, *An Essay on Free Will*, Oxford 1983; Jennifer Trusted, *Free Will and Responsibility*, Oxford 1984.

give the same affirmative answers to these questions as, according to a popular interpretation,[18] classical theologians such as Luther and Calvin did (but sometimes Aquinas is mentioned as well), but also argue for their position in comparable ways. The philosophers usually link moral responsibility to concepts as intention, spontaneity, effort, voluntariness, and non-compulsion rather than to avoidability, and argue that although our human actions are ensured by the laws of nature, they are not determined by them.[19] As to the theologians, their distinction between necessity and compulsion may be interpreted along similar lines: although necessitated by God, our actions are not compelled by Him. In a sense, then, this reading of the Reformers' position, according to which human beings are responsible for their actions although they cannot refrain from performing them, morally repulsive though it may be in the eyes of many, is revitalized wholly independently in present-day secular philosophy!

In this section I am not going to join the debate whether this interpretation of classical theology is correct; I think there are important reasons for doubt here. Luther at least acknowledged that human beings have freedom of choice in worldly affairs, and given Calvin's endorsement of Bernard's use of the distinction between necessity and compulsion, it seems that Calvin did acknowledge human freedom of choice as a formal prerequisite for human responsibility for sin.[20] However this may be, the pertinent question in the present context is, whether the position sketched above is conceptually tenable, i.e. whether we can reasonably ascribe moral responsibility to persons for actions with regard to which they had no freedom of choice, but only "freedom of spontaneity." Or, in the theological setting: whether we can consider human actions as free and their agents as responsible for them even though such actions are ensured by the power of God.

In his case for the compatibilist position, Harry Frankfurt asks us to imagine the existence of a "counterfactual intervener," who does not actually intervene to bring it about that Jones performs action A (consisting in, for example, the killing of the innocent Smith by firing a pistol), but who *would have* intervened to bring this about if Jones had not voluntarily performed A. In this situation, it is unavoidable that Jones brings about A; Jones has no choice, he will perform A anyway. So Jones is free on a compatibilist account of freedom only, since he has no freedom of choice. Des-

---

[18] See for this interpretation e.g. Antony Flew, "Divine Omnipotence and Human Freedom," as discussed above, § 3.3.4.

[19] Harry Frankfurt, "Alternate Possibilities and Moral Responsibility," *JP* 66 (1969), 829-839; repr. in John Martin Fischer (ed.), *Moral Responsibility*, Ithaca 1986, 143-152; Berofsky, *Freedom*, 3, 54, and passim.

[20] Cf. Luther, *De Servo Arbitrio*, WA 18, 634; Calvin, *Institutes* II 3, 5; cf. II 2, 7f., where Calvin rejects the word "free will" since it is open to misunderstanding, but at the same time agrees with the conceptual connotation given to it by the fathers.

pite the unavoidability of A, Jones is clearly responsible for the fact that he brings it about *voluntarily*. Although Jones would have brought about A anyway, we are justified in blaming him for the fact that he intended to do it, that he did it voluntarily, that he made no effort to avoid A, etc. That the counterfactual intervener would have forced him to kill Smith anyway, does not exonerate Jones (not even if Jones knew about the counterfactual intervener). So the compatibilist account of freedom can indeed carry the weight of the ascription of moral responsibility. Moreover, this case nicely demonstrates the difference between necessity and compulsion, or between ensuring A and determining A. Since the counterfactual intervener does not actually intervene, he does not *determine* A, or make A a compulsive action. At the same time, he *ensures* A, so that A is performed with necessity, because if Jones would not have done it freely the counterfactual intervener would have forced him to do it.

The theological parallel of Frankfurt's case amounts to the following. God's power ensures all our human actions. We have no choice to act otherwise than God wills us to act. At the same time, we are free in the relevant sense of morally responsible for our actions, since God does not actually intervene, but only counterfactually. We are the ones who voluntarily perform our actions and are therefore morally responsible for them, although we cannot avoid them. In this way, God's almightiness is compatible with a notion of human freedom, which is acceptable in that it at least satisfies a minimum condition for relevant freedom, viz. moral responsibility.

Unfortunately, however, this line of argument is seriously flawed. For consider again Jones's dilemma. Either he performs A voluntarily, or he is forced to perform A, but he cannot refrain from performing A anyway. No doubt, most of us will be inclined to hold Jones responsible for A if he performs it voluntarily. And the only reason why most of us will agree with this ascription of responsibility to Jones is precisely that Jones *had* a genuine choice! He could either choose to kill Smith freely, or to kill him as a result of a forcing intervention of the counterfactual intervener. But in the latter case it would be misleading to say that it was *Jones* who killed Smith, in the same sense in which it is misleading to say that the pistol killed Smith.[21] So the counterfactual interventionist case is insightful in that on closer scrutiny it shows us precisely the opposite of what it was intended to show, viz. that the notion of moral responsibility is inextricably linked

---

[21] This point is contested by Berofsky, *Freedom*, 33; Berofsky suggests that if the counterfactual intervener would act by inducing Jones' self to cause a bodily movement (e.g., to fire the pistol) rather than by bypassing Jones' self, Jones would perform 'the same action' as when he voluntarily moves his body. Even if this is correct, however, (which I doubt, since it is hard to imagine how the same action can be both caused and uncaused by external factors) the link between moral responsibility and avoidability would still stand: We would hold Jones morally responsible not for performing the action as such, but for the way in which he performed the action, since he could have acted otherwise.

with concepts such as avoidability, alternativity, and choice.

In theology very different conceptions of the nature of human freedom are embraced. Especially since the Enlightenment is has become common to emphasize the human autonomy and dignity as essential ingredients of a satisfactory concept of human freedom.[22] More traditionally orientated theologians, on the other hand, have always resisted this modern influence and pointed to the slavery of sin, death and devil, which demeans human freedom to the extent of abolishing the human dignity and autonomy. As a result, "the first thing which must be said of human freedom ... is that our freedom is in need of liberation."[23] Freedom is not an innate possession, but has to be given. Thus we are not free unless we are *set* free by God's justifying and sanctifying grace.[24] As it seems to me, the abysses of human sin and evil which our century has experienced during two world wars and beyond make clear that the largely uncritical adoption of a secular conception of human freedom in modern theology has been essentially wrongheaded.[25] There is, however, one element of freedom which has to be ascribed to human beings even if we fully allow for the fact that we live in the state of sin, and that is moral responsibility. I know of no theologian who denies that in general human beings are morally responsible for at least some of their actions. This is understandably so, since such a denial would make our active life (including the way we relate to God) ultimately meaningless.

So in this minimum sense at least human beings are free by nature rather than by grace:[26] they are in principle[27] morally responsible for their actions. Now what I have tried to establish above is that this moral responsibility conflicts with both determinist and compatibilist accounts of human agency. A necessary condition for ascribing moral responsibility to someone for an action is that she could have done otherwise (in the contra-causal sense of "could"). If she had no genuine choice, she cannot be held morally

---

[22] On the bearing of the Enlightenment and subsequent religion criticism on the relation between divine and human free agency, see e.g. Wilfried Härle, "Werk Gottes - Werk des Menschen," *NTT* 34 (1980), 213-224, esp. 215f.

[23] Daniel L. Migliore, "God's Freedom and Human Freedom," in: H. Deuser et al., *Gottes Zukunft - Zukunft der Welt*, München 1986, 247.

[24] Cf. Colin Gunton, *The Promise of Trinitarian Theology*, Edinburgh 1991, 126: "The Reformers are right to hold that we are not free unless we are set free."

[25] Cf. in this connection the revival of Luther's doctrine of the *unfreedom* of the will in the thinking of present-century German theologians such as H.J. Iwand. Cf. G.C. den Hertog, *Bevrijdende kennis. De 'leer van de onvrije wil' in de theologie van Hans Joachim Iwand*, Den Haag 1989. A similar case against the modern conception of human freedom is in Robert W. Jenson, *America's Theologian: A Recommendation of Jonathan Edwards*, New York 1988.

[26] For a classical defence of this point, see Bernard of Clairvaux, *De Gratia et Libero Arbitrio*.

[27] In practice, of course, most of us will grant that there may be relevant facts (e.g., mental disease, or blameless ignorance of some of the consequences) which may exonerate people from moral responsibility for an action.

responsible for the action. For this reason I reject the compatibilist concept of freedom.

Notice that this rejection is not based upon a straightforward refutation. It is notoriously difficult to refute compatibilism and determinism straightforwardly, i.e. simply to show that these are false positions (as it is, for that matter, difficult for their adherents to show the opposite). We are nevertheless entitled to reject both views due to the fact that we have shown that if either of them were true, an unacceptable conclusion would follow. Following W.S. Anglin, we may say that a conclusion is unacceptable if (1) it is not known to be true, (2) its truth would contradict assumptions and attitudes which go deep in our lives, and (3) it would contradict them in such a way that life would become unthinkable.[28] The statement that we are never morally responsible for our actions is disqualified as an acceptable statement because it satisfies all of these conditions.

Another qualification which may be helpful here is the following. The contra-causal concept of freedom defended here does not commit us to a Sartrean philosophical anthropology, according to which human beings are entirely autonomous. On the contrary, contra-causal freedom is compatible with all the kinds of reasons, influences, temptations and addictions which are so manifestly present in our world and lives. Arguably, these pressures may even become so overwhelming, that as soon as we yield to them we virtually loose the opportunity or ability (or both) to do otherwise, thus becoming the slaves of sin and misery. Still, we are morally responsible for our actions, since there was a moment when we were not forced to give in to those pressures, but could have acted otherwise (in the contra-causal sense). In this way, it seems to me that a contra-causal notion of freedom can do full justice to the doctrine of sin; the Anselmian complaint *nondum considerasti quanti ponderis peccatum sit* does not apply to the defender of contra-causal, libertarian freedom. In fact, since only this concept of freedom allows for moral responsibility, it is *only* this concept which does full justice to the doctrine of sin. This may also have been the view of Calvin, who aligns himself to the Fathers here. As Jacob Klapwijk says: "To Calvin's perception, bondage to sin is actually *confirmed* by what a person does on his or her own free initiative with the gifts and possibilities which God bestows."[29]

There is, however, one other theological objection which is often put forward against the contra-causal view of human freedom. We must consider

---

[28] Anglin, *Free Will*, 2. Anglin argues that if human beings do not have libertarian free will, eight unacceptable conclusions follow. I have elaborated only one of them, not because I consider the other seven conclusions to be entirely acceptable, but because I am specifically concerned here with the *theological* viability of accounts of human freedom. (Thus, for my present purposes the notion of "life" in Anglin's conditions for unacceptability might be substituted by "theology").

[29] Jacob Klapwijk, "John Calvin," in: J. Klapwijk, S. Griffioen & G. Groenewoud (eds.), *Bringing into Captivity every Thought*, Lanham 1991, 139 (my italics); cf. n.24 above.

this objection carefully, because if it holds this could imply that also the contra-causal view of freedom has unacceptable consequences for theology, so that a stalemate would have been reached, which leaves the issue of the nature of human freedom unresolved after all.[30] According to this objection, the contra-causal notion of freedom is incompatible with God's almightiness. Let us discuss this issue in the next subsection.

4.2.4 *The compatibility of almightiness and freedom*

The reason why it is sometimes held that God's almightiness or omnipotence and human freedom are incompatible, is that omnipotence is (implicitly or explicitly) equated with omnidetermination. Clearly, if God determines every state of affairs, including the outcome of human actions, then these actions are not free in the sense required by a contra-causal notion of freedom. So if we define omnipotence in this way it is incompatible with human freedom, and we are forced to sacrifice either our belief that such a God exists or our belief in human freedom and responsibility. Confronted with this choice, modern atheist religion criticism has a point in that it concludes from the experience of human freedom, the denial of which would contradict "assumptions and attitudes which go deep in our lives," to the non-existence of an omnidetermining God.

But does the doctrine of God's almightiness imply omnidetermination?[31] In order to answer this question, let us recapitulate the results of our account of the historical development of the doctrine. In chapter 2 we established that the omnipotence-doctrine comprises three essential elements: God's sovereign government of the universe and its history, God's actual preservation of the world, and God's ability to realize all logically possible states of affairs which are compatible with His nature. The first two of these elements are also aspects of the traditional doctrine of divine providence, the third is a distinctive part of the omnipotence-doctrine.

Does any of these three elements require that God determine every single state of affairs in the course of history? As to the third, this is a statement about God's abilities, not about the scope of His activities, so the possibility of a conflict seems absent here. As to the second, it is very well possible to preserve an object without determining all the events which happen in or upon it. Only events which would result in the annihilation of the object should be prevented, all other events may come about without divine determination. As to the first, God's universal lordship over history seems the most plausible candidate for implying omnidetermination. But consider a nice example of Kenneth Foreman:

---

[30] Cf. Anglin's procedure in *Free Will*, 25-28.

[31] For discussions of this question from the perspective of biblical theology and exegesis, see e.g. P.W. Gooch, "Sovereignty and Freedom: Some Pauline Compatibilisms," *SJTh* 40 (1987), 531-542; George Mavrodes, "Is There Anything Which God Does Not Do?," *CSR* 16 (1987), 384-391 (cf. the subsequent discussion with Clark H. Pinnock and John Feinberg, ibid., 392-404).

Let us imagine two horsemen. One sits on a horse every movement of which he controls absolutely. The horse does not move a fraction of an inch in any part unless the rider decides it shall move and sees to it that the movement is made. Here we see absolute control. Another man sits on another horse. This horse makes various movements which the rider does not command, does not initiate, cannot even predict in detail. But the rider is in control. The first horse is a hobbyhorse; the second is a spirited five-gaited showhorse. But which is the better horseman? ... Is it actually more to the credit of God that He shall ride this universe like a hobbyhorse, or like a real, living creature of intelligence and spirit? ... we do not have to suppose that God cannot be sovereign without robbing His creatures of all their freedom.[32]

Surely, as Kierkegaard already suggested, a God who remains in control on the whole while granting His creatures a considerable degree of freedom is far more powerful than a God who stays in control by determining every single event. Unless, of course, the first option is incoherent (in which case it is logically impossible even for God to bring it about). This is what has been claimed by a number of philosophers and theologians. Let us try to find out whether their arguments are convincing.

Wolfhart Pannenberg, to begin with, writes as follows:

If the eternity of God is thought of as the unlimited continuance of a being which has existed from the first, then the omnipotence and omniscient providence of this God must have established the course of everything that takes place in the universe in all its details from the very first.[33]

He goes on to reject traditional solutions such as that God only foresees free actions without determining them, or that God's eternity has to be thought of as simultaneous at any point in time rather than as everlasting.[34] Pannenberg concludes that

... it is this very monstrous conception of a God who is an existent being equipped with omnipotence and omniscience, which atheist criticism attacks in the name of human freedom. ... Here atheist criticism is justified. An *existent* being acting with omnipotence and omniscience would make freedom impossible.[35]

Pannenberg's remedy for this conflict is his well-known proposal to con-

---

[32] K.J. Foreman, *God's Will and Ours*, Richmond 1954, 30; quoted by Samuel Fisk, *Divine Sovereignty and Human Freedom*, Neptune 1973, 55.

[33] W. Pannenberg, "Speaking of God in the Face of Atheist Criticism," in: id., *Basic Questions in Theology* Vol.3, London 1973, 108.

[34] Ibid., 108; for recent adoptions of the latter solution, see John C. Yates, *The Timelessness of God*, Lanham 1990; Brian Davies, *Thinking about God*, 170ff.; Soskice, "God of Power," 936 (and other Catholic authors mentioned there); cf. from a Protestant point of view, Helm, *Eternal God*; B. Loonstra, *Verkiezing - verzoening - verbond*, 's Gravenhage 1990, 330f., 387.

[35] Ibid., 109; cf. Suurmond, *God is machtig*, 45 ("Elk denken dat uitgaat van een goddelijke almacht als domweg 'alles kunnen' ... reduceert de menselijke vrijheid tot illusie"); Louw, "Omnipotence (Force)," 55.

ceive of God not as an existent being but as the power of the future.[36]

At first sight, it seems that Pannenberg's criticism consists in sweeping statements rather than sound arguments. We should keep in mind, however, that Pannenberg starts from his definition of the concept of God as "the Reality that determines everything" (die alles-bestimmende Wirklichkeit), and it is this definition which permeates his understanding of omnipotence. This "strong" view of God's omnipotence, equating omnipotence with omnidetermination, is fundamental to the whole of Pannenberg's theological enterprise.[37] This being so, it is easy to see why Pannenberg's own solution to the conflict between God's power and human freedom fails. For as long as God's power is conceived of as determining every single event, there can be no genuine room for human freedom and responsibility. It does not matter in this connection whether God is seen as active in past and present or only in the future. Pannenberg simply substitutes for divine predeterminism "an equally odious divine postdeterminism which amounts to the same thing."[38] If anything is monstrous here, it is not the traditional concept of an omnipotent, presently existent God as such, but Pannenberg's interpretation of this God's omnipotence in terms of omnidetermination. For the consequence of this interpretation must be that human beings are not free in the contra-causal sense. Remarkably, this is precisely what Pannenberg implicitly acknowledged in his rejection of the idea of free will.[39]

In response to this charge, Pannenberg has denied the deterministic interpretation of his position, and taken up an idea which he had sometimes hinted at but never fully developed in detail in his earlier work, viz. that it might belong to God's all-determining power to leave some degree of self-determination to the creature. Pannenberg now emphasizes that the Power of the future determines the present not by preventing human freedom in terms of contingent decisions, but, on the contrary, by making such freedom of decision possible. "... God creates his creatures as they are, which means in the case of the human creature that human freedom itself is to be conceived as God's creation."[40] This reference to the divine act of creation,

---

[36] Ibid., 110-115; cf. Brinkman, Gods- en mensbegrip, 34f. Remarkably, this idea is absent from Pannenberg's doctrine of God as expounded in his Systematic Theology, Vol.1, Edinburgh 1991.

[37] For a sample of places where in various ways Pannenberg describes God as the all-determining reality, see David R. Polk, "The All-Determining God and the Peril of Determinism," in: C.E. Braaten & P. Clayton (eds.), The Theology of Wolfhart Pannenberg, Minneapolis 1988, 159-163; cf. most recently Pannenberg's Systematic Theology Vol.1, 159.

[38] Ibid., 163.

[39] David McKenzie, "Pannenberg on God and Freedom," JR 60 (1980), 324-326; McKenzie rightly questions the compatibility of this rejection with Pannenberg's adoption of the existentialist account of freedom as Weltoffenheit: "If we have no free will, we are really bound to the past and have no freedom in the sense of a transcending openness to the future" (326).

[40] Pannenberg, "A Response to My American Friends," in: Braaten & Clayton, Theology, 322f.; cf. also his Systematic Theology I, 420 ("The goal of the act of creation is the independent

however, leaves us at a loss with regard to the specific contribution of Pannenberg's conception of God as the Power of the *future* to the solution of the almightiness-freedom dilemma. Moreover, it suggests that Pannenberg has by now given up his interpretation of omnipotence as omnideter-mination, which originally prompted him to his provocative denial of the compatibility of human freedom with the existence of an omnipotent God.[41]

In their criticisms of Pannenberg both McKenzie and Polk insist that if Pannenberg really wants to incorporate the modern preoccupation with human freedom in his theology, he should align himself with process theol-ogy on this point. According to them, process theology, in distinction to Pannenberg, does succeed in safeguarding human freedom, precisely because it does not shrink from the task of revising the ideas of the omnipotence and almightiness of God. Indeed, process theologians usually hold that it is inconsistent to ascribe contra-causal freedom to human beings while at the same time maintaining a traditional account of divine power. In order to find out whether they are right, we will now turn to an examination of their arguments. In fact, I will concentrate upon one argument, which occurs in the writings of most process theologians, and which I therefore consider to be the typical process-approach to the problem.[42] The first one to develop this approach was Charles Hartshorne,[43] but since Hartshorne's doctrine of God's power has recently been highlighted more than once,[44] I will refer to David Griffin's equally forceful presentation of the argument.

A central assumption in process thinking ever since Whitehead is that we cannot think of individuals as essentially existing independently from their activities and their exercise of power. As Griffin recently put it, "ac-tual things differ from nonactual things by having power."[45] Accordingly, all actual entities in the world have power. Now Griffin, following Harts-horne, claims that the traditional doctrine of omnipotence (or almightiness; process theologians do not usually differentiate between both) implies that God has all the power in the world.[46] But this, he argues, is inconsistent

---

existence of creatures. But in fact this means that they have to be independent of God.").

[41] In his response to Polk, Pannenberg tries to combine both claims by declaring that God and the human person "do not act on the same level" (ibid., 323). Unfortunately, he makes no attempt to spell out this claim further.

[42] I realize that it is hard to isolate the process-argument from the entire scheme of White-headian metaphysics. It may be that in the end we can only accept the claim if we are prepared to accept the comprehensive metaphysical scheme. See on this e.g. D.R. Griffin, "Actuality, Pos-sibility, and Theodicy," *PrS* 12 (1982), 168-179. Since I am not concerned here with assessing process thought as a whole, I will test the plausibility of its omnipotence-argument largely on its own terms.

[43] See esp. his *Divine Relativity*, ch.2, and for a recent restatement his *Omnipotence*, 10-26.

[44] See for literature below, §4.4 n.68.

[45] D.R. Griffin, "Preface to the UPA Edition" in his *God, Power, and Evil*, Lanham 1991[2], 2.

[46] Griffin, ibid., 268.; cf. Hartshorne, "Omnipotence," in: Vergilius Ferm (ed.), *An En-*

with the existence of other actual beings, since it implies that such beings are totally devoid of power. Therefore, the traditional doctrine should be revised in such a way that God possesses the greatest possible power *given the existence of other actual beings*. This means that God does not have all the power; He does not have the power to totally determine all the activities of actual beings in the world. What is more, "if there are many centres of power, then no state of affairs in which these entities are involved can be completely determined by any one of them"[47] - not even by God, we should add. In short, in terms of our discussion, Griffin argues that the only way to solve the conflict between God's almightiness and creaturely freedom is to redefine the concept of God's almightiness so as to allow for the fact that God is at least partly dependent upon the power of creaturely beings.

To my opinion, this line of argument is unconvincing for a number of reasons. First, from the fact that an omnipotent being cannot completely determine all the activities of actual beings, it does not follow that an omnipotent being cannot unilaterally (i.e., "on its own") bring about *any* state of affairs. It is perfectly conceivable that, due to its greater power, an omnipotent being is able to bring about some but not all states of affairs. To give an analogy: while my stronger brother lacks the power to control all the activities of the muscles, the blood vessels, and their constituent molecules in my arm, he certainly has the power to raise my arm (apart from my cooperation).[48] So the cherished process-thesis that God's activity should be conceived of in terms of persuasion rather than in terms of coercion does not follow from the sole assumption that actual beings by definition have some degree of power.

Second, it does not follow from the assumption that every actual being has power, that an omnipotent being cannot completely determine all the activities of that being. What follows from this assumption is simply that if an omnipotent being chooses to determine all of this being's activities so as to rob it of all its power, this being ceases to exist. An appeal to another assumption of process thinking, viz. that it is a metaphysical (and, therefore, a necessary) truth that there is a world, does not help here.[49] For this assumption does not imply that such a world must necessarily contain this particular (or, for that matter, any other particular) actual being.

Third, there is nothing in the traditional view of almightiness which implies that God has all the power there is.[50] Nor does it follow from any

---

cyclopedia of Religion, New York 1945, 545.

[47] Griffin, *God, Power*, 270.

[48] I borrow this example from Griffin himself ("Actuality," 175), who employs it to make another point, however.

[49] For the claim that there *must* be a world, see Griffin, *God, Power*, 279; for the necessary status of metaphysical truths, see his "Actuality," 170-172.

[50] This is not to say that the traditional view has not often been interpreted in this way; it is

of the three elements of which the traditional view consists that actual beings are completely devoid of power. From the fact that God is almighty in the traditional sense one cannot conclude that other beings are utterly powerless. Griffin's suggestion to the contrary results from a misunderstanding of the nature of power which goes back to Hartshorne, and which underlies both his criticism of the traditional doctrine as his alternative conception of divine power. Nelson Pike has lucidly put this point as follows:

> With respect to marbles or pineapples, ownership is exclusive - if I have them all, you have none. But power doesn't work that way - nor (so far as I know) has anyone prior to Hartshorne supposed that it does. I possess the power to shatter the glass sitting on my desk and so does my son. The fact that I possess that power does not mean that others do not possess it as well.[51]

A consequence of this, let us say, substantialist misunderstanding of power on the part of process thought is that the difference between the possession and the exercise of a power is obscured.[52] Griffin even explicitly denies this distinction, arguing that whether someone chooses to raise his arm, or chooses not to, he is still choosing. This may be true, but clearly there is a third option here: choosing not to raise your arm differs from not choosing to raise your arm! If I don't choose to raise my arm, nor choose not to raise my arm, I have the power to raise my arm but don't exercise it.

Given these shortcomings of the process objection against our hypothesis that God's almightiness may be compatible with human contra-causal freedom, is it possible to substantiate this hypothesis in a more positive way? Is it possible to give an account of the relation between omnipotence and freedom which on the one hand does not (if not verbally then in practice) deny human freedom and responsibility and on the other hand does not make God partially dependent upon the world? I think it is. A good starting-point for such an account is precisely the difference between having and exercising a power. God may have the power to bring about every state of affairs which it is logically possible for Him to bring about, without exercising this power. It is from God's refraining from exercising this power that our freedom stems. In this sense, God is indeed the origin and ground

---

to say, that this interpretation is not necessitated by the view itself. Cf. Griffin, "Actuality," 169f.

[51] Nelson Pike, "Process Theodicy and the Concept of Power," *PrS* 12 (1982), 154. In fact, Pike is refuting here the so-called zero-sum view of power; cf. my own refutation of this view above, §3.2.1.

[52] A partial reflection of the substantialist misunderstanding which does not have this consequence can be found in David Pailin, *Groundwork of Philosophy of Religion*, London 1986. Pailin does not explicitly accuse the tradition of holding an incoherent concept of divine power, but by stipulatively defining omnipotent as "having all power" and subsequently rejecting this notion as self-contradictory he implicitly suggests the tradition to be incoherent (153f.; cf. 52). On the other hand, Pailin's alternative proposal (154f.), which maintains the distinction between having and using power (154), comes close to what (in my view) the traditional doctrine really intends to say.

of our human freedom.[53] Note that this is not so because of some limitation of God's power.[54] That would mean that God had become less powerful than almighty. What God limits is only the *exercise* of His power, i.e. the scope of His activities.

At the same time, God is able to remain the fully sovereign Lord of history, since He has the power to suspend our freedom as often as He wishes. Some argue that such interventions contradict the original creative act of God by means of which He constituted us as free persons.[55] But this is unconvincing. As William Alston points out, we have no reasons to assume "that God would prefer to attain His goals only by working through the natural order,"[56] or, we might add, by always respecting the free decisions of human beings. We simply lack such insight into the divine order of preferences. Others have argued that God will not overpower human freedom since by doing so He would destroy our very personhood, treating us as objects rather than as persons. But first, this does not follow, as long as God intervenes only incidentally, restoring our freedom afterwards. Second, we are simply not in a position to issue a new commandment with which God has to comply: "Thou shalt not overpower our freedom"![57] And third, as David Basinger has pointed out, it is very doubtful whether God is able to realize all of His intentions if He is bound not to circumvent or suspend the human freedom at least occasionally.[58]

4.2.5 *Conclusion*

This account of the relation between divine almightiness and human freedom has been aptly illustrated by Nelson Pike by means of the following diagram, which represents this relation in the form of an electrical circuit:[59]

---

[53] Pannenberg, "Speaking about God," 110; Härle, "Werk Gottes," 218-220; cf. Gunton, *Promise*, 126: "... should it not be possible to conceive our freedom as a function of our *createdness*, of the relation we have to our creator by virtue of being made in the image of God?"

[54] The idea that God has limited his omnipotence is a fairly popular one; cf. e.g. John Lucas, *The Freedom of the Will*, Oxford 1970, 75; Bruce Reichenbach, "God Limits His Power," in: Basinger & Basinger (eds.), *Predestination*, 99-124; Maurice Wiles, *God's Action in the World*, Oxford 1986, 63, 67, 80. For a critique of this idea, see Marcel Sarot, "Omnipotence and Self-Limitation," in: Van den Brink, Van den Brom & Sarot, *Christian Faith*, 172-185; see also Kenny, *God of the Philosophers*, 60f.

[55] E.g. Härle, ibid., 217; Wiles, *God's Action*, passim.

[56] W.P. Alston, *Divine Nature*, 210.

[57] Here lies my difficulty with Luco van den Brom's paper "Gottes Welthandeln und die Schachmetapher," *G&D* 3 (1990), 125-151 (cf. his *Creatieve twijfel*, Kampen 1991, 127-144). In personal communication, however, Van den Brom has made clear that the reason for God's not overpowering human creaturely freedom is not that this would be impossible or immoral, but that He has wilfully decided to respect this freedom, at least until an eschatological moment.

[58] D. Basinger, "Human Freedom and Divine Providence. Some New Thoughts on an Old Problem," *RS* 15 (1979), 491-510.

[59] Nelson Pike, "Over-Power and God's Responsibility for Sin," 17; I have replaced the letters

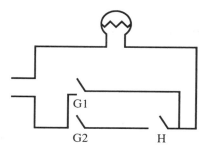

In this picture, G1 and G2 are switches operated by God, whereas H stands for a switch operated by a human agent. The lighting up of the bulb represents any possible event caused by God or the human agent. Assume that G1 is fixed in the open and G2 is fixed in the closed position. In that case, it is the human agent who may use his freedom to determine whether the bulb lights up or not. But now suppose that G2 is opened. Now H is bypassed, and whether the bulb goes on or not wholly depends upon the position of G1, which is determined by God. Moreover, by fixing G2 in the closed position or G1 in the open position God can grant the human agent different forms of partial control.

Now this seems to me a perfectly consistent way of picturing the relation between God's almightiness and human freedom. It solves the problem with the exposition of which started the present discussion, viz. that of the common arbitrary appeal to T1 and T2, i.e. to the human moral responsibility and the divine sovereignty. For what we are doing by appealing to T1 for clarification of a particular event is to claim that this event is one in which G1 is fixed in the open and G2 in the closed position, so that its occurrence is due to an action of H. When we appeal to T2, on the other hand, we are claiming that G2 is opened, so that the occurrence of the event is the result of an active handling of G1 by God. Such appeals need not be arbitrary, but may rather express interpretations of different situations with the "eyes of faith."[60] I conclude that the traditional doctrine of almightiness, with its stress on God's "ultimate mastery over all existence" (Austin Farrer), is adequate to the demands of life which require us to see human beings as free and responsible persons.

I do not claim, however, that the account which I give here solves all problems without further consideration. On the contrary, at least two age-old problems are elicited by it, and therefore require explicit discussion. First, it must be shown how the present section's construal of the divine-human relationship bears upon the question of the authorship of faith. For it may seem that the ascription of freedom and responsibility to human beings threatens the priority of God's grace in the work of salvation. How can this suggestion be avoided? How do God's sovereignty and grace relate to

used by Pike.
[60] V. Brümmer, *Personal God*, 125-127.

human responsibility in these soteriological affairs? And second, on the construal of the divine-human relationship which I propose it seems impossible to avoid the conclusion that God is at least co-responsible for sin and evil. To many thoughtful people, this consequence is so unpalatable that they reject the whole scheme for this sole reason. Therefore, we must address the implications which our defence of the compatibility of almightiness and freedom has for the problem of evil. In short, we must show that a credible form of theodicy can be formulated from the perspective we have reached in the present section. Let us now discuss these issues in turn.

4.3 PERSPECTIVISM AND THE AUTHORSHIP OF FAITH

4.3.1 *Perspectivism as a heuristic tool: Donald MacKay*

There is one objection to my defence of the compatibility of almightiness and freedom which is so obvious that I cannot ignore it. I have argued that human beings as creatures of God must be endowed with freedom of choice, since otherwise it would be wrong to hold them morally responsible for their actions. This point of view has unwelcome ramifications, however, in the sphere of soteriology. For it seems to cut the Gordian knot of the "freedom and grace" debate in a purely Arminian way. The problems of such an Arminian position are well-known. To cite only three of the most obvious ones: it gives credit to human persons rather than to God for salvation, it makes salvation depend upon the decision and steadfastness of sinful, fickle-minded human beings, and it conflicts with both the claim of revelation and the experience of many believers that faith is a sheer gift of God, wholly a matter of grace. It was precisely these soteriological and doxological concerns which led Luther, Calvin and many others to their vehement rejection of free will.

One possible response to this objection would be to consider matters of salvation as examples, perhaps even as the paradigmatic examples of God overruling human freedom. When developing my proposal for harmonizing almightiness with freedom, I have argued that such occasional overrulings of human freedom do not destroy this freedom. So perhaps we can incorporate the priority of God in bringing about salvation into our general account of the relation between God's almightiness and human freedom. A moment's reflection makes clear, however, that this response will not do. For if we suppose that people only come to faith if God causally brings about their act(s) of faith by overpowering their free choice, the necessary consequence is that if people do not come to faith they are not responsible for this. Since faith can only be God's doing, they simply cannot help it. And this, again, runs counter to what Christian theists are committed to hold.

In short, it seems that there are religiously compelling reasons for each of two diametrically opposed views. Is it possible to overcome this dilemma? Well, the conditions look unfavourable. Perhaps, however, it would help us if we found a way not so much to overcome the dilemma as to come to terms with it, to handle it in a fruitful way, and to see *why* it is so paradoxical. This would offer us an intelligible explanation - though, admittedly, not a solution - for the paradox of faith's authorship. I believe that such an explanation is possible, and that it is offered by a theory which I will call perspectivism. The hinge of this theory is that whether two paradoxical claims form a genuine contradiction or only reveal disparities which are complementary at another level depends upon whether the disparities come about from a different *perspective*. I think that the paradox of the authorship of faith is provoked by such a difference of perspective. Let me explain.

For a start, consider the following simple experiment. If we hold up a finger and a thumb at some distance of our face, one 10 or 15 cm behind the other, we see both in line with each other. But if we close one eye in turn, we see the finger to the left and right side of the thumb respectively (or in reverse). Clearly, a finger cannot be simultaneously to the right and to the left side of a thumb. Thus, we seem to have two mutually exclusive experiences. As soon as we open both eyes, however, we see-in-depth a single finger, displaced from the thumb in a third dimension. This latter experience integrates at another level the paradoxical experiences of looking at finger and thumb with only one eye, and shows that these are complementary rather than logically contradictory.

Donald MacKay, to whom I owe this example,[1] makes a number of pertinent comments in this connection with regard to theological paradoxes. First, he suggests that the being of God is to such a degree a complete mystery to us, that far from having to be embarrassed by them, we may simply *expect* paradoxes to arise when we try to do justice to all aspects of what He has disclosed about His being and activities. Second, in order to make sense of such paradoxical statements about God, "it is essential to identify as well as we can the *standpoint* for which it claims to be a valid 'projection'." We are entitled to dismiss two verbally disparate theological statements as mutually exclusive only after having established that they are not framed for (and from) different perspectives, and may therefore be logically complementary at some higher level.[2] Third, the integration of complementary experiences is not an easy task, to be fulfilled merely at an intellectual level. Rather, it requires a change in my "perceptual set" which cannot be brought about in me by others, although they can help me by telling me what to look for. In the end, a change has to happen in *me* as a whole human being. But it may be postponed indefinitely as a result of the

---

[1] Donald M. MacKay, *Science, Change and Providence*, Oxford 1978, 44.
[2] Ibid. See also his "Complementarity in Scientific and Theological Thinking," *Zygon* 9 (1974), 225-244.

wrong perceptual set.[3]

Two related questions emerge if we want to apply MacKay's argument to our present discussion. First, is it possible to identify the difference between the perspectives from which the authorship of faith is ascribed to God and man respectively? And secondly, are we able to transcend this paradox-creating difference, and to reach (or at least hint at) one single integrating and unifying perspective from which it may be possible to redescribe the conflicting statements as complementary in one and the same universe of discourse? No doubt, this second question is the more difficult one; but at the same time, it is especially this question which we need to answer in order to validate the usefulness of perspectivism in our context.

4.3.2 Historical perspectivism: Sallie McFague

One possible way to identify the difference between the two perspectives of God's almightiness and human freedom with regard to the appropriation of salvation is to appeal to *temporal* categories. This is the way in which Sallie McFague proceeds.[4] According to McFague, previous ages asked for a strong doctrine of divine providence. In a situation characterized by continual threats of epidemic diseases, feudal oppression, death-through-war etc. it was of great help in facing the demands of life to emphasize that in the end it is God who is in control of all that really matters. Salvation ultimately depends on God, not on human beings. In our nuclear age, on the other hand, this emphasis would be quite counterproductive, since it is now no longer we who are threatened by the world, but the world which is threatened by us. Stressing the divine almightiness in this situation would only confirm our self-indulgence and stimulate us to escape our responsibility for the world. Therefore, we should now propagate discourse which underscores the human freedom and responsibility with regard to the salvation of the world and of human life.[5]

As it seems to me, this account should not be too easily dismissed. There is much in it which deserves careful consideration, since the doctrine of divine almightiness can indeed be abused in such a way as to obscure our responsibility as human beings. Nevertheless, McFague's view can hardly be deemed a satisfactory account of the relation between God's power and human freedom in matters of salvation. For it obviously implies an agnosticism or relativism with regard to the question whether *in fact* God's sovereign agency or the self-determining power of human creatures is ultimately

---

[3] Ibid., 46f.

[4] It should be noted that McFague's conception of salvation is broader than the one under consideration, since McFague does not link salvation with personal faith but thinks of it largely in this-worldly communal categories. Since I am concerned here with the origin and authorship of salvation rather than with its nature and scope, this difference does not affect my argument.

[5] Sallie McFague, *Models of God*, London 1987, 14-21; cf. 29f.; see also §1.3.3 above.

decisive with respect to salvation. Unless we suppose that God's power has diminished and given way to human self-determination in the course of history (which apparently is not the point McFague is making), we are still at a loss about which of both perspectives is ontologically true. What reason do we have to suppose that our contemporary human predicament offers the best prospective of conceptualizing the divine-human relationship? McFague wrote her book before the breakdown of the Eastern communist world. Since this breakdown, the threat of a nuclear annihilation of the world (which plays an important role in the background of McFague's project of re-thinking theology[6]), has diminished considerably. Does this mean that God's power is increasing again at the moment?

Perhaps such objections can be countered in the following way. McFague is not arguing that theological truth *itself* is changing, but that it depends upon the particular situation in which we find ourselves which *aspects* of this truth should be highlighted because of their contextual *relevance*. Now this claim is certainly true, and therefore this reading would offer us a more rational interpretation[7] of McFague. It is not a more plausible interpretation, however. For this to be so McFague should at least have indicated how divine power and human responsibility go together in a way which makes it possible to highlight each of them in different situations. But there is no hint at an overarching perspective in McFague which integrates the partial truths of both seemingly exclusive points of view. Let us therefore now examine the work of Kathryn Tanner, in order to find out whether she helps us further at this point.

4.3.3 *Functional perspectivism: Kathryn Tanner*

A second version of perspectivism, which may be labelled functional perspectivism (as distinct from McFague's temporal perspectivism) has recently been defended in a fascinating study by Kathryn Tanner.[8] The fascination of this study lies in the fact that, while sticking to its subject matter throughout the book, it succeeds in avoiding a straightforward answer to the question which is pivotal to this subject matter, viz. the question of decisiveness. Let me elaborate this point in some detail.[9]

According to Tanner, it is the task of theology to show the coherence of Christian claims by isolating meta-level rules for the formation of proper theological first-order statements. The modern conviction that traditional assertions about God's absolute sovereignty and human self-determination are incompatible is a typical result of the unconscious distorting transfor-

---

[6] Cf. the subtitle of her *Models of God: Theology for an Ecological, Nuclear Age.*

[7] See on the concept of a rational interpretation Brümmer, *Wijsgerige Begripsanalyse*, 96.

[8] Kathryn E. Tanner, *God and Creation in Christian Theology: Tyranny or Empowerment?*, Oxford 1988.

[9] I discuss Tanner's version of perspectivism more extensively than the others, since Tanner has devoted a full-length monograph to its exposition and defence.

mation of these rules, ensuing from the historically conditioned body of interrelated assumptions that form the modern framework for discussion of the topic.[10] As a result of this modern misconstrual of the character of traditional Christian discourse, this discourse has lapsed into incoherence, which is clear from its fragmentation within the Christian Church since the Reformation.

In order to re-establish its coherence, we must therefore trace the rules at work in traditional discourse on the divine-human relationship. These rules all have a positive and a negative side. The positive side is that God grants us our own value and powers, including some sort of capacity for free self-determination.[11] The negative side is that human beings are immediately and totally dependent upon God's universal and unconditional agency, which is required for any particular power, operation and efficacy of created beings.[12] Together, the rules for coherent Christian discourse guarantee that God founds rather than suppresses created being, and that He empowers rather than tyrannises created causes to bring about by their own power all those effects which are included in God's transcendent agency - for God must be said to directly establish every aspect of created reality. In this way, genuine efficacy must be predicated of both God and the creature, and the Christian theologian who sacrifices the one in behalf of the other is mistaken. As Bernard of Clairvaux has it, "it is not as if grace did one half of the work and free choice the other; but each does the whole work, according to its own peculiar contribution. Grace does the whole work, and so does free choice."[13]

Major divergent theological strands within the Christian tradition agree with each other in conforming to these rules for coherent Christian discourse, but differ from each other in emphasizing either the positive or the negative side of the rules. Because of their fundamental agreement on the propriety of those rules the theologies of Aquinas, Suarez, Luther, Calvin, Barth, Rahner and others can be considered as "functional equivalents" in spite of their material differences.[14] These differences have to do with what is called in my terminology the particular *perspective* of the theologian in question. This perspective is in turn determined by the theologian's philosophical milieu, his metaphysical commitments, conceptual categories, theological method, the particular topics and issues which have priority in his thinking, but above all by the theologian's estimation of which sort of

---

[10] Tanner, *God and Creation*, 4-9; cf.27-29.

[11] Ibid., 105, 122.

[12] Ibid., 105, 91, and passim.

[13] Bernard of Clairvaux, *De Gratia et Libero Arbitrio* XIV, 47 (tr. Daniel O'Donovan, *On Grace & Free Choice*, Kalamazoo 1988, 106); cf. Tanner, *God and Creation*, 92.

[14] Tanner, *God and Creation*, 104ff., cf. 30-32; Suarez (108) is a dubious example, however, since later on (146) Tanner includes him along with Molina among those who violated the rules for proper Christian discourse.

claims must have priority, depending upon the particular audience addressed, the particular historical situation etc. Both the positive and the negative sides of the rules are prone to illicit inferences which might be drawn from them. A climate in which the human power and freedom tends to be over-emphasized might promote self-reliance and lack of trust in God, self-satisfied pride, ingratitude to God, but also, in cases where human efforts fall short, anxiety about the future. On the other hand, a situation in which exclusively the total-working agency of God is emphasized may incite moral indifference and torpor, suspicion of divine injustice, and a lack of love and gratitude towards God.[15] This kind of illicit implications can only be headed off by emphasizing the opposite side of the rules.

In this way, what matters in theology is not so much the material content of the claims which are made but the *functions* they fulfill. Functional equivalence does not require descriptive equivalence. Semantically very diverse accounts can convey the same message. Luther may differ widely from Aquinas in extending as far as possible the negative side of the rules, by stressing the pervasive effects of sin, the bondage of the human will, the *simul iustus ac peccator*-status of the faithful etc., since neither he nor Aquinas violates the rules for coherent Christian discourse, they convey basically the same message.[16] In modern times, however, traditional theological discourse breaks down, because modern methods of inquiry obscure the fact that the traditional formulations were conditioned by the *functions* they were designed to serve within the context of Christian communities; instead, these formulations were interpreted as referentially adequate, i.e. as the results of a "pure" inquiry into the nature of the divine-human relationship. But viewed as ontological descriptions, the positive and negative side of the rules become incoherent![17] Thus, the modern difficulties with traditional theological discourse are the result of a "curious forgetfulness about the nature of the rules for proper Christian talk."[18]

This may suffice as a summary of Tanner's argument, which strikes me as extremely powerful and convincing except for one crucial element. Tanner severs the connection between the regulatory and referential functions of theological statements. According to her, meta-level rules governing theological statements mainly have a negative role, they rule out inadmissible claims without singling out any one for acceptance. So they do not indicate whether a particular statement is ontologically true or false. Tanner does not say that ontological or referential questions are unimportant or wrong-headed in theology, but modestly sees her functional approach as a propaedeutic for the actual recovery of the coherence of traditional claims, which is, she admits in the end, a matter of first-order theological construc-

---

[15] Ibid., 114f.
[16] Ibid., 31, 112.
[17] Ibid., 155.
[18] Ibid., 5.

tion.[19]

The problem here is, however, that the formal rules which regulate theological discourse can only be coherent if the first-order statements which they permit are coherent. It is easy to see the logic of this point. Formal recommendations for *talk* about God and the world do not hang together coherently if they produce incoherent material statements about these matters. The rules

R1   Avoid in talk about God's creative agency all suggestions of limitations in scope or manner

and

R2   Avoid talk which assumes that God's agency takes away from what the creature does

can only be considered as coherent if the material statements

S1   God's creative agency has no limitations in scope or manner

and

S2   God's agency does not take away from what the creature does

are coherent.[20] If S1 and S2 are incoherent, however, then the formal rules R1 and R2 are so too.

How do we know whether the material statements concerning the divine-human relationship are coherent? Well, they are coherent if the concepts involved do not logically exclude each other. But clearly the concepts of divine omnidetermination (which is implied in Tanner's rule for God's agency) and human self-determination (which is implied in Tanner's rule for talk of the creature in relation to God's agency) logically exclude each other. Though the occurrence of an event can surely be over-determined by God's and the creature's simultaneous agency (a possibility classically expressed in the notion of divine "concursus"), it cannot be wholly *and* decisively determined by them together. If both are working to the same effect, it does not matter if one of them decides to stop. It is significant in this connection that Tanner, in the few passages in which she feels pressed to take side on the issue of the nature of human freedom, seems to reject the contra-causal notion of freedom in favour of the compatibilist one, at least in matters of salvation.[21] So it seems that in the end only God's agency is

---

[19] Ibid., 12, 29, 169.
[20] See for these rules ibid., 47, 85.
[21] Ibid., 29, 178 n.11, 179 n.29.

decisive, and that human agency is covertly manipulated by it. But this result runs counter to what Tanner verbally suggests.

Tanner might respond to the charge of incoherence by arguing that she need not address these issues for her purposes to be fulfilled. She might do this in either one of two ways. First, she might argue that the question of coherence cannot be settled on neutral ground. Coherence in Christian theology is determined by conformity with the Christian form of life. And since in the Christian form of life both claims about God's unlimited agency and claims about the creature's own free agency (however "freedom" is defined) have a proper function, such claims and the rules by which they are structured are coherent. Any implications which would entail their incoherence in non-theological contexts should simply be blocked and declared invalid in the theological context.[22] However, this reply overlooks the fact that the structured ways in which we use our concepts and assess their implications, presuppositions etc. in non-theological contexts are not arbitrary. On the contrary, these are the well-tested ways which enable us to deal with reality and practical life in a fruitful way. To the extent that they are changed for theological reasons, theology threatens to loose contact with reality and become speculative. Clearly, this is not what Tanner wants, but she cannot have it both ways.

Second, Tanner might argue that the rules for the formation of coherent Christian discourse may permit more material statements than the ones which are referentially true. Not every set of legitimate material instantiations of these rules has to be coherent. The scope of the rules may be wider than the body of referentially true statements, since the only function of the rules is to head off all statements which are *known* to be incoherent and false. We simply don't know whether the statements which are allowed by the rules really apply to the nature of the divine-human relationship, because in virtue of God's transcendence this relationship remains in the end a mystery to us. But we at least *approximate* a proper account of it if we stick to the rules.[23] This kind of agnosticism, informed by our consciousness of the limitations of our capacities for comprehension, is no

---

[22] This line of argument is suggested by Tanner in some passages; see ibid., 9 ("Christian claims ... can be coherently maintained together in theologies that restrict in certain ruled ways the implications their language would suggest in non-theological contexts"), and 26f. ("The appearance of inconsistency that haunts theological statements is the result of [the] struggle with previous linguistic habits. ... If those statements are to hang together consistently, the theologian must restrict apparent but nevertheless inappropriate implications of the language he or she presses into service").

[23] There are also passages in Tanner's book which suggest this argument; see e.g. 11f. ("Theologians ... may abjure all positive knowledge of the nature of God and insist that their statements tell us nothing but what God is not"), 26 ("Because of the theologian's failure of comprehension, the compatibility of divine and created agencies cannot be established in any positive fashion that specifies the 'how' of their interaction"), 31 ("identical rules may operate even in schemes of thought that conflict on the level of first-order claims").

doubt a respectable and careful position. The price we have to pay for it, however, is that the suspicion of incoherence on the material level still remains unchallenged. Perhaps this price is lower than the loss of contact with reality; nonetheless, it should only be payed after all the alternative possibilities have been examined.

We conclude, then, that Tanners version of perspectivism ultimately turns out to be of little help to us. It does not establish and elucidate the compatibility of God's sovereignty and human freedom in matters of salvation by showing that both are affirmed from different perspectives, which can be reconciled in one overarching perspective. Nor does it do so in any other way. In fact, the situation is comparable to the situation which exists in physics with respect to the complementarity of wave-models and particle-models in explaining the behaviour of light rays: both models are needed for different reasons, to illuminate different aspects of the rays' behaviour etc., but at the same time each seems to contradict the other, since a unifying perspective is lacking. In the same way, we need statements highlighting God's sovereignty as well as claims stressing the human responsibility and efficacy, but we are unable to view them in a single perspective.

4.3.4 *Personal perspectivism: William Sessions*
Perhaps a third version of perspectivism shows us the way out. This version has recently been put forward by William Sessions, and might be labelled "personal perspectivism" since it hinges on the *person* who perceives the relation between freedom and grace. Sessions' main distinction - I leave his more intricate subdistinctions aside - is between a first-person and a third-person perspective on faith. From a first-person perspective there are very good reasons to ascribe all the glory, and hence all the authorship of faith to God. Believers are so overwhelmed by the goodness and grace of God towards them as to give all credit for their faith and conversion to God. Conversely, "one who insists on her own agency in faith ... will inevitably be excluded from the fullness and maybe even the fact of faith."[24] So from a first-person standpoint, faith is essentially and completely authored by God. From a third-person perspective (i.e., from the perspective of someone who tries to understand the nature of faith from outside, as an observer rather than a participant[25]), on the other hand, the act of faith can only be seen as co-authored by the believer. If the act of faith would have been wholly authored by God, it would wholly *be* His act and in no sense the act of the believer. Moreover, in so far as faith involves a personal relationship

---

[24] W.L. Sessions, "The Authorship of Faith," *RS* 27 (1991), 90f. Cf. John R. Lucas, *Freedom and Grace*, London 1976, 13: lest by "arrogating to himself a credit that is God's," the Christian "attributes all to the grace of God rather than himself." This is also the main trust in Rudolf Bultmann's paper "Grace and Freedom," in his *Essays Philosophical and Theological*, 168-181.

[25] Cf. Ingolf U. Dalferth's distinction between "participant theology" and "observer philosophy" in his *Theology and Philosophy*, Oxford 1988, 56-58, and part II as a whole.

it logically requires two persons, each of whom is related to the other *qua* person. This entails that each of the persons must be actively involved in establishing the relationship, since free agency is an essential characteristic of personhood.[26]

These, then, are the two perspectives which give rise to the paradox of the authorship of faith. As soon as the two views are conflated because their specific *points of view* are ignored, this paradox gets a flavour of irresolvability. All this is lucidly set out by Sessions. But the question which he still has to answer is how to reach the vantage-point from which both conflicting perspectives can be seen "in-depth" as complementary parts of an encompassing perspective. It is here that Sessions begins to waver. At first, he argues that the *divine* first-person perspective may coincide with the human third-person perspective. Since it would be preposterous to think of God's view as partial and limited, this suggests that the third-person view is *objectively* true, whereas the first-person human view, inspired as it is by pietistic and pragmatic motivations, is useful but not truthful. There is no over-arching perspective, but the perspective which allows us to see all sides is the third-person one, whereas the first-person human perspective is one-sided and therefore in fact false.

Then, however, Sessions realizes that on this resolution perspectivism collapses back into Arminianism, which was one of the positions he intended to avoid and overcome.[27] Therefore, he goes on to explore another avenue of thought, and argues that the superiority of the third-person over the first-person viewpoint is by no means obvious. Appealing to Kierkegaard's concept of "truth as subjectivity," Sessions suggests that, on the contrary, the truth of having faith may be superior to the truth of knowing about faith. It is clear, however, that this move does not provide him with an over-arching perspective either. It simply consists in a shift from the third-person back to the first-person human perspective, and makes it difficult to account for the element of truth in the former.

Apparently discontented with this result, Sessions hints at two other possible options, both of which avoid the dilemma without solving it. First, he recognizes the danger of confusing his own philosophical perspective with the divine perspective. For "no human could possibly reach or occupy such a perspective. I certainly don't claim to have done so myself."[28] But this comes near to the agnostic position with which we ended our discussion of Tanner's view, and which prompted our present search for a more informative account. Rather than providing us with a perspective which unifies the contrasting aspects of the origin of faith, this option explains nothing at all, and leaves us at a loss about "how things really are." Second, Sessions suggests that those who adopt an Anselmian conception of faith-as-seeking-

---

[26] Sessions, "Authorship," 92; cf. 82.

[27] Ibid., 93.

[28] Ibid., 95.

understanding may combine in themselves the first-person and the third-person perspective. From an Anselmian first-person standpoint of faith, taking a third-person reflective standpoint and engaging in acts of reflection on one's faith is not merely permitted, but devoutly desired.[29] Now this is certainly true, but it by no means clarifies the crucial issue, viz. how the conflicting first-person and third-person perspectives are *related* to each other. I conclude that all of Session's attempts to solve the paradox of the authorship of faith fail. In the end, he does not succeed in developing a transcending perspective which illuminates and unifies both of the legitimate but conflicting strands of thought concerning the origin of faith.

4.3.5. *The perspective of the beggar*
The upshot of our discussion of perspectivism thus far is rather disappointing. Nevertheless, Sessions' contribution contains one element which sets the stage for the development of a version of perspectivism which could succeed in overcoming the paradox of the conflicting partial perspectives. Sessions' personal perspectivism focuses on the personal and relational character of faith. The act of faith occurs in the context of a personal relationship between the divine and a human person. As has been displayed in some recent studies on the subject,[30] interpreting faith in terms of a personal rather than a merely causal relationship provides us with a much richer conceptuality, and therefore enhances our opportunities for clarifying the issue of the authorship of faith. Moreover, it is widely acknowledged that the predominance of causal conceptuality in theology has been provoked by Aristotelian metaphysics and enhanced by mechanistic interpretations of the universe in the Enlightenment.[31] Interpreting faith in personal terms, on the other hand, has a solid biblical background, and is therefore much more in line with our project of developing a biblical conception of God's power.

This does not mean, I hasten to add, that the shift from causal to personal language yields an easy solution to our problem. For personal relationships do not simply rule out questions of causality and authorship, but rather include them. As Sessions rhetorically asks:

> What, exactly, is each person in the personal relationship *doing*? *Who* authors the various acts in the relationship? Does one initiate, the other respond, both authoring different types of actions? Or is the human person only a kind of logical place-marker in a relation in which the divine agent completely authors everything?[32]

---

[29] Ibid., 96.

[30] Christoph Schwöbel & Colin E. Gunton (eds.), *Persons: Divine and Human*, Edinburgh 1991; Vincent Brümmer, *Personal God*.

[31] Cf. for the latter influence e.g. Jenson, *America's Theologian*, 23-34.

[32] Sessions, "Authorship," 84 (italics by the author). Brümmer, *Personal God*, 139f. also acknowledges that causal and personal relationships are not mutually exclusive.

Such questions suffice to show that the original paradox can easily be restated in terms of a personal relationship. How, then, might conceiving faith as a personal relationship help us to solve this paradox?

In order to answer this question we should keep in mind two characteristics of perspectivism in general as it functions in science. First, the different perspectives which play a role (e.g. in light ray-theories) usually have a metaphorical character; they are described in terms of metaphors and models rather than by straightforward referential description (whatever that may be). Thus, in some situations light rays behave like gulfs (e.g. of water), in other situations like particles.[33] Hence, especially in looking for an overarching perspective, we may expect that it can most easily and convincingly be disclosed by means of metaphors. Second, as Mackay already pointed out, the integration of conflicting perspectives in an in-depth perspective which makes them complementary rather than conflicting cannot be brought about on a merely intellectual level. Rather, it requires a change in one's "perceptual set" which pertains to all aspects of one's personality, including one's will and emotional life.

Bearing these provisos in mind, let us now state as precisely as possible what we are looking for. We are looking for one or more - perhaps somewhat shocking - metaphors in the sphere of personal relations which show us how the authorship of an event may be ascribed partially to one and partially to the other person involved in the relationship, whereas at the same time only one person is wholly to be credited for the event. These two requirements seem to be contradictory, for if the authorship of an event is divided between two persons then it would seem that credit for the event is equally divided. This suspicion of contradiction can only be removed if we succeed in finding at least one such a metaphor which shows that they may complement rather than rule out each other.

I believe that at least one such a metaphor is to be found in the figure of the beggar. Imagine a beggar who lives in extremely miserable circumstances, and who is offered a gift by a rich benefactor great enough to make him live without material worries for the rest of his life. Suppose that the beggar hates his poverty, and therefore accepts the gift. Let us refer to the whole of the benefactor's offer and the beggar's acceptance as "the event." Since he accepts the gift, the beggar is no doubt actively involved in bringing about the event. His accepting the gift is his own act, not the act of his benefactor. Nevertheless, it is crystal-clear that only the benefactor is to be credited for the event. If the beggar would even to the slightest degree take credit for himself, e.g. by boasting "I have accepted the gift," we would rightly consider him to be insane. It would have been so unreasonable for him to refuse the gift,[34] that his acceptance can in no way

---

[33] Note that this metaphorical character of the observations does not imply that they are not reality-depicting. Both the gulfs and the particles are encountered as real and objective phenomena!

[34] For an interpretation of the impossibility to resist the divine grace as *rational* impossibility

be interpreted as an achievement. On the other hand, if he would unreasonably have refused the gift, he and only he would be responsible for this. Let me now make a couple of additional comments in order to establish the explanatory adequacy of the beggar-perspective, and at the same time forestall some obvious objections against it.

First, it is clear that the beggar-metaphor is superior to Sessions' personal perspectivism, since it succeeds in transcending the conflicting first-person and third-person standpoint. It is not the case that the benefactor is wholly to be credited for the event only from a first-person, internal perspective, whereas from the more objective third-person perspective both the beggar and the benefactor are to be credited for it. Nor is the beggar only for pietistic or pragmatic reasons obliged to ascribe full credit to his benefactor, while he tacitly knows that *in fact* it is of course also due to him that his miserable circumstances have changed. On the other hand, the beggar will not deny that it was he who accepted the gift. So neither does the beggar-perspective reduce to the "Kierkegaardian" view that *in fact* the event is to be ascribed fully to the benefactor. Finally, it clearly overcomes agnostic solutions such as the appeal to mystery etc.

Second, the idea that such a simple, outworn analogy as the beggar-metaphor adequately solves our complicated problem may initially strike most of us as counter-intuitive. But this only demonstrates MacKay's point that an in-depth perspective cannot be reached merely at an intellectual level. We will only accept the beggar-metaphor as an adequate overarching perspective on matters of freedom and grace if we are prepared to give up our emotional repugnance and volitional unwillingness to ourselves being compared to a poor beggar. At the same time, if we are not prepared to give up these non-intellectual attitudes because we think our freedom, autonomy and self-determination vis-à-vis God exceed those of the beggar vis-à-vis his benefactor to such a degree that the comparison must fail, we show thereby that we are infected by modern conditions of thought which make us unable to solve the dilemma in any other way than by cutting the Gordian knot in the Arminian way. In this connection, Kathryn Tanner rightly observes that the apparent incoherence of traditional Christian language is a result of the distorting impact of modernity![35] Tanner is wrong, however, in suggesting that the contra-causal conception of freedom is also a heritage of modernity; as the beggar-example shows, this conception of freedom is indispensable for ascribing responsibility to human beings for their refusal to accept God's grace.[36]

(i.e. "unreasonability"), see Brümmer, *Personal God*, chapter 3 (esp. 80-82).

[35] Tanner, *God and Creation*, chapter 4 ("The Modern Breakdown of Theological Discourse").

[36] Cf. Thomas Tracy's criticism in his review of Tanner's book, *F&P* 9 (1992), 120-124. "Against this, however, there appear to be considerations *internal* to Christianity that might lead to the affirmation of such creaturely freedom, even if one resists the enchantment of Enlightenment claims about autonomy ..." (123).

Third, the beggar-analogy has an interesting tradition in the history of (especially protestant) theology. Let me confine myself to mentioning two famous theologians, representing diametrically opposed positions on the authorship of faith, both of whom employed the beggar-metaphor. The last words of Martin Luther, author of *De Servo Arbitrio*, are reported to have been: "Hoc est verum: wir sind bettler."[37] Luther's conviction that our anthropological status before God might most adequately be compared with the status of beggars has been a central spiritual insight of his.[38] On the other hand, the analogy of the beggar is employed in the post-Reformation debates on predestination and free will by James Arminius.[39] The fact that both Luther and Arminius positively affirmed the propriety of the beggar-metaphor illustrates that it does justice to central concerns on both sides of the scene. Unfortunately, neither Luther nor Arminius developed the beggar-metaphor into a systematic model for interpreting other claims. If Luther, Arminius and many others would have used the beggar-metaphor more systematically as a hermeneutical grid for bringing order and in-depth perspective in the whole nexus of problems and concepts related to the grace and freedom debate, perhaps some ecclesiastical fragmentation could have been avoided. Presumably, however this fragmentation became unavoidable precisely because of the fact that in practice not everybody *wanted* to abide by the humility of the beggar-metaphor!

Fourth, I do not claim that the metaphor of the beggar is the only one which may be developed into a satisfactory model for showing the complementarity of freedom and grace. There are of course more metaphors which may be employed to illuminate the event of coming to faith. For example, an analogy which is often drawn is the analogy with entering in a relationship of love or friendship with another person.[40] The advantage of the beggar-metaphor, however, is that it underlines the asymmetrical nature of the divine-human relationship. It shows that the bringing about of salvation is a "one-sided act of God," for which He and He alone is to be credited and praised. But at the same time it demonstrates how it is possible that God's power, which is so overwhelmingly present in the conversion of a human being, does nevertheless not remove the human freedom of choice, nor, for that matter, the human responsibility for eventually not coming to faith after having been sincerely offered the gift of grace.

Fifth, I do not claim that the metaphor of the beggar can be de-

---

[37] M. Luther, *WAT* 5, 318.

[38] Cf. H.A. Oberman, "Wir sein pettler. Hoc est verum.," in: id., *Die Reformation*, Göttingen 1986, 90-112. A similar characterization can be given of the theology of H.F. Kohlbrugge; see A. de Reuver, *'Bedelen bij de Bron'*, Zoetermeer 1992, 626.

[39] J. Arminius, *Apologia*, in: id., *Opera Theologica*, Leiden 1629, 176; cf. James Nichols & William Nichols, *The Works of James Arminius*, Vol.2, Kansas City 1986², 52. I am indebted for these references to Eef Dekker; cf. his forthcoming *Rijker dan Midas*, Den Haag 1993, esp. §9.3, for a positive evaluation of Arminius' theological concerns.

[40] Cf. e.g. Bultmann, "Grace and Freedom," 178f.

veloped into an appropriate model which covers all aspects of the relationship between God and human beings. Rather, there are many other complementary analogies and metaphors which express equally significant but different aspects of this relationship. Believers rightly see themselves as the children of God, the servants, the friends, the beloved ones, and even the co-operators of God (cf. e.g. 1 Cor.3:9). Vice versa, God is related to them as a father or mother (Is.49:15; 66:13), a king or Lord, a friend, a bridegroom or lover etc.[41] No doubt, some of these images are more prominent than others, and all of them highlight different features of the relationship between God and His people. All I claim is that when it comes to the way in which the relationship between God and human beings is *established and constituted in time*, the metaphor of the beggar offers us an appropriate perspective to capture the paradox of the authorship of faith.

In short, the model of the beggar shows how a sovereign God does all that is necessary for my salvation, whereas at the same time I am involved as a person in coming to faith.

4.4 ALMIGHTINESS AND THE PROBLEM OF EVIL

4.4.1 *Evil, almightiness and the goal of theodicy*
We must now address what is no doubt the most incisive and enduring challenge to the Christian doctrine of divine almightiness: the problem of evil. We need not deny that the problem of evil is a perennial problem, which has always troubled thoughtful believers, in order to acknowledge that its existential force has increased considerably in recent times. I will not investigate here the no doubt complex causes of this process, but I conclude from it that coming to terms with the problem of evil is one of the most pressing demands of life for contemporary believers. More specifically, any viable doctrine of God's power should pass the test of being able to cope satisfactorily with the problem of evil in order to be theologically acceptable. Here, then, we are at the point where our third criterion for systematic theology, viz. adequacy to the demands of life, comes in most emphatically.[1]

Although most of us will intuitively feel that the experience of evil forms a challenge to the doctrine of God's almightiness, it is important to spell out as precisely as possible in what sense this is the case. In fact, according to many people it is not so much the almightiness of God which is at stake here as it is His very existence. They consider the vast amount of human experiences of evil and suffering as "the rock of atheism."[2] As

---

[41] See for an elaboration of some of these models Sallie McFague, *Models of God*, esp. 91-180.

[1] Cf. § 1.3.3. and §1.4 above.

[2] Georg Büchner, "Dantons Tod. Ein Drama" (1835), to be found in: id., *Werke und Briefe*,

Eugene Borowitz says in relation to the Holocaust:

> Any God who could permit the Holocaust, who could remain silent during it, who could "hide His face" while it dragged on, was not worth believing in. There might well be a limit to how much we could understand about Him, but Auschwitz demanded an unreasonable suspension of understanding.[3]

Those who are not Jews have their own perplexing experiences of evil and affliction, in the face of which they may come to hold that "God's only excuse is that He does not exist" (Stendhal). Whereas belief in God seems to imply at the very least belief in the ultimate rationality of the universe, the experience of evil and extreme suffering brings all rationality to an end.

The theistic response to this kind of challenges has usually taken the form of some kind of *theodicy*, i.e. an attempt to explain the ways of God in view of the world's evils.[4] Some theologians and philosophers (apparently a growing number of them), however, have argued that the enterprise of theodicy is inappropriate, since the only proper responses to experiences of evil and suffering are practical ones.[5] Abstaining from any explanation of the co-existence of God and evil, they focus on practical strategies for coping with and fighting against evil. As it seems to me, however, although such practical responses to evil are of primary importance indeed, this does not mean that all systematic and reasoned reflection on God and evil is inherently flawed. On the contrary, it belongs to the proper task of systematic theology to demonstrate the plausibility of belief in God in view of our human experiences of evil and suffering. Let us pause to explore the nature of this task a little further by briefly reviewing the main arguments which are put forward against it.[6]

First, there are *theological* objections against theodicy. It is often argued that the project of theodicy is wrong-headed since we as tiny and sinful human beings are not in a position to justify God, whose perfect justice is beyond doubt.[7] This is certainly true, but putting it forward as an

---

München 1965, 40; quoted by Hans Küng, *Christ Sein*, München 1974, 524 (the phrase was not invented by Küng himself, as Peterson et al., *Reason & Religious Belief*, Oxford 1991, 93 suggest). On the philosophical significance of Büchner's text, see Wilfried Härle, "Leiden als Fels des Atheismus?," in: W. Härle, M. Marquardt & W. Nethöfel (eds.), *Unsere Welt - Gottes Schöpfung*, Marburg 1992, 127-143.

[3] E. Borowitz, *The Masks Jews Wear*, New York 1973, 99, as quoted in Peterson et al., *Reason & Religious Belief*, 92.

[4] Literally, of course, the word "theodicy" refers to *justifying* the ways of God; understood in this sense, however, as I will point out in a moment, the program of theodicy is unacceptable. Therefore I prefer a definition of theodicy centring around the concept of explanation.

[5] The most radical exponent of this development is Terrence Tilley's *The Evils of Theodicy*, Washington 1991.

[6] I have dealt with this issue more extensively in my paper "Over de (on)mogelijkheid van een theodicee," *TR* 32 (1989), 194-210.

[7] E.g. G.C. Berkouwer, *The Providence of God*, Grand Rapids 1974[4], 246-249; cf. also P.T.

argument against theodicy betrays a misconception of the task of theodicy, which is not to justify God but to justify *our talk of* God in the face of evil. In order to be credible, our talk of God should not only be internally consistent and coherent, but also adequate to the demands of life, and therefore among other things adequate with regard to the evils life is so replete with.[8] A kindred theological argument frequently advanced against theodicy is that we cannot know why God permits evil, since His plans and thoughts are inscrutable for us, exceeding the grasp of puny human intellects. The latter should also be granted. But it should not be interpreted in a way that runs counter to a cornerstone of theistic belief, viz. belief in God's self-revelation. It is on the basis of God's having revealed Himself and having given us at least glimpses of His purposes with the world that it is appropriate to ask how our experiences of evil fit in with these.[9]

Second, theodicy is sometimes criticized for *epistemological* reasons. According to this criticism, the construction of a theodicy is unnecessary, since theists have sufficient independent epistemological warrant for their belief in God. They may take their religious belief as basic, i.e. as rational in itself (because of certain circumstances which confer warrant upon it) rather than dependent for its rationality upon *arguments* in favour of it. Therefore, the only thing which is incumbent upon theists in relation to evil is to show that their beliefs are not logically inconsistent with the existence of evil in the world. They should not fulfil the further task of elaborating a theodicy (since a theodicy is intended to give rational support to theistic belief and thus suggests that theism is in *need* of such support, quod non), but rather restrict themselves to the more modest task of formulating a defence.[10] Even if we grant that this account of the basicality of religious belief is correct, there is an important reason to reject the epistemological objection against theodicy. In our secularized society it is important for theists to demonstrate that theistic belief in God is not only rational in the

---

Forsyth, *The Justification of God*, London 1916, 130: "The Church, starting from the Holy One, asks how man shall be just with that God... But the world, with its egoist start, asks how God shall be just with man. The one brings man to God's bar, the other brings God to man's."

[8] Cf. for these criteria section 1.3.3 of this study.

[9] Cf. Peterson et al., *Reason & Religious Belief*, 101.

[10] This criticism is ascribed to Plantinga by Peterson et al., *Reason*, 101-103, and by David Griffin, *Evil Revisited*, Albany 1991, 42-49; it is by no means explicit in Plantinga's writings on the subject, however. As far as I know Plantinga has only argued three things in this connection: first, that in addressing the *logical* problem of evil considerations of plausibility are beside the point, which is indubitably true; second, that it *might* be possible that the reasons why God permits evil and therefore the construction of a theodicy transcend our limited human mental capacities; and third, that none of the existing theodicies has convinced him. The fact that Plantinga has involved himself in also trying to rebut the *evidential* argument from evil shows, that he is certainly interested in the probability and plausibility of theistic beliefs. In his "response to Alvin Plantinga" (ibid., 42) Griffin is therefore largely committing the straw man fallacy. See e.g. Plantinga, *God, Freedom, and Evil*, 9-11, 28f; "Reply to the Basingers on Divine Omnipotence," *PrS* 11 (1981), 25-29; "Epistemic Probability and Evil," *AdF* 56 (1988), 558-565.

rather thin sense of being non-contradictory, but also in the sense of being *plausible* in comparison to alternative world views.[11] In religion's struggle to keep naturalistic and atheistic views of life and their implications from controlling the common sense, theoretical theodicy plays a crucial role.[12] Moreover, theodicy is also appropriate in the context of the search of theistic believers for better understanding the implications of their own beliefs, especially when those beliefs are questioned by life's experiences (such as experiences of evil).[13]

Third, theodicy is rejected for *methodological* reasons: because of its abstraction from concrete instances of evil in their sheer particularity, theodicy is supposed to be irrelevant to the real problem and to be undermined by the ongoing reality of evil. It "requires us to be articulate, rational and reasonable in the face of the unspeakable."[14] The theodicist does not observe evil, but an objectification of it. In removing himself from the concreteness of evil, he "becomes akin to the pilot of a small plane who wants to understand a certain African tribe by flying over them at 10,000 feet."[15] As a result, the theodicist's arguments are untenable and worthless in the eyes of the victims of evil. But this charge again stems from a misunderstanding of the aim of theodicy. Theodicy is not aimed at ministering or consoling the afflicted, but at trying to understand God in the face of evil in the world, and vice versa. It is a response to the conceptual dimensions of the problem of evil rather than to its existential dimensions — and these different dimensions should be carefully distinguished.[16] It is the community of faith at which theodicy is directed, and concrete sufferers only in so far as they want to make sense of their suffering in the light of faith.

Fourth, closely affiliated to this is the *moral* objection against theodicy. According to this objection, theodicy's address to the problem of evil is immoral because it implies a tacit endorsement of evil. It tries to make sense of evil, and thus provides - albeit unwittingly - a tacit sanction of the myriad of evils that exists on this planet. As a result, it "legitimizes and mystifies the social processes that block the transformation of life and reality."[17] Now this objection is surely to the point with regard to some forms

---

[11] See on these two kinds of rationality Richard Swinburne, *Faith and Reason*, Oxford 1981, chapter 2.

[12] This point is aptly made by David O'Connor, "In Defense of Theoretical Theodicy," *MTh* 5 (1988), 61-74; see esp. 69.

[13] Peterson et al., *Reason*, 103. Thus, theodicy is not a part of natural theology's quest for a rational foundation of faith, but rather a part of "positive theology" in the Anselmian sense of *fides quaerens intellectum*.

[14] Kenneth Surin, *Theology and the Problem of Evil*, Oxford 1986, 155.

[15] Stephen J. Vicchio, *The Voice from the Whirlwind*, Westminster 1989, 88.

[16] This does not mean that there is no relation at all between the existential and conceptual problems of evil. For a careful assessment of the nature of this (indirect) relation, see David O'Connor, "Theoretical Theodicy," 61-74. Cf. also John Hick, *Evil and the God of Love*, 10.

[17] Surin, *Theology*, 50. See also Peter L. Berger, *The Social Reality of Religion*, London 1967,

of theodicy. It does not affect the project of theodicy (or even theoretical theodicy) as such, however, because, as I hope to show below, it is equally possible to adhere to a form of (theoretical) theodicy which does not explain evil away by giving a point to what is utterly pointless.

Having thus elucidated what is and what is not implied by the enterprise of theodicy, in what follows I propose a form of theodicy which is not only viable as a response to atheist criticism, but also spells out what seem to me the intellectual corollaries and commitments of Christian theistic belief in relation to the conceptual problem of evil. Before setting off, however, I want to make one more introductory observation, pertaining to the role of the doctrine of divine almightiness in theodicy.

It is often tacitly assumed that the only alternatives in the debate on the conceptual problem of evil are classical theism and atheism. This can be seen from the odd way in which atheological arguments from evil[18] are sometimes formulated. Assuming throughout the theistic conception of God as both omnipotent and perfectly benevolent, they conclude that evil counts against the existence of this God, and is therefore an argument for atheism. In this way, William Rowe sets forth a version of the empirical argument to the effect that "the world contains evils that render the existence of the theistic God unlikely."[19] After having presented his argument, Rowe concludes: "So I would say that the problem of evil can legitimately function as an argument for atheism."[20] But that is a biased conclusion. If Rowe's argument has succeeded, it is an argument against classical theism but not necessarily an argument for atheism. For the argument leaves open whether atheism or some other version of theism should be adopted instead of the classical one.

There are at least two possible ways of revising classical theism in order to neutralize atheological arguments from evil against it. The first is to deny God's perfect goodness and the second to deny God's omnipotence. The first way is not very promising, since it casts serious doubts on God's worshipfulness. I will therefore not pursue it here.[21] The second revision, on the other hand, is of course of special interest in the context of the

---

59. Surin makes an exception for what he calls "practical theodicy" (as opposed to theoretical theodicy), which is directed at the overcoming of evil in the world. Cf. Odo Marquard's concept of "Weltverbesserungstheodizee" (H. G. Janssen, *Gott-Freiheit-Leid*, Darmstadt 1989, 189; A.H. van Veluw, *God en de zinloosheid van het kwaad*, Nijkerk 1991, 56f.) as what he claims to be the only tenable form of theodicy.

[18] For my use of the term "atheological", see Plantinga, God, Freedom, and Evil, 2f., 7.

[19] William L. Rowe, "The Empirical Argument from Evil," in: Audi & Wainwright (eds.), *Rationality, Religious Belief, & Moral Commitment*, 227.

[20] Ibid., 247.

[21] Nevertheless, the denial of God's goodness as a response to the problem of evil is certainly a live option. A recent example is in the work of the Dutch theologian A. van de Beek, most explicitly in his *Rechtvaardiger dan God*, Nijkerk 1992, in which he claims that Job not only *thought* himself to be more righteous than God, but really was.

present study. Moreover, it is not merely a theoretical possibility but a very popular way of reconciling belief in God with the existence of evil.[22] In this connection, David Griffin's complaint that this in-between option between atheism and classical theism is so often unduly ignored or quickly dispensed of in the literature is entirely to the point.[23]

An additional motive for rethinking the concept of divine omnipotence in response to the problem of evil is inspired by the results of our study thus far. I have tried to show that from a biblical point of view we should not ascribe omnipotence to God, but rather almightiness. And I have pointed out that one of the differences between omnipotence and almightiness is in the modal status which is usually associated with them. Whereas (according to the Anselmian tradition) omnipotence is a necessary property of God, almightiness is not. From a biblical perspective, it is not logically impossible for God to lose (part of) His power and at the same time continue to be God. It would be a quite natural elaboration of this view to argue that God *did* lose His power to the extent of not being able to prevent the many occurrences of evil in our world. This would offer us a fairly simple solution to the conceptual problem of evil.

There are two initial reasons, however, for not following this path too eagerly. First, we have also seen that although from a biblical perspective God is not omnipotent, He certainly is almighty. He is able to do all the things which He wants to do, His intentions cannot be thwarted. In this sense, our replacing the doctrine of omnipotence by a more biblical perspective on God's power does not prima facie alleviate (let alone solve) the conceptual problem of evil. And many Christian theists, including myself, consider such data of revelation as "non-negotiable." Second, solving the conceptual problem of evil by renouncing God's almightiness is a way of cutting the knot rather than unravelling it. In general, we should only cut knots after it has been assessed that they cannot be unravelled. So I will first try to unravel this knot. More specifically, I will argue that a theodicy which leaves the doctrine of divine almightiness as spelled out above intact is not only possible, but in the end also more adequate than theodicies which reject or reinterpret this doctrine.[24]

The core of the theodicy proposed below, as of so many current theodicies, is formed by a version of the free will defence. But I will develop this free will defence in a particular direction which makes it fit to function in the larger framework of a theodicy (§ 4.4.2). Then I will demonstrate that this theodicy does indeed leave the doctrine of divine almightiness intact (§ 4.4.3). Next, I will try to point out its advantages in comparison to theodicies which deny or revise this doctrine, especially to

---

[22] Cf. the success of Harold Kushner's famous *When Bad Things Happen to Good People*.

[23] David Griffin, *God, Power, and Evil*, 256ff.

[24] Note that since I hope to show this latter point, I do not join the ranks of those who quickly dispense of theodicies which deny or reinterpret divine almightiness.

process theodicy (§ 4.4.4). Finally, I will show how other central tenets of Christian trinitarian theology fit in with the theodicy and in general with the understanding of divine power which I propose (§ 4.4.5).

4.4.2 *The free will defence and gratuitous evil*

If one thing has become clear in the on-going post-war debate on the problem of evil, it is that the atheist challenger of theism has no easy victory. Atheological arguments from evil have succeeded each other, but up to now none of them has been generally convincing. On the contrary, with regard to some developed atheological arguments from evil it is now quite generally acknowledged that they are unsuccessful. I have in mind, of course, the attempts to show that there is a logical inconsistency in holding that both the theistic God and evil exist. There are still what should perhaps be considered as rear-guard actions in this field,[25] but most philosophers, both theistic and atheistic, have become convinced that the logical argument from evil has failed to do what it was intended to do, viz. to establish the claim that the existence of evil is *logically inconsistent* with the existence of the theistic God.[26]

A prominent role in countering this inconsistency-charge was played by the so-called "free will defence," as developed most energetically by Alvin Plantinga.[27] From the perspective of our study it is important to note that the nub of the free will defence turns on two crucial assumptions, one of which is a particular understanding of God's omnipotence. According to this understanding, God is able to bring about all those states of affairs which are logically possible *for Him* to bring about. This entails that there might be logically possible and perhaps even actual states of affairs which nevertheless cannot be brought about by God, in spite of His omnipotence. The other crucial assumption of the free will defence is that human freedom should be understood along libertarian lines, which is to say (among other things) that it is logically impossible to *make* a person do something *freely*. Given these assumptions, here is a succinct statement of the strategy followed by the free will defender:

---

[25] Such as Ian Markham's "Hume Revisited," *MTh* 7 (1991), 281-290 and Robert M. Gale's "Freedom and the Free Will Defense," *ST&P* 16 (1990), 397-423. For rebuttals, see respectively Gerard Loughlin, "Making a Better World" *MTh* 8 (1992), 297-303 and James M. Humber, "Response to Gale," *ST&P* 16 (1990), 425-433.

[26] Cf. Peterson et al., *Reason*, 97. For an atheist conceding this point, see William L. Rowe, "The Problem of Evil and Some Varieties of Atheism," now in: M.M. Adams & R.M. Adams (eds.), *The Problem of Evil*, Oxford 1990, 126, footnote 1. On the recent shift in interest towards different sorts of argument and different problems of evil than the logical one, see my "Natural Evil and Eschatology," in: Van den Brink et al., *Christian Faith*, 39.

[27] Cf. Richard Gale's assessment: "Plantinga's version of the free will defense is a thing of beauty that, it is safe to say, will serve as one of the cornerstones of theism's response to evil not just for many years to come but for many centuries" (R.M. Gale, *On the Nature and Existence of God*, Cambridge 1991, 113).

A world containing creatures who are sometimes significantly free (and freely perform more good than evil actions) is more valuable, all else being equal, than a world containing no free creatures at all. Now God can create free creatures, but he cannot *cause* or *determine* them to do only what is right. For if he does so, then they are not significantly free after all; they do not do what is right *freely*. To create creatures capable of *moral good*, therefore, he must create creatures capable of moral evil; and he cannot leave these creatures *free* to perform evil and at the same time prevent them from doing so. God did in fact create significantly free creatures; but some of them went wrong in the exercise of their freedom: this is the source of ... evil. The fact that these free creatures sometimes go wrong, however, counts neither against God's omnipotence nor against God's goodness.[28]

There has been much discussion both about the soundness of the reasoning in the quotation as about the plausibility of the two assumptions.[29] Since Plantinga's sophisticated elaboration of the argument has convinced many, I shall take its validity for granted here. As to the assumption on the nature of human freedom, I shall do the same since I have already argued for a libertarian account of freedom above.[30] As to the omnipotence-assumption, I shall discuss it in the next subsection.

First, however, I want to point out one important limitation of the free will defence and discuss its consequences.[31] The free will defence is a defence, not a theodicy. Accordingly, it only shows that theism is *possibly* true, without establishing anything at all with regard to its plausibility and probability. Those interested in the construction of an atheological argument from evil have exploited this limitation by shifting their strategy. Rather than contending that there is a logical problem of evil for theism, many of them now argue that theism faces an *evidential* problem of evil.[32] The challenge here is not that theism is inconsistent, but that it is implausible or unlikely, since the evils in the world count as evidence against it. There are different ways in which this charge may be fleshed out, yielding different evidential arguments from evil.[33] It may, for example, be argued that the sheer *existence* of evil forms evidence against theism; alternatively, the *amount* of evil in the world, or the *intensity* of so many forms of evil, or the *innocence*[34] of so many of its victims may be referred to as the real evidence against theism.

---

[28] Plantinga, *Nature of Necessity*, 166f.

[29] For a recent survey, see Gale, *Nature and Existence of God*, 115-151.

[30] See § 4.2.

[31] In the course of this section I will note some other limitations of the free will defence as well.

[32] Other labels referring to essentially the same sort of argument include: the inductive (Reichenbach), probabilistic (Plantinga), and empirical (Rowe) argument from evil.

[33] Michael Peterson, *Evil and the Christian God*, Grand Rapids 1982, 66f., distinguishes three of them.

[34] Cf. e.g. Moltmann, *Trinity*, 63: "The suffering of a single innocent child is an irrefutable rebuttal of the notion of an almighty and kindly God in heaven. For a God who lets the innocent suffer and who permits senseless death is not worthy to be called God at all."

I believe, however, that the most powerful evidential argument from evil appeals to another fact in relation to evil, viz. the fact that so many evils strike us as utterly *pointless*. To see this we must make a distinction between on the one hand justified or instrumental or prima facie or apparent evil, and on the other hand (ab)surd or pointless or genuine or gratuitous evil.[35] It is generally agreed that some of the evils we experience in the world belong to the first category. There are evils which are justified because of some greater good unobtainable or some greater evil unavoidable without their occurrence. For example, dentists may inflict some pain upon their patients in order to guarantee the greater good of a healthy set of teeth. Even intense forms of pain and suffering may be justified for this reason. Usually we do not blame surgeons for the amputation of a child's leg if this operation was necessary in order to avoid death from cancer. Despite the intense suffering which is presumably caused by the amputation, there are situations in which we hold this intense evil for justified, because it is instrumental in avoiding a greater evil. Applied to our context, if God has a *morally sufficient reason* for permitting or bringing about evil and suffering, nothing is wrong with theistic claims about God and evil.[36]

The problem, however, is caused by those instances of evil with regard to which we have not the slightest idea what kind of morally sufficient reason might be involved. Each of us will know countless cases of evils in which we are hardly able to conceive of any greater good served or any greater evil avoided by it. It is this group of evils which forms the real problem for theism. To be sure, it cannot be *disproved* that such evils are connected to greater goods which are beyond our ken. That is why the argument from so-called "apparently pointless evil" has no logical but only evidential force. But according to proponents of an evidential argument from evil such as William Rowe, the great number and variety of apparently pointless suffering in our experience makes it difficult to maintain that no genuinely pointless suffering exists, and thus constitutes compelling evidence against theism.

The most common theistic reply to this charge consists in a withdrawal into agnosticism: we do not know what reasons God has for permitting apparently pointless evils, and we should not even expect this situation to be otherwise.[37] In a much-discussed paper Stephen Wykstra has even argued that we are not entitled to claim that there is *apparently* pointless evil in the world. Carefully analyzing what could be called "the logic of appearance," Wykstra concludes that we are only entitled to say "it appears

---

[35] These adjectives reflect the different ways in which basically the same distinction figures in the literature.

[36] Nelson Pike, "Hume on Evil," now in: Adams & Adams, *Problem of Evil*, 41.

[37] Plantinga, "Epistemic Probability," 561f.; S.T. Davis, "Free Will and Evil," in: id. (ed.), *Encountering Evil*, Edinburgh 1981, 81f.; cf. 95, 97; in response, John Roth mockingly labels Davis's policy as the "I Just Don't Know Defence" (90).

that p" if we can reasonably hold that, if p were not the case, we would be likely to discern that. So in order to be justified in saying: "it appears that this particular evil is pointless," it must be reasonable for us to believe that, were it to have a point, we would be likely to discern it.[38] But this is clearly unreasonable for us to believe. For

> ... the outweighing good at issue [which prevents the evil from being pointless] is of a special sort: one purposed by the Creator of all that is, whose vision and wisdom are therefore somewhat greater than ours. How much greater? A modest proposal might be that his wisdom is to ours, roughly as an adult human's is to a one-month old infant's. (You may adjust the ages and species to fit your own estimate of how close our knowledge is to omniscience.) ... If such goods as this exist, ... that we should discern most of them seems about as likely as that a one-month old should discern most of his parents' purposes for those pains they allow him to suffer - which is to say, it is not likely at all.[39]

In my opinion Wykstra attacks the evidential argument from evil in its Achilles' heel. Its crucial problem is that "we couldn't reasonably be expected to know what God's reason is for permitting a given evil."[40] Given our limited epistemic resources we humans are simply not in a position to have strong opinions here, and our search for a theodicy may very well be in vain. Wykstra's conclusion is of course a very startling one: not even the most terrible horrors, the most large-scale and innocent sufferings can be of such a kind that they *appear* to be pointless! There is not even any *possible* instance of intense suffering which would be prima facie evidence for there really being pointless evil, and so for theism being false. All this may strike us as highly counter-intuitive. But of course, if the argument is sound, we have some reason to distrust our intuitions at this point.

Nevertheless, I will not follow Wykstra's line of argument here. Not only has it been subject to severe criticisms,[41] but it also draws too heavily on agnosticism and suspension of our natural judgments to be of much use in the struggle to keep naturalistic and atheistic estimations of evil from controlling common sense. Therefore, theists should only withdraw to some Wykstraen position if all attempts to give a more informed account of theism's plausibility in the face of evil have failed.

---

[38] I leave aside technical details such as Wykstra's "Condition of Reasonable Epistemic Access" or CORNEA.

[39] S.T. Wykstra, "The Humean Obstacle to Evidential Arguments from Suffering: On Avoiding the Evils of Appearance," now in: Adams & Adams (eds.), *Problem of Evil*, 155f.

[40] Plantinga, "Epistemic Probability," 562, and cf. 565 for the way he relates this point to the free will defence. Cf. Phillips, "On Not Understanding God," *AdF* 56 (1988), 597.

[41] E.g. by W.L. Rowe, "Evil and the Theistic Hypothesis," now in: Adams & Adams, *Problem of Evil*, 161-167; Richard Swinburne, "Does Theism Need a Theodicy?" *CJP* 18 (1988), 298-300; Daniel Howard-Snyder, "Seeing through CORNEA," *IJPR* 32 (1992), 25-49. Swinburne and Howard-Snyder attack Wykstra's CORNEA as a general principle, Rowe its application to the evidential argument from evil.

But is it possible to give such a more informed account? The most common policy in this respect has been to suggest what kind of greater goods may conceivably be connected to the evils we experience in the world. Some have been very inventive in imagining greater goods necessarily related to the most diverse sorts of moral and natural evil. Richard Swinburne is a typical representative of this approach, and he indeed thinks that a theodicy, i.e. "a justified account of how ... evils do (contrary to appearance) serve a greater good" is not only needed in order to uphold theism, but also can be provided.[42] The result of such an approach is that evil is not only explained, but also explained *away*. In fact, there is no genuine evil in the world, since every evil we experience is related to a higher good unobtainable without it.

No doubt there are many instances of evil and suffering which are retrospectively seen to have led to precious higher goods that would not have obtained if the evil or suffering had not taken place. It is, however, very difficult to believe that *all* evils we experience in the world are all needed by the almighty God to fulfil His purposes, and thus serve a higher goal. To say this is to generalize and absolutize what is only a partial truth.[43] At least countless "epicycles" must be invented in order to sustain this position. With regard to Rowe's fawn which is trapped in a forest fire, horribly burned and lying in terrible agony for several days before death relieves its suffering[44] as well as with regard to little children dying from starvation in the third world, it should not only be pointed out what greater goods are obtained by these cases of suffering, but also that there was no other way even for God to obtain these goods. These being only two rather arbitrary examples from the myriad of evils we know of, the prospects for a satisfactory rebuttal of the evidential argument from evil along these lines do not seem very promising.

Therefore, I want to explore a third and often overlooked alternative besides agnosticism in theodicy and a greater good theodicy. This alternative becomes available as soon as we simply acknowledge that there is pointless, genuine evil in the world. Not every suffering in the world serves a greater good. Indeed, it belongs to the very nature of genuine evil that it is not good for anything, and therefore should not have happened. All this should be granted by the theist. Although some evils are surely willed by God as the necessary means to achieve some higher goal, it is not the case that *all evils can be explained in this way*. But if there is pointless evil, doesn't this fact count evidentially against theism? Taking up some insights of Michael Peterson which have recently been developed in more detail by William Hasker,[45] I will argue that the contrary is the case. That is to say,

[42] Swinburne, "Does Theism Need a Theodicy?," 292, 310f.

[43] Cf. Härle, "Leiden als Fels des Atheismus?," 141.

[44] Rowe, "Problem of Evil," 129f.

[45] M. Peterson, *Evil and the Christian God*, Grand Rapids 1982, 93ff.; W. Hasker, "The

in so far as the free will defence is an integral part of theism, the occurrence of pointless evil is evidence *in favour of* theism rather than against it.

This point of view is not initially very plausible of course. Initially, it seems much more plausible to suppose that in His wisdom and power, God would permit only those evils brought about by human free will which lead to a greater good, and prevent all other ones. This would reduce the range of human freedom, but it is reasonable to suppose that not every evil (nor permitting every evil) is justified by the simple fact that it is freely chosen. The value of free will should not be over-estimated.[46] But now consider what would happen if God were indeed to prevent every instance of pointless evil, so that every evil which took place were connected with some greater good unobtainable without its occurrence. In that case, it would be impossible for us to harm each other. For "one may undergo physical and mental suffering, torture, degradation, and death, but all of this will be more than compensated for by the benefits ... which will come to one as a result of that suffering..."[47] This, in turn, has perplexing consequences, for it implies that on any viable ethical theory morality is undermined.[48] No matter what we do, we are not in a position to harm other persons, nor presumably to harm animals or the environment. All evils we inflict upon them are needed by God to bring about greater goods - otherwise He would have prevented the evil from taking place.

It needs little argument to demonstrate that all this is quite alien to classical Christian theism. Its manifold moral prohibitions, prescriptions and exhortations, as well as the fact that in each of its branches it includes some form of ethics, are enough to show that it considers it all too possible for us to harm other persons etc. Accordingly, it is all too possible for us to bring about gratuitous evil, evil which isn't good for anything. This is the implication of God having created us as moral persons, i.e. as persons who have the ability to make morally significant free choices between good and evil. As a result, it belongs to the constitutive core of Christian theism that things can go fundamentally wrong due to evil human choices. There is no obligation (moral or otherwise) for God to prevent such cases of gratuitous evil, for this would undermine God's own purposes in creating human beings as moral persons. In this sense, then, gratuitous evil is evidence in favour of theism rather than against it.

In order to see more precisely what is and what is not entailed by this response to the evidential argument from evil, let us now discuss the

---

Necessity of Gratuitous Evil," *F&P* 9 (1992), 23-44. It seems to me that Hasker's point can be assessed independently of his rejection of divine middle knowledge and his view that God does take risks, as defended most extensively in his *God, Time, and Knowledge*, Ithaca 1989.

[46] Cf. Brümmer, *Personal God*, 132f.

[47] Hasker, "Necessity," 27f.

[48] See for detailed argumentative support of this point (taking into account both consequentialist and deontological forms of ethical theory) Hasker, "Necessity," 27-29.

most natural objection against it. This objection points to an alleged equivocation in the meaning of "gratuitous." On the one hand, gratuitous evil is opposed as unjustified evil to evil which is deemed to be justified because of its serving some greater good. On the other hand, however, an attempt is made to justify the existence of gratuitous evil by pointing out that it is a prerequisite for morality. But then morality *is* the greater good which justifies all evils, and consequently what has been demonstrated is not that gratuitous evil does not count against theism, but that prima facie gratuitous evil is in fact not gratuitous at all. For it is indispensable if morality is to have its proper place in our lives. After all, then, what we have here is simply another attempt to explain evil *away* by pointing out that it is good for something. This kind of theodicy boils down to dissolving the problem of evil by denying the reality of evil.[49]

I think the best way to counter this objection is to distinguish between the possibility and the actuality of gratuitous evil. It is the *possibility* of gratuitous evil which is an indispensable prerequisite for a properly functioning morality. In this way, the fact that gratuitous evil is pointless does not imply that its non-prevention is pointless. Although gratuitous evil has no point, not preventing it may have one. More specifically, the possibility of gratuitous evil is not itself gratuitous, because it is necessary for the higher goal of constituting human moral responsibility. The *actuality* of gratuitous evil, on the other hand, is not necessary for achieving this goal. In fact, it is not necessary for any higher goal. Hence any actual instance of gratuitous evil is really gratuitous and therefore really evil. It should not have happened, and isn't good for anything. Far from explaining evil away, this theodicy refuses to give a point to what is utterly pointless. As Vincent Brümmer puts it:

> It follows that the free will defence can explain no more than the *possibility* of evil and not its *actuality*! This distinguishes the free will defence ... from all forms of theodicy which claim ... that evil has a point. From the point of view of faith, this is a perverse claim since evil can never have a point in the eyes of a loving God.[50]

So the moral objection against theodicy does not apply to this form of theodicy. But its point is, of course, that logically you cannot have the possibility of gratuitous evil without seriously taking the risk of getting its actuality. According to Christian theism, God wanted to have the possibility of gratuitous evil but not its actuality.

That this is indeed the mainstream position in the Christian theistic

---

[49] This argument is brought in against Peterson by Keith Chrzan, "When is Gratuitous Evil Really Gratuitous?," *Sophia* 30.2/3 (1991), 23-27, and against Hasker by William Rowe in an unpublished "Reply to Hasker's 'The Necessity of Gratuitous Evil'," discussed by Hasker in "Necessity," 30ff.

[50] Brümmer, *Personal God*, 144.

tradition can neatly be seen from another perspective. When discussing the question whether God has willed sin, theologians have always been reluctant to answer this question with an unequivocal "yes" or "no." Rather, they have always distinguished between what God wills antecedently and consequently, or between His hidden and revealed or commanding will, or, more enigmatically, between what God wills positively and what He wills as non-willing.[51] This sort of distinction is clearly intended to maintain that, as Augustine says, "in a strange and ineffable fashion even that which is done against His will is not done without His will."[52] I suggest that the strangeness and ineffability mentioned by Augustine might perhaps be diminished if we interpret the distinctions in the way outlined above. On the one hand, gratuitous evil is against God's will; He does not want or cause it, neither overtly nor covertly. This seems to me simply a consequence of the doctrine of *sin*, for sin is by definition that which runs counter to God's will. On the other hand, God does not prevent gratuitous evil, because what He *does* will is that gratuitous evil is *possible*; for only in this way God can secure the morally responsible character of creaturely life and action. Clearly, these two kinds of will in God are not contradictory, but perfectly compatible. The interpretation which I propose therefore also safeguards the traditional concern for the unity of God's will, which should "not be considered as at war with itself."[53] In short, far from being "illicit distinctions,"[54] the traditional ways of distinguishing between different kinds of will in God in relation to evil express a very sound intuition and legitimate concern.

I realize that much should be added in order to elaborate this approach to the problem of evil in sufficient detail and to defend it against some obvious further objections. One such objection is that there seem to be much *more* actual instances of gratuitous evil than are needed for maintaining the moral significance of human life. So why doesn't God deplete the class of gratuitous evils until the point is reached where further depletion would undermine morality? Another objection is that my approach deals exclusively with moral evil, whereas an adequate theodicy should account for natural evil as well. Now although I think that these objections can be met by extending the outlined position, I will not pursue this line of argument here.[55] Rather, having sketched the main lines of the sort of theodicy I advocate, I will try to further elucidate its contours by returning

---

[51] The first distinction can be found in Aquinas, the second in Luther and Calvin, the third in Barth. See for references e.g. Griffin, *God, Power, and Evil*, 83f., 108, 119f., 164-167; for the roots of these distinctions in Augustine, ibid., 66f.

[52] Augustine, *Enchiridion* XXVI, 100. The statement is quoted with approval by Calvin in his *Institutes* I 18, 3.

[53] Calvin, ibid.

[54] Griffin, *God, Power, and Evil*, 250.

[55] For responses to both these objections, see Hasker, "Necessity," resp. 33-37 and 37-40; I have myself addressed the problem of natural evil in "Natural Evil and Eschatology," in: Van den Brink et al., *Christian Faith*, 39-55.

to the proper object of my concerns, viz. the role played by the concept of divine power.

4.4.3 *Divine power as specific sovereignty*

In contemporary philosophical theology the notion of divine power which is presupposed in the theodicy the main lines of which I traced in the former subsection, is criticized for two mutually exclusive reasons. Some people argue that God can do more than this theodicy allows for, others argue that He cannot do as much as it implies.[56] Let us discuss the former charge in this section, the latter in the next. One remark may be appropriate in advance: both of these charges are usually not directed at the theodicy I outlined in the former subsection, but at the free will defence. Since the free will defence forms the core of my own proposal, however, it is clear that criticisms of the free will defence equally apply to my extended version of it.

There are several variants of the argument aimed at showing that the free will defence unacceptably compromises God's power. One of them attempts to demonstrate that the free will defence is incompatible with the ascription of omnipotence to God. Roughly,[57] this is how the argument runs. Consider the following counterfactual conditionals (P being a possible person, E an evil act):

(1)   If P were created, P would freely do E at t

and

(2)   If P were created, P would freely refrain from doing E at t

Granted that counterfactuals of freedom such as these have a definite truth-value,[58] it is clear that only one of them is true. According to the free will defence, God cannot bring it about that P freely does E or that P freely refrains from doing E (for if He would bring about an action of P, this action would not be free). So far so good, for, given a libertarian account of freedom, this inability is only an imaginary limitation of God's power, since it is logically impossible for Him (as for anybody else save P) to bring about any free actions of P. But now consider that whether (1) or (2) is true

---

[56] Cf. for the terminology Gale, *Nature and Existence of God*, 114f.

[57] For more detailed (and slightly different) accounts, see William Wainwright, "Freedom and Omnipotence," *Noûs* 2 (1968), 293-301; Peter Y. Windt, "Plantinga's Unfortunate God," *PS* 24 (1973), 335-342; Wesley Morriston, "Is Plantinga's God Omnipotent?," *Sophia* 23.3 (1984), 50-55; cf. also Gale, *Nature and Existence of God*, 139-146.

[58] This is a controversial point, which I shall nevertheless grant for the sake of argument; the most well-known attempt to refute it is Robert M. Adams's article "Middle Knowledge and the Problem of Evil," *APQ* 14 (1977), 109-117, reprinted in Adams & Adams (eds.), *Problem of Evil*, 110-125.

is a contingent fact, depending upon the choice of P. It is logically possible that (1) is true and it is logically possible that (2) is true. Hence in creating P, it is logically possible for God to bring it about that (1) is true and it is logically possible for God to bring it about that (2) is true. But since it depends solely on P's choice which of the conditionals is true, there is at least one of them which God cannot make true. So there are propositions which God cannot make true (and corresponding states of affairs which He cannot bring about), although it is logically possible for Him to do so. Now this is a nonlogical and therefore real limitation of God's power, which shows that on libertarian assumptions God cannot be omnipotent.

The soundness of this conclusion depends, of course, on the correctness of the presupposed definition of omnipotence. We have seen that many philosophers construe omnipotence in such a way, that "there are no nonlogical limits to what an omnipotent being can do."[59] In order to be omnipotent, God must be able to do all things which are logically possible for Him to do. On such a definition, it is clear that the conclusion holds, and that given the free will defence God cannot be omnipotent. But note that we have already come across independent reasons for not ascribing this kind of omnipotence to God. Instead, I have made a plea for a notion of omnipotence which I preferred to call *almightiness*, and which differed in some significant respects from traditional philosophical notions of omnipotence.[60] First, almightiness includes the ability to give up part of one's power, or rather to refrain from exercizing part of one's power. It is this kind of self-imparted limitation of power which plays a crucial role in the free will defence, for what God does in creating free persons is exactly giving up part of His power in order to make room for their free decisions. Second, we have seen that almightiness does not include the ability to bring about literally all logically possible states of affairs. Perhaps we should add to the list of things which an almighty being need not be able to bring about the truth-value of freedom-conditionals like those spelled out above.

However this may be, it is clear that our notion of almightiness is far more fit to accommodate the sort of limitations which the free will defence impinges on God's power than the philosophical notion of literal omnipotence. This has to do, I suggest, with the biblical background of both the notion of almightiness and the free will defence. In the Bible it is abundantly clear from the way in which God addresses Himself to human beings (and especially to His people) that in a sense He has made Himself dependent upon their choices. All Old Testament exhortations to conform to the Law and live in the right relationship with God, as well as all New Testament appeals to accept the Gospel and live in a restored relationship with God give ample testimony to the fact that God has endowed human beings

---

[59] Plantinga, *God and Other Minds*, 118; cf. *God, Freedom, and Evil*, 17f.

[60] See §3.4.5 above (esp. the third and fourth differences between the philosophical and the biblical conception of divine power).

with freedom and responsibility, and that He cannot keep this intact while at the same time *causing* them to use it only for the good.[61]

There is, however, another variant of the argument aimed at showing that the free will defence unacceptably compromises God's power, which, if valid, cannot be accounted for by substituting the notion of almightiness for that of omnipotence. Let me introduce this argument by conjuring up the picture of the kind of power which the free will defence suggests God to have. It is as if the contingent decisions of free human beings confront God with a kind of *ananke*, or fate, or recalcitrant material with which He can only do the best He can.[62] The free will defence seems to exonerate God for tolerating evil by suggesting that there were so many contingent facts over which God had no control (viz. all the freedom-conditionals made true by the evil actions of moral agents), that He was unable to realize the kind of world He desired most, i.e. a world in which all moral agents always freely choose to do good instead of evil. But clearly such a God looks more like a finite, limited craftsman such as Plato's Demiurge than like the all-sovereign Judaeo-Christian God, who has control over every event which takes place in the universe.

David Basinger has recently rationalized this intuition by moulding it into an argument against the free will defence. Basinger concedes that "omnipotence" has had no constant, specified meaning in the Christian tradition, so that it is difficult to show that the free will defence presupposes the wrong notion of omnipotence (thus, he implicitly endorses the plausibility of the response I gave above to that kind of criticism). He goes on to argue, however, that there is a specific aspect of God's power with regard to which such an unambiguous authentically Christian position exists, and this is that God has what he calls "specific sovereignty" over events:

> When orthodox Christians contend that God is in control of each contingent action (X) performed by a moral agent they mean (have meant) that, if God did not desire X to occur, he could prohibit it. ... orthodox Christian theism has never interpreted the free agency of moral agents as a limitation on God's sovereignty. Man is accorded freedom of a sort, but God is clearly seen as a being who, if not the cause of all contingent events, at least possesses total "veto power" over all such occurrences (i.e., God is accorded specific sovereignty).[63]

---

[61] Strangely enough, Richard Gale, *Nature and Existence of God*, 145f. draws precisely the opposite conclusion from what he calls the "omnipotence objection" against the free will defence. Acknowledging that Plantinga is not "fully facing up to the extent of the limitations he places on God's omnipotence," Gale nevertheless asserts that Plantinga's account of omnipotence, as distinct from e.g. the Old Testament notion of "God Almighty," "... might be the one that will prove most digestible and healthy for theism in its effort to construct an adequate defense" (viz. against arguments from evil). Gale even thinks that evolution from the Old Testament notion towards Plantinga's account of omnipotence forms a fine illustration of scientific progress! I hope to have shown that he is entirely misguided here.

[62] See for these terms respectively Wainwright, "Freedom," 300; Windt, "Unfortunate God," 340f.; Morriston, "Is Plantinga's God Omnipotent?," 55.

[63] David Basinger, "Christian Theism and the Free Will Defence," *Sophia* 19.2 (1980), 25.

According to Basinger, God as envisioned by the free will defence (for short: the free will God) has no such specific sovereignty, since He has no way to control the free choices of the moral agents He created. Basinger's point is not that the nature of freedom limits the free will God's power[64] - for this is a *logical* limit on God's power, which therefore does not count against it. Rather, Basinger's point is that the free will God's *character* limits His power to such an extent as to rule out specific sovereignty. For, assuming that a universe containing more moral good than evil is more valuable than a universe containing only robots who cannot perform morally good actions at all, the free will God is necessitated by His goodness to create the set of free moral agents which He foreknows will contain the greatest possible amount of good over evil.[65] And since God cannot causally determine the decisions of the moral agents participating in this best creatable set, it is possible that the moral agents actually created by God, despite their many evil actions, together constitute this best creatable set. Then the only way for God to prevent specific evils we experience would be by bringing about a less valuable overall state of affairs, which would conflict with His goodness. So given the recalcitrant contingent facts of free moral decisions, which deprive God of His specific sovereignty, God has created the best possible universe He could, or so Basinger's rendition of the free will defence goes.

However, is this rendition of the free will defence correct? I think not. It contains at least one crucial assumption which rests on a serious misinterpretation of this defence.[66] This is the assumption that God must bring about the most valuable overall state of affairs which He can. Clearly, if this assumption were true it would entail a serious limitation on God's power indeed, for it would imply that God had no control over the actualization of any individual state of affairs. In every situation, He had no choice but to create the best He could. But first, as it stands this is a dubious assumption, since it is not clear at all that the concept of a most valuable overall state of affairs (like that of a "best possible world," which seems identical to it) is a coherent one. Isn't it more plausible to think that, whatever the value of the actual world, God could have made a more valuable world in innumerably different ways, e.g. by creating more free agents who would all in all perform more moral good than evil? And second, even if we grant for the sake of argument that this assumption is a rational one, it is not one which is presupposed by the free will defence. For the free will

---

Basinger quotes Augustine, Aquinas, Luther, Calvin and G.C. Berkouwer in support of this contention.

[64] One who argues that the free will defence conflicts with divine specific sovereignty for this reason is Dewey Hoitenga, "Logic and the Problem of Evil," *APQ* 4 (1967), 121f.

[65] Basinger, "Christian Theism," 24.

[66] For the following criticism I am indebted to an instructive paper of Thomas Flint, "Divine Sovereignty and the Free Will Defence," *Sophia* 23.2 (1984), 41-52; see esp. 47-50.

defence does not attempt to excuse God for the existence of evil by arguing that God had *no choice* but to create our world. On the contrary, part of the faith that it wants to defend is precisely that God is a *free* Creator, i.e. that each contingent being owes its existence to a truly and fully gracious act of God. That is precisely why believers thank and praise God for having created them and caring for them (cf. e.g. Psalm 8); these would be odd actions if God were *necessitated* to create and care for us. In short, God's creative goodness is a matter of grace rather than necessity.[67] What the free will defence puts forward is only that *one* of the valuable things which a wholly good God *might* want to see exemplified in the world, viz. moral good, is logically related to creaturely freedom, and that this relation explains why God permits evil. The free will defence does not presuppose that God was *compelled* to actualize moral good, and therefore to permit the evils we experience.

Once freed from the restrictions of the assumption that God must create the best possible world, it is easy to see that the free will defence is compatible with divine specific sovereignty. Not being necessitated to create any being, God could simply have decided not to create a moral agent whom He foreknew would freely bring about one or more events which He did not want to take place. Moreover, after having created such a moral agent, God might decide to occasionally overrule its creaturely freedom in order to prevent some undesirable event. Thus, the free will God has the power to prevent all contingent events which actually occur, including those brought about by the free agency of His creatures. In short, God has specific sovereignty, and the second argument intended to show that the free will defence (and any theodicy based upon it) unacceptably waters down God's power fails.

4.4.4 *Must we ascribe less power to God?*

At this point, we must turn to the opposite objection which is often put forward against the free will defence, viz. that it ascribes *too much* power to God rather than too little. For it is precisely at this juncture that this objection is likely to be raised. If the free will defence indeed grants God the power to create freely (rather than restricted by some hidden *ananke*), as well as the "veto power" by which He can overrule creaturely freedom at any moment, then it seems to ascribe too much power to God. Like the God-can-do-more objection discussed in the previous subsection, the God-cannot-do-as-much objection may take two forms. First, it is sometimes argued that it is *incoherent* to hold that God has these sorts of power. Second, it is sometimes contended that if coherent, the sorts of power ascribed to God in the free will defence exacerbate the problem of evil instead of

---

[67] See for more argument to this effect Robert M. Adams, "Must God Create the Best?," *PR* 81 (1972), 317-332, also in T.V. Morris (ed.), *Concept of God*, 91-106. Cf. also David Brown, "Why a World at All?," forthcoming in *NTT*.

contributing to its solution. Both objections are typically put forward by process thinkers, although the second is also often raised by others. Let us discuss them by concentrating on the thought-provoking work of process theologian David Griffin, who has offered a detailed and complete elaboration of process theodicy and is no doubt its most energetic and combative advocate.[68]

Drawing upon Whiteheadian/Hartshornian metaphysical principles, Griffin argues that the notion of divine power which is implicit in free will theodicy is deficient. As he sees it, this notion is based upon the problematic assumption that

> it is possible for one actual being's condition to be completely determined by a being or beings other than itself.[69]

Let me follow Griffin in labelling this assumption "premise X." It is premise X which Griffin designates as the source of all misery in traditional theodicies, and which he denounces as meaningless, metaphysically false, and logically false. Before discussing this remarkable compilation of charges, let me first make two other observations.

First, on a natural interpretation of "traditional" Griffin seems right that the truth of premise X is assumed in all traditional theodicies, including the free will theodicy as discussed and elaborated above. As we have seen, a free will theodicy holds that God controls every contingent event, and it is plausible to suggest that this makes it possible for Him to completely determine any actual being's condition. As to free moral agents, He is able to do this both by His decision to create that particular being and by His decisions to allow or prevent its free decisions from being executed. The free will defence does not necessarily imply that God actually makes such decisions on all particular occasions, but it does imply that God has the ability to do so.

Second, at first sight Griffin's objections against premise X are highly abstruse. For it seems perfectly possible for one being to have its condition (which for Griffin amounts to: all of its activities) totally determined by another being. Consider an example put forward by Nelson Pike to this

---

[68] This is not to say that Griffin also ranks as the most *original* process-theodicist. Rather, the most original and fundamental work in creating the process-view of divine power has been done by Charles Hartshorne, from whom Griffin borrows many insights. Hartshorne's position with regard to the power of God and the problem of evil, however, has been extensively described and discussed several times in recent literature. See Barry L. Whitney, *Evil and the Process God*, New York 1985; Sheila G. Davaney, *Divine Power*, Philadelphia 1986; Case-Winters, *God's Power*, 129-170. Cf. more generally on Hartshorne's doctrine of God Colin E. Gunton, *Becoming and Being*, London 1978; Santiago Sia (ed.), *Charles Hartshorne's Concept of God*, Dordrecht 1990. For this reason I prefer to focus on the way in which Hartshorne's work is applied and elaborated by David Griffin.

[69] Griffin, *God, Power, and Evil*, 264.

effect: a father has the power to move his arm, but allows his daughter to move it for him.[70] It is not clear why this example could not be extended to all bodily movements which the father has the power to bring about. In such a case, it seems that an actual being (viz. the daughter) has the power to completely determine all the activities of another being (the father), simply because the latter has granted this power to the former. Hence, far from being meaningless or logically or metaphysically false, premise X seems to express a fully consistent state of affairs.

In his response to Pike,[71] however, Griffin offers some additional information which clarifies his position. Pike's main mistake turns out to be that he has misunderstood the concept of an "actual being" in premise X. This concept should be defined along the lines of Whiteheadian metaphysics as an "occasion of experience." Examples of enduring temporal societies of such occasions are the human soul or mind, electrons, atoms, molecules and cells, but not *aggregates* of actual beings such as sticks and stones or, for that matter, human arms. One of the characteristics of all actual beings, as distinct from their aggregates, is that they are partially self-determining. The primary form of self-determination is choice. According to Whitehead and process theologians, all actual beings have freedom of choice to some degree.[72]

On this interpretation, it is clear why Pike's example fails. First, to move an arm is not to move an actual being, but an aggregate of actual beings (which as such lacks the power of self-determination). In order to completely determine the activities of these actual beings, the daughter would need to be able to determine all the activities of all the arm's cells etc. And second, in order to be able to determine her father's activities with regard to his arm, the daughter would have to have full control over the father's *choice* to have his arm moved by her. But it is of course logically impossible for one being to determine the free choice of another. Apart from Pike's example, we can easily see why any example adduced against premise X must fail. For substituting the definition we have just found for the term "actual being," this is how premise X should be read:

X'   It is possible for the condition of one by definition partially self-determining occasion of experience to be completely determined by a being or beings other than itself

X' being the correct reading of premise X, it is evident that premise X is

---

[70] Nelson Pike, "Process Theodicy," 157. Pike has elaborated the theological ramifications of this example with regard to the problem of evil in his paper "Over-Power."

[71] David R. Griffin, *Evil Revisited*, Albany 1991, chapter 7; this chapter goes back to Griffin's earlier separate rejoinder to Pike, "Actuality, Possibility."

[72] This paragraph draws upon Griffin's exegesis of Whitehead, as presented in *Evil Revisited*, 127-129; see also *God, Power, and Evil*, 268, 277f. and, for a more extensive exposition, J.B. Cobb & D.R. Griffin, *Process Theology*, Philadelphia 1976, 16-18, 63-79.

false, since a being which is by definition partially self-determining cannot be fully determined by another being. Thus, Griffin's charges against it are not so easily falsifiable as it seemed at first sight.

Nevertheless, it can be shown that they are mistaken after all. To see this, note that the validity of Griffin's defence against Pike depends on X' being the correct interpretation of X. The crucial step in the transition from X to X' is the assumption that there are no actual beings that do not have at least some power of self-determination, a power which they cannot refrain from exercising. Griffin's allegations against premise X can only hold if this further premise is not only true, but indeed true *by definition*, i.e. necessarily true. Only in that case Griffin's charges that premise X is meaningless and logically false are justified. So Griffin must hold not only that there are no actual beings devoid of self-determining power, but that there *cannot* be such beings. Although he is not quite so explicit, it seems that this is indeed Griffin's position.[73]

How does Griffin know that there are no actual beings without self-determining power? Griffin answers this question by invoking what he calls the experiential criterion of meaning, i.e. the principle that "the meaningful use of terms requires an experiential basis for those terms."[74] Starting from his own experience, Griffin argues that he does not experience powerless actualities. Next, he states the point more broadly, arguing that in the common experience of all humanity there is nothing that we would call an actuality and that we would directly experience as being devoid of power.[75] But this seems obviously false. There are people who experience actualities that are devoid of self-determining power, viz. philosophical determinists (or compatibilists).[76] They usually claim to have an experiential basis for their position that human beings are entities which have no self-determining power in Griffin's sense of the term. And in Griffin's metaphysics a human being (in opposition to the human *arm* we encountered before), is not an aggregate, but a structured society of actual beings unified by one centre of

---

[73] Griffin is not explicit here, because he refuses to disconnect metaphysical and logical truth. What he explicitly says is this: "If the Whiteheadian view of actual entities is correct about the ... power of all actual entities, then ... [t]here would be no possible worlds with actualities devoid of ... the power of self-determination" (*Evil Revisited*, 135). Since Griffin holds the Whiteheadian view of actual entities to be correct, he therefore holds that there are no possible worlds with actual beings devoid of self-determining power.

[74] *God, Power, and Evil*, 266; *Evil Revisited*, 141; in the latter work (cf. also 123-125, 252f. n.24) Griffin prefers the term "experiential" above "empirical" in order to fend off the charge of endorsing a naive sensationist form of empiricism, which has been falsified by the breakdown of logical positivism. According to the experiential theory of meaning the meaningful use of terms is not primarily based on sensory perception, but on a "deeper" mode of perceptual experience which Griffin does not further define, but which he suggests to include e.g. religious experience.

[75] *Evil Revisited*, 141.

[76] As we saw in §4.2, esp. n.21, philosophers who deny the reality of free will are far from extinct.

experience, viz. the mind or soul.[77] As such, the individual human being shares the basic characteristics of singular actual beings. Griffin himself hints at this counter-example when he mentions Spinoza's view that we as human beings have no power of self-determination. According to Griffin, however, this counter-example is wrong-headed, since the view of Spinoza "is based upon argumentation, not direct experience."[78]

The difficulty here is, of course, that Griffin completely overlooks what has almost become a matter of common opinion in contemporary philosophy, viz. the fundamental unity of experience and interpretation. In short: There is no experience without interpretaion.[79] The concept of "direct experience" is therefore misleading. The fact that the view of philosophical compatibilists differs from Griffin's experience is not the result of the argumentation of the former, but has to do with the *different interpretations* of what is experienced. We cannot get beyond these interpretations to something called "pure" or "direct" experience, and therefore an appeal to this alleged sort of experience as a criterion for meaningfulness is misplaced. Thus, even the refined version of Griffin's experiential criterion of meaning must still be rejected as rather naive. Whether our terms are meaningful or not does not depend upon whether we experience them or not - for example, has anyone ever directly experienced the term "greater"? - but upon whether it can be made clear without contradiction what we intend them to *do*.

However, let us grant for a moment for the sake of argument that both Griffin's criterion of meaning and his contention that we do not experience powerless actualities are correct. Even in that case the claim which should be supported remains without warrant. For what we experience is that there *are* no powerless actualities, not that there *cannot* be such actualities.[80] Hence, the claim which is shown to be meaningless is "there are powerless actualities" rather than "it is possible that there are powerless actualities." Suppose that we had the opportunity to experience all actualities which exist or have existed in the world, and that we found out that none of them was powerless. In such a situation we would perhaps be entitled to hold that it is a metaphysical truth that there are no powerless actualities. But still, we would not be entitled to claim that this is a *logical* truth. For how would we know that a world exemplifying other metaphysical

---

[77] *Evil Revisited*, 111; cf. 102f.

[78] *God, Power, and Evil*, 267. The suggestion is that Spinoza's claim is meaningless, since it lacks this experiential basis.

[79] See for this point e.g. John Hick, *Faith and Knowledge*, Ithaca 1966², 95-148; Christoph Schwöbel, *God: Action*, 103-112. Schwöbel's observation that the tendency to ignore the complexity of the concept of experience, and to reduce it by proposing a simplified account of experience is one of the main reasons for the manifold difficulties which have accompanied reflection on the concept in modern theology (103), is pertinent here.

[80] For a somewhat similar argument, see Bruce Reichenbach, *Evil and a Good God*, New York 1982, 180; cf. the evasive comments of Griffin, *Evil Revisited*, 141f.

(i.e. basic ontological) truths would be impossible?

I conclude, then, that Griffin's attempt to show that there logically cannot be actualities that lack self-determining power fails. Even if we share Griffin's Whiteheadian metaphysics, we are at best entitled to the claim that premises X' and X are metaphysically (and not logically) false. But this conclusion falls short of satisfying Griffin's needs. For if premise X is only metaphysically false, this means that it is only metaphysically impossible for one being's activities to be completely determined by another. Unlike logical impossibilities, however, metaphysical impossibilities are not usually supposed to set limits to God's power. So there is no apparent reason to suppose that it is not within God's power to completely determine each of the activities of all other beings.[81] In short, then, the sort of power ascribed to God in traditional theodicies such as the free will theodicy advocated above, is not incoherent.

The second form taken by the objection that the free will God can do too much is, that by ascribing to God the power to control every contingent event the problem of evil is exacerbated rather than solved. For if God has the power to control every contingent event, He has the power to prevent every evil which takes place in the world (provided that there are no necessary evils). But if God has such power, He should use it much more frequently than He actually does. The fact that He does not do so counts against Him. This objection is far more widespread than the former, which is mainly raised by process thinkers. And it must be acknowledged that it has an important intuitive force. Nevertheless, I shall argue that it is mistaken.

To begin with, let me point out why a fairly common strategy to forestall this objection does not work. It is often suggested, especially in contemporary theology and philosophy, that God has limited His power and therefore is not responsible for the evil in the world. The claim that God has limited His power can be elaborated in either of two ways. First, it can be held that God has limited His power in such a way that He is no longer able to intervene in worldly affairs. This kind of divine self-limitation is e.g. defended by Hans Jonas, who argues in relation to the experiences of the Jewish people during the Second World War that

> ... not because he chose not to, but because he *could* not intervene did he fail to intervene. ... God ... has divested himself of any power to interfere with the physical course of things.[82]

---

[81] Cf. for this conclusion Pike, "Process Theodicy," 162.

[82] Hans Jonas, "The Concept of God after Auschwitz," *JR* 69 (1987), 10; Jonas restricts this self-limitation, however, to "the time of the ongoing world process," and thereby approaches the second form of self-limitation. For a discussion of Jonas's paper from a Christian point of view, see Eberhard Jüngel, "Gottes ursprüngliches Anfangen als schöpferische Selbstbegrenzung," now in Jüngel, *Wertlose Wahrheit*, München 1990, 151-162.

Second, it can be held that God has limited His power in such a way that He has not given up His ability to intervene, but has resolved not to use this ability on certain occasions and during a certain time. This second conception of divine self-limitation, which is e.g. implied by free will theodicies and which we have therefore implicitly endorsed above, is explained as follows by Thomas Tracy:

> This amounts to a purposeful limitation of the scope of his own activity, but it does not nullify his omnipotence ... Intentional self-restraint does not represent a renunciation of omnipotence, but rather a renunciation of certain uses of power.[83]

Let us, following a proposal of Marcel Sarot,[84] call this form of self-limitation "self-restraint," and allot the term "self-limitation" to the former. Further, we will use the notion of "self-restriction" as an umbrella term covering both forms. Now the point I want to make in this connection is that *neither of these forms of self-restriction would absolve God from all responsibility in relation to evil*. It may seem that since God has restricted His power in either of these ways, He is not responsible for the evil events which have subsequently taken place in the world. Indeed, especially in the case of self-limitation it is clear that God cannot prevent such events. However, He could have prevented the fact that He cannot prevent them, viz. by not limiting or restraining His power in the first place! Since God is responsible for doing that, He is equally responsible for all that follows from it. If we hold (as I do) that God has foreknowledge, He knew what would be the results of His self-restriction; if we assume that He has no foreknowledge, He knew at least that He did not know the results of His self-restriction. In either case, His responsibility is not mitigated in the slightest. On the contrary, in the case of self-limitation the act by which God limited His power would have been an entirely irresponsible act of self-mutilation! And in the case of self-restraint, God is responsible for not abrogating the restraint.

One of the merits of process thinkers is that they have recognized this point. Instead of trying to absolve God from responsibility for evil by invoking some concept of self-restriction, they argue that the concept of divine power is restricted *in itself*. "Instead of saying that God's power is limited, suggesting that it is less than some conceivable power, we should rather say: his power is absolutely maximal, the greatest possible, but even the greatest possible power is still one power among others, it is not the only."[85] If this is true, process theism at any rate succeeds in offering an

---

[83] Thomas F. Tracy, *God, Action, and Embodiment*, Grand Rapids 1984, 143f. (instead of "omnipotence" we can also read "almightiness" here).

[84] Marcel Sarot, "Omnipotence and Self-Limitation," 182; Sarot also lists more literature in which both positions are defended, cf. resp. 177 n.16, 183 n.23, but he groups authors who do not explicitly indicate the kind of divine self-restriction they advocate too easily among those endorsing divine "self-limitation."

[85] Hartshorne, *Divine Relativity*, 138; cf. his "Omnipotence," in: Vergilius Ferm (ed.), *An*

argument which shows that God is not responsible for evil. We have already seen that if God's power is limited in the way defended by process thinkers (i.e. limited to what is metaphysically possible), it is certainly not the greatest possible power, since God is not omnipotent in the sense of being able to do all that is logically possible for Him to do. I have already substituted the concept of almightiness for that of omnipotence as defined in terms of logical possibility, and therefore this is not the point I want to take issue with.

What is problematic in the process conception, however, is that the limitations attributed to God's power are far more serious than those suggested by what we found in relation to the biblical conception of divine almightiness. To be sure, given this latter conception we may grant that there are logically possible states of affairs which God is unable to bring about. But this inability has nothing to do with the influence exerted by other centres of power existing independently of God's creative activity. To claim the latter, as process theists do, is to embrace a metaphysical dualism which cannot escape in the end from making God the victim of evil. As John Hick explains in connection with the dualism of J.S. Mill, this amounts to renouncing the Christian understanding of God:

> From the point of view of Christian theology, however, a dualism of this kind is unacceptable for the simple but sufficient reason that it contradicts the Christian conception of God. ... Dualism avoids the problem - but only at the cost of rejecting one of the most fundamental items of the Christian faith, belief in the reality of the infinite and eternal God, who is the sole creator of heaven and earth and of all things visible and invisible. The belief is so deeply rooted in the Bible, in Christian worship, and in Christian theology of all schools that it cannot be abandoned without vitally affecting the nature of Christianity itself. The absolute monotheism of the Judeo-Christian faith is not, so to say, negotiable; it can be accepted or rejected, but it cannot be amended into something radically different. This then is the basic and insuperable Christian objection to dualism; not that it is intrinsically impossible or unattractive, but simply that it is excluded by the Christian understanding of God and can have no place in Christian theodicy.[86]

Encyclopedia of Religion, New York 1945, 545f.

[86] Hick, *Evil and the God of Love*, 35; for Hick's rejection of process theodicy in particular, cf. his *Philosophy of Religion*, Englewood Cliffs 1990[4], 48-55. Griffin, *Evil Revisited*, 23, tries to rebut the charge that the process view entails a dualism by arguing that in this view no particular being exists eternally over against God; but this is not the decisive point. The decisive point is whether there are necessarily other centres of power (either eternal or not) in the universe which limit God's power and upon which God is therefore dependent. Even if such centres are conceived of as participating in God, so that God is dependent upon them in the same way as human beings are upon their bodies (a view recently defended by Sarot, *God, Passibility*, 234-243; see esp. 239), the charge of dualism still stands. For these powers, which are not wholly controllable by God, are the only possible candidates to be blamed for evil. For a fine exposition of the way in which the radical contingency of all creaturely reality is fundamentally entailed by Christian faith, see Schwöbel, *God: Action*, 148.

There is, however, a second argument against the acceptance of a metaphysical dualism, which is in a sense more forceful since it may also convince those who do not accept the implicit appeal to revelation theology of this first argument.[87] This second argument is that it is inappropriate (if not self-contradictory) to invest faith as unconditional and absolute trust in someone or something which is not itself unconditioned and infinite. Notice that this principle is not derived from revelation, but evident in itself. Following Luther, we may use this principle to distinguish between superstition and "right" or "real" faith. Christoph Schwöbel neatly puts this distinction as follows:

> As "superstition" appear all forms of faith where someone invests unconditional and absolute trust in a finite and conditioned entity. This attitude, however, appears self-contradictory, because unconditional trust can only rationally be directed at something or someone that is itself unconditioned and infinite. Therefore only a form of faith can without contradiction be unconditional faith if its "object" is indeed the unconditional ground of all being, meaning, and truth...[88]

In other words, a God who is conditioned by certain metaphysical principles and as a result of this conditionedness has become the victim of evil, is worthy neither of our faith nor of the worship to which only this kind of faith can lead. He may be worthy of our admiration, compassion and love etc., it is definitely irrational to judge such a conditioned and in that sense imperfect being worthy of our faith and worship, i.e. to call such a being God.[89]

The great advantage of a free will theodicy in comparison to process theodicy and all kinds of finitist theodicies is that the former succeeds in holding creaturely agents responsible for evil *without thereby making God the victim of evil*. The reverse side of this medal is, of course, that a free will theodicy cannot escape from ascribing a form of responsibility for evil to God as well as to creaturely beings. For in creation God freely restrained His own power, thus making room for free moral agency and for the *possibility* of the occurrence of evil. Moreover, even if we think it incoherent to ascribe detailed foreknowledge to God, God knew at any rate the possible

---

[87] Cf. Griffin's criticism of the passage quoted from Hick in his *God, Power, and Evil*, 202f.

[88] Schwöbel, *God: Action and Revelation*, 146; cf. Ward, *Divine Action*, 6f.

[89] Griffin, *God, Power, and Evil*, 256-258 lists a series of authors (including e.g. C.A. Campbell, M.B. Ahern, Terence Penelhum, but also atheists like J.N. Findlay and Roland Pucetti) who endorse this argument in some form or another. Interestingly, both in his criticism of Brightman's finitist concept of God (*ibid.*, 246; cf. the restatement in *Evil Revisited*, 199f.) and in his crucial chapter on "Worshipfulness and the Omnipotence Fallacy" (*God, Power, and Evil*, 261), Griffin himself concedes that this line of argument is valid. Still, Griffin denies that it is sound since according to him the premise that omnipotence in the traditional sense is the highest conceivable form of power - and therefore a necessary condition for divine perfection and worshipfulness - is false. I have already shown, however, that Griffin is mistaken in holding that the traditional concept of almightiness is inconceivable.

266

consequences of His self-restraint, and presumably also their relative probabilities. In that sense, God is also partially responsible for the *reality* of evil. But if we must concede that God is fully responsible for the possibility of evil and co-responsible for its reality, then surely we are faced with an enormous perplexity. For then it seems that we can no longer consistently uphold God's perfect *goodness*. That would mean that we have unwittingly done the same thing which dualist theodicy do openly, viz. resolving the problem of evil by cutting the knot rather than unravelling it. More seriously, of course, we would implicitly be guilty of denying another central tenet of Christian faith, viz. belief in the absolute goodness of God.

I think that this suspicion can be removed, however, by distinguishing between the ascription of responsibility and the ascription of *blame* to someone.[90] In holding God co-responsible for evil we do not necessarily blame Him for it. Let us grant for the sake of argument that we are right in applying our imperfect human moral standards of good and evil to God. This is of course a problematic position, but to deny any relation between our moral standards and the ascription of goodness to God would involve an absolute voluntarism, which is an equally problematic position. Now even if we are in a position to pass moral judgements on the ways of God, we would only have reason to blame God for evil, if it would be impossible for Him to make good out of evil. Only in that case we would be justified in concluding that God is to be blamed for what He did in creating free moral agents. Now the impossibility of making good out of evil is of course often affirmed by anti-theodicists. One of the tenets of the Christian doctrine of God's almightiness, however, is to articulate the faith that this is *not* impossible for God, but that, on the contrary, God is constantly and actively involved in the redemption of evil. This conclusion, however, finally leads us to a novel nexus of issues, which can be most properly assessed in the universe of discourse which is provided by trinitarian Christian faith. Let us now pass on to a discussion of these issues.

4.4.5 *Evil and the power of the trinitarian God*

The conclusion of the previous subsection leads us to the formulation of a very important point: it is impossible to offer an adequate theodicy from an existentially neutral perspective. In the end, either we trust that God is able to make good out of all the evils we experience, and learn to share His purposes in realizing this good. Or we refuse to trust that God is able to make good out of so much havoc, and follow the protest-atheism of Ivan Karamazov in Dostoyevsky's novel, most respectfully returning God our ticket of admission. In this sense, Vincent Brümmer points to the fact that

---

[90] This distinction was suggested to me by Nelson Pike, "Over-Power and God's Responsibility for Sin," 26ff. I do not share Pike's conclusion, however, that in order for God not to be blamed for evil, every evil must be justified by its serving a higher goal. This would amount to a negation of gratuitous evil, and does not necessarily follow from Pike's assumptions.

the acceptability of a theodicy such as the free will theodicy depends upon whether we can make the "moral universe" of which this theodicy is a part existentially our own.[91] This universe differs from the utilitarian moral universe in which the prevention of evil and suffering is the highest moral value. The moral universe presupposed by the free will defence is character-ized by another hierarchy of values, which has e.g. living in a relationship of love with God as its highest value. If the realisation of such a value is to be possible, the possibility of evil side-effects is unavoidable, given the fact that love is connected with freedom and freedom with the ability to do evil.[92] In this way, a theodicy can only properly function within the encom-passing framework of faith.

Note that this position does not imply that all evil which takes place in the world *in itself contributes* to this highest good. That would again imply a denial of the existence of gratuitous evil, a position which we have found wanting. It is not the case that all evil is good for something. What is the case, however, as seen from the point of view of faith, is that God is able to turn even evil into good (Gen.50:20), and to let evil work for good (Rom.8:28). Indeed, this is one of the most profound implications of the belief that God is almighty. The paradigmatic example of this almighty agency of God, and at the same time the most powerful invitation to share the perspective of faith, is the cross of Christ. Here we see how God is able to make good out of the most horrendous evils, how He becomes Himself involved in suffering and evil in order to effect redemption and reconcili-ation. Here it is the utter weakness of God which is stronger than all human strength (1 Cor.1:25).

Thus we find that a truly Christian theodicy cannot in the end do without an appeal to God's working in Christ to overcome evil. "My Father works hitherto, and I work," Jesus responds to the accusation that He has healed a paralytic on the sabbath (John 5:17). It is this redemptive, saving agency of God which forms the way in which God justifies Himself for allowing evil. This is not to say that God *had* to become engaged in over-coming evil in order to justify Himself. Redemption, like creation, is a matter of grace not necessity; in the cross God does not justify Himself, but sinful human beings. But it is to say that in this way God *shows* how His justice, goodness and power go together without the one having priority over the other.

A similar point must be made with regard to the Holy Spirit. The question: why does God permit so much evil if He is almighty? can only be answered by referring to the work of the Spirit. After the resurrection of Christ God fulfill His purposes predominantly by working through the Holy Spirit, and has to a large extent limited (in the sense of self-restraint) His

---

[91] Brümmer, *Personal God*, 149-151.
[92] Ibid., 145-147; cf. Redmond, *Omnipotence of God*, 163: "Forced love would be as self-contradictory as square circles."

power to this work. He fights evil neither by forcing people to refrain from doing evil nor by placing them in an environment in which evil cannot come to them, but by confronting them with the Gospel of God's work in Christ, summoning them to live in faith and convincing them of its truth. In this way, we are enabled by the Spirit to interpret our experiences of evil in a way which does not block the future, but which, on the contrary, strengthens us to share the purposes God has in bringing about His Kingdom. In the *school of faith* it is the Spirit who may show us "fragments of meaning"[93] in the suffering that befalls us. In this way, a Christian theodicy, which leads to an adequate practical response to evil, not only presupposes an sound doctrine of divine almightiness, let alone a consistent philosophical account of God's omnipotence and goodness, but also the christological, pneumatological and eschatological dimensions of Christian theology.[94]

In relation to these christological, pneumatological and eschatological aspects of theodicy a final remark must be made. It is often argued that the cross of Christ makes clear that it is wrong to define God's power in terms of an alleged sovereignty to control all contingent states of affairs. Rather, it is held, the cross of Christ should incite us to redefine the concepts of omnipotence and almightiness. As Geddes MacGregor says:

> The power of God is not to be conceived as ... the ability to do everything (omni-potere) or to control everything (pantokratein). ... The divine power should be conceived as, rather, the infinite power that springs from creative love. ... God does not control his creatures. He graciously lets them be.[95]

The result of such a redefining procedure may be that we are left with a truncated notion of almightiness. Surely God's almightiness is shown *sub specie contrarii* in the cross of Christ, but it is also shown in Christ's resurrection.[96] Therefore, even God's weakness at the cross is one of the manifold manifestations of His power.[97] Here, we get a glimpse of the way in which the *weakness* of God (cf. § 3.4.5), far from detracting from his power, should be affirmed as one of the forms in which He is actively

---

[93] For this well-chosen expression I am indebted to J. Westland, *God onze troost in noden*, Kampen 1986, 11; cf. the examples elaborated in the final chapter, 118-143.

[94] For an instructive proposal of the way in which a Christian theodicy has to integrate philosophical and theological strands of thought, see David Brown, "The Problem of Pain," in: Robert Morgan (ed.), *The Religion of the Incarnation*, Bristol 1989, 46-59

[95] Geddes MacGregor, *He Who Lets Us Be*, New York 1975, 15; it is fairly popular to oppose God's power and God's love to each other in this way. Cf. also, e.g. Grace M. Jantzen, *God's World, God's Body*, London 1984, 152; Jüngel, "Gottes Ursprüngliches Anfangen".

[96] Cf. Van Ruler, *Ik geloof*, 28f. Van Genderen, *Beknopte gereformeerde dogmatiek*, 178, admits that the older reformed dogmatics has one-sidedly described God's almightiness in terms of His creation and preservation of the world, but warns for the opposite danger of describing it only in christological terms.

[97] Cf. Biard, *Puissance de Dieu*, 184: "Il fallait cette extrémité de la faiblesse pour que toutes les virtualités de la puissance de Dieu fussent manifestées."

involved in the redemption of human sin and misery. Similarly, God's almightiness is shown in the way in which believers sometimes find themselves able to bear their sufferings in the Spirit of Christ, but also in the way in which God reveals Himself to Job, as the sovereign creator of heaven and earth.[98] As Newbigin says: "The power that controls all the visible world, and the power at work in the human soul, is one with the man who went his way from Bethlehem to Calvary."[99] In this way a trinitarian understanding of the power of God, which takes the work of the Father, the Son and the Spirit equally seriously, enables us to avoid the suggestion of a tension within the being of God between His power and His love.[100]

I consider it an area for further inquiry to elaborate such a trinitarian understanding of God's power in more detail than can be done here.[101] This is ground almost untrodden, but it is both necessary and worthwhile to make a few remarks on the theme in passing. For it can be argued against the present study that I have taken the power of the Father (or of the one divine being) far more seriously than that of the Son and the Spirit. In a sense, this is indeed the case, but not without good reason. For in contemporary theological and spiritual literature it is especially the power exemplified in the creating and sustaining work of the Father which is highly contested. Hence, in spelling out the doctrine of divine almightiness it belongs to the present "demands of life" to give special attention to the almightiness of the Father.[102] In laying this emphasis I have not intended to deny that the Son and the Spirit are equally almighty,[103] nor that their almightiness is realized in different ways and works than the Father's. But the "demands of life" in the Early Church, when subordinationism was the most virulent threat, were different from those in our time.

Moreover, in another sense it is by no means clear that the power of God which has been studied in this book should be associated exclusively with the Father. If we take the three modes of divine power which we found in §2.2, we may wonder whether these should not rather be related to the different persons of the trinity. For example, God's authority may be conceived as primarily exercised through the second person of the trinity, the eternal Word of God, who has become the King and Lord of the world in the way of His incarnation, redemption and resurrection. God's sustaining power may be seen as the energy of the Spirit, who keeps the earth in exist-

---

[98] Cf. Vicchio, *Voice from the Whirlwind*, esp. chapters IV and V.

[99] Lesslie Newbigin, *Truth to Tell*, Grand Rapids 1991, 37.

[100] In this sense, Moltmann is right in claiming: "If we see the Almighty in trinitarian terms, he is not the archetype of the mighty ones of this world"; *Trinity*, 197. Unfortunately, Moltmann goes on to develop this idea in a way which again threatens to sacrifice God's power to God's love.

[101] I have myself made a small beginning in my paper "Theodicee en Triniteit," *Theologia Reformata* 33 (1979), 7-27.

[102] Cf. the Luther-example quoted in §1.3.3 above.

[103] Cf. the Athanasian Creed, which goes back to Augustine here.

ence from the moment of its creation. God's infinite abilities to bring about unexpected states of affairs can be considered as the specific power of the Father, for whom nothing is impossible. In this way, trinitarian theology may integrate the different modes of the divine power, and bring to light that the divine activities are unified rather than uniform. If Pannenberg is right that, on the ground of the New Testament witness, the doctrine of the trinity should be unfolded in Christian doctrine *before* that of the divine unity and attributes, we must at least ask *how* trinitarian thinking affects our conception of God's almightiness.[104]

However this may be, taking into account the trinitarian character of the Christian doctrine of God enables us to see that God's power and God's love do neither compete with each other nor detract from each other. There is nothing wrong with the claim that God's power is the power of His love,[105] as long as we do not suggest by this that the power of love is a weaker or softer form of power than the almightiness traditionally ascribed to God. As Vernon White has neatly pointed out, it is precisely the logic of God's love which *requires* a strong notion of divine power:

> If divine action can secure good ends in all the world's conditions (for individuals, in particular events), in and through the worlds freedom, *then it ought to*. If it cannot, its creative endeavour is suspect, no longer responsible love. The meaning of love itself demands the "full" meaning of initiative and sovereignty, not a qualified meaning.[106]

The reason why the relation between power and love is so often portrayed as a necessary compromise in the literature is no doubt that the traditional notion of almightiness is still very often misunderstood. This misunderstanding always has to do with a dissolution of the different aspects which were captured by the traditional notion, a dissolution which may take two different forms. On the one hand, it may be that the aspect of divine government is abstracted from God's creative power to bring about what He wants to bring about. In this way, God's almightiness becomes one-sidedly conceived of in terms of power-over (which in turn is one-sidedly conceived as an *oppressive* form of power) rather than in terms of creative power-to. Above I have attempted to show that this understanding draws upon a misconceived definition of the concept of power in general.[107] As to its application to the doctrine of God, the consequences

---

[104] Pannenberg, *Systematic Theology*, 280-399; cf. also 415-422 (on omnipotence). A trinitarianly structured theory of divine action was rejected by Augustine and first developed by the Cappadocian Fathers. According to Schwöbel, *God: Action*, 101, it was rediscovered for the theology of the Reformation by John Calvin. Cf. in general Gunton, *Promise*, e.g. 1-15, 162-176.

[105] Cf. e.g. A.A. Spijkerboer, "De almacht van de liefde," in: D. van Weerlee et al., *Het verschijnsel godsdienst*, Amsterdam 1986, 61-66.

[106] White, *Fall of a Sparrow*, 164 (italics by the author); cf. 92.

[107] See above § 3.2.

of this misconception are pernicious, leading to what Whitehead and Hartshorne have referred to as the tyrant-image of God.[108] I have also tried to show, however, that this image was not implied in the traditional conceptions of omnipotence and almightiness, since both of these operate with the notion of creative power to fulfill one's purposes. As far as the power-over aspect is included in the ascription of almightiness to God, it is always power as *authority*, which is or should be recognized by the human beings created by God.

On the other hand, it may be that the aspect of creative power-to is isolated from God's concrete acts in the history of salvation. In this way, God's almightiness becomes one-sidedly conceived of in terms of an abstract power to do everything which is logically possible, rather than as the power by means of which God realizes His purposes in history. Above, I have attempted to show that this understanding draws upon a misconceived definition of the concept of almightiness as synonymous to the philosophical concept of omnipotence.[109] Again, as to its application to the doctrine of God, the consequences of this misconception are pernicious. The pale notion of divine power as ability to do everything not only leads (as we have seen) to many logical and conceptual problems, but also makes the problem of evil absolutely intractable, since it prevents us from relating God's power to His love and to His involvement in the struggle against evil. This struggle and God's involvement in it should not be docetically interpreted as merely apparent![110]

Once we see this double danger of isolating the different aspects of God's almightiness from each other, we understand how important it is to avoid all competition-language which plays off God's love against His power. The third aspect which we have distinguished in the traditional understanding of God's power, God's providential care for and sustainment of His creation,[111] can be interpreted as an expression of precisely this concern, since it combines the notions of power and love in itself. However this may be, only when we avoid talk of one attribute of God as having priority over another we can affirm the fundamental unity of God's character,[112] which gives us the most trustworthy ground for belief in the ultimate eschatological overcoming of evil in the Kingdom of God. That the

---

[108] Cf. § 1.1.1 above.

[109] See above § 3.3.

[110] Cf. e.g. J.J. Buskes, *God en het lijden*, repr. Kampen n.d., 18. Buskes points to the fact the in the Apostles' Creed "almighty" is not a noun, but an adjective before the noun "Father," thus expressing God's powerful care rather than an abstract notion of omnipotence. Cf. his comment: "De almacht van God, die daarin bestaat dat God zomaar alles kan, is een onbijbelse abstractie" (ibid.). See also J. Westland, *God onze troost*, 66: "Gods almacht is Góds almacht. Het is de almacht van die God, van Wie wij op grond van zijn openbaring ook belijden, dat Hij heilig is, rechtvaardig en goed."

[111] This is the aspect which we called "B-power" in § 2.2 above.

[112] Cf. Wiles, *God's Action*, 23 (in response to Jantzen as cited in n.95 above).

God whose holy love transcends our capacities for understanding is at the same time almighty, and that the Almighty God is at the same time the God in whom there is no darkness (1 John 1:5), is the only reason for hope in history.

Epilogue

At the end of this book it may be useful to recapitulate briefly what has been done and, equally important, what has not been done. This book presents itself as a study of the Christian doctrine of divine omnipotence. After having made explicit some of the assumptions and presuppositions embedded in this study, I have outlined its method by developing three criteria which must be fulfilled by a study in philosophical theology: consonance with the religious tradition, comprehensive conceptual coherence, and adequacy to the demands of life.

In order to satisfy the criterion of consonance with the tradition, I have investigated the history of the formation of the doctrine of divine omnipotence. I have not, however, provided an exhaustive survey of this history, but a cursory one, especially concentrating upon three issues which I hope to have shown were of paramount importance to its development, and to the development of the doctrine of God as a whole.

Second, I have attempted to fulfill the criterion of conceptual coherence by analysing the concept of omnipotence. I have examined the notion of power in its diverse connotations, as well as the way in which its meaning is affected by adding the prefix "omni." It turned out, however, that this theologically neutral and, in a sense, context-free analysis led us into almost intractable conceptual puzzles, thus confusing rather than illuminating the Christian doctrine of God's power. The reason for this confusion, I have suggested, is that this doctrine is rooted in and determined by the biblical revelation of God's words and actions. I have therefore started to explore the biblical notion of divine almightiness. What I have not done in this context, however, is elaborating this biblical conception (or conceptions) in extenso, since that would have compelled me to exchange the field of philosophical for that of biblical theology. Nevertheless, I have explored the biblical material to such a degree as to be able to roughly distinguish a biblical notion of divine almightiness from the philosophical notion of divine omnipotence. Next, from the perspective of the former, I have revisited the conceptual puzzles which plagued the latter, and indicated how they can now be adequately dealt with.

Third, turning to the criterion of adequacy to the demands of life, I have tested this concept of divine almigtiness on its systematic relevance by confronting it with two of the most generally experienced demands of contemporary life, namely the need to emphasize human responsibility and freedom, and the need to find an adequate response to the problems of evil and suffering. In selecting these issues I have chosen not to discuss all possible objections which could be raised against the ascription of almightiness to God. For example, the Freudian objection that the omni-potence-doctrine is a projection of human wishful thinking has been passed over, whereas the suspicion of some feminist theologians that the ascription of power to God is inextricably connected with images of oppression and masculinity has only been marginally reviewed. Rather, I have restricted myself to what I think to be two of the most natural candidates for discrediting the doctrine of divine almightiness. In addressing them I hope to have shown not only that the doctrine of divine almightiness can stand up to the criticisms that it obscures human responsibility and freedom and that it aggravates the problem of evil, but that the classical doctrine is to be preferred above its modern alternatives, i.e. that it is theologically compelling to hold fast to it.

In the foregoing chapters much has been said or implied about the being of God. It is good to remind ourselves in the end of the *Deus semper maior*, the fact that the living God always exceeds the grasp of our finite human intellect. There are strict limits to what we may claim to know about God. In speaking about God, there is always the theological peril that we transgress these limits by making Him the object of our intellectual speculations, thus treating Him as an impersonal and abstract construction. Doing theology, either philosophical theology or one of its other branches, is always a risky enterprise, and can never be equated with a mere harmless playing with concepts. On the other hand, there is also the theological danger, inspired or intensified by the current pluralist and agnostic trends in society, of claiming that we know too little about God to make truth claims about Him at all. Here lies the weakness of so much modern theology, in reducing the knowledge of God to talk *about* ourselves and our experiences rather than *from* God and His revelation.[1] It is only from the perspective of a personal relationship with God as He has made known Himself in His revelation and as He is experienced in the community of faith, that we can steer between the Scylla and the Charybdis of these opposite theological dangers. What I hope to have done in this book is to show where this way leads us in speaking of the power of God.

---

[1] Cf. Gunton, *Promise*, 162.

Bibliography of Literature
Referred to in the Text

- Abelard, Peter, *Introductio ad theologiam* (PL 178)
- Adam, Charles, & Tannery, Paul (eds.), *Oeuvres de Descartes* (12 vols.), Paris 1897-1913
- Adams, Marilyn McCord, *William Ockham*, Notre Dame 1987
- Adams, Robert Merrihew, "Must God Create the Best?," *Philosophical Review* 81 (1972), 317-332, reprinted in: Morris (ed.), *Concept*, 91-106
- Adams, Robert Merrihew, "Middle Knowledge and the Problem of Evil," *American Philosophical Quarterly* 14 (1977), 109-117, reprinted in: Adams & Adams (eds.), *Problem*, 110-125
- Adams, Marilyn McCord & Adams, Robert Merrihew (eds.), *The Problem of Evil*, Oxford 1992^2 (1990)
- Adriaanse, H.J., "Theses on Philosophy of Religion and Theology," unpublished paper presented at the "Symposion on the Nature and Rationality of (Philosophical) Theology," Utrecht 9 September 1992
- d'Ailly, Peter, *Quaestiones super libros sententiarum cum quibusdam in fine adjunctis*, repr. Minerva 1964 (1490)
- Alanen, Lilli, "Descartes, Duns Scotes and Ockham on Omnipotence and Possibility," *Franciscan Studies* 45 (1985), 157-188
- Alanen, Lilli, "Descartes, Omnipotence, and Kinds of Modality," in: P.H. Hare (ed.), *Doing Philosophy Historically*, Buffalo (N.Y.) 1988, 182-196
- Allen, Diogenes, *Philosophy for Understanding Theology*, London 1985
- Alston, William P., "Christian Experience and Christian Belief," in: Plantinga & Wolterstorff (eds.), *Faith and Rationality*, 103-134
- Alston, William P., *Divine Nature and Human Language: Essays in Philosophical Theology*, Ithaca 1989
- Alston, William P., "Referring to God," in: id., *Divine Nature*, 103-117
- Alston, William P., "God's Action in the World," in: id., *Divine Nature*, 197-222
- Ames, William, *Medulla Theologiae*, 1629^3; ET: J.D. Eusden, *The Marrow of Theology*, Philadelphia 1968
- Anderson, C. Anthony, "Divine Omnipotence and Impossible Tasks: An Intentional Analysis," *International Journal for Philosophy of Religion* 15 (1984), 109-124
- Anglin, W.S., *Free Will and the Christian Faith*, Oxford 1990
- Ansaldi, Jean, "La toute-puissance du Dieu du theisme dans le champ de la perversion," *Laval théologique et philosophique* 47 (1991), 3-11
- Anselm of Canterbury, *Cur Deus Homo?*
- Anselm of Canterbury, *Proslogion*; ET in: Charlesworth, *St. Anselm's* **Proslogion**
- Aquinas, Thomas, *Quaestiones disputatae de potentia Dei*
- Aquinas, Thomas, *Summa contra Gentiles*
- Aquinas, Thomas, *Summa Theologiae*; ET in: Thomas Gilby (ed.), *St. Thomas Aquinas: Summa Theologiae* (Blackfriars edition), London 1964-1981
- d'Arcy, C.F., "The Theory of a Limited Deity," *Proceedings of the Aristotelian Society* 18 (1917-18), 158-184
- Arendt, Hannah, *On Violence*, London 1970
- Aristeas, *Ad Philocratem Epistula* (SC 89)
- Arminius, J., *Apologia*, in: id., *Opera Theologica*, Leiden 1629, 134-183; ET in: Nichols,

James & Nichols, William (eds.), *The Works of James Arminius: The London Edition*, repr. C. Bangs (ed.), 2 vols., Kansas City 1986[2]
- Asmussen, H., *Über die Macht*, Stuttgart 1960
- Athanasius, *Epistula ad Serapionem* (PG 26)
- Athanasius, *Orationes contra Arianos* (PG 26)
- Augustine of Hippo, *Confessiones* (CSEL 33)
- Augustine of Hippo, *Contra Faustum* (CSEL 25)
- Augustine of Hippo, *De fide et symbolo* (CSEL 41); ET in: Meijering, *Augustine*
- Augustine of Hippo, *De Genesi ad litteram* (CSEL 28)
- Augustine of Hippo, *De Trinitate* (CCL 50)
- Augustine of Hippo, *Enchiridion* (CCL 46)
- Augustine of Hippo, *Sermones* (PL 38; CCL 46)
- Augustine of Hippo, *Tractatus in Johannis Evangelium* (CCL 36)
- Austin, John L., "Performative Utterances," in: id., *Philosophical Papers*, eds. J.O. Urmson & G.J. Warnock, Oxford 1970[2] (1961), 232-252
- Avis, Paul, *The Methods of Modern Theology: The Dream of Reason*, Basingstoke 1986
- Bach, U., "Schüttet das Kind nicht mit dem Bade aus! Zur Notwendigkeit der Rede von der 'Allmacht Gottes'," *Evangelische Kommentare* 24 (1991), 289-292
- Bakker, F.L., *De verhouding tusschen de almacht Gods en de zedelijke verantwoordelijkheid van den mensch in den Islam*, Amsterdam 1922
- Bannach, K., *Die Lehre von der doppelten Macht Gottes bei Wilhelm von Ockham*, Wiesbaden 1975
- Barnes, Barry, "On Authority and its Relationship to Power," in: J. Law (ed.), *Power, Action and Belief: A New Sociology of Knowledge?*, London 1986, 180-195
- Barnes, Barry, *The Nature of Power*, Oxford 1988
- Barth, Karl, *Dogmatics in Outline*, London 1949
- Barth, Karl, *Church Dogmatics* II.1, eds. G.W. Bromiley & T.F. Torrance, Edinburgh 1957
- Barth, Karl, *Anselm: Fides Quaerens Intellectum*, London 1960
- Basinger, David, "Human Freedom and Divine Providence: Some New Thoughts on an Old Problem," *Religious Studies* 15 (1979), 491-510
- Basinger, David, "Christian Theism and the Free Will Defence," *Sophia* 19.2 (1980), 20-33
- Basinger, David, *Divine Power in Process Theism: A Philosophic Critique*, Albany 1988
- Basinger, David & Basinger, Randall, "In the Image of Man Create They God: A Challenge," *Scottish Journal of Theology* 34 (1981), 97-107
- Basinger, David & Basinger, Randall (eds.), *Predestination & Free Will: Four Views of Divine Sovereignty and Human Freedom*, Downers Grove 1986
- Bavinck, H., *Gereformeerde Dogmatiek* Vol.II, Kampen 1928[4] (1897)
- Bavinck, H., *The Doctrine of God*, Edinburgh 1977[2]
- Bayles, M.D., "The Function and Limits of Political Authority," in: R. Baine Harris (ed.), *Authority: A Philosophical Analysis*, Alabama 1976, 101-111
- Beek, A. van de, *Why? On Suffering, Guilt, and God*, Grand Rapids 1990
- Beek, A. van de, *Rechtvaardiger dan God: Gedachten bij het boek Job*, Nijkerk 1992
- Beerling, R.F., *Niet te geloven: Wijsgerig schaatsen op godgeleerd ijs*, Deventer 1979
- Bellarmine, Robert, *De gratia et liberum arbitrium*, in: id., *Disputationes de controversiis christianae fidei adversus huius temporis haereticos* IV, repr. Paris 1608
- Benn, S.I., "Power," in: P. Edwards (ed.), *Encyclopedia of Philosophy*, New York 1967, Vol.6, 424-427
- Berger, P.L., *The Social Reality of Religion*, London 1969
- Berger, P.L., *The Heretical Imperative: Contemporary Possibilities of Religious Affirmation*, Garden City (N.Y.) 1979
- Berkhof, Hendrikus, *Christian Faith: An Introduction to the Study of the Faith*, Grand Rapids

1986² (1979)
- Berkouwer, G.C., *The Providence of God*, Grand Rapids 1974² (1952)
- Bernstein, Richard J., "Introduction," in id., *Philosophical Profiles: Essays in a Pragmatic Mode*, Cambridge 1986, 1-20
- Bernstein, Richard J., *Beyond Objectivism and Relativism: Science, Hermeneutics, and Praxis*, Philadelphia 1983
- Berofsky, Bernard, *Freedom from Necessity: The Metaphysical Basis of Responsibility*, London 1987
- Bertocci, Peter A., *Introduction to the Philosophy of Religion*, New York 1951
- Beukel, A. van den, *More Between Heaven and Earth*, London 1992
- Beyssade, J.-M., *La philosophie première de Descartes: Le temps et la cohérence de la métaphysique*, Paris 1979
- Beyssade, J.-M., "Création des vérités éternelles et doute métaphysique," in: *Studia Cartesiana* 2 (1981), 86-105
- Biard, Pierre, *La Puissance de Dieu*, Paris 1960
- Blaakmeer, F. et al. (eds.), *Philosophy of Religion: A Select Bibliography 1974-1986*, Groningen 1988
- Blumenberg, H., *Die kopernikanische Wende*, Frankfurt 1965
- Blumenfeld, D., "On the Compossibility of the Divine Attributes," *Philosophical Studies* 34 (1978), 91-103, reprinted in: Morris (ed.), *Concept*, 201-215
- Bocheński, J.M., *Was ist Autorität? Einführung in der Logik der Autorität*, Freiburg i.Br. 1974
- Bochenski, J.M., "An Analysis of Authority," in: F.J. Adelmann, *Authority* (Boston College Studies in Philosophy III), The Hague 1974, 56-85
- Boer, Theo de, *De God van de filosofen en de God van Pascal: Op het grensgebied van filosofie en theologie*, 's Gravenhage 1989
- Bonhoeffer, Dietrich, *Letters and Papers from Prison*, London 1970¹² (1953)
- Bonifacio, A.F., "On Capacity Limiting Statements," *Mind* 74 (1965), 87-88
- Borowitz, E., *The Masks Jews Wear*, New York 1973
- Bos, A.P., "World-Views in Collision," in: D.T. Runia (ed.), *Plotinus amid Gnostics and Christians*, Amsterdam 1984, 11-28
- Bouveresse, J., "La théorie du possible chez Descartes," *Review Internationale de Philosophie* 37 (1983), 293-310
- Braaten, Carl E. & Clayton, Philip (eds.), *The Theology of Wolfhart Pannenberg: Twelve American Critiques, with an Autobiographical Essay and Response*, Minneapolis 1988
- Bréhier, E., "The Creation of the Eternal Truths in Descartes's System," in: W. Doney (ed.), *Descartes: A Collection of Critical Essays*, London 1968, 192-208
- Brightman, E.S., *A Philosophy of Religion*, New York 1946³ (1940)
- Brink, G. van den, "Over de (on)mogelijkheid van een theodicee," *Theologia Reformata* 32 (1989), 194-210
- Brink, G. van den, "Theodicee en Triniteit," *Theologia Reformata* 33 (1990), 7-27
- Brink, G. van den, "De absolute en geordineerde macht van God. Opmerkingen bij de ontwikkeling van een onderscheid," *Nederlands Theologisch Tijdschrift* 45 (1991), 204-222
- Brink, G. van den, "Natural Evil and Eschatology," in: Van den Brink et al. (eds.), *Christian Faith*, 39-55
- Brink, G. van den, "Almacht bij Anselmus en Abraham: Bijdrage tot het debat over de God van de filosofen versus de God van de Bijbel," *Kerk en Theologie* 43 (1992), 205-225
- Brink, G. van den, "Allmacht und Omnipotenz: Einige Bemerkungen über ihr gegenseitiges Verhältnis im Rahmen der christlichen Gotteslehre," *Kerugma und Dogma* 38 (1992), 260-279
- Brink, G. van den, "Lesslie Newbigin als postmodern apologeet," *Nederlands Theologisch Tijdschrift* 46 (1992), 302-319
- Brink, G. van den, "Descartes, Modalities, and God," *International Journal for Philosophy of Religion* 33 (1993), 1-15

- Brink, Gijsbert van den, Brom, Luco J. van den, Sarot, Marcel (eds.), *Christian Faith and Philosophical Theology: Essays in Honour of Vincent Brümmer*, Kampen 1992
- Brinkman, M.E., *Het Gods- en mensbegrip in de theologie van Wolfhart Pannenberg: Een schets van de ontwikkeling van zijn theologie vanaf 1953 tot 1979*, Kampen 1980² (1979)
- Brinton, Alan, "Omnipotence, Timelessness, and the Restoration of the Virgins," *Dialogos* 45 (1985), 149-156
- Broek, R. van den, "The Theology of the Teachings of Silvanus," *Vigiliae Christianae* 40 (1986), 1-23
- Brom, L.J. van den, *God Alomtegenwoordig*, Kampen 1982
- Brom, L.J. van den, "Hermeneutics as a Feedback System for Systematic Theology," in: *Proceedings of the Seventh European Conference on Philosophy of Religion*, Utrecht 1988, 178-182
- Brom, L.J. van den, "Gottes Welthandeln und die Schachmetapher," *Glaube und Denken* 3 (1990), 125-151
- Brom, L.J. van den, *Creatieve twijfel: Een studie in de wijsgerige theologie*, Kampen 1991
- Brom, L.J. van den, "En is Hij niet een God voor filosofen? God, filosofie en almacht," in: H.M. Vroom (ed.), *De God van de filosofen en de God van de Bijbel: Het christelijk Godsbeeld in discussie*, Zoetermeer 1991, 99-113
- Brown, Colin, *Christianity and Western Thought: A History of Philosophers, Ideas & Movements*, Vol.I, Leicester 1990
- Brown, David, "The Problem of Pain," in: Robert Morgan (ed.), *The Religion of the Incarnation: Anglican Essays in Commemoration of LUX MUNDI*, Bristol 1989, 46-59
- Brown, David, "Why a World at All?," forthcoming in *Nederlands Theologisch Tijdschrift*
- Brown, Robert F., "God's Ability to Will Moral Evil," *Faith and Philosophy* 8 (1991), 3-20
- Brümmer, Vincent, *Theology and Philosophical Inquiry*, London 1981
- Brümmer, Vincent, "Divine Impeccability," *Religious Studies* 20 (1984), 203-214
- Brümmer, Vincent, *What are We Doing When We Pray? A Philosophical Inquiry*, London 1985
- Brümmer, Vincent, *Wijsgerige Begripsanalyse: Een inleiding voor theologen en andere belangstellenden*, Kampen 1989³ (1975)
- Brümmer, Vincent, "Metaphorical Thinking and Systematic Theology", *Nederlands Theologisch Tijdschrift* 43 (1989), 213-228
- Brümmer, Vincent, "A Dialogue of Language Games," in: id., (ed.), *Interpreting the Universe as Creation: A Dialogue of Science and Religion*, Kampen 1991, 1-17
- Brümmer, Vincent, *Speaking of a Personal God: An Essay in Philosophical Theology*, Cambridge 1992.
- Brümmer, Vincent, "Theology and Philosophical Inquiry," unpublished paper presented at the "Symposion on the Nature and Rationality of (Philosophical) Theology," Utrecht 9 September 1992
- Brunner, Emil, *The Christian Doctrine of God*, London 1949
- Brunschvicq, L. (ed.), *Blaise Pascal: Pensées et opuscules*, Paris 1951
- Büchner, Georg, "Dantons Tod: Ein Drama," in: Georg Büchner, *Werke und Briefe*, München 1965
- Buckley, Michael J., *At the Origins of Modern Atheism*, Yale 1987
- Bultmann, Rudolf, "Grace and Freedom," in: id., *Essays Philosophical and Theological*, London 1955, 168-181
- Bultmann, Rudolf, "Welchen Sinn hat es von Gott zu reden?," in: id., *Glauben und Verstehen: Gesammelte Aufsätze* I, Tübingen 1954² (1933), 26-37
- Burkle, Howard R., *God, Suffering & Belief*, Nashville 1977
- Burrell, David B., "Theology and the Linguistic Turn," *Communio* 6 (1979), 95-112
- Burrell, David B., "Religious Belief and Rationality," in: Delaney (ed.), *Rationality*, 84-115
- Buskes, J.J., *God en het lijden*, repr. Kampen n.d. (Den Haag 1948¹)

- Calvin, John, *Institutes of the Christian Religion*, 2 Volumes, ed. John T. McNeill, Philadelphia 1960
- Calvin, John, *De aeterna Dei praedestinatione* (1552), in: *CO* 8, 248-366
- Campbell, Richard, *From Belief to Understanding: A Study of Anselm's Proslogion Argument on the Existence of God*, Canberra 1976
- Cantin, A. (ed.), *Pierre Damien: Lettre sur la toute-puissance divine* (SC 191), Paris 1972
- Capizzi, C., *Pantokrator: Saggio d'esegesi letterario-iconografica*, Roma 1964
- Cargile, James, "On Omnipotence," *Noûs* 1 (1967), 201-205
- Carson, D.A., *Divine Sovereignty and Human Responsibility: Biblical Perspectives in Tension*, London 1981
- Carter, W.R., "Omnipotence and Sin," *Analysis* 42 (1982), 102-105
- Carter, W.R., "Impeccability Revisited," *Analysis* 45 (1985), 52-55
- Case-Winters, Anna, *God's Power: Traditional Understandings and Contemporary Challenges*, Louisville 1990
- Charlesworth, M.J., *St. Anselm's Proslogion with a Reply on Behalf of the Fool and the Author's Reply to Gaunilo*, Oxford 1965
- Chisholm, R.M., *Person and Object: A Metaphysical Study*, London 1976
- Chrzan, Keith, "When is Gratuitous Evil Really Gratuitous?," *Sophia* 30.2/3 (1991), 23-29
- Clairvaux, Bernard of, *De Gratia et Libero Arbitrio*; ET: Daniel O'Donovan (ed.), *On Grace & Free Choice*, Kalamazoo 1988
- Clegg, S.R., *Power, Rule and Domination: A Critical and Empirical Understanding of Power in Sociological Theory and Organizational Life*, London 1975
- Clegg, S.R., *Frameworks of Power*, London 1989
- Clement of Alexandria, *Stromateis* (GCS 15)
- Clouser, Roy, "Religious Language: A New Look at an Old Problem," in: H. Hart et al. (eds.), *Rationality in the Calvinian Tradition*, Lanham 1983, 385-407
- Cobb, J.B. & Griffin, D.R., *Process Theology: An Introductory Exposition*, Philadelphia 1976
- Cook, E.D., "Weak Church - Weak God," in: Nigel M. de S. Cameron (ed.), *The Power and Weakness of God: Impassibility and Orthodoxy*, Edinburgh 1990, 69-92
- Copleston, F., *A History of Philosophy* Vol.II, London 1964[3] (1950)
- Cottingham, John (ed.), *Descartes' Conversation with Burman*, Oxford 1976
- Courtenay, W.J., *Covenant and Causality in Medieval Thought: Studies in Philosophy, Theology and Economic Practice*, London 1984
- Courtenay, W.J., "The Dialectic of Divine Omnipotence in the High and Late Middle Ages," in: T. Rudavsky (ed.), *Divine Omniscience and Omnipotence in Medieval Philosophy*, Dordrecht 1985, 243-269
- Cowan, J.L., "The Paradox of Omnipotence," *Analysis*, Supplement to Vol.25 (1964/1965), 102-108, reprinted in: Urban & Walton (eds.), *Power*, 144-152
- Cowan, J.L., "The Paradox of Omnipotence Revisited," *Canadian Journal of Philosophy* 3 (1974), 435-445
- Craig, W.L., *Divine Foreknowledge and Human Freedom: The Coherence of Theism. Omniscience*, Leiden 1991
- Cremer, H., *Die christliche Lehre von den Eigenschaften Gottes*, 1917[2], repr. H. Burkhardt (ed.), Giessen 1983
- Croix. R.R. la, "The Incompatibility of Omnipotence and Omniscience," *Analysis* 33 (1972/1973), 176
- Croix, R.R. la, "Omnipotence, Omniscience and Necessity," *Analysis* 34 (1973/1974), 63-64
- Croix, R.R. la, "Swinburne on Omnipotence," *International Journal for Philosophy of Religion* 6 (1975), 251-255
- Croix, R.R. la, "The Impossibility of Defining 'Omnipotence'," *Philosophical Studies* 32 (1977), 181-190
- Croix, R.R. la, "Failing to Define Omnipotence," *Philosophical Studies* 34 (1978), 219-222

- Croix, R.R. la, "Descartes on God's Ability to Do the Logically Impossible," *Canadian Journal of Philosophy* 14 (1984), 455-475
- Curley, E.M., "Descartes on the Creation of the Eternal Truths," *Philosophical Review* 93 (1984), 569-597
- Cyril of Jerusalem, *Catecheses* (PG 33; ET: NPNF II,8)
- Dahl, R.A., "Power," *International Encyclopedia of the Social Sciences*, New York 1968, Vol.12, 405-415; reprinted as "Power as the Control of Behaviour," in: S. Lukes (ed.), *Power*, Oxford 1986, 37-58
- Dalferth, Ingolf U., *Existenz Gottes und christlicher Glaube: Skizzen zu einer eschatologischen Theologie*, München 1984
- Dalferth, Ingolf U., *Theology and Philosophy*, Oxford 1988
- Dalferth, Ingolf U., "Gott und Sünde," *Neue Zeitschrift für systematische Theologie und Religionsphilosophie* 33 (1991), 1-22
- Dalferth, Ingolf U., "Historical Roots of Theism," in: Dalferth et al., *Traditional Theism and its Modern Alternatives*, papers held at the 9th European Conference on Philosophy of Religion, Aarhus 1992, 20p. (unpublished)
- Damian, Peter, *De divina omnipotentia* (PL 145; SC 191)
- Davaney, Sheila G., *Divine Power. A Study of Karl Barth and Charles Hartshorne*, Philadelphia 1986
- Davidson, Donald, *Inquiries into Truth and Interpretation*, Oxford 1984
- Davies, Brian, *Thinking about God*, London 1985
- Davies, Paul C.W., *God and the New Physics*, London 1983
- Davies, Paul C.W., *The Mind of God: Science and the Search for Ultimate Meaning*, London 1992
- Davis, Stephen T., "Free Will and Evil," in: id. (ed.), *Encountering Evil: Live Options in Theodicy*, Edinburgh 1981, 69-99
- Davis, Stephen T., *Logic and the Nature of God*, London 1983
- Davison, Scott A., "Could Abstract Objects Depend upon God?," *Religious Studies* 27 (1991), 485-497
- Dekker, Eef, *Rijker dan Midas: Vrijheid, genade en predestinatie in de theologie van Jacobus Arminius (1559-1609)*, forthcoming 1993
- Delaney, C.F. (ed.), *Rationality and Religious Belief*, Notre Dame 1979
- Desharnais, R.P., *The History of the Distinction between God's Absolute and Ordained Power and its Influence on Martin Luther*, diss. Washington 1966 (unpublished)
- Devenish, Philip E., "Omnipotence, Creation, Perfection: Kenny and Aquinas on the Power and Action of God," *Modern Theology* 1 (1985), 105-117
- Dillenberger, J., *God Hidden and Revealed: The Interpretation of Luther's Deus absconditus and its Significance for Religious Thought*, Philadelphia 1953
- Dodd, C.H., *The Bible and the Greeks*, London 1954² (1935)
- Doney, W. (ed.), *Eternal Truths and the Cartesian Circle: A Collection of Studies*, New York 1987
- Doorn, J.A.A. van, "Sociology and the Problem of Power," *Sociologia Neerlandica* 1 (1963), 3-51
- Double, Richard, *The Non-Reality of Free Will*, Oxford 1991
- Driel, L. van, *Over het lijden en God: Tussen Kushner en Calvijn*, Kampen 1988
- Dummett, Michael, "On Bringing About the Past," *Philosophical Review* 73 (1964), 338-359
- Duns Scotus, J., *Ordinatio*, in: id., *Opera omnia* I-VII, Vatican City 1950-1973
- Duns Scotus, J., *Lectura*, in: id., *Opera omnia* XVI-XVIII, Vatican City 1960-1982
- Eichenseer, C., *Das Symbolum Apostolicum beim heiligen Augustinus mit Berücksichtigung des dogmengeschichtlichen Zusammenhangs*, St. Ottilien 1960
- Elders, L.J., & Tukker, C.A., *Thomas van Aquino: Zijn leven, leer en invloed*, Leiden 1992
- Englebretsen, George, "The Incompatibility of God's Existence and Omnipotence," *Sophia* 10.1

(1971), 28-31

- *Epistula ad Diognetum*; ET: Kirsopp Lake, *The Apostolic Fathers with an English Translation* (LCL) Vol. 2, London 1913, 348-379
- Evans, Donald D., *The Logic of Self-Involvement: A Philosophical Study of Everyday Language with Special Reference to the Christian Use of Language about God as Creator*, London 1963
- Evans, G.R., *Anselm*, London 1989
- Farley, B.W., *The Providence of God*, Grand Rapids 1988
- Farnell, Lewis R., *The Attributes of God*, Oxford 1925
- Feinberg, John, "God Ordains All Things," in: Basinger & Basinger (eds.), *Predestination*, 17-43
- Fiddes, Paul S., *The Creative Suffering of God*, Oxford 1988
- Fisher, Simon, *Revelatory Positivism? Barth's Earliest Theology and the Marburg School*, Oxford 1988
- Fisk, Samuel, *Divine Sovereignty and Human Freedom*, Neptune (N.J), 1973
- Fitch, Frederic B., "A Logical Analysis of Some Value Concepts," *Journal of Symbolic Logic* 2 (1963), 135-142
- Flew, A. "Divine Omnipotence and Human Freedom," in: A. Flew & A. MacIntyre (eds.), *New Essays in Philosophical Theology*, London 1955, 144-169
- Flew, Antony, *God and Philosophy*, London 1966
- Flew, Antony, "Compatibilism, Free Will and God," *Philosophy* 48 (1973), 231-244
- Flew, Antony, *A Dictionary of Philosophy*, London 1983² (1979)
- Flew, Antony, "Freedom and Human Nature," *Philosophy* 66 (1991), 53-63
- Flint, Thomas P. & Freddoso, Alfred J., "Maximal Power," in: Freddoso (ed.), *Existence*, 81-113, reprinted in: Morris (ed.), *Concept*, 134-167
- Flint, Thomas P., "Divine Sovereignty and the Free Will Defence," *Sophia* 23.2 (1984), 41-52
- Flint, Thomas P., Review of E.R. Wierenga, *Nature of God*, in: *Faith and Philosophy* 9 (1992), 392-398
- Forcellini, A., *Lexicon totius latinitatis*, repr. F. Corradini & J. Perin (eds.), Vol.3, Padoue 1940 (1771)
- Forsyth, P.T., *The Justification of God: Lectures for War-Time on a Christian Theodicy*, London 1916
- Foreman, K.J., *God's Will and Ours*, Richmond 1954
- Foucault, M., "The Subject and Power," in: H.L. Dreyfus & P. Rabinow, *Michel Foucault: Beyond Structuralism and Hermeneutics*, Chicago 1983² (1982), 208-226
- Francks, Richard, "Omniscience, Omnipotence and Pantheism," *Philosophy* 54 (1979), 395-399
- Frankfurt, Harry G., "The Logic of Omnipotence," *Philosophical Review* 73 (1964), 262-263, reprinted in: Urban & Walton (eds.), *Power*, 135-137
- Frankfurt, Harry G., "Alternate Possibilities and Moral Responsibility," *Journal of Philosophy* 66 (1969), 829-839, reprinted in: J.M. Fischer (ed.), *Moral Responsibility*, Ithaca 1986, 143-152
- Frankfurt, Harry G., "Descartes and the Creation of the Eternal Truths," *Philosophical Review* 86 (1977), 36-57
- Frankfurt, Harry G., "Descartes on the Consistency of Reason," in: M. Hooker (ed.), *Descartes: Critical and Interpretive Essays*, Baltimore 1978, 26-39
- Freddoso, A.J., "Accidental Necessity and Power over the Past," *Pacific Philosophical Quarterly* 63 (1982), 54-68
- Freddoso, A.J. (ed.), *The Existence & Nature of God*, Notre Dame 1983
- Friedman, Richard B., "On the Concept of Authority in Political Philosophy," in: Richard E. Flathman (ed.), *Concepts in Social & Political Philosophy*, New York 1973, 121-145
- Funkenstein, Amos, "Descartes, Eternal Truths, and the Divine Omnipotence," *Studies in the History and Philosophy of Science* 6 (1975), 185-199

- Funkenstein, Amos, *Theology and the Scientific Imagination from the Middle Ages to the Seventeenth Century*, Princeton 1986
- Gadamer, H.G., *Philosophical Hermeneutics*, ed. David E. Linge, Berkeley 1977
- Gale, Robert M., "Freedom and the Free Will Defense," *Social Theory and Practice* 16 (1990), 397-423
- Gale, Robert M., *On the Nature and Existence of God*, Cambridge 1991
- Gallie, W.B., "Essentially Contested Concepts," *Proceedings of the Aristotelian Society* 56 (1955-56), 167-198
- Garcia, Laura L., "The Essential Moral Perfection of God," *Religious Studies* 23 (1987), 137-144
- Geach, Peter T., "Omnipotence," *Philosophy* 43 (1973), 7-20; reprinted in: id., *Providence and Evil*, 3-28
- Geach, Peter T., "Can God Fail to Keep Promises?," *Philosophy* 52 (1977), 93-95
- Geach, Peter T., *Providence and Evil*, Cambridge 1977
- Gelber, H.G., review of M.M. Adams, *William Ockham*, in: *Faith and Philosophy* 7 (1990), 246-252
- Gellman, Jerome, "The Paradox of Omnipotence, and Perfection," *Sophia* 14.3 (1975), 31-39
- Gellman, Jerome, "Omnipotence and Impeccability," *New Scholasticism* 51 (1977), 21-37
- Gellman, Jerome, "The Limits of Maximal Power," *Philosophical Studies* 55 (1989), 329-336
- Genderen, J. van & Velema, W.H., *Beknopte gereformeerde dogmatiek*, Kampen 1992
- Gendin, S., "Omnidoing," *Sophia* 6.3 (1967), 17-22
- Genest, J.-F., "Le *De Futuris contigentibus* de Thomas Bradwardine," *Recherches Augustiniennes* 14 (1979), 249-336
- Genest, J.-F., "Pierre de Ceffons et l'hypothèse du Dieu trompeur," in: Z. Kaluza & P. Vignaux (eds.), *Preuve et raisons à l'Université de Paris*, Paris 1984, 197-214
- Gennep, F.O. van, *De terugkeer van de verloren Vader: Een theologisch essay over vaderschap en macht in cultuur en christendom*, Baarn 1990³ (1989)
- Gibbs, B., "Can God Do Evil?," *Philosophy* 50 (1979), 466-469
- Gibson, Q.,"Power," *Philosophy of the Social Sciences* 1 (1971), 101-112
- Glymour, Clark N., *Theory and Evidence*, Princeton 1980
- Godbey, John W., "On the Incompatibility of Omnipotence and Omniscience," *Analysis* 34 (1973/1974), 62
- Goldstick, D., "Could God Make a Contradiction True?," *Religious Studies* 26 (1990), 377-387
- Gooch, P.W., "Sovereignty and Freedom: Some Pauline Compatibilisms," *Scottish Journal of Theology* 40 (1987), 531-542
- Gordon, C. (ed.), *Power/Knowledge: Selected Interviews and Other Writings by Michel Foucault, 1972-1977*, New York 1980
- Graafland, C., *Van Calvijn tot Barth: Oorsprong en ontwikkeling van de leer der verkiezing in het Gereformeerd Protestantisme*, 's Gravenhage 1987
- Grant, E., "The Condemnation of 1277, God's Power and Physical Thought in the Late Middle Ages," *Viator* 10 (1979), 210-244
- Grant, Robert M., *Miracle and Natural Law in Graeco-Roman and Early Christian Thought*, Amsterdam 1952
- Grant, Robert M., *Gods and the One God*, Philadelphia 1986
- Gregory of Nyssa, *Contra Eunomium*, in: W. Jaeger (ed.), *Gregorii Nysseni Opera* II, Leiden 1960
- Gregory, T., "La tromperie divine," in: Z. Kaluza & P. Vignaux (eds.), *Preuve et raisons à l'Université de Paris*, Paris 1984, 187-195
- Griffin, David Ray, "Actuality, Possibility, and Theodicy," *Process Studies* 12 (1982), 168-179
- Griffin, David Ray, *Evil Revisited: Responses and Reconsiderations*, Albany 1991
- Griffin, David Ray, *God, Power, and Evil: A Process Theodicy*, Lanham 1991² (1976)
- Groot, Joh. de & Hulst, A.R., *Macht en wil*, Nijkerk n.d.

- Grundmann, Walter, *Der Begriff der Kraft im neutestamentlichen Gedankenwelt*, Stuttgart 1932
- Grundmann, Walter, "dynamai ktl.," in: G. Kittel (ed.), *Theological Dictionary to the New Testament* Vol.2, ET edited by G.W. Bromiley, Grand Rapids 1964, 284-317
- Gueroult, M., *Descartes selon l'ordre des raisons*, Vol.2, Paris 1953
- Gunton, Colin, *Becoming and Being: The Doctrine of God in Charles Hartshorne and Karl Barth*, Oxford 1978
- Gunton, Colin, *The Promise of Trinitarian Theology*, Edinburgh 1991
- Gutting, Gary, *Religious Belief and Religious Skepticism*, Notre Dame 1982
- Härle, Wilfried, "Werk Gottes - Werk des Menschen," *Nederlands Theologisch Tijdschrift* 34 (1980), 213-224
- Härle, Wilfried, "Lehre und Lehrbeanstandung," *Zeitschrift für evangelisches Kirchenrecht* 30 (1985), 283-317
- Härle, Wilfried, "Leiden als Fels des Atheismus?," in: W. Härle et al. (eds.), *Unsere Welt - Gottes Schöpfung*, Marburg 1992, 127-143
- Hahn, A. & Hahn, G.L. (eds.), *Bibliothek der Symbole und Glaubensregeln der alten Kirche*, Breslau 1897³ (1877), repr. Hildesheim 1962
- Haldane, E.S., & Ross, G.R.T., *The Philosophical Works of Descartes*, 2 vols. repr. vol.1 Cambridge 1973, vol.2 New York 1955 (1911)
- Halleux, André de, "'Dieu le Père tout-puissant'," *Revue Théologique de Louvain* 8 (1977), 401-422; reprinted in: id., *Patrologie et oecuménisme: Recueil d'Études*, Louvain 1990, 68-89
- Hamm, B., *Promissio, Pactum, Ordinatio: Freiheit und Selbstbindung Gottes in der scholastischen Gnadenlehre*, Tübingen 1977
- Hardy, Daniel W. & Ford, David F., *Jubilate: Theology in Praise*, London 1984
- Harré, R. & Madden, E.H., *Causal Powers: A Theory of Natural Necessity*, Oxford 1975
- Harrison, Jonathan, "Geach on God's Alleged Ability to do Evil," *Philosophy* 51 (1976), 208-215
- Harrison, Jonathan, "Geach on Harrison on Geach on God," *Philosophy* 52 (1977), 223-226
- Harrison Wagner, R., "The Concept of Power and the Study of Politics," in: R. Bell et al. (eds.), *Political Power: A Reader in Theory and Research*, New York 1969, 3-12
- Hart, Hendrik, "On the Distinction between Creator and Creature," *Philosophia Reformata* 44 (1979), 183-193
- Hartshorne, Charles, *Man's Vision of God and the Logic of Theism*, Hamden (Conn.) 1964² (1941)
- Hartshorne, Charles, "Omnipotence," in: Vergilius Ferm (ed.), *An Encyclopedia of Religion*, New York 1945, 545-546
- Hartshorne, Charles, *The Divine Relativity: A Social Conception of God*, New Haven 1948
- Hartshorne, Charles, *Omnipotence and Other Theological Mistakes*, Albany 1984
- Hasker, W., *God, Time and Knowledge*, Ithaca 1989
- Hasker, W., "The Necessity of Gratuitous Evil," *Faith and Philosophy* 9 (1992), 23-44
- Hebblethwaite, Brian, "God and Truth," Presidential Address at the Conference of the Society for the Study of Theology, Oxford, April 1989.
- Heering, H.J., "God de almachtige," in: H.J. Heering et al. (eds.), *Dogmatische verkenningen*, Den Haag 1968, 74-84
- Heering, H.J., "Schepping en almacht," *Wending* 17 (1962), 328-339
- Heidegger, J.H., *Corpus Theologiae* III, Zürich 1700
- Helm, Paul, "God and the Approval of Sin," *Religious Studies* 20 (1984), 215-222
- Helm, Paul, *Eternal God: A Study of God Without Time*, Oxford 1988
- Helm, Paul, "The Power and Weakness of God," unpublished paper
- Henderson, Edward, "A Critique of Religious Reductionism," *Philosophical Research Archives* 8 (1983), 429-456
- Henle, Paul, *Language, Thought and Culture*, Ann Arbor 1966
- Heppe, Heinrich, *Reformed Dogmatics Set Out and Illustrated from the Sources* (ed. E. Bizer),

repr. Grand Rapids 1978
- Hertog, G.C. den, *Bevrijdende kennis: De 'leer van de onvrije wil' in de theologie van Hans Joachim Iwand*, Den Haag 1989
- Hesselink, I. John, "The Providence and Power of God," *Reformed Journal* 41 (1988), 97-115
- Hick, John, *Faith and Knowledge*, Ithaca 1966² (1957)
- Hick, John, *Evil and the God of Love*, London 1977² (1966)
- Hick, John, *An Interpretation of Religion*, London 1989
- Hick, John, *Philosophy of Religion*, Englewood Cliffs (N.J.) 1990⁴ (1963)
- Hintikka, J., "Gaps in the Great Chain of Being: An Exercise in the Methodology of the History of Ideas," in: Knuuttila, *Reforging*, 1-17
- Hoffman, Joshua, "Can God Do Evil?," *Southern Journal of Philosophy* 17 (1979), 213-220
- Hoffman, Joshua, "Mavrodes on Defining Omnipotence," *Philosophical Studies* 35 (1979), 311-313
- Hoitenga, Dewey, "Logic and the Problem of Evil," *American Philosophical Quarterly* 4 (1967), 114-126; reprinted in: K. Yandell (ed.), *God, Man, and Religion: Readings in the Philosophy of Religion*, New York 1973, 334-351.
- Holcot, Robert, *In Secundum Sententiarum*, Lyon 1518
- Holland, D.L., "Pantokrator in New Testament and Creed," in: E.A. Livingstone (ed.), *Studia Evangelica* Vol.VI, Berlin 1973, 256-266
- Hommel, Hildebrecht, "Pantokrator," in: Harald Kruska (ed.), *Theologia Viatorum: Jahrbuch der kirchlichen Hochschule Berlin* Vol.V, Berlin 1954, 322-378
- Hommel, Hildebrecht, *Schöpfer und Erhalter*, Berlin 1956
- Hospers, John, *An Introduction to Philosophical Analysis*, London 1967² (1953)
- Howard-Snyder, Daniel, "Seeing through CORNEA," *International Journal for Philosophy of Religion* 32 (1992), 25-49
- Hubbeling, H.G., *Principles of the Philosophy of Religion*, Assen 1987
- Hudson, A, & Wilks, M. (eds.), *From Ockham to Wyclif*, Oxford 1987
- Humber, James M., "Response to Gale," *Social Theory and Practice* 16 (1990), 425-433
- Huyssteen, W. van, *Theology & the Justification of Faith: Constructing Theories in Systematic Theology*, Grand Rapids 1989
- Hygen, J.B., *Guds allmakt og det ondes problem*, Oslo 1973
- Immink, F.G., *Divine Simplicity*, Kampen 1987
- Immink, F.G., "Theism and Christian Worship," in: Van den Brink et al. (eds.), *Christian Faith*, 116-136
- Inwagen, Peter van, *An Essay on Free Will*, Oxford 1983
- Ishiguro, Hide, "The Status of Necessity and Impossibility in Descartes," in: Amélie Oksenberg Rorty (ed.), *Essays on Descartes' Meditations*, Berkeley 1986, 459-471
- Jammer, Max, *Concepts of Force: A Study in the Foundations of Dynamics*, New York 1957
- Janßen, H.G., *Gott-Freiheit-Leid: Das Theodizeeproblem in der Philosophie der Neuzeit*, Darmstadt 1989
- Jantzen, Grace M., *God's World, God's Body*, London 1984
- Jantzen, Grace M., "Could There be a Mystical Core of Religion?," *Religious Studies* 26 (1990), 59-72
- Jenkins, David E., *God, Miracle and the Church of England*, London 1987
- Jenson, Robert W., *America's Theologian: A Recommendation of Jonathan Edwards*, New York 1988
- Jerome, *Epistulae* (CSEL 54; ET: F.A. Wright, *Select Letters of St. Jerome*, London 1963)
- Jonas, Hans, "The Concept of God after Auschwitz: A Jewish Voice," *Journal of Religion* 67 (1987), 1-13
- Jonkers, Peter, "God en macht," in: F. Vosman (ed.), *God en de obsessies van de twintigste eeuw*, Hilversum 1990, 9-28
- Joyce, G.H., *Principles of Natural Theology*, London 1923

- Jüngel, Eberhard, "Gottes ursprüngliches Anfangen als schöpferische Selbstbegrenzung: Ein Beitrag zur Gespräch mit Hans Jonas über den 'Gottesbegriff nach Auschwitz'," in: id., *Wertlose Wahrheit: Zur Identität und Relevanz des christlichen Glaubens* (Theologische Erörterungen Vol.3), München 1990, 151-162
- Kahn, A.H. (ed.), Papers from the Canadian Symposium on the Relationship of the Philosophy of Religion to Theological Studies, *Toronto Journal of Theology* 5 (1989), 3-56
- Kasper, Walter, "Zustimmung zum Denken: Von der Unerlässlichkeit der Metaphysik für die Sache der Theologie," *Theologische Quartalschrift* 169 (1989), 257-271.
- Kattenbusch, F., *Das Apostolische Symbol: Seine Entstehung, sein geschichtlichen Sinn, seine ursprungliche Stellung im Kultus und in der Theologie der Kirche. Ein Beitrag zur Symbolik und Dogmengeschichte* I, Leipzig 1894, repr. Hildesheim 1962
- Katz, S.T., "Language, Epistemology and Mysticism," in: id. (ed.), *Mysticism and Philosophical Analysis*, London 1978, 22-71
- Kaufman, Gordon D., *An Essay on Theological Method*, Missoula 1979[2] (1975)
- Keene, G.B., "A Simpler Solution to the Paradox of Omnipotence," *Mind* 69 (1960), 74-75
- Keene, G.B., "Capacity Limiting Statements," *Mind* 70 (1961), 251-252
- Keene, G.B., "Omnipotence and Logical Omniscience," *Philosophy* 62 (1987), 527-528
- Kelly, J.N.D., *Early Christian Creeds*, London 1972[3] (1950)
- Kelsey, David, *The Uses of Scripture in Recent Theology*, Philadelphia 1975
- Kennedy, L.A., *Peter of Ailly and the Harvest of Fourteenth-Century Philosophy*, Queenston 1986
- Kennedy, L.A., "The Fifteenth Century and Divine Absolute Power," *Vivarium* 27 (1989), 125-152
- Kenny, Anthony, "The Cartesian Circle and the Eternal Truths," *Journal of Philosophy* 67 (1970), 685-700
- Kenny, Anthony (ed.), *Descartes: Philosophical Letters*, Oxford 1970
- Kenny, Anthony, *The God of the Philosophers*, Oxford 1979
- Kenny, Anthony, *What is Faith? Essays in the Philosophy of Religion*, Oxford 1992
- Kerr, Fergus, *Theology after Wittgenstein*, Oxford 1986
- Khamara, E.J., "In Defence of Omnipotence," *Philosophical Quarterly* 28 (1978), 215-228
- Kierkegaard, S., *Papirer* VII; ET: H.V. Hong & E.H. Hong (eds.), *Søren Kierkegaard's Journals and Papers*, Vol.2, London 1970
- Klapwijk, Jacob, "John Calvin (1509-1564)," in: J. Klapwijk, S. Griffioen & G. Groenewoud (eds.), *Bringing into Captivity every Thought: Capita Selecta in the History of Christian Evaluations of Non-Christian Philosophy*, Lanham 1991, 123-142
- Knuuttila, Simo, "Time and Modality in Scholasticism," in: id. (ed.), *Reforging*, 163-257
- Knuuttila, Simo (ed.), *Reforging the Great Chain of Being: Studies of the History of Modal Theories*, Dordrecht 1981
- Koningsveld, Herman, *Het verschijnsel wetenschap: Een inleiding tot de wetenschapsfilosofie*, Meppel 1980[5] (1976)
- Koyré, A., *Essai sur l'idée de Dieu et les preuves de son existence chez Descartes*, Paris 1922
- Kripke, Saul A., *Naming and Necessity*, Oxford 1980[2] (1972)
- Kuhn, Thomas S., *The Structure of Scientific Revolutions*, Chicago 1970[2] (1962)
- Kuitert, H.M., *Wat heet geloven? Structuur en herkomst van de christelijke geloofsuitspraken*, Baarn 1977
- Kuitert, H.M., "Het geloven waard: Een intellectuele verantwoording van het geloof in de christelijke traditie," in: Maurice & Noorda (eds.), *Onzekere zekerheid*, 99-125
- Kuitert, H.M., *Het algemeen betwijfeld christelijk geloof: Een herziening*, Baarn 1992
- Küng, Hans, *Christ sein*, München 1974
- Kuntz, Paul G., "The Sense and Nonsense of Omnipotence," *Religious Studies* 3 (1967), 525-538
- Kuntz, Paul G., "Omnipotence: Tradition and Revolt in Philosophical Theology," *New Scholas-*

ticism 42 (1968), 270-279
- Kunze, J., *Glaubensregel, Heilige Schrift und Taufbekenntnis*, Leipzig 1899
- Kushner, Harold, *When Bad Things Happen to Good People*, New York 1981
- Lackey, D., "The Epistemology of Omnipotence," *Religious Studies* 15 (1979), 25-30
- Lake, Kirsopp, *The Apostolic Fathers with an English Translation* (LCL), vol.1, repr. London 1975 (1914)
- Leeuw, G. van der, *Religion in Essence and Manifestation*, repr. Princeton (N.J.) 1986 (1938)
- Leff, Gordon, *Medieval Thought from Augustine to Ockham*, St. Albans 1958
- Leff, Gordon, *William of Ockham*, Manchester 1975
- Leftow, Brian, "God and Abstract Entities," *Faith and Philosophy* 7 (1990), 193-217
- Leumann, M. (ed.), *Lateinische Laut- und Formenlehre*, 1928⁵, repr. München 1963
- Lewis, C.S., *The Problem of Pain*, London 1946¹⁷ (1940)
- Lewis, C.S., *Miracles: A Preliminary Study*, New York 1960² (1947)
- Lewis, David, "The Paradox of Time Travel," *American Philosophical Quarterly* 13 (1976), 145-152
- Lindbeck, George A., *The Nature of Doctrine: Religion and Theology in a Postliberal Age*, Philadelphia 1984
- Loonstra, B., *Verkiezing - verzoening - verbond: Beschrijving en beoordeling van de leer van het pactum salutis in de gereformeerde theologie*, 's Gravenhage 1990
- Loughlin, Gerard, "Making a Better World," *Modern Theology* 8 (1992), 297-303
- Louw, D.J., "Omnipotence (Force) or Vulnerability (Defencelessness)?" *Scriptura* 28 (1989), 41-58
- Lovejoy, Arthur O., *The Great Chain of Being: A Study of the History of an Idea*, New York 1960
- Lucas, J.R., *The Freedom of the Will*, Oxford 1970
- Lucas, J.R., *Freedom and Grace*, London 1976
- Ludolphy, I., "Zu einer fraglichen Verwendung des Begriffes 'potentia absoluta' bei Luther," in: M. Hager et al., *Ruf und Antwort*, Leipzig n.d., 540-543
- Lukes, S., *Power: A Radical View*, London 1974
- Lukes, S., "Power and Authority," in: T. Bottomore & R. Nisbet (eds.), *A History of Sociological Analysis*, London 1978, 633-676
- Luscombe, D.E., *The School of Peter Abelard: The Influence of Abelard's Thought in the Early Scholastic Period*, Cambridge 1970
- Luther, Martin, *De Servo Arbitrio*; WA 18, 551-587
- Luther, Martin, *Die kleine Catechismus für die gemeine Pfarrherr und Prediger* (= *Smaller Catechism*); WA 30-1, 239-425
- Maas, W., *Unveränderlichkeit Gottes: Zum Verhältnis von griechisch-philosophischer und christlicher Gotteslehre*, Paderborn 1974
- Mackie, J.L., "Evil and Omnipotence," *Mind* 64 (1955), 200-212; reprinted in: Urban & Walton (eds.), *Power*, 17-31
- Mackie, J.L., "Omnipotence," *Sophia* 1.2 (1962), 13-25, reprinted (slightly revised) in: Urban & Walton (eds.), *Power*, 73-88
- MacBeath, Murray, "Geach on Omnipotence and Virginity," *Philosophy* 63 (1988), 395-400
- McCabe, Herbert, "The Involvement of God," in: id., *God Matters*, London 1987, 39-51
- McFague, Sallie, *Metaphorical Theology: Models of God in Religious Language*, London 1983
- McFague, Sallie, *Models of God: Theology for an Ecological, Nuclear Age*, London 1987
- McGrath, Alister E., *The Genesis of Doctrine: A Study in the Foundations of Doctrinal Criticism*, Oxford 1990
- MacGregor, Geddes, *He Who Lets Us Be: A Theology of Love*, New York 1975
- MacKay, Donald M., "Complementarity in Scientific and Theological Thinking," *Zygon* 9 (1974), 225-244
- MacKay, Donald M., *Science, Change and Providence*, Oxford 1978

- McKenzie, David, "Pannenberg on God and Freedom," *Journal of Religion* 60 (1980), 307-329
- MacKinnon, Alistair, *Falsification and Belief*, The Hague 1970
- McLean, M., "The Unmakable-Because-Unliftable Stone," *Canadian Journal of Philosophy* 4 (1975), 717-721
- Macquarrie, John, "Divine Omnipotence," *Proceedings of the Seventh Inter-American Congress of Philosophy* I, Quebec 1967, 132-137
- McTaggart, J.M.E., *Some Dogmas of Religion*, London 1906
- Malcolm, Norman, *Thought and Knowledge: Essays*, Ithaca 1977
- Mann, W.E., "Ross on Omnipotence," *International Journal for Philosophy of Religion* 8 (1979), 142-147
- Mann, W.E., "Divine Simplicity," *Religious Studies* 18 (1982) 451-471
- Mann, W.E., "God's Freedom, Human Freedom, and God's Responsibility for Sin," in: T.V. Morris (ed.), *Divine & Human Action*, Ithaca 1988, 182-210
- Marion, J.-L., *Sur la théologie blanche de Descartes: Analogie, création des vérités éternelles et fondement*, Paris 1981
- Markham, Ian, "Hume Revisited," *Modern Theology* 7 (1991), 281-290
- Matthews, J.T., *The Pantocrator: Title and Image*, New York 1976
- Maurice, M.A. & Noorda, S.J. (eds.), *De onzekere zekerheid des geloofs: Beschouwingen in het spanningsveld van geloven en denken*, Zoetermeer 1991
- Mavrodes, George I., "Some Puzzles Concerning Omnipotence," *Philosophical Review* 72 (1963), 221-223, reprinted in: Urban & Walton, *Power*, 131-134
- Mavrodes, George I., *Belief in God: A Study in the Epistemology of Religion*, New York 1970
- Mavrodes, George I., "Defining Omnipotence," *Philosophical Studies* 32 (1977), 191-202
- Mavrodes, George I., "Necessity, Possibility and the Stone which Cannot be Moved," *Faith and Philosophy* 2 (1985), 265-271
- Mavrodes, George I., "Is There Anything Which God Does Not Do?," *Christian Scholar's Review* 16 (1987), 384-391
- Mayo, B., "Mr. Keene on Omnipotence," *Mind* 70 (1961), 249-250
- Meierding, Loren, "The Impossibility of Necessary Omnitemporal Omnipotence," *International Journal for Philosophy of Religion* 11 (1980), 21-26
- Meijering, E.P., *God Being History: Studies in Patristic Philosophy*, Amsterdam 1975
- Meijering, E.P., *Augustine: De Fide et Symbolo*, Amsterdam 1987
- Mele, Alfred J. & Smith, M.P., "The New Paradox of the Stone," *Faith and Philosophy* 5 (1988), 283-290
- Michaelis, W., "Pantokrator," in: G. Kittel (ed.), *Theological Dictionary of the New Testament* III, ET edited by G.W. Bromiley, Grand Rapids 1965, 914-915
- Miethke, O., *Ockhams Weg zur Sozialphilosophie*, Berlin 1969
- Migliore, Daniel L., *The Power of God*, Philadelphia 1983
- Migliore, Daniel L., "God's Freedom and Human Freedom," in: H. Deuser et al., *Gottes Zukunft - Zukunft der Welt*, München 1986, 240-249
- Mill, John Stuart, *Three Essays on Religion*, London 1874
- Mills, C. Wright, *The Power Elite*, London 1956
- Miskotte, K.H., *Bijbels ABC*, Amsterdam 1966[2] (1940)
- Mitchell, Basil, *The Justification of Religious Belief*, London 1973
- Moltmann, Jürgen, *The Crucified God: The Cross of Christ as the Foundation and Criticism of Christian Theology*, London 1982[5] (1974)
- Moltmann, Jürgen, *The Trinity and the Kingdom of God: The Doctrine of God*, London 1986[3] (1981)
- Montevecchi, Orsolina, "Pantokrator," in: *Studii in onore di A. Chalderini et R. Paribeni*, Milan 1957, 401-432
- Moonan, Lawrence, "Impossibility and Peter Damian," *Archiv für Geschichte der Philosophie* 62 (1980), 146-163.

- Moor, J.C. de, *Gods macht en liefde, probleem? of uitdaging!*, Kampen 1988
- Morris, T.V., "Properties, Modalities, and God," *Philosophical Review* 93 (1984), 35-55
- Morris, T.V. & Menzel, C., "Absolute Creation," *American Philosophical Quarterly* 23 (1986), 353-362, reprinted in: Morris, *Anselmian Explorations*, 161-178
- Morris, T.V., "Perfection and Power," *International Journal for Philosophy of Religion* 20 (1986), 165-168, reprinted in: id., *Anselmian Explorations*, 70-75
- Morris, T.V., *Anselmian Explorations: Essays in Philosophical Theology*, Notre Dame 1987
- Morris, T.V., "On God and Mann: A View of Divine Simplicity," in: id., *Anselmian Explorations*, 98-123
- Morris, T.V. (ed.), *The Concept of God*, Oxford 1987
- Morriss, Peter, *Power: A Philosophical Analysis*, Manchester 1987
- Morriston, Wesley, "Is Plantinga's God Omnipotent?," *Sophia* 23.3 (1984), 50-55
- Muller, R.A., "Incarnation, Immutability and the Case for Classical Theism," *Westminster Theological Journal* 45 (1983), 22-40
- Muller, R.A., *Dictionary of Latin and Greek Theological Terms: Drawn Principally from Protestant Scholastic Theology*, Grand Rapids 1985
- Murphy, Nancey & McClendon, Jamens Wm. Jr., "Distinguishing Modern and Postmodern Theologies," *Modern Theology* 5 (1989), 191-214
- Nash, Ronald H., *The Concept of God: An Exploration of Contemporary Difficulties with the Attributes of God*, Grand Rapids 1983
- Newbigin, Lesslie, *Foolishness to the Greeks: The Gospel and Western Culture*, Grand Rapids 1986
- Newbigin, Lesslie, *The Gospel in a Pluralist Society*, London 1991³ (1989)
- Newbigin, Lesslie, *Truth to Tell: The Gospel as Public Truth*, Grand Rapids 1991
- Nielsen, Kai, "Religion and Groundless Believing," in: Frederick Crosson (ed.), *The Autonomy of Religious Belief*, Notre Dame 1981, 93-107
- Oakley, Francis, "Jacobean Political Theology: The Absolute and Ordinary Powers of the King," *Journal of the History of Ideas* 29 (1964), 323-346
- Oakley, Francis, *The Western Church in the Later Middle Ages*, Ithaca 1985² (1979)
- Oakley, Francis, *Omnipotence, Covenant and Order: An Excursion in the History of Ideas from Abelard to Leibniz*, Ithaca 1984
- Oberman, H.A., *Archbishop Thomas Bradwardine*, Utrecht 1957
- Oberman, H.A., *The Harvest of Medieval Theology: Gabriel Biel and Late Medieval Nominalism*, Cambridge (Mass.) 1963
- Oberman, H.A., "Wir sein pettler. Hoc est verum," in: id., *Die Reformation: Von Wittenberg nach Genf*, Göttingen 1986, 90-112
- Oberman, H.A., "*Via Antiqua* and *Via Moderna*: Late Medieval Prolegomena to Early Reformation Thought," in: Hudson & Wilks (eds.), *From Ockham*, 445-463
- Ockham, William, *Opus Nonaginta Dierum*, in: *Opera Politica* II, Manchester 1963
- Ockham, William, *Tractatus contra Benedictum*, in: *Opera Politica* III, Manchester 1956
- Ockham, William, *Quodlibeta Septem*, in: *Opera Theologica* IX, St. Bonaventure (N.Y.) 1980
- O'Connor, David, "In Defence of Theoretical Theodicy," *Modern Theology* 5 (1988), 61-74
- Ogilvy, J., "Understanding Power," *Philosophy and Social Criticism* 1 (1978), 129-144
- Oppenheim, Felix E., *Political Concepts: A Reconstruction*, Oxford 1981
- Origen, *Contra Celsum* (SC 136); ET: H. Chadwick, *Origen: Contra Celsum*, Cambridge 1953
- Origen, *De Principiis* (SC 252)
- Origen, *Excerpta in Psalmos* (PG 17)
- Ozment, S., *The Age of Reform 1250-1550: An Intellectualist and Religious History of Late Medieval and Reformation Europe*, New Haven 1980
- Packer, J.I., *Evangelism and the Sovereignty of God*, Downers Grove 1961
- Pailin, David, *Groundwork of Philosophy of Religion*, London 1986

- Pannenberg, Wolfhart, *Die Prädestinationslehre des Duns Skotus*, Göttingen 1954
- Pannenberg, Wolfhart, *Basic Questions in Theology* Vol. I, London 1970; Vol. II, London 1971; Vol.III, London 1973
- Pannenberg, Wolfhart, *The Apostles' Creed in the Light of Today's Questions*, Philadelphia 1972
- Pannenberg, Wolfhart, "A Response to My American Friends," in: Braaten & Clayton, *Theology*, 313-336
- Pannenberg, Wolfhart, *Metaphysics and the Idea of God*, Edinburgh 1990
- Pannenberg, Wolfhart, *Systematic Theology* Vol.1, Edinburgh 1991
- Parsons, Talcott, "On the Concept of Political Power," *Proceedings of the American Philosophical Society* 107 (1963), 232-262, reprinted in: S. Lukes (ed.), *Power*, Oxford 1986, 94-143
- Parsons, Talcott, *Sociological Theory and Modern Society*, New York 1967
- Partridge, P.H., "Some Notes on the Concept of Power," *Political Studies* 11 (1963), 107-125
- Pascal, Blaise, *Pensées*, tr. A.J. Krailsheimer, New York 1985¹⁴ (1966)
- Penelhum, Terence, *Religion and Rationality: An Introduction to the Philosophy of Religion*, New York 1971
- Pentz, Rebecca D., *A Defense of the Formal Adequacy of Saint Thomas Aquinas' Analysis of Omnipotence*, diss. Irvine 1979 (unpublished)
- Pernoud, M.A., "Innovation in William of Ockham's References to the '*Potentia Dei*'," *Antonianum* 45 (1970), 65-97
- Pernoud, M.A., "The Theory of the *Potentia Dei* according to Aquinas, Scotus and Ockham," *Antonianum* 47 (1979), 69-95
- Peters, Richard S., "Authority," in: Richard E. Flathman (ed.), *Concepts in Social & Political Philosophy*, New York 1973, 146-156
- Peterson, Michael, *Evil and the Christian God*, Grand Rapids 1982
- Peterson, Michael et al., *Reason & Religious Belief*, Oxford 1991
- Peursen, C.A. van, *Cultuur in stroomversnelling*, Leiden 1992⁸ (1975)
- Phillips, D.Z., *Faith and Philosophical Enquiry*, New York 1971
- Phillips, D.Z., *Religion without Explanation*, Oxford 1976
- Phillips, D.Z., *Faith after Foundationalism*, London 1988
- Phillips, D.Z., "On Not Understanding God," *Archivio di Filosofia* 56 (1988), 597-612
- Pike, Nelson, "Hume on Evil," reprinted in: Adams & Adams (eds.), *Problem*, 38-52
- Pike, Nelson, "Omnipotence and God's Ability to Sin," *American Philosophical Quarterly* 6 (1969), 208-216
- Pike, Nelson, "Process Theodicy and the Concept of Power," *Process Studies* 12 (1982), 148-167
- Pike, Nelson, "Over-Power and God's Responsibility for Sin," in: Freddoso (ed.), *Existence*, 11-35
- Plantinga, Alvin, "The Free Will Defence," in: Max Black (ed.), *Philosophy in America*, London 1965, 204-220
- Plantinga, Alvin, *God and Other Minds: A Study of the Rational Justification of Belief in God*, Ithaca 1967
- Plantinga, Alvin, "Is Belief in God Rational?," in: Delaney, *Rationality*, 7-27
- Plantinga, Alvin, *God, Freedom, and Evil*, Grand Rapids 1974
- Plantinga, Alvin, *The Nature of Necessity*, Oxford 1974
- Plantinga, Alvin, "Aquinas on Anselm," in: C. Orlebeke & Lewis B. Smedes (eds.), *God and the Good*, Grand Rapids 1975, 122-139
- Plantinga, Alvin, *Does God Have a Nature?*, Milwaukee 1980
- Plantinga, Alvin, "Reply to the Basingers on Divine Omnipotence," *Process Studies* 11 (1981), 25-29
- Plantinga, Alvin, "How to Be an Anti-Realist?," *Proceedings and Addresses of the American*

Philosophical Association 56 (1982), 47-70
- Plantinga, Alvin, "Reason and Belief in God," in: Plantinga & Wolterstorff (eds.), *Faith and Rationality*, 16-93
- Plantinga, Alvin, "Epistemic Probability and Evil," *Archivio di Filosofia* 56 (1988), 558-565
- Plantinga, Alvin & Wolterstorff, Nicholas (eds.), *Faith and Rationality: Reason and Belief in God*, Notre Dame 1983
- Plato, *Timaeus*, ET: R.G. Bury (ed.), *Plato* (LCL) Vol.9, London 1981
- Plotinus, *Enneads*
- Polk, David R., "The All-Determining God and the Peril of Determinism," in: Braaten & Clayton (eds.), *Theology*, 152-168
- Popper, K.R., *Conjectures and Refutations: The Growth of Scientific Knowledge*, New York 1965² (1963)
- Powell, Cyril H., *The Biblical Concept of Power*, London 1963
- Pražić, A., "An Argument against Theism," in: A. Pavković (ed.), *Contemporary Yugoslav Philosophy: The Analytical Approach*, Dordrecht 1988, 251-262
- Proudfoot, W., *Religious Experience*, Berkeley 1985
- Pseudo-Tertullianus, *Carmen adversus Marcionem* (PL 2)
- Pucetti, Roland, "The Concept of God," *Philosophical Quarterly* 14 (1964), 237-245
- Purtill, Richard L., *Thinking about Religion: A Philosophical Introduction to Religion*, Englewood Cliffs (N.J.) 1978
- *Quaestiones in epistolam ad Romanos* (PL 175)
- Quine, W.V.O, "Two Dogmas of Empiricism," *Philosophical Review* 60 (1951), 20-43, reprinted in: id., *From a Logical Point of View*, London 1980³ (1953), 20-46
- Quine, W.V.O. & Ullian, J.S., *The Web of Belief*, New York 1978² (1970)
- Ramsey, Ian T., "The Paradox of Omnipotence," *Mind* 65 (1956), 263-266
- Randi, E., "A Scotist Way of Distinguishing between God's Absolute and Ordained Power," in: Hudson & Wilks (eds.), *From Ockham*, 43-50
- Randi, E., "Ockham, John XXII and the Absolute Power of God," *Franciscan Studies* 46 (1986), 205-216
- Redmond, H.A., *The Omnipotence of God*, Philadelphia 1964
- Reichenbach, B.R., "Mavrodes on Omnipotence," *Philosophical Studies* 37 (1980), 211-214
- Reichenbach, B.R., *Evil and a Good God*, New York 1982
- Reichenbach, B.R., "God Limits His Power," in: Basinger & Basinger (eds.), *Predestination*, 99-124
- Rescher, Nicholas, *Rationality: A Philosophical Inquiry in the Nature and the Rationale of Reason*, Oxford 1988
- Resnick, Irvin Michael, *Divine Power & Possibility in St. Peter Damian's De Divina Omnipotentia*, Leiden 1992
- Reuver, A. de, *'Bedelen bij de Bron': Kohlbrugge's geloofsopvatting vergeleken met Reformatie en Nadere Reformatie*, Zoetermeer 1992
- Reve, Karel van het, "De ongelofelijke slechtheid van het opperwezen," in: D. van Weerlee et al., *Het verschijnsel godsdienst*, Amsterdam 1986, 26-32
- Rijk, L.M. de, *Middeleeuwse wijsbegeerte: Traditie en vernieuwing*, Assen 1981² (1977)
- Röttgers, K., *Spuren der Macht: Begriffsgeschichte und Systematik*, Freiburg i.Br. 1990
- Rolt, C.E., *The World's Redemption*, London 1913
- Rorty, Richard, "Intuition," in: Paul Edwards (ed.), *The Encyclopedia of Philosophy*, vol.3, New York 1967, 204-212
- Rorty, Richard, *Philosophy and the Mirror of Nature*, Princeton 1980² (1979)
- Rosenkrantz, Gary, Review of E.R. Wierenga, *Nature of God*, in: *Philosophy and Phenomenological Research* 51 (1991), 725-728
- Rosenkrantz, Gary & Hoffman, Joshua, "The Omnipotence Paradox, Modality, and Time," *Southern Journal of Philosophy* 18 (1980), 473-479

- Rosenkrantz, Gary & Hoffman, Joshua, "What an Omnipotent Agent Can Do," *International Journal for Philosophy of Religion* 11 (1980), 1-19
- Rosenkrantz, Gary & Hoffman, Joshua, "Omnipotence Redux," *Philosophy and Phenomenological Research* 49 (1988), 283-301
- Ross, James F., *Philosophical Theology*, Indianapolis 1969 (1980²)
- Ross, James F., "Creation," *Journal of Philosophy* 77 (1980), 614-629
- Ross, James F., "Creation II," in: Freddoso (ed.), *Existence*, 115-141
- Ross, James F., "God, Creator of Kinds and Possibilities: *Requiescant universalia ante res*," in: Robert Audi & William J. Wainwright (eds.), *Rationality, Religious Belief & Moral Commitment*, Ithaca 1986, 315-335
- Rowe, William L., "The Problem of Evil and Some Varieties of Atheism," reprinted in: Adams & Adams (eds.), *Problem*, 126-137
- Rowe, William L., "Evil and the Theistic Hypothesis: A Response to Wykstra," reprinted in: Adams & Adams (eds.), *Problem*, 161-167
- Rowe, William L., "The Empirical Argument from Evil," in: Audi & Wainwright (eds.), *Rationality, Religious Belief*, Ithaca 1986, 227-247
- Rufinus, *Expositio Symboli* (CCL 20; ET: NPNF 3)
- Ruler, A.A. van, *Ik geloof: De Twaalf Artikelen van het geloof in morgenwijdingen*, Nijkerk n.d. (1968)
- Russell, B., *Power: A New Social Analysis*, London 1938
- Ryle, Gilbert, *The Concept of Mind*, London 1966¹¹ (1949)
- Sanders, Andy F., *Michael Polanyi's Post-Critical Epistemology: A Reconstruction of Some Aspects of 'Tacit Knowing'*, Amsterdam 1988
- Sarot, Marcel, "Omniscience and Experience," *International Journal for Philosophy of Religion* 30 (1991), 89-102
- Sarot, Marcel, *God, Passibility and Corporeality*, Kampen 1992
- Sarot, Marcel, "Omnipotence and Self-Limitation," in: Van den Brink et al. (eds.) *Christian Faith*, 172-185
- Savage, C. Wade, "The Paradox of the Stone," *Philosophical Review* 76 (1967), 74-79, reprinted in: Urban & Walton (eds.), *Power*, 138-143
- Schillebeeckx, Edward, "Overwegingen rond Gods 'weerloze overmacht'," *Tijdschrift voor theologie* 27 (1987), 370-381
- Schiller, F.C.S., *Riddles of the Sphinx*, London 1894² (1891)
- Schiller, F.C.S., "Omnipotence," *Proceedings of the Aristotelian Society* 18 (1917-18), 247-270
- Schrader, David E., "A Solution to the Stone Paradox," *Synthese* 42 (1979), 255-264
- Schrader, David E., "Frankfurt and Descartes: God and Logical Truth," *Sophia* 25.1 (1986), 4-18.
- Schwöbel, Christoph, "Exploring the Logic of Perfection," in: Van den Brink et al. (eds.), *Christian Faith*, 197-217
- Schwöbel, Christoph, *God: Action and Revelation*, Kampen 1992
- Schwöbel, Christoph & Gunton, Colin E. (eds.), *Persons: Divine and Human*, Edinburgh 1991
- Seeberg, R., *Lehrbuch der Dogmengeschichte* Vol.3, Leipzig 1930⁴ (1898)
- Sessions, W.L., "The Authorship of Faith," *Religious Studies* 27 (1991), 81-97
- Shaw, D.W.D., "Omnipotence," *Scottish Journal of Religious Studies* 13 (1992), 103-113
- Shestov, Leo, *Athens and Jerusalem*, Athens (Ohio) 1966
- Sia, Santiago (ed.), *Charles Hartshorne's Concept of God: Philosophical and Theological Responses*, Dordrecht 1990
- Smulders, P., "The *Sitz im Leben* of the Old Roman Creed," in: E.A. Livingstone (ed.), *Studia Patristica* Vol.XIII, Berlin 1975, 409-421
- Smulders, P., "'God Father All-Sovereign': New Testament Use, the Creeds and the Liturgy. An Acclamation? Some Riddles in the Apostles' Creed III," *Bijdragen* 41 (1980), 3-15
- Sölle, Dorothee, *Suffering*, London 1975

- Sölle, Dorothee, "Vom Gott-über-uns zum Gott-in-uns," *Evangelische Kommentare* 23 (1990), 614-615
- Sontag, Frederick, "Omnipotence Need not Entail Omniscience," *Sophia* 29.3 (1990), 35-39
- Soskice, Janet Martin, "God of Power and Might," *The Month* 21 (1988), 934-938
- Spanneut, M., *Le stoïcisme de pères de l'Eglise: De Clément de Rome à Clément d'Alexandrie*, Paris 1957
- Spijkerboer, A.A., "De almacht van de liefde," in: D. van Weerlee et al., *Het verschijnsel godsdienst*, Amsterdam 1986, 61-66
- Stannard, Russell, *Grounds for Reasonable Belief*, Edinburgh 1989
- Stauffer, R., *Dieu, la création et la providence dans la prédication de Calvin*, Bern 1978
- Steel, Carlos, *Proslogion gevolgd door de discussie met Gaunilo*, Bussum 1981
- Strehle, Stephen, "Calvinism, Augustianism, and the Will of God," *Theologische Zeitung* 47 (1992), 221-237
- Stump, Eleonore, Review of A. Plantinga, *Does God Have a Nature?*, in: *The Thomist* 47 (1983), 617-620
- Suarez, F., *Disputationes Metaphysicae*, in: *Opera omnia* XXVI, Paris 1861
- Surin, Kenneth, *Theology and the Problem of Evil*, Oxford 1986
- Suurmond, P.B., *God is machtig - maar hoe? Relaas van een Godservaring*, Baarn 1989⁵ (1984)
- Swinburne, Richard, "Omnipotence," *American Philosophical Quarterly* 10 (1973), 231-237
- Swinburne, Richard, *The Coherence of Theism*, Oxford 1977
- Swinburne, Richard, *Faith and Reason*, Oxford 1981
- Swinburne, Richard, "Does Theism Need a Theodicy?," *Canadian Journal of Philosophy* 18 (1988), 287-312
- Taliaferro, Charles, "The Magnitude of Omnipotence," *International Journal for Philosophy of Religion* 14 (1983), 99-106
- Taliaferro, Charles, "The Limits of Power," *Philosophy & Theology* 5 (1990), 115-124
- Tanner, Kathryn E., *God and Creation in Christian Theology: Tyranny or Empowerment?*, Oxford 1988
- Theodore of Mopsuestia, *Homilia catechetica*, in: R. Tonneau & R. Devreesse (eds.), *Les Homélies Catéchétiques de Théodore de Mopsueste*, Roma 1949
- Theophilus, *Ad Autolycum*, in: G. Bardy (ed.), *Trois livres à Autolycus* (SC 20), Paris 1948
- Thiemann, Ronald F., *Revelation and Theology: The Gospel as Narrated Promise*, Notre Dame 1985
- Thorburn, W.M., "Omnipotence and Personality," *Mind* 29 (1920), 159-185
- Tilley, Terrence, *The Evils of Theodicy*, Washington 1991
- Tillich, Paul, *Systematic Theology* I, Chicago 1951
- Tillich, Paul, *Love, Power and Justice*, Oxford 1954
- Timmer, John, *God of Weakness: How God Works Through the Weak Things of the World*, Grand Rapids 1988
- Torrance, Thomas F., *The Ground and Grammar of Theology*, Belfast 1980
- Torrance, Thomas F., *Divine and Contingent Order*, Oxford 1981
- Tracy, David, *Blessed Rage for Order: The New Pluralism in Theology*, New York 1975
- Tracy, Thomas F., *God, Action, and Embodiment*, Grand Rapids 1984
- Tracy, Thomas F., Review of K. Tanner, *God and Creation*, in: *Faith and Philosophy* 9 (1992), 120-124
- Triplett, Timm, "Recent Work on Foundationalism," *American Philosophical Quarterly* 27 (1990), 93-116
- Trusted, Jennifer, *Free Will and Responsibility*, Oxford 1984
- Urban, Linwood & Walton, Douglas N., "Freedom within Omnipotence," in: id. (eds.), *Power*, 192-207
- Urban, Linwood & Walton, Douglas N. (eds.), *The Power of God: Readings on Omnipotence*

and Evil, New York 1978.
- Veluw, A.H. van, *God en de zinloosheid van het kwaad, oftewel: waarom is er zoveel pijn en lijden in deze wereld?*, Nijkerk 1991
- Vetesse, A. (ed.), *Sopra la volta del mundo: Omnipotenza e potenza assoluta di Dio tra medioevo e età moderna*, Bergamo 1986
- Vicchio, Stephen J., *The Voice from the Whirlwind: The Problem of Evil and the Modern World*, Westminster 1989
- Vignaux, P., "Nominalisme," in: *Dictionnaire de Théologie Catholique*, Vol.XI^1, Paris 1931, 717-784
- Vignaux, P., *Philosophy in the Middle Ages*, New York 1959
- Vos, Antonie, "De theorie van de eigenschappen en de leer van de eigenschappen van God," *Bijdragen* 42 (1981), 75-102
- Vos, Antonie, *Kennis en noodzakelijkheid: Een kritische analyse van het absolute evidentialisme in wijsbegeerte en theologie*, Kampen 1981
- Vos, Antonie et al. (eds.), *Johannes Duns Scotus: Contingentie en Vrijheid. Lectura I 39*, Zoetermeer 1992
- Vos, Arvin, *Aquinas, Calvin, and Contemporary Protestant Thought: A Critique of Protestant Views on the Thought of Thomas Aquinas*, Grand Rapids 1985
- Vroom, H.M., *Religions and the Truth: Philosophical Reflections and Perspectives*, Grand Rapids 1989
- Vroom, H.M., "Gods goedheid en het menselijk tasten," in: Maurice & Noorda, *Onzekere zekerheid*, 50-68
- Vroom, H.M., "God and Goodness," in: Van den Brink et al. (eds.), *Christian Faith*, 240-257
- Wainwright, Geoffrey, *Doxology: The Praise of God in Doctrine, Worship and Life. A Systematic Theology*, London 1980
- Wainwright, William J., "Divine Omnipotence: A Reply to Professors Kuntz and Macquarrie," *Proceedings of the Seventh Inter-American Congress of Philosophy*, Vol.1, Quebec 1967
- Wainwright, William J., "Freedom and Omnipotence," *Noûs* 2 (1968), 293-301
- Wainwright, William J., "Christian Theism and the Free Will Defence," *International Journal for Philosophy of Religion* 6 (1975), 243-250
- Wainwright, William J., *Philosophy of Religion: An Annotated Bibliography of Twentieth-Century Writings in English*, New York 1978
- Walton, Douglas, "The Omnipotence Paradox," *Canadian Journal of Philosophy* 4 (1975), 705-715, reprinted in: Urban & Walton (eds.), *Power*, 153-164
- Walton, Douglas, "Some Theorems of Fitch on Omnipotence," *Sophia* 15.1 (1976), 20-27, reprinted in: Urban & Walton (eds.), *Power*, 182-191
- Ward, Keith, *Rational Theology and the Creativity of God*, Oxford 1985^2 (1982)
- Ward, Keith, *Divine Action*, London 1990
- Warfield, B.B., "Calvin's Doctrine of God," in: id., *Calvin and Calvinism*, New York 1931, 133-185
- Watson, Gary (ed.), *Free Will*, Oxford 1982
- Weber, M., *The Theory of Social and Economic Organization*, ed. T. Parsons, New York 1947
- Wells, H.G., *God the Invisible King*, New York 1917
- Wendel, F., *Calvin: Sources et évolution de sa pensée religieuse*, Paris 1950
- Wentsel, B., *God en mens verzoend: Godsleer, mensleer en zondeleer* (Dogmatiek vol. 3a), Kampen 1987
- Werner, L., "Some Omnipotent Beings," *Critica* 5 (1971), 55-69, reprinted in: Urban & Walton, *Power*, 94-106
- Westland, J., *God onze troost in noden: Een gesprek met hedendaagse theologen over de vragen rond God en het lijden*, Kampen 1986
- White, Roger, "Notes on Analogical Predication and Speaking about God," in: B. Hebblethwaite & S. Sutherland (eds.), *Philosophical Frontiers of Christian Theology: Essays*

Presented to D.M. MacKinnon, Cambridge 1982, 208-221
- White, Vernon, *The Fall of a Sparrow: A Concept of Special Divine Action*, Exeter 1985
- White, Vernon, *Atonement and Incarnation: An Essay in Universalism and Particularity*, Cambridge 1991
- Whitehead, Alfred North, *Process and Reality: An Essay in Cosmology*, Corrected Edition, eds. David Ray Griffin & Donald W. Sherburne, New York 1978 (1929)
- Whitney, Barry L., *Evil and the Process God*, New York 1985
- Wierenga, Edward, "Omnipotence Defined," *Philosophy and Phenomenological Research* 43 (1983), 363-375
- Wierenga, Edward, *The Nature of God: An Inquiry into Divine Attributes*, Notre Dame 1989
- Wiles, Maurice, *God's Action in the World*, Oxford 1986
- Wilson, M.D., *Descartes*, London 1978
- Windt, Peter Y., "Plantinga's Unfortunate God," *Philosophical Studies* 24 (1973), 335-342
- Wittgenstein, Ludwig, *Philosophical Investigations* I, Oxford 1976³ (1953)
- Wittgenstein, Ludwig, *On Certainty*, eds. G.E.M. Anscombe & G.H. von Wright, Oxford 1969
- Wolfe, Julian, "Omnipotence," *Canadian Journal of Philosophy* 1 (1971), 245-247
- Wolter, A.B., *Duns Scotus on the Will and Morality*, Washington 1986
- Wolterstorff, Nicholas, *On Universals*, Chicago 1970
- Wolterstorff, Nicholas, "God Everlasting," in: C. Orlebeke & Lewis B. Smedes (eds.), *God and the Good*, Grand Rapids 1975, 181-203
- Wolterstorff, Nicholas, *Reason within the Bounds of Religion*, Grand Rapids 1984² (1976)
- Wolterstorff, Nicholas, "The Migration of Theistic Arguments," in: R. Audi & W.J. Wainwright (eds.), *Rationality, Religious Belief*, Ithaca 1986, 38-81
- Wood, Charles M., *Vision and Discernment: An Orientation in Theological Study*, Atlanta 1985, 304-305
- Wood, R., "Intuitive Cognition and Divine Omnipotence," in: Hudson & Wilks (eds.), *From Ockham*, 51-61
- Wright, Georg Henrik von, *Truth, Knowledge and Modality* (*Philosophical Papers*, Vol.3), Oxford 1984
- Wrong, Dennis H., *Power: Its Forms, Bases and Uses*, Oxford 1979
- Wykstra, S.T., "The Humean Obstacle to Evidential Arguments from Suffering: On Avoiding the Evils of 'Appearance'," in: Adams & Adams (eds.), *Problem*, 138-160
- Yates, John C., *The Timelessness of God*, Lanham 1990
- Young, Robert, *Freedom, Responsibility and God*, London 1975
- Young, Robert, "Omnipotence and Compatibilism," *Philosophia* 6 (1976), 49-65
- Zeis, John & Jacobs, Jonathan, "Omnipotence and Concurrence," *International Journal for Philosophy of Religion* 14 (1983), 17-23
- Zobel, H.-J., "Seba'ot," in: G.J. Botterweck, H. Ringgren & H.-J. Farby (eds.), *Theologisches Wörterbuch zum Alten Testament* VI, Lieferung 8-10, Stuttgart 1989, 876-892
- Zwingli, Ülrich, *Sermonis de providentia Dei anamnema*, in: *Huldrich Zwinglis Sämtliche Werke* Bd.VI III. Teil, Zürich 1983, 64-230

List of Abbreviations

AA	Analecta Anselmiana
AdF	Archivio di Filosofia
AGP	Arciv für Geschichte der Philosophie
APQ	American Philosophical Quarterly
CCL	Corpus Christianorum, Series Latina
CJP	Canadian Journal of Philosophy
CO	G. Baum, E. Cunitz, E. Reuss (eds.), *Ioannis Calvini Opera quae supersunt omnia* (Brunsvigae 1863ff.)
CSEL	Corpus Scriptorum Ecclesiastorum Latinorum
CSR	Christian Scholar's Review
EK	Evangelische Kommentare
F&P	Faith and Philosophy
FS	Franciscan Studies
GCS	Griechisch christlichen Schriftsteller der ersten drei Jahrhunderte
G&D	Glaube und Denken
IJPR	International Journal for Philosophy of Religion
JHI	Journal of the History of Ideas
JP	Journal of Philosophy
JR	Journal of Religion
JSL	Journal of Symbolic Logic
K&Th	Kerk en Theologie
K&D	Kerugma und Dogma
LCL	Loeb Classical Library
LThP	Laval Théologique et Philosophique
MTh	Modern·Theology
NPNF	Philip Schaff (ed.), A Select Library of Nicene and Post-Nicene Fathers of the Christian Church, second series, Grand Rapids 1976-1983
NS	New Scholasticism
NTT	Nederlands Theologisch Tijdschrift
NZSTh	Neue Zeitschrift für systematische Theologie und Religionsphilosophie
PAS	Proceedings of the Aristotelian Society
PAPS	Proceedings of the American Philosophical Society
PG	J.P. Migne (ed.), Patrologiae cursus completus, series Graeca
PL	J.P. Migne (ed.), Patrologiae cursus completus, series Latina
PPQ	Pacific Philosophical Quarterly
P&PR	Philosophy and Phenomenological Research
PQ	Philosophical Quarterly
PR	Philosophical Review
PRA	Philosophical Research Archives
PRef	Philosophia Reformata
PrS	Process Studies
PS	Philosophical Studies
P&SC	Philosophy and Social Criticism
PSS	Philosophy of the Social Sciences
P&Th	Philosophy and Theology
RA	Recherches Augustiniennes

RIP	Revue Internationale de Philosophie
RJ	Reformed Journal
RS	Religious Studies
RThL	Revue Théologique de Louvain
SC	Sources Chrétiennes
SHPS	Studies in the History and Philosophy of Science
SJP	Southern Journal of Philosophy
SJRS	Scottish Journal of Religious Studies
SJTh	Scottish Journal of Theology
SN	Sociologia Neerlandica
ST&P	Social Theory and Practice
ThDNT	*Theological Dictionary of the New Testament*
ThQ	Theologische Quartalschrift
TJTh	Toronto Journal of Theology
ThR	Theologia Reformata
TvTh	Tijdschrift voor Theologie
ThZ	Theologische Zeitung
TWAT	*Theologisches Wörterbuch zum Alten Testament*
VC	Vigiliae Christianae
WA	*D. Martin Luthers Werke*, Kritische Gesamtausgabe, Weimar 1883ff.
WAB	Luther, Weimarer Ausgabe Briefwechsel
WAT	Luther, Weimarer Ausgabe Tischreden
WThJ	Westminster Theological Journal
ZEK	Zeitschrift für evangelisches Kirchenrecht

Index of Names

Index of Subjects

DATE DUE

Demco, Inc. 38-293